THE IDEA
by Nick Heath

THE IDEA

by Nick Heath

Just Books Publishing

Published by Just Books, 2022

Just Books
PO Box 258
Newtownabbey
BT36 9FQ

https://organiseanarchistsireland.com/shop/

ISBN 978-1-7397237-1-2

© 2022 Nick Heath

Illustrations by kind permission of Clifford Harper
Design and DTP by Jayne Clementson

Printed on sustainably sourced paper by
Kerschoffset
Zagreb, Croatia

Contents

Acknowledgements 13

Anarchist communism: a birth of fire and rain 15

Foreword 17

Chapter One
Prehistory of the Idea: part one 23

Chapter Two
Prehistory of the Idea: part two 47

Chapter Three
Proudhon – Anarchist? 57

Chapter Four
Marx and Engels and the Communist Movement 63

Chapter Five
Bakunin and the First International 77

Chapter Six
The First International 83

Chapter Seven
The Struggle within the International 87

Chapter Eight
The Emergence of Anarchist Communism 91

Chapter Nine
Elisée Reclus 99

Chapter Ten
James Guillaume 103

Chapter Eleven
Gustave Lefrançais: A Link to The Past 105

Chapter Twelve
Estrangement 109

Chapter Thirteen
Paul Brousse 115

Chapter Fourteen
The Idea of the Commune and its Effect on Anarchist
Communism...127

Chapter Fifteen
Anarchist Communism and Anarchosyndicalism 133

Chapter Sixteen
Kropotkin and his ideas 147

Chapter Seventeen
Malatesta: the Pragmatist 157

Chapter Eighteen
The Yellow Fever of Disorganisation: Individualist
Anarchism 165

Chapter Nineteen
Johann Most, Peukert and the German exile movement 173

Chapter Twenty
German Anarchist Communism from the 1890s to the
1930s: the AFD and the FKAD 183

Chapter Twenty One
Erich Mühsam 193

Chapter Twenty Two
The movement within the Austro-Hungarian Empire 201

Chapter Twenty Three
Anarchist communism in the Low Countries 209

Chapter Twenty Four
Stormy Petrel: Anarchism within the Russian Empire
and in exile 219

Chapter Twenty Five
Anarchist Communism in the USA 235

Chapter Twenty Six
Murray Bookchin 247

Chapter Twenty Seven
Social anarchism re-emerges within the United States 251

Chapter Twenty Eight
The Organisational Platform of the Libertarian Communists
and the Synthesis 255

Chapter Twenty Nine
Anarchist communism in Britain 273

Chapter Thirty
Spain: a flickering flame 301

Chapter Thirty One
Anarchist communism in Portugal 323

Chapter Thirty Two
Anarchist Communism in France: part one 331

Chapter Thirty Three
The Second World War and Its Aftermath in France 341

Chapter Thirty Four
May 1968 and After in France 361

Chapter Thirty Five
Anarchist Communism in Italy 381

Chapter Thirty Six
Anarchist Communism in Bulgaria 407

Chapter Thirty Seven
Anarchist Communism in Latin America 417

Chapter Thirty Eight
Cocks crowing in the dark: anarchist communism
in China 447

Chapter Thirty Nine
Anarchist communism in Japan 457

Chapter Forty
Anarchist Communism in Korea 465

Chapter Forty One
The future 469

Appendix One
Anarchist Communist Manifesto 473

Appendix Two
Platform of the Anarchist Communist Federation
of Bulgaria (1945) 477

Index 485

Dedication

This book is dedicated to John Clipsham, carpenter.
Meeting with one hundred others in the woods outside Hastings, in Sussex, he called for the deposition of Henry VI and that all goods be held in common, during the 1450 Jack Cade revolt, to my comrades of the Anarchist Communist Federation/Anarchist Federation, the late Colin Parker and Bob Miller, and also to the late Peter Ridpath, anarchist communist and IWW militant and a close friend.

About the author

Nick Heath, born in Brighton, East Sussex in 1948, began his political career at the age of 14 as a supporter of first the Labour Party and then the Communist Party. In 1966, following readings of anarchist books from the public library, he became an anarchist communist and participated in the formation of the Brighton Anarchist Group (1966-1972) he helped edit local anarchist magazines.

In 1969 he was also part of a campaign to help homeless families occupy empty homes. During a protest in 1971 he was arrested with thirteen other participants at a street party in a slum area of Brighton. He also briefly joined the Anarchist Syndicalist Alliance, where he participated in the publication of *Black and Red Outlook*.

In the early 1970s he went to Paris for a year and participated in the activities of the libertarian movement and in support for persecuted Spanish anarchists. Returning to England in 1972, he joined the Organisation of Revolutionary Anarchists (ORA) and became an editor of its paper *Libertarian Struggle*, where he wrote under the name *Ron Allen*. When the British ORA became the Anarchist Workers Association (AWA) and then the Libertarian Communist Group (LCG), he continued to campaign and participate in the editing of its papers *Anarchist Worker* and then *Libertarian Communist*. In the early 1980s, he was briefly a member of the libertarian socialist organisation Big Flame. Then for three years he went to live in Toulouse where he was a member of the Union of Libertarian Communist Workers (UTCL).

Returning to London in the mid-1980s, he was one of the founders of the Anarchist Communist Federation (ACF), which later became the Anarchist Federation. He remains an active member of the

Anarchist Communist Group, founded in 2018. He is the author of numerous biographies of anarchist militants and articles on the Hungarian Revolution and the Third Russian Revolution.

Acknowledgements

This book could not have been written without the many discussions and articles of the last 45 years. So, I am grateful to fellow members of the Brighton Anarchist Group of the late 60s/early 70s but above all to Ted Kavanagh and the late Jim Duke. I am also grateful to discussions with comrades of the Organisation of Revolutionary Anarchists, the Anarchist Workers Association and the Libertarian Communist Group. My years in the Anarchist Federation (formerly the Anarchist Communist Federation) were also highly educational.

I would also like to thank the comrades of the French anarchist movement. In the early seventies I attended meetings of the Alliance Syndicaliste Révolutionnaire et Anarcho-Syndicaliste (ASRAS) in Paris, among whom was Alain Pecunia, who had been imprisoned in Spain for anti-Franco activity. Also, in the seventies I made several visits to France to attend conferences of the Organisation Révolutionnaire Anarchiste, and I warmly remember comrades like the late Jan Van Zaanen and Michel Ravelli. In the 80s, during a three year sojourn in France, I was a member of the Union des Travailleurs Communistes Libertaires. Also highly educational and informative have been my contacts with the Organisation Communiste Libertaire, including one of their summer camps and meetings in Paris and Boulogne, above all the OCL comrade and veteran soixantehuitard Jean Pierre Duteuil.

I have had other helpful discussions of the last 45 years with many other activists. I did not necessarily always see eye to eye with these individuals, in fact I have had sharp disagreements with some of them. These disagreements have helped clarify and firm up my own politics. It would be naïve to think that political outlooks can be formed by constant agreement. The body of revolutionary anarchist communist thought was created by struggle, contradiction and acute dissensions.

I would particularly like to thank my friend and comrade Dek Keenan, who painstakingly read through the manuscript of The Idea, making corrections and political comments. I would also like to heartily thank Jayne Clementson for her voluntary work on layout and design of the book.

Finally, I would like to thank mi compañera de vida, Bonnie, whose love, patience and encouragement have helped this book come about.

Anarchist communism: a birth of fire and rain

On 19th October 1876, delegates of the Italian Federation of the First International attempted to meet in Florence for their third national congress. Andrea Costa was arrested straightaway. Four others joined him in jail the following day. Those who had eluded the dragnet attempted to convene. The meeting hall booked for the congress was occupied by the State authorities, so they moved to neighbouring Pontassieve. This town was swarming with State forces. Undeterred, the delegates of the International set off over mountain paths, in complete darkness and teeming rain.

They eventually arrived at the mountain village of Tosi. Here on 21st October 38 delegates assembled in the morning. However, a patrol of carabinieri was seen approaching and the delegates had to retreat to the nearby woods, where they reconvened in the pouring rain.

Here, revolution was reaffirmed as the only solution to the social question. Electoralism was rejected. So far, this merely reaffirmed the anarchist outlook of the Italian section. Where the Tosi congress broke with previous orthodoxy, that of Bakuninism, was the affirmation of the maxim 'From each according to his ability, to each according to his needs' over the collectivist 'From each according to his ability, to each according to his productivity'.

Thus, a national congress representing a national body was the first to accept anarchist communism. The difficult circumstances under which this was accomplished point not only to the straitened conditions which anarchist communism has always found itself in, but also to its hardiness.

Foreword

"Their learned tomes leave the reader with a feeling of diffusion, almost incoherence, still asking himself what anarchism really is." (Guérin, *Anarchism*, 1970, p.5)

"We have just been told of two different Anarchisms, of which the one, we are assured, is none at all. I know but one; that is Communistic Anarchism, which has grown among workingmen into a party, and which alone is known in 'larger circles,' as we say. It is as old, yes, older than the present century: Babeuf already preached it. Whether a few middle-class liberals have invented a new Anarchism is entirely immaterial to me, and does not interest me any more than any other workingman. As regards Proudhon, to whom comrade Auban again and again refers, he has long ago been disposed of and forgotten even in France, and his place has everywhere been taken by the revolutionary, Communistic Anarchism of the real proletariat." (Otto Trupp in *The Anarchists*, John Henry Mackay, 1999)

"For what has to be recognised is that anarchism is fundamentally a historical movement and political tradition that emerged only around 1870, mainly among the working class members of the International Working Men's Association, widely known as the First International. Although they did not initially describe themselves as anarchists but rather as "federalists" or as "anti-authoritarian socialists," this group of workers adopted the label of their Marxist opponents and came to describe themselves as "Anarchist Communists." Anarchism as a political movement and tradition thus emerged among the workers of Spain, France, Italy, and Switzerland in the aftermath of the Paris Commune, and among its more well-known proponents were Élisée Reclus, Francois Dumartheray, Errico Malatesta, Carlo Cafiero, Jean Grave, and Peter Kropotkin". (Brian Morris, *The Revolutionary Socialism of Peter Kropotkin*, 2010)

Why this book? Surely enough general works on anarchism have appeared in the last 40 years, it could be argued. But many of these represent academic interpretations of the idea and the movement. The label of anarchist appears to count more than the place of different currents in the class struggle. An idealist outlook has emerged, more concerned with the "eternal struggle of humanity for freedom" than the concrete struggle of the exploited and the social conditions which have permitted the emergence of an anti-authoritarian point of view within the working-class. So this type of historian has gone off in search of anarchist ideas among the Greek philosophers and the French Encyclopaedists.

Whilst Woodcock may have had some involvement with the British anarchist movement in the 1940s, his attitude to the movement is dismissive, with the general hypothesis that it had died by the end of the Spanish Civil War. Though he was forced to revise this hypothesis to a certain extent under evolving circumstances, it essentially remains the same. The 'liberal' outlook of Woodcock has little to do with the class struggle anarchist movement, as people like Meltzer were quick to point out.

Others like Joll and Kedward reiterate Woodcock's hypothesis that if the anarchist idea has survived in one form or another, then the movement itself has been virtually moribund since the late 1930s.

All of these essentially bourgeois historians have wilfully furthered an eclectic vision of anarchism as encompassing many ideas, philosophers and movements, from Jesus Christ and Karpocrates and Zeno to Gandhi and Vinobha Bhave. Indeed, Peter Marshall, who claims some connection with anarchism, has produced a massive tome where the eclecticism remarked upon above has reached absurd levels in his inclusion of a chapter on "anarcho-capitalism" and where he states that the "line between anarchist and libertarian is thin, and in the past the terms have often been used interchangeably. But while all anarchists are libertarian, not all libertarians are anarchists. Even so, they are members of the same clan, share the same ancestors and bear resemblances" (p.xiii, Demanding the Impossible. 2000).

There is a lucid passage in a bulletin of Union des Travailleurs Communistes Libertaires (special no. 5 for the Third Congress of the UTCL):

"Synthesist anarchism inspires a certain conception of history. For it, it is the label which counts, and not the place of different currents in the class struggle. It is an idealist fashion of thinking more preoccupied with the 'eternal struggle' of humanity for liberty' than the concrete struggle of the exploited and the social conditions which have permitted the emergence of an antiauthoritarian point of view in the proletariat. In this logic one goes very far back in the history of the 'idea'. The Greek philosophers, the Encyclopaedists, and others mark out this long search. I understand well enough: one should not play at blind workerism. This philosophic research has its value. What is lamentable is to drown in a humanist saga that is possibly interesting, the birth of an essentially working class movement. In continuity, the traditional anarchist historian brackets together in a vast imaginary current working class components and petty bourgeois individualists like Stirner: the importance is the label. Secondarily, the same historian can push to the periphery of the movement currents not judged to be truly libertarian..."

Woodcock himself recognises that: "In general, the anarchist historians have confused certain attitudes which lie at the core of anarchism – faith in the essential decency of man, a desire for individual freedom, an intolerance of domination – with anarchism as a movement and a creed appearing at a certain time in history and having specific theories, aims, and methods. The core attitudes can certainly be found echoing back through history at least to the ancient Greeks. But anarchism as a developed, articulate, and clearly identifiable trend appears only in the modern era of conscious social and political revolutions." (Anarchism, Woodcock, 1992, p. 38)

But what about those books written by activists in the movement? Daniel Guérin's work is excellent in many ways, but he spends too much time on Max Stirner and Proudhon and ends his book with spurious notions of 'self-management' in Yugoslavia and Algeria. Although Guérin held a libertarian communist outlook, he was too much under the influence of views held within the Federation Anarchiste at that time, of which he was a member when he wrote Anarchism.

Meltzer and Christie's book the Floodgates of Anarchy, has a refreshing affirmation of class struggle anarchism. It was influential in introducing a layer of newcomers to the movement who were attracted by this approach, and its influence lives on in the English-speaking movement today. However, in other ways it is too idiosyncratic and discursive.

As to Black Flame, the book by Michael Schmidt and Lucien van der Walt, controversy still hangs over it like a dark cloud, due to the discovery of Schmidt's covert racist and pro-fascist opinions. However, quite correctly their history of the movement includes only class struggle currents, stating, "Class Struggle" anarchism, sometimes called revolutionary or communist anarchism, is not a type of anarchism; in our view it is the *only* anarchism. We are aware that our approach contradicts some long-standing definitions, but we maintain that the meaning of anarchism is neither arbitrary nor just a matter of opinion – the historical record demonstrates that there is a core set of beliefs." But they too quickly identify syndicalism as the main current within anarchism, and distinguish between a "mass" and an "insurrectionist" current, at the same time making something monolithic out of anarcho-syndicalism and revolutionary syndicalism, when history shows us the existence of many divergent currents within these movements. For example, they state, "That some syndicalists described themselves as Marxists or rejected the anarchist label does not invalidate their place in the broad anarchist tradition; we do not use self-identification but rather ideas as the basis for inclusion." They go so far as dubiously identifying non-anarchist proponents of syndicalism like James Connolly, Big Bill Haywood and Daniel de Leon as part of this "mass" current, whilst at the same time excluding Proudhon. Another dubious assertion made by Schmidt elsewhere is that nationalists like Phan Bôi Châu of Vietnam were anarchists, because they had some nodding associations with the movement. However, I agree with the premise of the book, that class struggle anarchism is the only anarchism, against the criticisms of Robert Graham, who seeks to distinguish, in my opinion falsely, between anarchism, as a broad body of ideas, and anarchist movements. The historic current of anarchism emerged from the slow development of the working class, and to look elsewhere for anarchist ideas, I would reiterate, amongst Lao Zi, Stirner, Tolstoy etc, might be a diverting pastime, but has little value in contributing towards the construction of a revolutionary theory and practice.

This book does not intend to offer a comprehensive overview of the anarchist movement from its inception. For that you would be better off reading Max Nettlau, or indeed, Woodcock's book, as long as you do so critically. Neither is it intended to give a detailed historical account of anarcho-syndicalism. There are many works on this subject already, either offering world surveys or detailing particular movements in different countries.

Spanish anarchists talked about 'The Idea', in the same way as they talked about the Especifico, the specific anarchist organisation. By the idea they meant "communismo libertario", libertarian or anarchist communism. Hence the title of this work – with acknowledgements as well to the wonderful graphic novel The Idea by Frans Masereel!

This work is intended as a specific look at the history and development of that idea. It includes a prehistory – a look at how the idea of communism developed. Its main sections deal with:

1. The antiauthoritarian wing of the First international.
2. The development of the specific idea of anarchist communism.
3. The troubled relationship of anarchist communism with anarcho-syndicalism and revolutionary syndicalism.
4. Platformist anarchist-communism.
5. The post-war platformist movement.
6. An anarchist communism for the present and future.

Finally, let me say that in these pages I am not attempting to develop a "libertarian Marxism" as both Daniel Guérin and Maximilien Rubel have each in their own ways set out to do.

I think that such a synthesis would be neither fish nor fowl, some sort of absurd Pushmipulyu that would not be able to walk in any direction. At the same time, I must point out that Bakunin himself saw himself as having 'gone to the school' of Karl Marx and wrote the first translation of both the Communist Manifesto and sections of Capital into Russian. The Italian anarchist Covelli produced the first discussion on Capital in Italian and his comrade Carlo Cafiero wrote a summary of the first book of Capital whilst in prison for his part in the Matese insurrection. Marx himself considered this the best yet written. It was then edited, introduced and annotated in French by Bakunin's closest associate James Guillaume.

As the Reponse de Quelques Internationaux (1872) noted, many of the Jura Internationalists had read Capital: "They have read it, and all the same they have not become Marxists; that must appear very singular to these naïve types. How many, on the contrary, in the General Council, are Marxists without ever having opened the book of Marx".

Anarchist communism often hides in the shadows in the general works on anarchism available, only clearly emerging when the ideas of Kropotkin, Reclus and Malatesta are discussed. All too often, apart from the worthless speculations on various philosophers outside of the historic anarchist movement, anarchist communism is rejected as a poor relation to the mass movements launched by anarcho-syndicalism and revolutionary syndicalism – see for example Alain Pengam, Anarchist-Communism (1999) where anarchist communism is referred to as a "poor and despised relation". Brian Morris in his Anthropology, Ecology, and Anarchism: A Reader (2015), replies that this is misleading and asserts that anarchist communism is the main current within anarchism. Pengam further states that the accommodation of anarchist communism to syndicalism, made it a "simple variant of anarcho-syndicalism", that it failed to discover the causes of the counter-revolution initiated by the Bolsheviks, and that it died as a credible current with the aftermaths of the Mexican and Russian Revolutions and that it was absorbed or replaced by anarcho-syndicalism. This book will seek to counter these assertions.

Anarchist communism, as opposed to anarchist collectivism, is the only anarchist current that specifically argues for the end of the market economy and of exchange value. It has survived down to the present day and features, I would argue, as an important current in Russia, France, Latin America, Ukraine, China and Japan amongst other countries. This book seeks to rehabilitate the current of anarchist communism and make it better known and understood; and to renovate and modernise it.

Chapter One
Prehistory of The Idea: Part One

"The first appearance of a really active communist party is found within the framework of the bourgeois revolution, at the moment where the constitutional monarchy is suppressed. The most consistent republicans, in England the Levellers, in France Babeuf, Buonarroti are the first to have proclaimed these 'social questions'. The 'Conspiracy of Babeuf' written by his friend and comrade Buonarroti, shows how these republicans derived their social insight from the movement of history. It also demonstrates that when the social question of princedom versus republic is removed, not a single social question of the kind that interests the proletariat has been solved." (Karl Marx 1847 Moralising criticism and critical morality in Marx/Engels *Sur la Revolution Française*, Paris, Messidor/Editions Sociales, 1985 p. 91)

"True religion and undefiled is this, to make restitution of the Earth which hath been taken and held from the common people by the power of Conquests formerly and so set the oppressed free" (Gerard Winstanley, *A New Yeers Gift for the Parliament of the Armie*, 1650)

Anarchism is not the product of the minds of a few intellectuals divorced from the great mass of the people. It springs directly from the struggle of workers and the oppressed against capitalism, from their needs and necessities, and their unrealised desires for freedom, equality, happiness and self-fulfilment. Whenever revolutions challenged the old order, anarchist ideas and forms of organisation emerged, if only briefly, and often without calling themselves such.

In the English revolution, groups on the radical fringe of Puritanism, the Levellers and Diggers, developed libertarian ideas and during the French bourgeois revolution, those workers and artisans who were developing their own class consciousness began to evolve anarchist ideas.

The Levellers, in some ways ancestors of the Chartists, represented the 'left' of Puritan republicanism. They did not believe in universal suffrage, excluding servants, paupers, farm labourers, Catholics, Episcopalians, 'heretics' and women. However, some on their left, like Walwyn, did advance ideas of community of property. One of them,

William Everard, who had been a soldier in the New Model Army, had been dismissed from it for spreading Leveller ideas. It was he and Gerard Winstanley who helped found the movement known as the Diggers. This group made up mainly of landless farm workers and out of work labourers, assembled at St. George's Hill near Walton-on-Thames in 1649 and began to dig up the common land to sow vegetables. Unremitting prosecution, including beatings and trampling of Digger crops, led to the abandonment of the Digger experiment by March 1650. This minor event in the English Revolution would have become a mere footnote if not for the writings of Gerard Winstanley, who attempted to continue on from the ideas of the early Digger example of propaganda by the deed by a sustained propaganda by the word. During the land experiment Winstanley issued a flurry of pamphlets, which as "his ideas rapidly evolved, came to constitute the first systematic exposition of libertarian communism in English". (Rexroth, Communalism).

Winstanley was the son of a Wigan mercer and continued in this trade until bankrupted in the depression which began in 1643.

Like previous writings of a socio-religious nature, Winstanley's writings have a large dose of chiliasm. But this chiliasm does not involve the saving of an Elect few, but the divinisation of 'Man', rejecting a patriarchal God as the "doctrine of a sickly and weak spirit who hath lost his understanding in the knowledge of the Creation and of the temper of his own Heart and Nature and so runs into fancies" (The Law of Freedom in a Platform or True Magistracy Restored, 1652). Rejection of heaven and hell was set alongside the conception of a communism of the land.

"The earth with all her fruits of Corn, Cattle and such like was made to be a common Store-house of livelihood, to all mankinde, friend and foe, without exception". (A Declaration from the Poor Oppressed People of England, 1649).

Equally alongside this development of communism of the land is a clear understanding of class and State oppression: "The power of the murdering and thieving sword formerly as well as now of late years hath set up a government and maintains that government; for what are prisons and putting others to death, but the power of the sword to enforce people to that Government which was got by Conquest and

Winstanley by Clifford Harper

sword and cannot stand of itself but by the same murdering power". (ibid.)

Winstanley believed that land communism if carried out would eventually lead to the communalisation of all the resulting wealth, including crafts and manufacture.

However, Winstanley's pacifism meant that no resistance was put up to the violent attacks on the Diggers, their houses and their crops and livestock. Like later rationalists, he believed that the pure example of the Diggers would lead even the rich and powerful to join them. A generous nature, but a poor understanding of the hold that riches and power have.

The Enragés

"Liberty is nothing but a vain phantom when one class of men can starve another with impunity. Equality is nothing but a vain phantom when the rich, through monopoly, exercise the right of life or death over their like. The republic is nothing but a vain phantom when the counter-revolution can operate every day through the price of commodities, which three quarters of all citizens cannot afford without shedding tears." (Roux, Address to the Convention, 1793)

The French Revolution was the second large scale attempt by the newly emerging bourgeoisie to overthrow the monarchy and aristocracy, and to establish itself as a new ruling class. In doing so, it needed new mechanisms of control, and as many historians have noted, the French Revolution was the cradle of parliamentary democracy. Like a previous experiment of the bourgeoisie, the English revolution, the French revolution offered the chance for other ideas to emerge. Just as radical, communistic ideas were espoused by John Clipsham and his friends during the Jack Cade uprising, an attempt by the merchant class to limit the power of the monarchy, and just as the Diggers and others were to advance radical ideas during the English Revolution, ideas that represented the interests of the rural and urban poor and dispossessed – so the French revolution offered the chance for an embryo of proletarian revolution to gestate.

Before looking at the Enragés, we should bear in mind a considerable anarchist mythology around this loose coalition which had its origins in late 19th century anarchist attempts to establish a lineage dating back to the French Revolution. Kropotkin and others looked towards the sans-culottes, the Sections (the committees that governed subdivisions of Paris from 1790 onwards), and the Enragés themselves. They tried to make out that they were closely akin to their predecessors. Jean Grave was to admit that little was known of Enragé programmes, but that they were closest to the people and advanced essentially anarchist ideas. This rather open armed welcome into the ranks of anarchism was repeated in later works like Woodcock's Anarchism.

The Enragés were a loosely knit group centred in the Gravilliers district of Paris, based upon the shoemakers and carpenters of that quartier. One of the foremost of them was Jacques Roux, a country priest who, it was alleged by a State official, had told his congregation in 1790 that "the land belongs to all equally".However, as R. B. Rose has noted, Roux's opinions on property appeared far more moderate and conformist in two tracts published in the same year (Roland B. Rose, Socialism and the French revolution: The Cercle Social and the Enragés. Bulletin of the John Rylands Library. 1958;41(1):139-166.). In one of them he wrote that: "Properties being an inviolable and sacred right, of which nobody can be deprived, except because of public necessity... and with just... indemnity", hardly different in any way from The Rights of Man declaration of 1789. He was to affirm the natural right of all to subsistence, referring to the "products of the earth, which like the elements, belong to all men" (in Publiciste, 28th July 1793, cited in Rose p.20)

Alongside Roux worked the orator Jean Varlet (though in an earlier time Roux had denounced Varlet as a "disorganiser" with the attempted insurrection of 10th March 1793). Roux had taken part in the agitation of the Gravilliers against price rises, Varlet had led attacks on the Girondins, the conservative group within the Convention. Now they collaborated in June 1973 in further agitation over price rises. To their numbers were added the activist Jean-Théophile Leclerc and the Society of Revolutionary Republican Women, among whom were Claire Lacombe and Pauline Léon.

Varlet talked about limiting the power of the rich in favour of the poor, and fulminated against "priests, the great, the financiers" (Plan for A New Organisation of Society, 1792). In a series of pamphlets, he stressed the need for direct democracy and for eternal vigilance. He was highly suspicious of representative assemblies, and was regarded with distaste by Robespierre and the rest of the Jacobin Montagne.

Leclerc in his paper L'Ami Du Peuple paired Roux's insistence on the natural right to subsistence with Varlet's views on limiting the power of the rich. He stated that "All men have an equal right to subsistence and to all products of the earth which are theirs from an indispensable need to assure their existence". In No 2 of L'Ami Du Peuple he wrote: "To the aristocracy of nobles has succeeded the bourgeois and mercantile class; this class which formed in several ways an intermediate caste between the first and the people, had acquired thanks to its riches, as much of the needs, and by consequence, as much of the vices as the superior class". He warned that these men would become the cruellest enemies of the people. Roux was to say in his Address to The Convention (1793) that: "It's the rich, who, for four years have profited from the Revolution. It's the merchant aristocracy, more terrible than the noble aristocracy which oppresses us".

The Enragés were closest to the masses and understood best their concerns. This realisation that the bourgeois class was superseding the monarchy and aristocracy was one of their greatest insights, as was their distrust of representative democracy and their reliance on the popular revolutionary bodies. But the masses they were relating to were not the working class, which barely existed, but the sans-culottes, made up of small masters, their journeymen employees and their apprentices. This class and their political spokespeople, the Enragés, agitated against the agioteurs, the money speculators, and against the accapareurs, the "cornerers" of supplies of food and raw materials. The outlook of Roux is revealed when he says that when he lets himself go against these people he was "very far from including in this infamous class a large number of grocers and merchants who have rendered themselves recommendable by their civicism and their humanity" (Address to The Convention, 1793). Thus the political outlook of the Enragés is not without problems, and in all truth the assertion that they were fully fledged anarchists or indeed communists has to be taken with caution.

One other important feature of the Enragés was the inclusion in the alliance of The Society of Revolutionary Women. This organisation insisted on the immediate involvement of women in political and social action. On the 12th May 1793 the Society had demanded the right for women to carry arms so that they could fight the reaction in the Vendée. From its beginnings one of the themes of the developing radical movement amongst the masses was that of women's liberation and this was to be seen repeatedly over the coming decades.

Jacobin repression fell heavily on the Enragés. The Society of Revolutionary Republican Women was banned, Roux and Varlet arrested. Roux cheated the guillotine blade by taking his own life. Varlet, a survivor of the Terror, witnessed the end of Robespierre, the Thermidor and the imposition of the Directory. Under the Thermidorean Convention in 1794, he was arrested with Babeuf for attempting to create an opposition movement, resulting in a year's imprisonment. After that, he was three times exiled from Paris. He re-emerged during the 1830 Revolution at Nantes, bringing out some small pamphlets. He was already 72 years old at the time and all trace of him is lost in 1832, until his death by drowning in 1837.

Varlet produced a pamphlet of 15 pages, Gare L'Explosion (Beware the Explosion) which appeared on 1st October 1794. A second edition with a slight change of words appeared on the 6th October. Varlet was already in prison. Mourning the end of revolutionary hopes and denouncing the Thermidorean Convention, he cried out: "For any reasoning being, Government and Revolution are incompatible, at least unless the people wishes to constitute the organs of power in permanent insurrection against themselves, which is too absurd to believe". Varlet had drawn the lessons of revolutionary defeat and developed an anarchist conclusion.

Babeuf

Gracchus Babeuf developed the ideas of his group in the aftermath of the crushing of the Enragés in 1793. But the ideas that he developed were to turn away from the mass action of the Enragés, rooted as they were in the popular quarters of Paris, towards conspiratorial action by small and secret enlightened elites, but it could also be argued that Babeuf represented the extreme wing of bourgeois republicanism. He attempted to amalgamate the revolutionary idea of the emerging bourgeoisie – democracy – with the revolutionary idea of the embryonic working class-communism. Babeuf wanted to introduce democracy and then to build communism, in small stages. The people, through a democratic Constitution, would veto all laws until the maintenance of all citizens should be assured by law, as Kropotkin notes. In fact, Babeuf thinks that an individual, if he has enough of a strong will, can introduce communism single-handedly.

It should be remembered that the principal subscribers to the Babouvists' paper were bankers, manufacturers, financiers, high officials, functionaries and professionals. They supported the Babouvist grouping because they had been closely linked with the Jacobin dictatorship and were fearful of the growing threat of White reaction. They supported Babeuf in spite of his avowed communism.

It is possible that a triumph of Babouvism would not have led to the establishment of a communist society, but would have speeded up the advancement of capitalist society, in the process bypassing the Bonapartist phrase, a costly and destructive phrase for emerging capitalist society. This is not to deny the courage and conviction of Babeuf, but to recognise that he could have quickly become a prisoner of these bourgeois forces. The Babouvists used every means possible at their disposal, means which became those of every succeeding revolutionary grouping – newspapers, posters, songs, public meetings.

Whilst people like Babeuf were to develop communist ideas, they linked this to a special elite carrying out a revolutionary dictatorship.

As Kropotkin notes:

"It is obvious that communism in 1793 did not appear with that completeness of doctrine which is found with the French followers of Fourier and Saint-Simon.... In 1793 communist ideas were not worked out in the quiet of a private study; they were born from the needs of the moment. This is why the social problem showed itself during the Great Revolution superior to the socialism of 1848 and of its later forms. It went straight to the root in attacking the distribution of produce.

"This communism certainly appears fragmentary to us, especially as stress was laid by its exponents upon its different separate aspects; and there always remained in it what we might call partial communism. It admitted individual possession side by side with common property, and while proclaiming the right of all to the entire sum of the fruits of production, it yet recognised an individual right to the "superfluous", by the side of all to the products of "first and second necessity". Nevertheless, the three principal aspects of communism are already to be found in the teachings of 1793: Land communism, industrial communism, and communism in commerce and credit" (The Great French Revolution, Elephant Editions, 1986, p.508).

Communist and anarchist ideas emerged from among the sans-culottes masses during the Revolution. They were to be formalised in writing and speeches in various ways by Babeuf, Maréchal and Buonarroti and to a lesser extent by the Enragés. The revolutionary tradition of the clubs managed to survive under the rule of Louis

Philippe, with the secret Communistes Materialistes groupings of the indefatigable Blanqui and Barbès. However, the outlook of these groupings was greatly affected by the radical Jacobinism of the Babouvists, not to mention the repressive conditions under which these groupings were forced to operate.

Sylvain Maréchal

Maréchal, whilst linked to Babouvism, deserves an individual mention. Sylvain Maréchal was born in 1750, the son of a wine merchant in the Les Halles district of Paris. He trained as a lawyer, but could not practice because of an acute stutter. He then obtained work in a library. His reading quickly led him to an atheist position. He began to write and publish on the subject. This lost him his job, and he was driven into poverty. He managed to get other library work and eventually pulled himself out of his straitened circumstances.

He wrote and published an almanac containing a revolutionary calendar, with a drastic revision and renaming of the months. This caused it to be burnt on the orders of the Parlement of Paris, and Maréchal to be condemned to three months imprisonment in 1788.

This confirmed his evolving republicanism, and he began to write on the subject. His The First Lessons of the Oldest Son of the King, which appeared later in the year, stated that there was no need for kings, even the best intentioned. "Misfortune to the people whose king is generous! The king can only give what he has taken from his people. The more the king gives, the more he takes from his people". Maréchal called for a general strike of producers and called for the earth to be taken in common by all who lived on it.

Maréchal continued his atheistic and anti-clerical agitation with the coming of the Revolution, through newspapers and pamphlets. He made the acquaintance of Babeuf in March 1793, supporting him financially and helping him to get out of prison on provisional liberty. He disapproved of the Terror, and used his standing as a revolutionary to help people avoid execution. He felt that the Terror had been an instrument to replace the rule of the monarchy and aristocracy with that of businessmen and landowners.

He kept in contact with Babeuf during the latter's protracted stays in prison and he eventually was involved in the Babouvist leadership.

He wrote the Manifeste des Egaux (Manifesto of the Equals) for the grouping, although the majority of Babouvists had not approved it.

In this Manifesto he argues for a stateless communism. "The French revolution is only the front runner of another revolution much grander, of much greater occasion, and which will be the last". He advances the notion of the common good, of a common wealth, where there will be "no more individual ownership of the land", because "the earth belongs to no one". He called for an end to a system where the vast majority "toils and sweats at the service of and for the pleasure of an extreme minority", and for the disappearance of "revolting distinctions between rich and poor...between governors and governed".

Maréchal avoided imprisonment with the repression of the Babouvist movement. He remained outspoken, using his book History of Russia to hide a veiled attack on Napoleon in 1802. He died the following year.

Whilst being at the forefront of those who were developing the idea of communism, it should be noted that he still could not shed all the prejudices of his age. Thus, one of his last works was Projet de loi portant défense d'apprendre à lire aux femmes (Law Project Prohibiting Women from Learning to Read), written in 1801. Nevertheless, Kropotkin was right in detecting in him a "vague aspiration to that which we call anarchist communism today" (The Great French Revolution, Elephant editions, 1796, p.509).

The emergence of the conception of Communism

It should be remembered that neither Babeuf nor Maréchal had invented the term "communism". The idea of a free and equal society brought about through the sharing of the fruits of the earth goes back to a multitude of religious and philosophical writings.

A first written mention of the word "communist" itself was found in the book of condolences of the parish of Guillestre (Hautes Alpes) in France in 1789. Babeuf, of course, never used the word himself, calling himself a communalist, believing that a community of goods would result from a community of work.

With the fall of Robespierre there is a mention of the word communism when Restif de la Bretonne talks about a general assembly of the Club du Pantheon, which was one of the most democratic in Paris. "A citizen demands the rejection of the Constitution and the establishment of communism. This eye-witness report was published in Paris in 1797". (Marius Berou in an article in Le Peuple no 1537 20th November 2002 p 8-9)

Buonarroti

Buonarroti produced a history of the Babeuf conspiracy in 1830 (followed by an English translation by the Chartist leader Bronterre O'Brien). This book was extremely influential in reviving the communist tradition as represented by Babouvism. As David Thomson notes in his The Babeuf Plot: "Revolutionaries of the July Monarchy, working in conditions that were new, strove to link their own efforts to the epic story of the Babouvists, and so emphasise the direct continuity of the revolutionary tradition." Buonarroti's book came at an appropriate time. The revolutionary events of 1830 from July 27th to August 20th were a result of an alliance between the radical bourgeoisie and the artisans and workers. Once the task of asserting their own interests was accomplished, the working class was abandoned by its erstwhile allies. Attempting to assert their own interests, several insurrections broke out with the demands for the establishment of a republic and the end of political monopoly. But the newly confident bourgeoisie had not only the Army on its side but had organised itself militarily in the National Guard. The risings were all crushed. A dawning realisation of the opposing interests of the working people and the 'middle class' led some republican workers and artisans to develop the need for their own political and organisational autonomy, and a link to the ideas of Babouvism was established with the fortuitous publication of Buonarroti's book. The 1830, 1832 and 1834 risings, the mass actions in Lyons by the workers there, the workers strikes in Paris, the circulation of the ideas of Saint-Simon, Fourier, and Owen all had their effect.

Buonarroti was still very much a prisoner of the radical Jacobinism of the most advanced bourgeois elements in his praise of Robespierre's Republic of Virtue. It was difficult for him to relate to the newly emerging urban working class, although elements in that class were able to recognise and make use of the ideas of any worth in his thinking and that of Babeuf and Maréchal et compagnie. Georges Duveau notes that "a kind of perfunctory communism was born and grew up which for that very reason was just the thing to spread through the workshops of the Temple, the Faubourg Saint-Antoine and the Faubourg Saint-Marcel". Thus came about a fusion of these advanced radical Jacobinist ideas with the aspirations of this new class, and the successor of Babeuf and Buonarroti, Auguste Blanqui, was to recognise and utilise this fusion, even though he too was a prisoner of the revolutionary conspiracy, the "temporary" revolutionary dictatorship, and the elite revolutionary group. At the same time, outside the self-educated urban workers and artisans, the main social groupings attracted to Blanquism were the declassed intellectuals and rootless bourgeois youth who were either unable or unwilling to subscribe to the project of the newly confident bourgeoisie of enriching themselves.

The Society of the Rights of Man and the Citizen which existed between 1832 and 1834 regrouped many of those Parisian workers who had been disillusioned by the events of the July Days. Operating in its radical wing was the law student Napoléon-Aimé Lebon. He has left few traces, but it appears that it was he who was to have an important role in developing both the idea of communism and the practice of its adherents in his two Aphorisms of 1834 written in the Sainte Pelagie prison – La propriété instrument de notre exploitation and Le capital social: nature, industrie, intelligence (Pour Une Généalogie du Communisme Français in Communisme and Cahiers d'Histoire N°77, Mouvements communistes dans la France des années 1830-1840. Table ronde: Louis Hincker, Alain Maillard, Claude Mazauric, Michèle Rio-Sarcey).

In the first of his Aphorisms he remarks: "you first and principally object, that our projects of community are inadmissible, in that they outweigh the abolition of individual property... but... where do you see that property is always the fruit of work? And if any man has to work to live, how did you understand that so many capitalists, entrepreneurs of industry can live off the work of others? Property! What else is it in their hands than the instrument of our exploitation?"

Born in Dieppe, Lebon was first a student of medicine and then a student of law (he still regarded himself as a law student at the age of 40!) A proponent of direct action within the Society, he however had opposed combinations (unions) of artisans and workers in 1833, returning to the same theme in 1848 when he stated: "A rise in wages, reduction in work, all that is a cause of ruin for manufacturers (entrepreneurs), and only gains insignificant relief. Furthermore, these actions have the harmful quality of perpetuating differences between classes" (Iorwerth Prothero, Radical Artisans in England and France, 1830-1870, p.111). Lebon epitomises a communism of sentiment which fails to connect with the situation of artisans and workers of the period.

The term 'communism' itself did not appear in print till the end of the 18th century in a book review by Restif de la Bretonne (the book has never been traced). It is an eyewitness account published in Paris in 1797 of a meeting of the Club du Pantheon where "A citizen demands the rejection of the Constitution and the establishment of communism". Babeuf never used the word in print or in any of his recorded speeches and it cannot be traced in the writings of any other radical before this mention. But now the term began to be used by this new generation of revolutionaries. During the trial on 22nd and 24th July 1835 of several militants involved in the attempted insurrection of April 1834 and accused of a plot and attentats against "internal State security", Victor Poinsot, the public prosecutor for the Department of the Seine, accused them of constituting "a sect of Communists and radicals". He defined this description by proposing that they aimed for: "by means of propaganda and of armed insurrection, the establishment of the most absolute social equality, on the ruins of all properties, without distinction or object" (cited in Mazauric).

Engels seemed to think that: "During this time (1834 or 1835) a new doctrine sprang up among the republican working men. They saw that even after having succeeded in their democratic plans they would continue the dupes of their more gifted and better educated leaders, and that their social condition, the cause of their political discontent, would not be bettered by any political change whatsoever. They referred to the history of the great revolution, and eagerly seized upon Babeuf's communism. This is all that can, with safety, be asserted concerning the origin of modern Communism in France; the subject was first discussed in the dark lanes and crowded alleys of the Parisian suburb, Saint-Antoine, and soon after in the secret assemblies of conspirators. Those who know more about its origin are very careful to keep their

knowledge to themselves, in order to avoid the "strong arm of the law""
(Friedrich Engels, Progress of Social Reform on the Continent, 1843).

There appears to have been a mass awakening by Parisian workers in the years 1839-40. The agent provocateur De La Hodde gives much information about the new groups created by Parisian workers in his Histoire des Societés Secretes (1850). He described the general strike that took place in 1840 in Paris as "inspired by communist ideas" and the creation of the Society of Egalitarian Workers, made up exclusively of workers founded in the same year with a clearly communist programme (Marius Darmès, a floor cleaner who attempted to assassinate Louis Philippe, appears to have belonged to this Society).

As well as being linked to the strike, the Society appears to have had two sets of demands, minimum with the idea of wages fixed by law and mutual aid societies, and maximum with the establishment of a popular dictatorship and an egalitarian society. Engels (ibid) says that "they purposed making the world a working-man's community, putting down every refinement of civilisation, science, the fine arts, etc, as useless, dangerous, and aristocratic luxuries….". A breakaway from this was the Revolutionary Communist Society, also exclusively made up of workers, which rejected the blind discipline among the Egalitarian Workers and above all the lack of discussion within it. Karl Marx in one of his first political articles on 16th October 1842 'Communism and the Augsburger Allgemeine Zeitung' was able to say that 'communism' had already become an international movement, appearing in Britain and Germany as well as France.

Socialism and Communism

The term 'socialism' first saw the light of day in England print in an Owenite publication of 1827, The Co-operative Magazine (see the section on William Thompson). It described the co-operative practices of the Owenites. In France it first appeared in Le Globe in 1832. This was a paper produced by the journalist Pierre Leroux, and was an official organ of the followers of Saint-Simon. Again, it was used to describe Saint-Simon's ideas for a collective plan of society. Leroux was later to rather inaccurately claim that he had first coined the term as a neologism to counter the other neologism individualism, which was increasingly being used because of the circulation of Jeremy Bentham's thought. Thus, it implied a quest for social solutions to the ills of society rather than Benthamite individualism. It was officially adopted as a term by the Owenites in 1841, and was often used to describe the followers of Saint-Simon and Fourier. As Corcoran notes (p3.) "...this innovation only incorporated the meanings already widely associated with le social, the complex of social concerns focused upon by several schools of 'social science' and an increasingly politically oriented literary and artistic romanticism".

Communism, for its part, referred to a belief in absolute social equality which must develop into the Communauté – the community of liberty, equality and fraternity. This term preceded that of communism and was used by Babeuf to describe his social vision, just as it was later used by the likes of Dézamy etc (note that Babeuf also used the terms "communautiste").

The term communist became more and more widely used under the July Monarchy as more and more political activists began to associate themselves with the concept of communism. On one hand were the revolutionary communists, from a Babouvist background, on the other were the followers of Cabet. At the trial of Darmès one witness testified that there were "two branches of the communists, one of which he did not think was in favour of violent means, the other, the communistes immédiats, who wished to overthrow the present government by any means."

Cabet-Communism Gets Religion

"It is indeed time that hatreds were forgotten and that all people rallied under a single flag. Shall that flag be Communism? The Icarians will enthusiastically answer yes" (Cabet, Journey to Icaria, English language edition, 1884, p.87).

Etienne Cabet was the son of a cooper from Dijon. His outspokenness and involvement in radical republicanism meant a long exile in England, and in the reading room of the British Museum, he discovered the ideas of Thomas More, as well as acquainting himself with the personage and the ideas of the cooperative thinker Robert Owen.

Cabet began to use Communism as an expression to describe a specific body of ideas and future society linked to those ideas. He broke with Buonarroti's and thus Jacobin theories of organisation. At this time Louis Philippe's regime was multiplying its provocations to legitimise its policies of repression. Cabet wished to avoid this. He contributed to the new interest in the most radical ideas of the French Revolution with his Histoire Populaire de la Revolution Française in 1840. The same year he produced his utopian novel Voyage en Icarie (Journey to Icaria) which depicted a future communist society. Unfortunately, this communist society was enclosed within a very authoritarian framework. Cabet had emerged from a radical Jacobin background, but his radicalism owed less to Babouvism than has sometimes been alleged. He had known Buonarroti in the Carbonari in the 1820s and was familiar with Babouvist ideas, but seems to have owed more to Thomas More and Robert Owen. Cabet, in Journey to Icaria, describes Christ as the leading teacher of communism and claims that the Icarian community "has fraternity as its basis, the love preached by the gospels and by Christianity". The society that Cabet describes is created by peaceful change after just two days of fighting which overthrew the tyrants. Cabet stated that he was "neither a Hébertist nor a Babouvist".

Cabet saw in his novel a modern version of More's Utopia as improved by the economic ideas of Owen. It is not particularly original, but it became the required reading of every French radical (and beyond). There is no money and all goods and property are shared in common, but it is a grim vision of communism, one where diet, clothing, furniture, housing, is uniform, where people work seven hours a day, and where women, apart from their seven hours in the workshops or fields, continue to carry out housework. There is no money and all goods and property are shared in common. Social life is closely supervised. Despite this the book caught the imagination of many.

In 1841 Cabet resurrected his paper Le Populaire. He called for the establishment of the community of goods "only by the power of public opinion, by the will of the nation, and by the rule of law".

Le Populaire did indeed become very popular and became one of the most widely read papers in France. This was against a backdrop of rising labour unrest in the country, with strikes in Belleville, in Lyon and Rouen in 1840. Cabet increasingly equated Communism with Christianity. He advanced the need for the abolition of private property, whilst warning artisans and workers away from demonstrations and from the revolutionary secret societies. The best strategy to accomplish the aims of communism was "civil courage", in other words passive resistance.

Cabetism became very popular, with Icarian chapters in many towns and cities, Lyon become a veritable stronghold of Icarian thought. It appealed above all to the artisan and not to the day labourer who was more likely to favour strikes and resistance to the authorities. For their part merchants, businessmen and shopkeepers were horrified by Icarianism and saw no difference between them and the revolutionary communists. Leading Icarians included a shoemaker, a shoemaker's tools salesman, a factory foreman, a cabinet maker, a tailor, a maker of artificial flowers, a physician, and a Polish mystic (!) but there were exceptions to the rule.

In Toulouse, another very strong chapter of Icarianism was organised, and participated in the census riots of July 1841. During the riots building workers were actively recruited to Icarianism. In July of the following year, the Icarians organised a demonstration of 600 at La Daurade church to commemorate the death of one of the rioters on the barricades. The police believed rightly or wrongly that the Icarians were planning for an armed insurrection and arrested leading Icarians in Toulouse in 1843. In a sign of increasing feeling of the need for autonomy from bourgeois republicans, they rejected their offer of legal aid and for a liberal republican deputy to serve as their defence lawyer. The Icarians were acquitted. Later on, the following year they organised an active boycott among artisans and workers of the funeral procession of a liberal republican leader (See Bullets and Barricades: Class Formation and Republican Politics in France,1830-1871, Ronald Aminzade, 1993).

Cabet had been able to create a mass movement that was estimated as from being as strong as anywhere between 100,000 and 400,000 with influence elsewhere – Germany, Switzerland, England. He and his paper Le Populaire had been able to favourably introduce the concept of communism to a large number of artisans and workers. Cabetism should not be characterised as standing aside in a sectarian manner from the developing workers' movement, as some Marxist historians like Michael Löwy have claimed (in The Theory of Revolution in the Young Marx). The mass base of Cabetism meant that it was sometimes in contradiction with the views of its leader, involving itself in riots, in workers' societies, in strikes etc. There was a dynamic to disengage with the pacifistic policies of Cabet and because of the mass nature of Icarianism it was pulled in different directions by the quite dramatic development of class struggle under the July Monarchy (Engels (ibid) was to say that "even the Icarians, though they declare in their publications that they abhor physical revolutions and secret societies, even they are associated in this manner, and would gladly seize upon any opportunity to establish a republic by force".). Cabet was also a great educator and advocate of the masses. His Citizen's Guide (1842) instructed on how to deal with the police and courts if arrested, house searches, temporary detentions, trials both secret and before an open court.

By 1844 Cabet began to emphasise his leadership more strongly. In 1846 he published another book Le Vrai Christianisme Suivant Jesus Christ (Real Christianity Following Jesus Christ). This was the beginning of the transformation of Cabetism from a political into one of a messianic religious movement. Cabet was elevated by some of his followers into the status of a Saviour, something which he increasingly appeared to believe himself. That year saw a severe depression in France as a result of a disastrous wheat harvest. Bread prices rose, as did unemployment. Bread riots became more frequent. The force of circumstances saw more Icarians abandoning their pacifism and taking part in the civil unrest. The artisan base of Icarian communism began to radicalise. Some, like Doctor Louis Desmoulins of the Tours chapter of Icarianism called on Cabet to abandon his doctrine of civil courage. Desmoulins told Cabet that rank-and-file Icarians were becoming increasingly frustrated by his failure to act and that he was seen as the "sole obstacle that prevents the Communist Party" from bringing about social change (letter to Cabet, November 26, 1846. See Introduction to Travels in Icaria by Robert Sutton, 2003, and Étienne Cabet and the Icarian Communist Movement in France 1839-1848 by Christopher H. Johnson, 1968. Desmoulins was known as "the doctor of the disinherited of fortune", for his good works among the working class of Tours. He was arrested as a member of the workers' unions after the grain riots in Tours of 21st to 23rd November 1846. He was deported by Napoleon III's regime to Lambessa in Algeria. He returned broken in health and died in poverty in 1858.)

In March 1847 repression began to fall upon the Icarians. Like so many others, Cabet soon succumbed to the call of setting up a utopian colony in America. Many Icarians refused to countenance this, seeing it as a cop-out. Subscriptions to Le Populaire fell by 30 per cent.

Before Cabet left for the States he was overtaken by events. Three weeks after the advance guard of colonists had left for Texas, revolution broke out in February 1848, overthrowing Louis Philippe. The second Republic was proclaimed. The Revolution was to dismantle Icarianism. A section of the Icarians called for the return of the advance guard, an end to the whole scheme of emigration, and a concentration on an effort to establish communism in France. Cabet attempted to do this, but by April a bourgeois administration led by Lamartine and Ledru-Rollin was in place and a backlash was whipped up against all socialists, radical republicans and communists. Cabet's house was besieged by a howling mob and many Icarians were persecuted. The growth of reaction pushed Cabet to cross the Atlantic himself.

The colonies established by Cabet, which took 5,000 Icarians out of France, soon foundered in futility and recrimination like so many others, and he became more eccentric and autocratic towards the close of his life. The development of the leadership cult may also have contributed to why so many Icarian communists began to move over to republican socialism during the last two years of Louis Phillippe's July Monarchy. These years were also ones of severe economic crisis. Republican socialist leaders said that they could solve the social question through reform of suffrage, cannily promising that such reform would lead on to right to work laws and full employment. The failure of the Icarian movement led many of its members away from its essentially anti-electoralist stance towards the promise of action through a mass mobilisation for electoral reform. The Icarian movement disappeared. However, Cabet's movement had helped bring about the idea of working-class autonomy (against the views of Cabet himself who favoured class conciliation) and led to the establishment of several important and persistent radical workers circles in France, including Lyon, and as we will see, later contributed towards the development of a specific anarchist communism.

Until very recently, Cabet, who has only been translated into English in the last few years, is associated more with the communal colonies set up in the USA than with the mass movement he created in France. Marx praised Cabet for his "practical attitude towards the proletariat" whilst later warning against the communal activities of the Icarians in this slightly inaccurate mention in the Communist Manifesto: "Therefore, although the originators of these systems were, in many respects, revolutionary, their disciples have, in every case, formed mere reactionary sects. They hold fast by the original views of their masters, in opposition to the progressive historical development of the proletariat. They, therefore, endeavour, and that consistently, to deaden the class struggle and to reconcile class antagonisms. They still dream of experimental realisations of their social Utopias, of founding isolated 'phalanstères', of establishing 'Home Colonies', of setting up a 'Little Icaria' – duodecimo editions of the New Jerusalem – and to realise all these castles in the air, they are compelled to appeal to the feelings and purses of the bourgeois."

As Johnson remarks "instead of a communist mass movement fortifying the far left of a unified social republican opposition in France, Icarian communism evolved into a semi-religious sect" (p.143).

Dézamy

It should be emphasised again that not all those who proclaimed themselves communists were Icarians, far from it. There were those who rejected the religiosity of Icarianism. The "communist party", this disparate body of thought, which developed in the 1840s was also made up of those who had been involved in the Carbonari with Buonarroti, those who had fought on the barricades of 1830, 1832 and 1834, who had taken part with Barbès and Blanqui in the Societé des Familles and the Societé des Saisons or in the Societé des Travailleurs Egalitaires.

The "utopian" socialism of the movements around Saint-Simon and Fourier had offered little to the urban artisans and newly developing working class, and as Max Nettlau, the Herodotus of anarchism, notes "it was really an act of independence on their part when many of them drew away from these to join a communism which proposed direct and voluntary action", in other words towards the ideas of Cabet and indeed to those more radical, like Théodore Dézamy, who had started as a Cabetian and had broken with him because of his authoritarianism and his turn towards the setting up of American colonies and away from action in France. Dézamy edited a paper Le Communitaire – in these early days communitarian was used as an alternative expression to communist just as later libertarian was used as an alternative to anarchist.

Dézamy had been Cabet's secretary. As well as being an animator of the aforementioned Communistes Matérialistes circles he was one of the main organisers of the Communist Banquet (banquets and speeches at banquets were a particular form of spreading radical ideas at the time) organised on the slopes of the Parisian working class quarter of Belleville on 1st July 1840 (another organiser was Jean-Jacques Pillot from the Babouvist current, a defrocked priest, who ended his life in prison as a result of his activity in the 1871 Paris Commune as a Blanquist activist). This banquet was a reply to those of the republican banquets which called for the extension of the vote. Under the auspices of the Communist Republicans 1,000 people took part in this banquet, including many artisanal workers. The orators, craftsmen, small shopkeepers, men of letters with no steady salary, proposed toasts to "real and perfect social equality", "the egalitarian community", "the abolition of free competition", "the abolition of the death penalty", "the emancipation of the worker", "egalitarian education", etc. The historian Jacques Grandjonc tells us that the German workers of the League of the Just that was animated by Wilhelm Weitling must have attended the banquet. (Interestingly, as a sign of a relationship between this emergent communism and the developing workers struggles, it appears that Weitling set up a soup kitchen a few days later to help the unemployed and strikers, as well as establishing a fund for striking tailors). The day after this banquet, a liberal journalist, Léon Faucher, perceived this as a split within the republican party (also called democratic party or radical party) and used the expression "communist party". The word then began to spread rapidly. Engels in his article "Progress of Social Reform on the Continent" written in 1843 notes that discussion of communism began between 1834-5. "This is all that can, with safety, be asserted concerning the origin of modern Communism in France; the subject was first discussed in the dark lanes and crowded allies of the Parisian suburb, Saint-Antoine, and soon after in the secret assemblies of conspirators. Those who know more about its origin are very careful to keep their knowledge to themselves, in order to avoid the "Strong arm of the law"".

Further banquets in Paris were sabotaged by the police though smaller ones took place in Rouen and Lyon. The banquet in Paris showed the popularity of communist ideas among artisans and workers. The Belleville banquet had certainly put communism on the map.

Dézamy's Code de la Communauté of 1843 was a mite less authoritarian than the concepts of Cabet, using a slogan borrowed from Rabelais "Do what you will!" It called for the abolition of money, and of commercial exchange. It advocated an economy that geared itself towards the satisfaction of the needs of all. It believed in the end of the division of labour, including between town and country, capital and provinces. Attractive work for all should be brought in progressively. The State and government should also be abolished progressively and any decisions made by these institutions should no longer be separate from the functioning of society as a whole. To bring this about a revolutionary government would oversee the introduction of communism into social relations.

Dézamy broke with Cabet over the division of labour, which the latter defended as necessary in the name of economic efficiency. The Code took a step forward in that it advocated no transition period between capitalism and communism. There would be no period in which exchange, buying and selling would continue. The immediate abolition of money would ensure that the ruling class would be disarmed socially and economically. Dézamy's Code called for the 'community of goods', opposing itself to the collectivist notion of the 'socialisation of property'.

L'Humanitaire

Cabet issued a refutation of these ideas in a series of pamphlets and he joined battle against another grouping in his Refutation of the Humanitaire. The Humanitaire group described themselves as egalitarian communists, and as a result of their refusing to register themselves as a legal body, suffered imprisonment. All the socialist and republican groups denounced them as immoral because they had advocated the abolition of marriage and the individual family and other interesting ideas in a group statement. One of these ideas was that travel would be a key feature of communist society; it would bring about the mixing of races, and a beneficial exchange between industrial and agricultural activities. Indeed, their journal went further and advanced "anti-political and anarchist ideas" which they believed Maréchal had advocated (quotation from the article on Maréchal in this journal, L'Humanitaire). Two issues of this journal, subtitled organe de la science sociale, were to appear in Paris in the summer of 1841.

This advanced group, which rejected the authoritarian and centralising ideas of most radical groups, was a herald of the anarchist communism to come, and was an isolated beacon in a period which produced a large number of radical publications. We should remember the names of some of those involved: Gabriel Charavay, Jean-Joseph May and Antoine-Pierre Page. Gabriel Charavay was born at Lyon in 1818. As a youth he had frequented communist and Babouvist circles, and was influenced by Maréchal, Babeuf and Buonarroti. He had proposed a toast at the first Communist Banquet in Belleville. Before becoming an editor of L'Humanitaire he had been involved in the workers' paper L'Atelier. He showed his appreciation for Maréchal by writing a biography of him in L'Humanitaire. Charavay was to receive a two year prison sentence not long after. May, like Charavay was a journalist and agronomist. Page was a jewellery worker, whilst another editor, Julien Galliard, was a plumber. Others named during the police investigation included the feminist Louise Dauriat, and bonnet-makers, jewellery workers, shoe-makers, and print workers. Only one of these workers was born in Paris, the others originating from many different regions of France. Cabet's denunciation of L'Humanitaire appears to have precipitated Dézamy's break with him.

The polemic between Cabet and Dézamy was also exacerbated by Cabet's denunciation of Dézamy's advocacy of the abolition of marriage. Dézamy firmed up his critique of Cabet in his Calomnies et Politique de M. Cabet when he wrote: "It is a capital error to believe that co-operation by the bourgeoisie is indispensable for the triumph of the community". He also took Cabet to task for the non-attendance of himself and his followers at the banquet in Belleville. "You refused to attend this banquet. You seemed from the start very unhappy because the proletarians were allowing themselves to raise the communist flag on their own, without having at their head some bourgeois, some well-known name". Dézamy emphasised the need for working class unity as well as the need for propaganda, affirming that "I will never stop crying: Propaganda, propaganda, propaganda". He warned against the perils of personality cults within the workers movement in his prescient address: "Proletarians! It is to you that I address these reflections, to you who, a thousand times already, have been betrayed, sold, handed over, slandered, tortured and mocked by alleged saviours! If you again submit to the cult of individuals, expect to experience once more cruel and poignant illusions". Perhaps Marx himself, who described Dézamy and Jules Gay as the "more scientific French communists" might have taken more notice of this warning.

References

Corcoran, Paul E. (ed). Before Marx: Socialism and Communism in France, 1830-1848

Grandjonc, Jacques. Communisme/Kommunismus/Communism

Guérin, Daniel. La lutte des classes sous la première république

Maillard, Alain Bref apercu historique du movement communiste en France in Cahiers d'Histoire No.77

Maillard, Alain La Communauté des Egaux. Le communisme neo-babouviste dans la France des années 1840

Mazauric, Claude. Une terre d'implantation et d'essaimage: Les origines françaises du communisme historique:
http://www.gabrielperi.fr/une-terre-d%E2%80%99implantation-et-d%E2%80%99essaimage-par-claude-mazauric.html

Pengam, Alain http://theanarchistlibrary.org/library/alain-pengam-anarchist-communism

Rose, R.B. Gracchus Babeuf: The First Revolutionary Communist. Stanford University Press. (1978)

Vanderort, Bruce. Babouvism (Babeuvism)

www.ohiou.edu/Chastain/ac/babouvis.htm

http://richardjohnbr.blogspot.co.uk/2007/07/chartist-lives-john-goodwyn-barmby.html

Chapter Two
Prehistory of the Idea: Part Two

One of the first to actually develop the idea of communism was the German Wilhelm Weitling. As Rexroth notes: "Quite independently of Hegel, and before Marx, he developed a theory of human self-alienation as the primary evil of capitalist production, and some years before Marx or Proudhon he was an avowed communist. In a sense, Marx and Engels joined his communist movement and took it over" (Communalism, Rexroth, 1842, p.294)

Weitling was a tailor who had painstakingly educated himself, had been involved in Blanqui's insurrections in Paris in the 1830s. He began to form secret groupings in Switzerland. Weitling preached that: "The perfect society had no government, but only an administration, no laws, but only obligations, no punishments, but means of correction". He attacked both the wages system and property, and in his early writings like Garantien den Harmonie und Freiheit (1842) he advanced a vision of a stateless communist society. Marx was to write of this work in 1844 in the German language paper Vorwärts based in Paris: "Where among the [German] bourgeoisie – including its philosophers and learned scribes – is to be found a work relating to the emancipation of the bourgeoisie – its political emancipation – similar to Weitling's Guarantees of Harmony and Freedom? If one compares the drab mealy-mouthed mediocrity of German political literature with this vehement and brilliant debut of the German workers, if one compares these gigantic infant shoes of the proletariat with the dwarfish political shoes of the bourgeoisie, one must prophesy that this Cinderella will one day have an athlete's figure". However, he had not broken completely with the influences of Saint-Simon and Fourier and there were authoritarian strains in this vision, for example the concept that: "Faculties can only be developed in so far as they do not disrupt the harmony of society", a concept which Max Stirner, the doyen of individualists, took issue with. At the same time as he preached the idea of an egalitarian and libertarian communist society as enunciated in the quotation above, he believed that a small group of wise men must be in control of this society, at least in the early stages. Like Cabet, he also equated the teachings of Christ with communism, seeing communism as equivalent to the early Christian Church before its degeneration.

Unlike other utopian thinkers of the period, Weitling did not believe that the transition to communism could come about through peaceful means. Armed force would be necessary, something he had imbibed from the traditions of Babeuf and Blanqui. He also believed that the most dispossessed elements, including those derogatorily described as the lumpenproletariat by Marx, would have a key role to play in an expropriating revolution. Bakunin met Weitling in Switzerland and it is likely from him that he gets many of his ideas on the revolutionary role of the most dispossessed.

Weitling had belonged to the League of the Just. This secret group of German workers, originally called the League of Outlaws (Bund der Gechteten), was formed in Paris in 1836, after an unsuccessful uprising in Frankfurt in 1833. The League of the Just was in fact a breakaway from the League of Outlaws, described as "democratic-republican" by Engels (On the History of the Communist League, 1885). It was influenced by an eclectic group of thinkers – Moses Hess, Weitling, Fourier, Proudhon, Blanqui, Cabet, Owen, Feuerbach, and the Left Hegelians. It had links with the Blanquist Societé des Saisons. In fact, Engels regards it as "not much more than the German branch of the French secret societies, especially the Societé des Saisons led by Blanqui and Barbès" (ibid). Following the crushing of the Blanquist uprising in Paris in 1839, one of its members, Carl Schapper, had ended up in London, where he formed the Workers' Educational Society in February, 1840. The League functioned in a semi-secret fashion within it. Schapper had evolved from "demagogue" to Communist, as Engels remarked (in this context demagogue was the term applied to those actively opposed to the reactionary German states and for the unification of Germany).

Weitling, expelled from Switzerland, joined Schapper in London. Schapper and his associates the shoemaker Heinrich Bauer and the watchmaker Joseph Moll had fallen under the influence of Robert Owen and the emerging British labour movement. The London Working Men's Association had called for increased international solidarity, as a result of which William Lovett set up the Society of the

Democratic Friends of All Nations in 1844. Its slogan was All Men are Brethren. In the same period the group around Julian George Harney, secretary of the Democratic Association, which held republican views and orientated itself to artisans and workers, set up the Fraternal Democrats two years later in 1846. It broke with the classless humanism of the Lovett grouping by calling for the oppressed countries of each land to come together. The League of the Just had loose links with both groups and they represented a first attempt at international organisation, calling for the coming together of revolutionaries of all nationalities, the strengthening of brotherhood among peoples, and the conquest of political and social rights.

The German Workers Educational Society adopted the slogan of Lovett's group – Alle Menschen Sind Brueder – and started emphasising the central role of the international proletariat. Through it, the Central Committee of the League of the Just in London was able to establish supremacy over other groups of the League in France, Germany and Switzerland.

Weitling had profound disagreements with this group. He denied the notion that the proletariat was a separate class with its own class interests. As far as he was concerned, it was only a section of the great mass of the oppressed. He reiterated his ideas that the poorest sections, including robbers and bandits, were its most revolutionary sections.

In later years, after the collapse of the revolutionary hopes of 1848, and his exile in the United States, Weitling increasingly turned away from communist ideas towards Proudhonist mutualism. After disillusionment with the colony of Communia set up mostly by German immigrants from the 1848 Revolution, his ideas became increasingly eccentric.

In a later chapter we will deal with the clash between Weitling on one hand and Marx and Engels on the other.

The 1848 upsurge produced other currents. Anselme Bellegarrigue published a pamphlet and series of articles followed by the first periodical that termed itself anarchist: L'Anarchie: journal de l'ordre which was first published in 1850. He was one of the first of that period to offer any criticisms of the dominant centralising and Statist trends within the radical movement. However, his rejection of communistic concepts meant that he put himself outside of that current, in his forthright statement that the free person: "works and therefore he speculates; he speculates and therefore he gains; he gains and therefore he possesses; he possesses and therefore he is free. By possession he sets himself up in an opposition of principle to the State, for the logic of the State rigorously excludes individual possession" (L'Anarchie, no.2)

Joseph Déjacque also participated in the 1848 events as well as in the insurrection the following year. Born in Paris on 27th December 1821, the death of his father left his mother to raise him alone. Throughout his life he worked as a decorator, house painter and paperhanger. Self-educated, he was in constant poverty, as, falling out with his employers, he was regularly sacked. Joining the French Navy, he journeyed to the Pacific, but came back a convinced antimilitarist and anti-authoritarian as a result of his experiences. He was imprisoned after 7th July 1848, first in Paris, and then in hulks at Brest and Cherbourg, under hellish conditions.

In often extremely violent and poetic language, he attacked religion, property, the family and the State, and advocated action by small groups who would hasten the end of the old hierarchical order. The massacres of June 1848 brought him not only to a rejection of exploitation and economic privilege, but equally to a rejection of all forms of authority.

In exile on Jersey in 1853 at the burial of a fellow exile, he confronted the writer Victor Hugo, accusing him of moderation, and ironising on his frequent mentions of God in the latter's funeral speech.

Whilst in the States he produced a journal in French, Le Libertaire, the first recorded use of the term libertarian as an alternative to that of anarchist. This first appeared on 9th June 1858, in New York, was subtitled Journal Du Mouvement Social, and had a print run of 1,000, and consisted of four pages in a large format. Thirty-eight issues of Le Libertaire appeared between 1858 and 1860. It was distributed in New Orleans, where it was often seized, as well as Belgium, Switzerland, England, and France. In this work Déjacque was aided by thirty sympathisers, although he had to write most of the copy, after working all day. continued the trailblazing work of the Humanitaire Group in his development of a kind of anarchist communism – "the anarchist community" (communauté anarchique). He used the term 'anarchist' in a favourable sense as in reports in Le Libertaire on "anarchist meetings" in New York and Paris. He rejected the strategy of Blanquism with its secret societies. Unlike Proudhon, he was able to reject the idea of the family. Indeed, he was able to offer fraternal criticisms of Proudhon himself, for his failure to carry his thoughts through to their ultimate conclusion. He rejects Proudhon's mutualism as much as he rejects the Statism of the inheritors of the Jacobin tradition. In reply to Proudhon's belief in the individual ownership of the products of labour, Déjacque replied that "it is not the product of his or her labour that the worker has a right to, but to the satisfaction of his or her needs, whatever may be their nature" ("l'Echange", article in Le Libertaire no 6, September 21, 1858, New York). It is true that he owed a great debt to Fourier – and this becomes apparent in his pamphlet L'Humanisphere: utopie anarchique – but his Fourierism is one stripped of all its reformist and authoritarian traits and he often makes criticisms of the prophet of social harmony, above all rejecting his religious ideas. He may be correctly cited as one of the grandparents of anarchist communism, his project of collective class emancipation was linked to complete liberty for the individual, thus being one of the first to redefine communism in opposition to the authoritarian concepts of Cabet et al.

Importantly, in opposition to Proudhon, he was deeply concerned with linking the emancipation of women to that of the working class. Castigating Proudhon for his rampant misogyny he was to say: "Is it possible, great publicist, that under your lion's skin so much of the ass may be found? Father Proudhon, shall I say it? When you talk of women you appear like a college boy who talks very loudly and in a high key, at random and with impertinence, in order to appear learned, as you do to your callow hearers, and who like you knows not the first thing of the matter he is talking about ...Listen, Master Proudhon! Before you talk of woman, study her; go to school. Stop calling yourself an anarchist, or be an anarchist clear through. Talk to us, if you wish to, of the unknown and the known, of God who is evil, of property which is robbery; but when you talk of man do not make him an autocratic divinity, for I will answer you that man is evil. Attribute not to him a stock of intelligence which belongs to him only by right of conquest, by the commerce of love, by usury on the capital that comes entirely from woman and is the product of the soul within her. Dare not to attribute to him that which he has derived from another or I will answer you in your own words: "Property is robbery!... Raise your voice, on the contrary, against the exploitation of woman by man... centre right anarchist, liberal and not libertarian you want free trade for cotton and the candle, and you advocate protective systems of man against woman in the movement of human passions; you shout against the barons of capital, and you want to rebuild the high barony of male over female vassal..." (On the Human Being, Male and Female, 1857).

At the speech he gave at the graveside of the feminist poet Louise Julien, who died in exile in Jersey, he said:

"Socialism does not take revenge; it destroys obstacles – whether men or things – without regard for their past. It does not chastise, it clears away. But, victim that we mourn, I wish at least to embalm you with this wish that I form; and it is to labour without rest and with all my strength for the realisation of my dream, the edification of your idea; it is, – contrary to paganism which denies one of the faces of human nature, to Christianity which denies the other, – it is – according to the new science which understands the individual with all its physical and moral sensations, the entire human being – it is, I say, to unite everywhere and always the cause of the proletarians to that of women, the emancipation, the liberation of the first to the emancipation, the liberation of the others; it is to push all those oppressed with the sabre and the strong-box, with the toga and the aspergillum, the disinherited of our terrestrial hell, to the hatred and scorn of the exploiters; it is to employ in the service of the social revolution, at the triumph of the egalitarian idea, thoughts and words, arms and action, ink and saltpetre; it is to march, finally, to the overturning of the old society and the promised land of liberty and harmony, the torch in one hand and the blade in the other: the light in one hand in order to spread it, and iron in the other, to guard the worker's way." (https://www.libertarian-labyrinth.org/working-translations/joseph-dejacque-discourse-pronounced-july-26-1853/)

Déjacque also frequented the Club Des Femmes, set up by the feminist Eugenie Niboyet in Paris in 1848. This was a club open to both men and women for a small admission charge. Unfortunately, there was heckling from men when women gave speeches there. We must assume that Déjacque was not among the hecklers!

In addition to his support for women's liberation, Déjacque was a passionate critic of racism, and was disgusted by the situation he encountered in the United States. He published a series of enthusiastic articles on John Brown and his actions at Harper's Ferry, where he sought to ignite a slave uprising throughout the South.

Déjacque and the International Association

Déjacque removed from Jersey to the United States in 1853, from where he edited his aforementioned newspaper. He was soon to support the founding of what can be seen as the precursor of the First International, the International Association.

An International Committee had been created in London, representing English, French, German, Polish and Italian sections. One of its members, the ex-Chartist Ernest Jones, described the committee as having a dual function, to propagate democracy in Europe and to attack capitalism. After French workers went to London in April 1856 to meet English workers and European exiles, the Committee called for the establishment of an International Association to coordinate the activity of "socialist and revolutionary national societies". As a result, several sections of the International Association were set up in Europe and the United States. Déjacque joined the International Association and propagated his views within it.

Anti-authoritarian and anarchist ideas were strong among the French workers in London and the USA. The International Association under their influence began also to develop anti-authoritarian perspectives. In its statement To the Republicans, Democrats and Socialists of Europe (1858) it declares that whether there was an absolute monarchy or a bourgeois republic, if there was still a class system, then there were "slavery and despotism". It went on to criticise the Italian nationalist Mazzini for his advocacy of support for bourgeois republicans. Similarly, the old triad of Liberty, Equality and Fraternity were rejected as events had transcended them, and they were worthless whilst capital and class rule existed.

Déjacque and his associates pushed for equal status for women in the International Association. They successfully argued for the replacement of the Association's Central Council with a secretariat that would act only as a correspondence committee to coordinate communication and activity between the different sections. This was adopted on 4th January 1859. The newly organised Association called for social revolution, "absolute negation of all privileges; absolute negation of all authority; liberation of the proletariat". Government would be replaced by administration created and controlled by the people and subject to recall at all times.

Opponents of these ideas within the Association set up the Central Council anew with the old rules, after the secession of the Polish section, the Polish Revolutionary Commune on 11th January, this section gathering around it those who dissented with the views of the decentralisers. After the amnesty of August 1859 in France, many French exiles returned there and both Associations withered away, in a chain of events that mirrored what was to happen in later years with the First International.

After the collapse of the International Association, the anti-authoritarian/anarchist French members in London set up the Club De La Discussion Libre (Club of Free Discussion). It held meetings on Sundays at 4 Marshall Street, Gordon Square. Its secretary was one A. Herben who had been a signatory of the statement To the Republicans, Democrats and Socialists of Europe. Another Club organiser's name is given in the pages of Le Libertaire as M. Calay. (Later Herben emigrated to America where he joined the First International. He was a member of its French speaking section in 1873). The Club also held regular public meetings. At its twelfth public meeting, on the 1848 Revolution," first stage of the proletariat towards real social progress" where the speakers remain anonymous, on 25th June 1860, the slogan, Liberty, Equality and Fraternity was rejected, and the provisional government, on the barricades, was denounced for its cowardice and treason and held responsible for the June massacre.

A report of the meeting appeared in Le Libertaire which ended with the words: "Long live the People, everything through labour, no more exploitation of the human being under any form that it can be represented. Long live anarchy!" (Robert Graham has misread this report, penned by Herben, mistakenly believing that meetings of the Club ended with the cry Long live anarchy). Nettlau regards the Club as the unification of the French anti-authoritarians, in which Déjacque's followers "also participated", seeming to draw a certain distinction between the two, but without going into any detail of any differences.

Forced to return to France in 1861 because of economic crisis which left him jobless, Déjacque died in poverty at the age of 43 in 1865 in Paris.

Couerderoy and Pignal

Like Déjacque, Ernest Couerderoy died in appalling conditions of poverty. Again, one of those moving from radical Jacobinism into Blanquism, he ended up rejecting the secret societies and conspiracies of these currents, and called for collective and mass insurrection as the means of bringing about a new civilisation.

Félix Pignal was a French exile in New York who in 1854 wrote Philosophie de L'insoumission ou pardon à Cain. Here he states that: "To cut off the head of a king, but allow the principle which requires him to remain, a principle which demands that so many other kinglets fatten themselves at the expense of the proletariat, is just like trying to stop the current in a rapidly flowing river with a sabre blow...". He exhorted workers to: "Establish yourselves in revolutionary communes; even in the smallest places always cry: Down with the governments! Let each of you participate in the discussions in their town, in order to debate their interests." He talks about producers freely exchanging their products and thus his concepts of a future society are closest to the mutualism of Proudhon than to the communist outlook of Déjacque, implying a self-managed market economy and the use of money. He later returned to France where in 1900, he was apparently a mayor in a village near Cluny.

The libertarian outlook of quarantehuitards (48ers) like Bellegarrigue, Déjacque, Couerderoy and Pignal owe a lot to the desperation and depression of the failed 1848 revolutions and the long and gloomy period of reaction that set in. At the same time just as after the defeat of the Enragés, the reversals of uprisings and insurrections of the 1830s, the collapse of 1848 engendered new waves of thinking.

But as Skirda points out: "To best measure the merit and the interest of these libertarian convictions, let us remember the context of the moment; the reaction of Louis Napoleon raged in France; black slavery continued in the United States; that of the Russian "white blacks" was not suppressed until 1861 in the Empire of the tsars; industrial mechanisation developed at a great pace, the prison of the factory too; the flattest academicism, and among the most advanced social doctrines, the church party and state socialism predominated." (My translation – see Paul Sharkey's translation of Skirda, Facing the Enemy).

References

Graham, Robert. We Do Not fear Anarchy We invoke It: The First International and the origins of the anarchist movement. (AK Press 2018)

Lehning, Arthur. From Buonarroti to Bakunin: studies in international socialism (E.J. Brill 1970)

Nettlau, Max. A Short History of Anarchism (PM Press 2020)

Pengam, Alain. Anarchist-communism on flag.blackened.net

Rexroth, Kenneth. Communalism (Peter Owen 1974)

Pignal, Felix. The Philosophy of defiance:
http://libertarian-library.blogspot.co.uk/2012/04/felix-p-philosophy-of-defiance-new-york.html

Chapter Three
Proudhon – anarchist?

"Marx was to the left of Proudhon, and Bakunin to the left of Marx". (*Obsolete Communism*, Daniel and Gabriel Cohn-Bendit, 1969, p.17 Penguin edition)

"Proudhon's use of the word "Anarchist" to designate his views must be taken with reservations". (Murray Bookchin, *The Spanish Anarchists*, 1976, p.20)

"Respect for his memory inhibits all but a passing reference to his "salute to war", his diatribes against women, or his fits of racism". (*Anarchism*, Guérin)

".... his words on women are still for all of us those which weigh most heavily." (Elisée Reclus, 1882)

Proudhon is a "complex and contradictory thinker" (David Stafford, 1972). He influenced Marx to a great extent, and Marx in a churlish fashion was to later totally repudiate any debt that he owed.

Proudhon's influence on the militants of the French labour movement in the decade preceding the Paris Commune was considerable. He was certainly no revolutionary, in the sense that we understand it, and he was certainly no communist. He was against violent revolution, and even saw bosses as being finally ready to be expropriated "at their solicitation and without indemnity". Some of his ideas were used by activists within the working class movement to develop their own theory. As David Stafford notes (p.16 From Anarchism to Reformism, 1972) the ideas he espoused can be summed up briefly as:

"(a) a belief in a peaceful social revolution and the replacement of the State by economic functional groups
(b) the demand for creation of free credit on a national basis which would enable small property owners to clear their debts and the workers to break free from the serfdom imposed on them by the wage system.
(c) The belief that this development would lead to a society based on freedom, justice and equality.

Towards the end of his political career Proudhon added to and reinforced these ideas with the concept of federalism. They were underpinned by a moral and ethical outlook that held up the patriarchal family unit as a model, alongside the idealisation of women, an idealisation that was restricted to family life and the home; and a strong belief in education, both professional and intellectual, as a prerequisite for freedom.

In their incessant attack on anarchism, all types of Marxist often first turn to Proudhon, seen as the founder of anarchism. In Proudhon, with his patriarchal and racist outlook, is to be found an easy target. It is conveniently forgotten that Proudhon was as much a forefather of socialism of all forms, including anarchism, and that he had a strong influence on Marx. Engels in a letter of 1843, regards (erroneously) Proudhon as the most important writer favourable to communism, and hails his What is Property? "as the most philosophical work, on the part of the Communists, in the French language; and, if I wish to see any French book translated into the English language, it is this…. he comes at last to the conclusion: "Nous voulons l'anarchie!"" Engels then enthusiastically continues: "What we want is anarchy; the rule of nobody, the responsibility of every one to nobody but himself".

The body of ideas represented by Proudhon reflect the consciousness of a class in formation and in search of its own identity. Proudhonism was on the one hand one of the first manifestations of an authentic working class socialism (as opposed to republicanism, or the ideas of Fourier and others, developed outside the workers' movement), and on the other hand the expression of the nostalgia of small producers who were becoming working class (progressive and pacifist 'obtaining' of the means of production through workers cooperatives; respect of private property; reactionary ideas about women).

At the same time, Proudhon was one of the first to revolt against the Statist and centralising ideas that Jacobinism had imprinted on Babouvism, and its successors in the Blanquist and communist currents, not to mention the strong centralisation that had been inflicted on France in the Napoleonic period, and his critique of the State can be cutting and trenchant. Equally, he was aware of the snares of parliamentary action.

"Democracy is nothing but a constitutional tyrant".

"The social revolution is seriously compromised if it comes about through the political revolution".

"To vote would be a contradiction, an act of weakness and complicity with the corrupt regime".

"We must make war on all the old parties together, using parliament as a legal battlefield, but staying outside it".

"Universal suffrage is the counter-revolution" and to develop and consolidate its own class interests the working class had to make an initial step of "seceding from" bourgeois democracy.

But in his typically contradictory fashion Proudhon allowed himself to be elected to Parliament in June 1848 for a short time. On two other occasions in the same year, he supported the extreme left candidate Raspail. Again, in contradiction to his espousal of working class autonomy, he was an advocate of the lesser evil, expressing preference for General Cavaignac, the June Days butcher, over the dictator in waiting Louis Napoleon.

Subsequently, in 1863 and 1864, he advocated returning blank ballot papers as a protest against Louis Napoleon's dictatorship and not as a rejection of universal suffrage.

In the 1860s French workers began to be conscious of their collective strength, and Napoleon III had to make concessions to them, sensing the fragility of his regime. Unions and producers' cooperatives were established as a result of the liberalisation of laws on association. Advanced workers respected Proudhon because he had been alone in taking their side in the 1848 events. As a result, a movement developed that looked to Proudhon's ideas. This was based on his free association and mutual credit. Proudhon reacted with this movement to theorise the actions of the French workers. In doing so he had to revise his own ideas on the French proletariat. He had seen them as manipulated by the rising bourgeoisie. He not only had to change his ideas on this, seeing the working class as a new and all-important force, but he revised his theories on class as well. He recognised the bourgeoisie as now being in the ascendant, as having won their battles with the monarchy and aristocracy. Now the "middle class" of shopkeepers, artisans and small businessmen and masters far from playing a key role in the struggle for Proudhon's mutualist society were now under siege. Proudhon predicted that it would be replaced by "officialdom, the bourgeoisie and the wage-earning class". He called for an alliance between the working class, the peasantry and what was left of the middle class, in which the workers had to take the leading role.

Proudhon then developed his theory of withdrawal, that is, working class autonomy. Since the 'old world' rejects the newly emergent working class, radical separation is required. Thus, by withdrawing from parliamentarism and the State, the working class would develop its own confidence and self-reliance. Death cut short his elaboration of any political abstentionism, but many in the First International, those that did not belong to Marx's camp, were to admit their debt to Proudhon on this score.

Proudhon also developed the idea of collective strength; "That immense force which results from workers' union and harmony, from the convergence and simultaneity of their efforts". This collective strength will increase workers' self-confidence and increase their independence and autonomy.

The mutualist movement that developed in France in the 1860s – and became dominant in the working class there – did not always follow these counsels of abstentionism. A group around Tolain and Limousin developed the need for workers' candidates to put forward the desires and rights of their own class "with moderation".

Proudhon had seized on the word anarchy and in his worldview, anarchie as he called it, encapsulates his views on the State and centralisation. Proudhon railed against what he saw as the communism of the times and particularly of the authoritarian schemes of Victor Considerant and the militaristic welfarism of Louis Blanc. "The communists cannot forgive me for having made a critique of community, as if a nation was one huge polyp and there were no rights of the individual alongside society's rights" (from The System of Economic Contradictions. 1847).

Proudhon shares much with Marx, as Skirda has pointed out. Not only were both atheists, they both theorised the need for the working class to emancipate itself. They were both influenced by the idealistic theories of Hegel (Proudhon at second-hand), as Skirda says: "the ideo-realist principle which developed in the materialist conception of History with Marx". They both venerated work as a principle (Proudhon: "Work is what confers dignity on man; only the productive worker is worthy of esteem"). They both believed in productivist ideas (Proudhon: "Have as much as possible produced and consumed, by the greatest possible number of men"). Long before Marx, Proudhon had coined the term "scientific socialism" in 1844. Where they parted company was on the role of the working class and the bourgeoisie. Marx believed that the bourgeois revolution had to be completed, and if the bourgeoisie was not up to the task, then the proletariat must accomplish it itself. Proudhon, as has been shown, eventually came to see that the bourgeoisie's interests were opposed in every way to those of the proletariat. Thenceforth, the working masses must separate themselves from the snares of bourgeois democracy and develop their own class self-organisation and their own autonomy.

There was much to criticise in Proudhon, above all his mutualism and his rejection of an insurrectionary revolution, his misogyny and his anti-Semitism. But Marx, at first an admirer of Proudhon, produced one of the most libellous, slanderous and vicious messes of abuse and misrepresentation in history in his The Poverty of Philosophy. "... in his attack on Proudhon, Marx made exclusive claim to ideas which Proudhon had also held, and perhaps even have invented" (Karl Marx and the Communist Manifesto, Elliott Erikson).

Proudhon wrote on his personal copy of Marx's book: "a tissue of insults, abuse, calumnies, falsifications and plagiarisms".

Confused and confusing as Proudhon is, he is still an original and interesting thinker. In a final summarising and appreciation of the pioneers of human liberty, Marx's actions on this score must be seen as unforgivable.

References

Erikson, Eliott. Karl Marx and the Communist Manifesto. Stanford University Press (1954, p.iv)

Pengam, Alain. Anarchist-communism on flag.blackened.net

Hilmer, Johannes Two views about socialism: why Karl Marx shunned an academic debate with Pierre-Joseph Proudhon on http://www.democracynature.org/dn/vol6/hilmer_proudhon.htm

The collectivist tradition: flag.blackened.net/asr/articles/llr13-8.html

Riazonov, David. Karl Marx and Frederick Engels: An introduction to their lives and work. Monthly Review Press (1973).

Stafford, David. From Anarchism to reformism Weidenfeld and Nicolson (1971)

Engels, Frederick Progress of social reform on the Continent 1843 Collected Works

Chapter Four
Marx and Engels and the Communist Movement

Marx was to reiterate his ideas and to put them into practice in all his time in the working class movement. "Without parties no development, without division no progress" he was to write (polemic with the *Kölnische Zeitung* newspaper, 1842). In a much later letter to Bebel written in 1873, Engels sums up this approach: "For the rest, old Hegel has already said it; a party proves itself a victorious party by the fact that it splits and can stand the split. The movement of the proletariat necessarily passes through stages of development; at every stage one section of the people lags behind and does not join in the further advance; and this alone explains why it is that actually the 'solidarity of the proletaria' is everywhere realised in different party groupings which carry on life and death feuds with one another".

The mythology of Marxism sometimes implies that the theory of communism was perfected by Marx and Engels without really taking into consideration all that had gone before and that communism, organised more or less into a loose movement, was created by artisans and workers as a result of their practical experiences in the French Revolution and the events of the 1830s, as well as their continuing theoretical labours. Marx and Engels' involvement in this communist movement was one of continual political struggle with what they saw as their opponents in it, a recurrent series of attacks often using slander as a weapon.

Marx was won over to communism in 1842 by Moses Hess. In the same year, Marx familiarised himself with the writings of Proudhon and Dézamy as well as Pierre Leroux and Considerant in order to gain a grasp of the currents of French socialism and communism. During a short stay in London in 1845, Marx and Engels made contact with the German exiles and radical elements among the British Chartist movement. After Marx had been kicked out of France, he made the acquaintance of Weitling in Brussels in 1846. Brussels acted as a focal point for the clandestine movement across Western Europe. Not only were there a number of exiles here from France and Germany, but it was a distribution point for the spreading of radical literature in

Germany, and was a stopping off point for German workers and intellectuals. Elliot Eriksson has argued that Marx did not fight his extradition from France, and was pleased to be exiled to Brussels, and that he was able to use its importance as a focal point to establish a stranglehold on all propaganda being smuggled into Germany. Marx put forward the idea of convening a congress of all communists to create the first international communist organisation. The Belgian city of Verviers was decided upon as the venue – it was close to the border with Germany and convenient too for those coming from France.

Before preparations for this could be finalised, delegates of the League of the Just arrived in Brussels and invited Marx and Engels to join their organisation. The League had, as we have seen, established itself as an international organisation, in contact with English and French revolutionaries. It now sought to enlist the mind of Marx.

Marx and Engels then entered into struggle with Weitling, who had defended Kriege. Up to then Weitling had been seen as the leading light of the League. The League had commissioned him in 1838 to write Mankind as It Is and As It Ought to Be, which had acted as a sort of Manifesto for the League. However, Weitling's ideas were increasingly being seen by others in the League as outmoded. The League's leading lights in London, Karl Schapper, Heinrich Bauer and Josef Moll had rejected the communist colonies advocated by Cabet, and now Weitling's concept of communism was in turn rejected as too militaristic and putschist. In addition, Weitling frequently made reference to Christ as a pioneer of communism, often quoting the Bible, and atheistic views were growing among League members. Weitling now advocated the need for a dictator to bring about the advent of communism, and he strongly implied this dictator should be himself. His self-importance alienated other communists like Schapper and Moll.

Both Weitling and the Russian Pavel Annenkov have left accounts of a plenary meeting in Brussels of the Communist League in spring 1846. Marx viciously attacked Weitling, whom before he had praised to the heavens for his Guarantee during his sojourn in Paris. Weitling's work Craft Workers' Communism was severely criticised. Both Annenkov and Weitling affirm that Marx demanded a thorough cleansing of the ranks of the communists, as Weitling says "human feeling must be derided". Despite the often asserted claim that Weitling was opposed to propaganda preparing the way for a social revolution, it was the Marx camp that opposed "oral propaganda, no provision for secret propaganda, in general the word propaganda not to be used in the future". Marx firmly stated that the realisation of communism in the near future was out of the question, and that first the bourgeoisie must be at the helm. (Letter from Weitling to Moses Hess April 1, 1846).

It's worth quoting extensively from this letter. "I believe Marx and Engels will end by criticising themselves through their own criticism. In Marx's brain, I see nothing more than a good encyclopaedia, but no genius. His influence is felt through other personalities. Rich men made him editor, voila tout (there you have it all, tr. NH). Indeed, rich men who make sacrifices have a right to see or have investigations made into what they want to support. They have the power to assert this right, but the writer also has this power, no matter how poor he is, not to sacrifice his convictions for money. I am capable of sacrificing my conviction for the sake of unity. I put aside my work on my system when I received protests against it from all directions. But when I heard in Brussels that the opponents of my system intended to publish splendid systems in well-financed translations, I completed mine and made an effort to bring it to the man (Karl Marx). If this is not supported, then it is entirely in order to make an examination. Jackass that I was, I had hitherto believed that it would be better if we used all our own qualities against our enemies and encouraged especially those that bring forth persecutions in the struggle. I had thought it would be better to influence the people, and, above all, to organise a portion of them for the propagation of our popular writings. But Marx and Engels do not share this view, and in this they are strengthened by their rich supporters. All right! Very good! Splendid!" This meeting was extremely acrimonious with both Marx and Engels arguing vehemently against Weitling, who responded in kind, Marx finally jumping up and down in his office.

The final break between the Marx group and Weitling came in the following month of May and only two years after Marx had called Weitling's book "an exuberant and brilliant debut of the German workers". Weitling soon left for the United States, from where he was not to return till the 1848 Revolution.

Marx and Engels next denounced the German communist Hermann Kriege, who had emigrated to America. Engels had at first put great faith in Kriege and had recommended him to Marx. When Kriege arrived in London shortly after he had joined the League of the Just. He then emigrated to New York in 1845. He led the League of the Just there into the Social-Reform Association, which advocated radical land reform. He brought out a paper called Volks-Tribun to support this move. There he wrote of a vague communism based on brotherly love, and came out with statements like "We have no wish to lay hands on the private property of any man; what the usurer now has, let him keep; we merely wish to forestall the further pillaging of the people's assets and prevent capital from continuing to withhold from labour its rightful property" and: "Every poor man... will instantly become a useful member of human society as soon as he is offered the opportunity of productive work." The land should be nationalised and then leased in rent free in plots of 150 acres to small holders.

On hearing of this Marx and Engels were quite rightly appalled. They issued a renunciation of Kriege's ideas, the 'Circular against Kriege', described by Gareth Stedman Jones as a "grossly self-important missive". What was disturbing about this was the viciousness of the attack, which was highly vitriolic and personalised. The Committee in London wrote to Marx: "aren't you being too harsh against Kriege?... Kriege is still young and can still learn." (Kriege was only twenty five years old). Another member of the League, Joseph Weydemeyer, wrote that there was "widespread regret that you have again got involved in such polemics" (Letter to Marx, 14 May 1846, Die Marx-Engels-Gesamtausgabe).

Moses Hess, who had been Marx's mentor, was next to be targeted, choosing to resign rather than be expelled. "In the struggle between Marx and Weitling, Hess had taken Weitling's side, and this was enough to infuriate Marx, and to make him look for a means of crushing Hess. Nevertheless, Moses Hess, despite many deviations and peculiarities had in the course of his socialist development come so near to Marx's standpoint, that, as late as July 28, 1846, Hess wrote to Marx: "I am in full agreement with your views concerning communist authorship. However necessary it may have been at the outset that communist endeavours should be linked to German ideology, it is no less necessary now that they should be based upon historical and economic premises, for otherwise we shall never be able to settle accounts either with the 'socialists' or with the adversaries of all shades of opinion" (Karl Marx, Rühle, 1928).

Marx and Engels now set up a Workers Educational Society in Brussels, modelled on the London organisation of the same name animated by Schapper. They gradually built up contacts in Britain, Germany, France and Switzerland, gathering those of like mind round them. They then decided to set up an international organisation, to create cells in Brussels, Paris and London. It seems likely that this, the second attempt at an international, was at the initiative of the London group around Schapper. These groups were to set up correspondence committees to maintain links with other communist groups. These became known as the Communist Correspondence Committees. One such Committee was established in Brussels by Marx, Engels and their associate Philippe Gigot. It would appear that the preparatory work for these committees had already been put into place by the middle of 1846 and that Joseph Moll, who came to Brussels to invite Marx and Engels to join the League of the Just, was acting as a representative of the Communist Correspondence Committee in London. The London group of the League of the Just had answered favourably to the idea of increased communication between communists and made clear that they had broken with the conspiratorial tactics of the Blanquists and the outlook of Weitling, which sought to rouse the masses through spiritual inspiration. However, they warned against the vicious denunciations that Marx had made against Weitling and Kriege and emphasised that correspondence between communists was to encourage ideas not to curb political debate. Later they wrote another letter where they stated:

"We believe that all these different orientations must be expressed and that only through a communist congress, where all the orientations are represented in a cold-blooded and brotherly discussion, can unity be brought to our propaganda...If people from all the communist positions were sent, if intellectuals and workers from all lands met together, then there is no doubt that a lot of barriers, which still stand in the way, would fall. In this congress all of the different orientations and types of communism would be discussed peacefully and without bitterness and the truth would certainly come through and win the day" (17th July. 1846, Die Marx-Engels-Gesamtausgabe).

After Marx had been persuaded by Moll that most of the London group had broken with the ideas of Weitling, a Congress was decided upon at the initiative of the Brussels Committee. For his part, Engels, active in the Paris Committee, used all the wiles of a politician to persuade those who had not broken completely with Weitling. Weitling was portrayed as a "reactionary" and falsely accused of not having written his books alone. In his reports back to Marx all the contempt of these two for workers is manifest with constant references to "those fools" "those asses", "those stupid workers who believe everything" with their "drowsiness and petty jealousy" In Engels' own words he was able "to put it over" with some and "bamboozled" others. Engels was able to report that "The remainder of the Weitlingites, a little clique of tailors, is on the point of being thrown out".

Karl Grün was next to be targetted. A populariser of Proudhon's ideas in Germany, he was not a member of the League, but had a following in its groups. He was accused of embezzling 300 francs on flimsy grounds by Marx and Engels. The Grünites explained that they had raised the money themselves, and considered it as a loan. First Eisermann, "Grün's chief follower" according to Engels, was expelled, followed in a few months by the most closet of the Grünites. "The last Grünites – a whole commune – were thrown out" crowed Engels. As a result, only 30 members of the League were left in Paris. Only two members survived in one Paris group of the League. The League was purged in Switzerland, Hamburg and Leipzig as well, and any supporters of Weitling, Proudhon and Karl Grün expelled or forced to leave.

Jonathan Sperber notes that:" Ideological differences do not entirely explain the vigour of Marx's attacks on Grün, since there was a lot in Grün's work on French and Belgian socialism that was congenial to Marx. Grün denounced the liberal regime in Belgium as facilitating capitalist exploitation of the workers, under the guise of protecting civil rights; he spoke of the concentration of capital and the impoverishment of the proletariat; he was critical of the efforts of Fourier and his followers to get wealthy individuals to finance his socialist schemes. Grün called for the abolition of wage labour, and for the proletariat to assume political power; he expressly associated his socialism with atheism."

The campaign against Hess did not proceed so well in Paris. Engels reported that: "Moses's tittle-tattle produces the devil of a confusion for me, and exposes me to the most long-winded counter-speeches from the workers. Whole meetings have been wasted over it, and it is not even possible to make a decisive attack on this stale nonsense".

The League of the Just had been decimated. As Otto Rühle remarked: "The net upshot of the visit was that Engels, though he did indeed put an end to Grün's influence, only increased the confusion, so that the "Straubinger" ceased to be possible recruits for an international communist league such as Marx and Engels already hoped to found" (Straubinger being Engels' put down term for travelling journeymen).

The projected Congress convened in London in 1847, without the presence of Marx, but with the participation of Engels. There were few delegates. Despite what Engels says, the League of the Just was not reorganised into the Communist League. The Communist League was a new organisation.

The Communist League established a constitution, and its first paragraph proclaimed that "The aim of the League is the overthrow of the bourgeoisie, the rule of the proletariat, the abolition of the old bourgeois society based on class antagonisms, and the establishment of a new society without either classes or private property". The organisation was based on "democratic centralism", with all members expected to espouse communism and to be in accordance with its aims. Groups of members, styled "communes" were the basic unit of the League. These made up into districts with their own committees. The districts were combined under the control of a special "leading district". These leading districts answered to a central committee.

The central committee itself was not elected by the conference of the League. Its powers were delegated to the district committee of any city appointed by the conference as the seat of the central committee. So, a district thus designated would elect a central committee of at least five members.

Marx and Engels suggest that the Communist League was the direct successor of the League of the Just, and its predecessor the League of Outlaws. We have seen that this is not completely true. They also give the impression that the lineage of these organisations was one of centralist organisation. But the central committee of the League of the Just was not just elected but broadly controlled by the membership as a whole. The original constitution of the Communist League was similar, and Marx and Engels' usurped this constitution, with the establishment of their highly centralised Central Committee in 1848. This arrangement was convenient for the perpetuation of a ruling clique.

The congress also decided to work on a programme for the League, and each district was to offer its own project at the next congress. Further, a paper was to be produced. Only one pioneer edition of the Kommunistische Zeitschrift appeared. It was the first paper that openly proclaimed itself communist on the masthead. It was mostly written by London members of the League. It quite correctly argued against Cabet, who was encouraging people to emigrate to America to found communist colonies there. It urged people to remain in Europe and fight for the establishment of communism there. The paper also distinguished its communism from that of Weitling and the French groups.

A second congress was held, at the end of 1847 with Marx present this time. There were days of violent disagreement over a programme (it appears both Engels and Marx had drafted separate proposals). The Paris groups had commissioned Hess to write a text, approving this by a large majority. As a member of the committee, Engels arranged that his own text, and not that of Hess, be sent to London contrary to the members' votes and as Engels admitted "behind their backs". "But of course, not a soul must notice this or we shall all be deposed and there will be an unholy row". The majority of the Congress was finally persuaded to accept Marx and Engels's proposals and Marx was charged by Congress to write a Manifesto in the name of the League.

It should be remarked upon that the Manifesto commissioned by the League took a considerable time to write. Schapper and his associates as members of the Central Committee had to write angrily to Marx that "If the Manifesto of the Communist Party does not reach us before Tuesday, February 1, further measures will be taken against him" (Marx, quoted in Hal Draper, The Adventures of the Communist Manifesto, Berkeley, 1994, p.10).

Marx and Engels argue in the Manifesto for a working class revolution in stages. Political power would be captured, all banks would be amalgamated into one State bank, and the means of production, transport and credit would also be controlled by the State. As Bakunin was to later comment: "This revolution will consist of the expropriation, either successive or violent of the actual landowners and capitalists, and in the appropriation of all the lands and all of capital by the State, which, so that it can fulfil its great economic as well as political mission, must necessarily be very powerful and very strongly concentrated. The State will administer and direct the cultivation of the land by means of its appointed engineers commanding armies of rural workers, organised and disciplined for this cultivation. At the same time, on the ruin of all the existing banks, it will establish a single bank, sleeping partner of all labour and all commerce of the nation" (1873, in Bakunin: Izbranniye sochineniya [Petrograd; 1919-22], Vol. I, p. 237)

It should be pointed out that the Manifesto should not be seen as completely Marx and Engels' work, as the input of other League members, notably Karl Schapper, can be detected. During the first months of 1848 Marx was an enthusiastic supporter of the section of the bourgeoisie that was struggling for democratic rights. At the same time, he had contempt for the democratic leaders, unlike some other members of the League, who admired their heroism and military capabilities (see Lattek). He clashed with Doctor Andreas Gottschalk and his grouping the Workers Association in Cologne for separating the proletariat from the democratic bourgeois camp (Gottschalk and co. were members of the Communist League). He accused this group of isolating itself from the struggle. The agitation of Gottschalk and his circle had increased the size of the Workers Society to 5,000 members. Finding himself in a minority, Marx first of all dissolved the Central Committee. Despite the Cologne group being a section of the Communist League, he set up a rival organisation, the Democratic Association and launched an electoral campaign for the Frankfurt Parliament, supporting a dubious left candidate. In June of the same year, he and Engels set up a daily paper the Neue Rheinische Zeitung: organ of democracy. Previously describing themselves as communists, Marx and his associates now described themselves as "we other democrats". They advocated a united front between the bourgeoisie and the proletariat, as long as the former remained on the "revolutionary" road, in other words as long as they struggled for a democratic society. There was not a word of the antagonism between the democracy of the bourgeoisie and the communism of the proletariat, and nothing about the immediate economic problems of the workers as the paper of the Workers Society was quick to point out. In fact, not once did the words "communist" or "communistic" "socialist" or "socialistic" appear in any article in the NRZ. During all of this, the Communist League was dropped and allowed to fizzle out.

As Marx said in an article in the paper (22nd January 1849) "The revolution must be first of all a revolution for the bourgeoisie. The revolution of the proletariat is solely possible after capitalist economy has created the conditions". Gottschalk responded in his own paper Freiheit, Arbeit (Freedom, Labour): "Must we, after finally escaping the hell of the Middle Age, throw ourselves voluntarily into the purgatory of a decrepit capitalist power?"

He went to say: "You have never been serious about the emancipation of the repressed. The misery of the worker, the hunger of the poor has for you only a scientific, a doctrinaire interest… You do not believe in the revolt of the working people, whose rising flood begins already to prepare the destruction of capital, you do not believe in the permanence of the revolution, you do not even believe in the revolution."

The criticisms of Gottschalk hit home among the German workers.

As Hunt says, "Gottschalk was unusually inconsistent and vacillating in his political views and could move from permanent revolution to social monarchism within a few weeks, but his popularity with and closeness to the Cologne working classes probably makes him a good weathervane of their sentiments". Gottschalk was close to the ideas of Hess and Grün. Devoid of notions of class struggle, he believed in a peaceful transition to communism. Nevertheless, his position vis-à-vis a united front with the progressive bourgeoisie put him on a collision course with Marx and Engels.

The German bourgeoisie signally failed in its endeavours to bring about a revolution for democracy and Marx was obliged to break with the bourgeois democrats in April 1849 and resurrect the Communist League. It had been a complete debacle for Marx and Engels. Not only had Marx and Engels attempted to hitch working class communism to the democratic desires of the bourgeoisie (already outlined in the

Babouvists' dangerous flirtation with it) but he had denounced the fundamental principles of international solidarity between the peoples. Positing the theory of "historic nations" – Germany, Poland, Hungary and Italy – and lesser nations doomed to be Germanised or disappear altogether, they argued that strong nation states had to be created in order to facilitate the fall of absolutism. The Poles were only useful as long as they fought against Russian despotism. After they had fulfilled this task, they would have to be relegated to the second division of nations doomed to extinction. In a totally inaccurate prediction, Engels foresaw the extinction of the Czechs and Slovaks and the South Slavs. Chillingly, he saw these nations as backwards and obsolete.

He warned in a veiled attack on the then Pan-Slavist Russian Bakunin that "We shall fight an 'implacable life-and-death struggle' with Slavdom, which has betrayed the revolution; a war of annihilation and ruthless terrorism, not in the interests of Germany but in the interests of the revolution!", that "we can only secure the revolution against these Slav peoples by the most decisive acts of terrorism". In a profoundly racist language against the Slavs, he belly-aches that no gratitude was shown "for the pains the Germans have taken to civilise the obstinate Czechs and Slovenes, and to introduce amongst them trade, industry, a tolerable agriculture and education!" (Democratic Pan-Slavism, 14th February 1848). Even more chilling was Engels' pronouncement that "the next world war will not only cause reactionary classes and dynasties to disappear from the face of the earth, but also entire reactionary peoples. And that too is an advance". (The Magyar struggle, 13th January 1850).

Just as appalling was Marx's belief in progressive wars. He was to support a war against Denmark by Germany in 1848 because it would strengthen the German nation and German democracy. "The real capital of Denmark is Hamburg, not Copenhagen" Marx blustered. This was to be a continuing policy of Marx's, as witness his support for Germany in the Franco-Prussian War in 1870.

Ending up in London later in the year, Marx formed an alliance with French Blanquist exiles and the revolutionary wing of Chartism to set up a Universal Society of Revolutionary Communists. The idea had come from Julian Harney, the communist Chartist leader. With Engels, Marx drafted an Address of the Central Committee to the Communist

League in 1850 refuting the opportunistic tactic of 1848-9, wrongly believing that a proletarian social revolution was about to break out, and developing the need for a Permanent Revolution until communism had been achieved. They linked to this the need for a dictatorship of the proletariat, a concept which had been invented by Blanqui and was sired by the Babouvists.

But soon Marx took a turn away from revolutionary activity, stating that no revolution was possible for the present because of the economic recovery. Further, a coming revolution did not just depend on another trade crisis, which he had seen as the cause of the 1848 Revolutions, but a massive development of the productive forces. Leading workers in the Communist League like Schapper, Fraenkel, Lehmann and Willich fell out with him over this. Worse was to follow. The communist Techow testifies that "Marx and his friends set Schramm, their champion, on to Willich. Schramm attacked him with the coarsest invective, and finally challenged him to a duel.... there are bound to be repercussions, not only in the local émigré set-up, but probably also in the Communist League. If this happens, then the disgusting intrigues and the mean gossip which Marx and Co. have been organising on a small scale will probably have a more far-reaching effect, principally on their literary activity. It is really too bad that men of such real talent should end by making it impossible for anyone but the dregs of humanity to make common cause with them". The duel was fought and Schramm was injured. This resulted in outrage against Marx. He was expelled from the German aid committee and from the Workers Educational Association. In behaviour that was echoed in Marx's later tactics in the First International, he had the Central Committee transferred to Cologne. As Schapper noted: "Just as the proletariat cut itself off from the Montagne and the press in France, so here the people who speak for the party on matters of principle are cutting themselves off from those who organise within the proletariat".

Harney had originally insisted that Willich be involved in the Universal Society. He refused to take sides now. Following this, Marx and Engels wrote to the Blanquists saying that as far as they were concerned the World Society was no longer existent. The Cologne section and indeed the whole German organisation of the minority section of the League controlled by Marx and Engels was closed down by police action, as was the German majority section in 1851. The police infiltrated both Leagues, but in his pamphlet on the Cologne events, Engels went out of his way to falsely blame the Willich group for shopping them to the police.

Marx followed this up with another pamphlet The Knight of the Noble Conscience attacking Willich in the most vicious way. Following this, Marx dissolved his section of the League in 1852. The German exiles found it hard to forgive his dismantling of the League. Being predominantly workers, it confirmed their suspicions of university-educated intellectuals and their "arrogance" (see Gareth Stedman Jones' preface to Christine Lattek's Revolutionary Refugees, 2006).

Marx and Engels had done considerable damage to important sections of the nascent communist movement with their tactic of allying the cause of the working class with that of the bourgeoisie. They had further strengthened the pro-Statist currents within this loose communist movement and had prepared the way for the mass social-democratic parties to come. They had separated off the different and loose currents of thought within the workers movement from each other by their purges of the League of the Just, thwarting fruitful dialogue and increasing division. None of the international endeavours had been at their instigation, though they claimed credit for them, and all had been sabotaged by them. Christine Lattek (2006) points out that it was never a case of the League having come under the sway of Marx and Engels, and that what occurred was a certain convergence of opinions between them.

The German Marxist Otto Rühle was to write: "Since Marx and Engels were ruthlessly endeavouring to reach self-understanding, self-laceration could not be avoided. This self-laceration conjured up an army of adversaries, and involved them for five years or more in the most venomous personal quarrels. A further result was that the proletarian united front, which was already in course of formation, was, prematurely and without any sufficient objective reason, broken for decades to come. The intolerant way in which the purging of the communist ranks was affected and in which the cleavage in the communist camp was brought about, was not the outcome of unavoidable necessity, not dependent upon the progress of economic evolution. Its primary cause was Marx's craving for exclusive personal predominance, which he rationalised into a fanatical confidence in the conquering power of his own idea."

Now they had the luxury of retreating into theoretical work until 1864, whilst communist workers endeavoured to carry on their organisational work within the working class.

On the positive side Marx and Engels had brought much clarity to the League with their ideas on class struggle and exploitation. With their departure many of the German communists returned to vague notions of oppression and tyranny, pointing to their influence being only passing.

It would be false to think that the communist movement vanished with the departure of Marx and Engels. Activities continued in London and elsewhere for decades to come, with the Willich League pursuing alliances with bourgeois democrats in efforts to overthrow the existing system in Germany. In addition, particularly in the two years after the 1848 defeat, the notion of a transitional dictatorship was taken up by these German exiles.

The exile German communist movement in London, embodied in the CommunistischerArbeiterBildungsVerein-(CABV)-Communist Workers Educational Association, established by Schapper and his associates in 1840, continued to exist and was still there when Johann Most – who was to turn it in an increasingly anarchist direction – and later Rudolf Rocker arrived in London.

References
Beamish, R. The Making of the Manifesto. Socialist Register, 1998.
Erikson, Eliott. Marx and the Communist Manifesto. Stanford University,1954.
Henderson, W.O. The life of Friedrich Engels.Routledge,1976.
Hunt, Robert Norman. The Political Ideas of Marx and Engels. Springer, 2016.
Lattek, Christine. Revolutionary Refugees: German socialism in Britain 1840-1860. Routledge,2006.
Lenin. VI. Marx on the American "General Distribution":
www.marxists.org/archive/lenin/works/1905/apr/20c.htm
Rühle, Otto. Karl Marx: His Life and Works. Routledge, 2011.
Schwarzschild, Leopold. The red Prussian: The Life and Legend of Karl Marx. Pickwick, 1986.
Sperber, Jonathan. Karl Marx: A Nineteenth Century Life. Liveright, 2014.
Stedman Jones, Gareth. Karl Marx, Belknap, 2016.

Chapter Five
Bakunin and the First International

"I will continue to be an impossible person so long as those who are now possible remain possible". (Bakunin, quoted by Eugene Pyziur in *The Doctrine of Anarchism of Michael A. Bakunin*, 1968, p.11)

It has to be reiterated that many of the 'great thinkers' of anarchism were not anarchists for all of their lives, and their writings may contain many passages that are contradictory, irrelevant, or reactionary. Such was the case with Mikhail Bakunin, of whom only the last twelve years of his life directly concern us. Bakunin's Hegelianism, his Panslavism, his impetuous immersion in the 1848 Revolutions, belong to a different existence. It was his appearance in Europe after the long years of prison, exile and then lengthy escape that began a process that was to bring him to revolutionary anarchism and his association with the working class movement. Indeed, without the developments that took place within that movement, Bakunin's revision of ideas would not have been possible.

The abortive Polish uprising of 1863 was the event that began his break with Pan-Slavism. His move to Italy was to begin the period of gestation for Bakunin's revolutionary outlook. Bakunin had learnt much from Karl Marx, in particular his 'scientific' approach to socialism, as opposed to his own previously 'purely instinctive' brand. Bakunin had also learnt much from Weitling, but he rejected both on grounds of their authoritarianism. It was Proudhon's anti-statist ideas that first confirmed Bakunin's own latent anti-authoritarianism.

The Polish fiasco had made Bakunin realise that a social revolution could only be achieved on an international level. He saw that the nationalist movements were under the ideological sway of bourgeois politicians, be they French, Prussian, Russian or Piedmontese. He looked towards the radical workers movements which were re-emerging.

Bakunin learnt much from the defeat of the 1848-9 revolutions. He saw that the behaviour of the bourgeois liberals, in first igniting uprisings and then moving over to supporting reaction meant that their class was irredeemably counter-revolutionary. It, and its institutions, which included parliamentarism and democracy, had to be destroyed. With Marx, he believed that the working class would carry this out.

He still shared with Weitling an obsession with secret societies, in contrast to the relatively open form of organisation that Marx posited with the First International. When that body was set up in 1864 Bakunin failed to join it immediately.

Bakunin's convictions on the need for secret societies were bolstered by the fact that it was impossible in any country to openly proclaim revolutionary views. He saw Italy as the best base from which to build his organisation of national and international networks.

In the period 1864-72 he wrote several programmes and statutes for secret societies, either on his own or with associates. These documents were often written in several languages. It was in Italy that the International Brotherhood was founded. Some of its first members appear to have been the French socialists the Reclus brothers, Elie and Elisée. The Reclus brothers had joined the First International in around 1865 but appear to have gone on to join both the International Brotherhood and the Alliance of Social Democracy.

It is in Bakunin's operations within the liberal democratic Congress for Peace and Freedom in September 1867 that his ideas on the form the new society would take can be observed. Bakunin intended to use this Congress as a platform for his revolutionary ideas, and win over individuals and hopefully sections to his Brotherhood. This failed to materialise, though he was elected to the central committee of the League founded by this Congress. To further his work in this body, he wrote a large text which was published later as Federalism, Socialism and Anti-Theologism.

Apart from the notable section on federalism, firmly basing itself on Proudhon's ideas on the subject, Bakunin's description of socialism also owes a great debt to Proudhon: "To organise a society which, rendering for each individual, whoever he may be, the exploitation of anybody else impossible, permits each to participate in social wealth – which, in reality, is never produced otherwise than by labour – only in so far as he has contributed to produce it by his own labour".

Bakunin still shared with Proudhon the admiration for physical labour that 'confers dignity on Man'.

But Bakunin broke with Proudhon over the question of property, of individualism, and the role of women. In fact, in the International, Bakunin and his followers were to cross swords with the mutualists, who in many ways were the real inheritors of Proudhon. As Bakunin said, the mutualists: "conceive society as the result of the free contract of individuals absolutely independent of one another and entering into mutual relations only because of the convention drawn up among them. As if these men had dropped from the skies, bringing with them speech, will, original thought, and as if they were alien to anything of the earth, that is, anything having social origins" (quoted by Bookchin, The Spanish Anarchists, 1976, p.29)

Bakunin, like other Russian radicals of the period, was a champion of the liberation of women (and here, of children) " Woman, different from man but not inferior to him, intelligent, working and free like him, must be declared his equal in all political and social rights; in free society, religious and civil marriage must be replaced by free marriage and care, education and instructing of all children must be done equally by all, at the expense of society, without the latter, in protecting them against either the stupidity, negligence or the bad will of their parents, having need to separate them from them, the children belonging neither to society, nor to their parents, but to their future liberty". (Programme of the Brotherhood, 1865).

As Skirda says, the Bakuninist organisation, the International Revolutionary Brotherhood, is seen as a permanent revolutionary organisation, exercising a critical and vigilant activity. The Bakuninist organisations were, for Skirda, constituted as specific anarchist organisations, given the circumstances of the period, "and even for some, the prototype of the libertarian communist organisations as conceived today".

For Bakunin, this specific organisation must develop its definite role as an 'invisible' general staff of the revolution. It must not attempt to take over and lead any mass movement that arose, but has the responsibility of clarifying goals, putting forward revolutionary propaganda, and working out ideas in correspondence with the revolutionary instincts of the masses. Bakunin saw revolutionary organisation in terms of offering assistance to the revolution, not as a substitute. Its other major task was that it would act as the watchdog for the working class, in opposition to new authoritarian groupings emerging and posing as the leaders of the revolution.

Bakunin had taken much from Proudhon in his belief in the self-organisation of the workers outside of bourgeois radicalism. The basis of this self-organisation had to be the workshops and the federation of workshops, the creation of funds of resistance, and federation on a national and international level, and the establishment of Chambers of Work, based on the Belgian model.

By 1867 Bakunin was to declare publicly "I am an anarchist" in the paper Liberta e Giustizia (August 23 and September 8th) which had been set up in Naples by him and his associates. At the same time, he attacked pan-Slavism, pan-Germanism and any other pan-isms as hostile to internationalism. He had transcended Marx, whose outlook was framed by the disastrous progressive nations theory, a theory which somehow almost always saw Germany as taking such a progressive role.

At the Congress of the League for Peace and Freedom which had been set up by J.S. Mill, Victor Hugo, Garibaldi and others with the express aim of stopping war between France and Prussia, Bakunin made an appearance on September 21st. It was his aim to attempt to spread his revolutionary ideas within this body, but he was forced to acknowledge that it was a bourgeois affair, liberal and pacifist in outlook, and certainly having no revolutionary potential. The following passage shows the stature that Bakunin had acquired as a result of his participation in the 1848 Revolutions and his 13 years of prison and banishment, as well as the bohemian traits he shared with Marx. (See Graham, Bakunin's Speech at the League of Peace and Freedom)

"As with heavy, awkward gait he mounted the steps leading to the platform where the Bureau sat, dressed as carelessly as ever in a sort of gray blouse, beneath which was visible not a shirt, but a flannel vest, the cry passed from mouth to mouth: "Bakunin!" Garibaldi, who was in the chair, stood up, advanced a few steps, and embraced him. This solemn meeting of two old and tried warriors of revolution produced an astonishing impression...Everyone rose and there was prolonged and enthusiastic clapping " (Vyrubov, quoted in Michael Bakunin, E.H. Carr).

In his speech to Congress Mikhail Bakunin articulated the cornerstone principles of his ideas. "We must abandon once and for all this false principle of nationality which has been invented in these last years by the despots of France, Russia and Prussia only in order to stifle the supreme principle of liberty. Nationality is not a principle. It is a fact as legitimate as individuality. Every nationality, small or great, has the incontestable right to be itself, to live according to its own nature; this right is merely a result of the universal principle of liberty... Universal peace will be impossible so long as the present centralised States exist. We must desire their destruction in order that, on the ruins of these forced unions organised from above by right of authority and conquest, there may arise free unions organised from below by the free federation of communes..."

Bakunin had taken a great step with his call for internationalism. He had broken irrevocably with nationalism, which in the past he – and others – had identified with revolution.

At the second Congress held in Berne in September 1868 he was accused of being a communist for advancing ideas of economic and social equality of classes and individuals. He was shocked, because whilst in the past he had associated with Weitling and had described himself as a communist, he now wished to distance himself and his ideas from those of Marx, which he regarded as authoritarian and statist.

"I hate communism because it is a negation of liberty... I am not a communist because communism concentrates all the powers of society and absorbs them into the State, because it leads necessarily to the centralisation of property in the hands of the State... I want society, and collective or social property, to be organised from the bottom up through free association and not from the top down by authority of any kind... In that sense I am a collectivist and not at all a communist" (September 23rd, 1868). He had made his first public declaration of anarchist collectivism. The radical bourgeoisie failed to appreciate the differences between communism and collectivism as outlined by Bakunin, and voted overwhelmingly against the motion which called for "the equalisation of classes and individuals". The motion had been devised by Elisée Reclus and Bakunin. The latter was disgusted enough by the rejection of the motion to wish to leave the Congress immediately. Reclus and Aristide Rey persuaded him to remain until the end. Reclus spoke on federalism on the fourth day.

Bakunin, Reclus and the others failed to push the League in a more radical direction. They had attempted to enlist the support of the First International but this had not been forthcoming. Reclus blamed this negative attitude on the Proudhonists within it, though Marx's hostile attitude should not be underestimated. He and 14 others quit the League signalling this with a Collective Protest. Among those who signed this were Reclus, who had independently developed anarchist ideas in the preceding years, Rey, Giuseppe Fanelli, and the worker from Lyons, Albert Richard, who met Bakunin for the first time at the Congress.

References

Graham, Robert Bakunin's Speech at the League of Peace and Freedom: https://robertgraham.wordpress.com/2018/09/24/bakunins-speech-at-the-league-of-peace-and-freedom/

Chapter Six
The First International

The first truly working class international was certainly not a socialist organisation and from the start identified itself as a combination of the working class. Again Marx had nothing to do with its inception. As a result of the agitation in many countries in favour of the Polish independence, London Trades Council organised a support meeting in 1863. Italian unification and the American Civil war had also been concerns of the English trade unionists and the labour revival of the early 1860s had also had its effect. Three mutualists, Henri Tolain, Charles Limousin and Perrachon, attended at their invitation, and the meeting appears to have been a cover for international talks. The previous year a French delegation had visited the International Exhibition in London and Tolain met the radical worker Ambrose Caston Cuddon among others there. In September 1864 the same three mutualists, together with Eugene Varlin, who had collectivist views, again visited London. Here at another mass meeting in support of the Poles, the French put forward the need for an International. Marx and Eccarius, his henchman from the days of the League, were invited to this meeting a few days beforehand and ended up being elected as representatives of Germany (even though both had been in London for many years). The task of setting up this International was left to a Central Committee in London, it being the safest place to organise at the time. Thus, it was directed by English trade unionists, Marx and co., some French Blanquists, and a Mazzinian. As for the French workers who had joined the new International, it should be noted that whilst many described themselves as mutualists, in the tradition of Proudhon, they were militants and were bound not by dogma but by doctrine as David Stafford in his work on Brousse has pointed out. The first Congress of the International was not to take place until 3rd to 8th September 1866 in Geneva, where a set of statutes was adopted.

The International was not to begin with a movement of young activists. Many of those involved were '48 veterans. The clash between Proudhonist mutualism on one hand and collectivism on the other was not as pronounced as Marx made out. The distinctions were often blurred, and the worker militants were men of practical outlook, not dogmatists. Many of the French had received their first schooling with Proudhon but had evolved a collectivist outlook.

As has been said, the First International was not a revolutionary organisation, it sought better wages and conditions for the working class. But as militancy increased, by 1868 so did the violent reaction by a union of the boss class and the State, and this inevitably led to a search for more radical solutions within the ranks of the working class and thus of the International. Whilst Marx might have boasted in 1865 that "I am in fact the head of the whole works" both the mutualists and collectivists were far more influenced by anti-Statist ideas than by any of Marx's.

In the same way as Marx should not be seen as the founder of communism, which sprang from the thought and action of German and French workers in the Communist League, neither can Bakunin be seen as the founder of anarchism within the International. Speaking of Andre Bastelica, one of the young workers who had entered the International, Antoine Olivesi notes that "There you have the man who constituted with Eugène Varlin and Benoît Malon at Paris, Émile Aubray at Rouen and Albert Richard at Lyons, the spontaneous generation of the renaissance of French socialism. Whilst Tolain, discouraged, thought that the International Association of Workers was dead in France, it was being reborn with new men and new ideas, young men coming out of workers' milieus. First of all isolated in clandestinity as a result of repression, little by little they got in contact with each other, united in the same cause and by a friendship never denied. Soon, they were going to coordinate their efforts in a perfect equality of action, without any among them trying to dominate the others and that as much in France as abroad, with the congresses of the International and that to such a point that an eminent historian could write: Their common, parallel, activity avoiding all hierarchy is a remarkable example of autonomy, of free initiative of voluntary decentralisation within a perfected system which dreamt precisely of founding the new society on federalist bases. (La Commune de 1871 à Marseille)". Olivesi, La Commune de 1871 à Marseille et ses origins (1946)

Bakunin by Clifford Harper

Bastelica had evolved his own ideas on anti-authoritarian socialism. He wrote to Albert Richard that: "We want non-government because we want non-property and vice versa. Human morality will destroy the revealed religions, socialism will suppress government and the political question." It was the encounter of Bakunin with this new wave of young militants that was to bring about a major evolution of anti-authoritarian socialist ideas.

And now Bakunin had succeeded in constructing his International Alliance of Socialist Democracy, numbering about 70 revolutionaries within the International Brotherhood and with its largest branch in Geneva consisting of 145 members. It had the large Spanish and Italian sections. The Geneva builders' strike in 1868 had been supported financially and otherwise by the International and Elpidin and other members of the Bakunin circle had given assistance. Bakunin soon enrolled as a member of the Geneva section of the International (this was two months before the Berne Congress of the League for Peace and Freedom). The Alliance was set up on the same day that Bakunin and his associates had quit the Congress. The Alliance applied to join the International late that year.

With the defeat of France in the Franco-Prussian War and the fall of Napoleon III, Bakunin was to enunciate his ideas on working class autonomy to his French contacts: "Are the workers going once more to play the part of victims? Abstain from all participation in bourgeois radicalism and organise the forces of the proletariat on the outside… when the hour of revolution strikes, proclaim the liquidation of the State and of bourgeois society. Proclaim juridical and political anarchism and the new economic organisation from the bottom up and from the circumference to the centre. And in order to save the revolution, to bring it to a good end, that is, to the focal centre of this anarchism, comes the action of a collective dictatorship of all the revolutionaries, not invested with any kind of official power whatsoever, yet all the more effective – the natural, free action of all energetic and sincere socialists, scattered all over the face of the country, of all countries, but strongly united by a common idea and a common will" (Quoted in Nettlau, 2020, p.118).

This passage reveals several developments of Bakunin's thought. Firstly, the concept of anarchism as a new description for a synthesis of mutualist, collectivist and communist ideas expressed in an anti-Statist socialism, secondly the need for action on an international level, and thirdly Bakunin's concept of a specific organisation of revolutionaries operating within a broader workers movement. This organisation was not one that intended to capture positions within a wider movement and to use an anachronistic expression, act as a Bolshevik-style vanguard within it, but to act as a leadership of ideas, that is to influence by propaganda and example. Bakunin's use elsewhere of the unfortunate phrase "the invisible dictatorship" should refer to the concept as articulated by him in the statement above and not to the interpretation of his detractors who gave it an authoritarian and manipulative sense.

Chapter Seven
The Struggle within the International

Initially composed of five national groupings, each with its own peculiar view of the means and ends of working class action, the General Council of the International, sitting in London, was intended to act as a centre of communication and coordination between them. They were not bound by any ideological viewpoint. Marx had drafted the inaugural Address and provisional rules of the International, and was quite aware of the difficulties inherent in this situation.

The impetus of the affiliation of the English trade unionists had been the issues of Italian and Polish independence and the American Civil War. The International was made possible by working class upsurge of the early 1860s which in turn had been triggered by the reaction of skilled craftspeople to the economic crisis of 1857-59. Around 1867 this had impelled a series of strikes in Britain and France, and a mass strike movement in Belgium ending in a massacre of workers by the State.

By 1871 circumstances led Marx to change his mind about the role of the General Council. One of these was the establishment of the Paris Commune, its bloody crushing, and the repression which followed. This led to a siege mentality which informed Marx's justification for a tightening of the ranks of the International. The projected Paris congress was unable to convene, and at the conference held in London in its lieu, the Jura Federation in which Bakunin's ideas were strong, was not invited. This allowed Marx and Engels to pass a resolution that the capture of political power was a necessary part of the programme of the International. At a speech after the Hague Congress of 1872 he said that at a time when the governments of Europe were planning a campaign of repression against the International, "it was wise and necessary to augment the powers of its General Council and to centralise for the struggle to come, an action that isolation would render impotent".

This move antagonised Bakunin and his associates. Bakunin was to write that Marx had established a personal dictatorship within the General Council. This antagonism came to the fore at the Hague Congress. There Bakunin and his closest associate James Guillaume were expelled from the International on spurious charges. This appalled not just the Bakuninists of Spain, Switzerland and Italy but also the Belgians around Caesar de Paepe, and socialists and trade unionists in Britain and the Netherlands.

The Jura federation had issued the Sonvillier Circular on 12th November 1871, contesting the developments within the General Council. They wrote: "We are not accusing the General Council of criminal intent. The personalities who make it up have found themselves succumbing to a fatal necessity: in good faith and to ensure the success of their own particular doctrine, they have sought to introduce the authority principle into the International; circumstances appeared to encourage this tendency and it strikes us as quite natural that this school, whose ideal is the conquest of political power by the working class, in the wake of recent developments, should have thought that the International should amend its original organisation and become a hierarchical organisation directed and governed by a Committee. But while we can understand such tendencies and such actions we are nonetheless compelled to combat them, on behalf of the Social Revolution, which we pursue, and its program: "Emancipation of the workers by the workers themselves," free of all directing authority, even should that authority be elected and endorsed by the workers. We ask for the retention within the International of that principle of autonomy of the Sections which has been the basis of our Association thus far; we ask that the General Council, whose powers have been rendered unnatural by the Basel Congress' administrative resolutions, should revert to its natural function, which is the function of a simple correspondence and statistical bureau; and we seek to found the unity some aim to build upon centralisation and dictatorship, upon a free federation of autonomous groups. The society of the future should be nothing other than the universalisation of the organisation with which the International will have endowed itself. We must, therefore, be careful to ensure that this organisation comes as close as possible to our ideal. How can we expect an egalitarian and free society to emerge from an authoritarian organisation? Impossible. The International, as the embryo of the human society of the future, is required in the here and now to faithfully mirror our principles of freedom and federation and shun any principle leaning towards authority and dictatorship".

The struggle between the "anti-authoritarians" and the "authoritarians" within the First International led to the publication of The Pretended Splits in the International by Marx. He attacked Bakuninism and the Sonvillier Circular. Here for the first time 'anarchist' was used as a term of abuse. The opposite of this was the development of the term 'Marxist'. First used in the same year in a letter which rebutted the charges brought against the brought against the Spanish Bakuninists by Marx's son in law, Paul Lafargue. Here the followers of Marx were described as Marxist, that is, those closely allied with Marx. The designation had little to do with theory as such. As this reply said, many of those in the Jura Federation had read Das Kapital, "They've read it, and they have not become Marxists. That must appear very singular to these naive people. How many of them on the other hand, in the General Council, are Marxists without ever opening the book of Marx".

The Jura Federation, after the expulsions of Bakunin and Guillaume at the Hague, convened a congress at St-Imier later that year. It was also attended by delegates from the Italian and Spanish sections of the International. Present were Bakunin, Cafiero, Malatesta, Costa, Guillaume, Schwitzguebel, Pindy, Lefrançais and other Bakuninists. This led to the birth of the St-Imier International, seen by its founders as the legitimate International. The following year, at Geneva, a further congress also attracted delegates from France, the Netherlands, Belgium and Britain. Thus a new International had developed with numbers far larger than that of Marx's rump International which had now moved its headquarters to New York. The St-Imier International sought to reconcile the different sections with their differing outlooks. Nevertheless, one resolution passed at St Imier was firmly against political action as put forward by Marx and his followers from the Lausanne Congress of 1867 onwards. "The aspirations of the proletariat can have no other aim than the creation of an absolutely free economic organisation and federation based upon work and equality and wholly independent of any political government, and that such an organisation or federation can only come into being through the spontaneous action of the proletariat itself, through its trade societies, and through self-governing communes, " whilst it was added that "the destruction of every kind of political power is the first task of the proletariat". This seemed to suit both the English trade unionists, who had been influenced by the ideas of Owenism, with its distrust of political action, and the Belgian and Dutch collectivists.

The specific anarchist organisation

The resolutions of Saint Imier were preceded by the setting up by Bakunin and others of the Revolutionary Socialist Alliance a week before in Zurich in Switzerland. Similar, if not identical to Bakunin's previous secret societies, they were founded on the belief that a revolutionary elite would act as the general staff of the Anti-Authoritarian International.

As Bakunin told Ceretti and other Italians two years later: "You do not need to recruit an army because your army is the people. What you must form are general staffs, a well-organized and well-inspired network of chiefs of the popular movement. And for that it is not necessary to have a great number of individuals initiated into the secret organisation". From the 13th to 27th March 1872, quoted in Italian Anarchism, p.6.

The struggle in the International between the "Marxists" and the Bakuninists and which was to wreck it, was over two fundamental positions.

Centralism versus federalism and the right of the local sections to operate autonomously versus the power of the General Council.

'Political' action, where the anti-parliamentary position began to develop against those who wanted to use 'political', that is, parliamentary actions.

In many ways the conference of St Imier which called for the destruction of political power and condemned the creation of any provisional revolutionary power and all compromise on the road to revolution, was the moment at which the historic class struggle anarchist movement became conscious of itself for the first time. Throughout the period 1874-6 in the course of dialogue with de Paepe and his Statist theories with a Jacobin concept of revolution, 'anarchist' became an accepted term, reflecting a degree of self-consciousness which permitted the Anarchists to distinguish themselves from other kinds of socialists and to denote a particular ideological position. This was something new. One further step was needed before the process of definition could be completed.

Chapter Eight
The emergence of anarchist communism

The death of Bakunin on 1st July 1876 left a legacy of a movement already well developed in Spain, Italy and Belgium, and with some support in France and Switzerland.

The anarchist movement, in many ways due to Bakunin's enormous efforts, had come into existence within the anti-authoritarian wing of the First International. Now this self-definition was to be further refined with the development of both the term and the theory of anarchist communism.

Kropotkin was to become its leading theorist, though not its originator. It was distinguished from the anarchism of Bakunin and co. by its emphasis on need rather than work as the criterion of distribution. Not just the instruments but in addition the products of society would be collectivised and at the free disposal of all of society, organised through a federation of communes, according to their individual needs. It would be argued by the anarchist communists that modern society created an interdependence. To insist on distribution based on contribution, as did the anarchist collectivists, would re-establish a new wages system as authoritarian as that existing in capitalist society.

It was a veteran of the Lyons commune who first used the term in print. François Dumartheray was born at Collonges, Haut-Saone in the Savoy on 27th January 1842. A member of an Icarian group in Lyons, he was one of those who fled to Geneva after the events of 1871. There he became a member of the L'Avenir group, a section of the International, along with Antoine Perrare, another participant in the Lyons Commune, composed mostly of workers who had their roots in the Cabetian strand of communism in Lyons but which also included participants in the Paris Commune like Charles Ostyn and Edouard Andignoux. Thus it can be seen that the development of the idea of anarchist communism in this group was brought about by familiarity with the concept of communism through the school of Icarianism together with practical experiences within the Lyons and Paris Communes. It was Dumartheray who penned a small pamphlet for the group, Aux travailleurs manuels partisans de l'action politique (To Manual Workers Partisans of Political Action) in 1876. In this pamphlet a further forthcoming pamphlet on anarchist communism is promised. This pamphlet has never been located and may never have appeared.

This is the first traceable mention of the term. Dumartheray and L'Avenir are the missing link, or rather the catalyst in the fusion of the best of the communist current that sprang from Babeuf, the Communist banquets of Belleville, Weitling and Cabet and the new anarchist current emerging from the First International. Dumartheray was a delegate to the anti-authoritarian International Congress in September 1873, and those to follow. In 1877 he helped Pindy, together with Paul Brousse, found a French-speaking section of the International in Switzerland with its newspaper L'Avant-Garde.

Woodcock makes the patronising comment that Elisée Reclus, who was in Geneva at the time, and who had a background in Fourierist phalansterism, was more likely to have introduced Dumartheray to a realisation of anarchist communism, saying, with no apparent evidence, that the worker Dumartheray "does not appear to have been a man of highly original mind". (p.189. Anarchism). Whether Reclus did indeed make such a contribution will be discussed below.

Kropotkin contradicts Woodcock on this. In his Memoirs of a Revolutionary, he writes warmly about Dumartheray: "with two friends, Dumartheray and Herzig, I started a new fortnightly paper at Geneva, in February, 1879, under the title of "Le Révolté." I had to write most of it myself. We had only twenty-three francs (about four dollars) to start the paper, but we all set to work to get subscriptions, and succeeded in issuing our first number.... Dumartheray and Herzig gave me full support in that direction. Dumartheray was born in one of the poorest peasant families in Savoy. His schooling had not gone beyond the first rudiments of a primary school. Yet he was one of the most intelligent men I ever met. His appreciations of current events and men were so remarkable for their uncommon good sense that they were often prophetic. He was also one of the finest critics of the current socialist literature, and was never taken in by the mere display of fine words or would-be science."

The Georgian Tcherkesov, active in Swiss revolutionary circles at that time, noted that the idea of anarchist communism had been adopted in the milieu of the revolutionary refugees, predominantly from the Lyons Commune, by 1877, although they were loath to use the word much in public.

In Italy the idea had developed rapidly and probably independently. Andrea Costa, close associate of Bakunin, claimed to have been "the first to speak openly of anarchist communism among the Italians" (in a three page pamphlet Ai miei amici e ai miei avversari, To my friends and to my enemies, Cesena, 1881).

The Bologna congress of July 1876 had remained loyal to Bakunin's concepts in endorsing collectivism. This had been a regional meeting representing 24 sections of the Romagna-Emilia province, at which Costa presided. Two months later, Costa stated in the paper Il Martello (The Hammer) that "any individual who gives to society according to his capacities must receive from it according to his needs", thus refuting collectivism and affirming an anarchist communist outlook. The anarchist historian Nettlau believes that another close associate of Bakunin, Carlo Cafiero, was the first to espouse anarchist communism, influenced as he was by James Guillaume's pamphlet Idées sur l'Organisation Sociale, published in 1875. Guillaume, generally regarded as closest to Bakunin, argued that an anarchist society would evolve from collectivism to communism with the achievement of material abundance. We see here a moving away from Bakunin's anarchist collectivism. Guillaume states that after the Revolution, consumption would not be related to work, but to a general sharing out of the common wealth. "We reckon, however, that the principle to which we should seek to approximate as closely as possible is this: from each according to ability, to each according to needs. Once – thanks to mechanical methods and these of industrial and agricultural science – production has been so increased that it far outstrips the needs of society – and the that result will be achieved within a few years of the Revolution – once we are at that point, shall we say, there will be an end of scrupulous measuring of the portion due each worker: each of them will be able to dip into the abundant social reserve , to meet all of his requirements, without fear of ever exhausting it, and the moral sentiment which will have grown up among free and equal workers will prevent abuse and waste".

However, Guillaume makes the reservation that: "In the interim, it is for each community to determine for itself during the transitional period, the method which it considers most appropriate for distributing produce among its members".

Cafiero translated the pamphlet into Italian and circulated it among his associates. It was this and/ or a discussion in the Jura Bulletin that, again according to Nettlau, that influenced Cafiero, with Errico Malatesta, Andrea Costa and Emilio Covelli to drop the term collectivism and to espouse anarchist communism. Born in Trani into a family of wealthy aristocrats on 5th August 1846 Emilio Covelli was a classmate of Carlo Cafiero in Molfetta. He studied for a law degree at the University of Naples in 1868 and then continued to study in Germany at the Universities of Heidelberg and Berlin. Here, according to Cafiero, he "tore off his bourgeois hide" and moved towards socialism. He wrote an essay on Eugen Duehring's Kritische Geschichte der Nationaloekonomie und des Sozialismus (Critical History of the National Economy and Socialism) which was the first discussion in Italian of the ideas of Marx. His next essay was L'economia politica e la scienza in 1874, again a first Italian article on scientific socialism. The same year he joined the International and began to be an important influence within it. His aristocratic bearing and his intellectualism made him an odd leader of the Neapolitan working class, and he was nicknamed Mephistopheles because of his dark and ascetic features.

Covelli's extensive knowledge of German communist literature made him a key figure in the development of anarchist communism in Italy and the move away from anarchist collectivism. His influence on Malatesta and Cafiero in regards to this should not be underestimated. Malatesta was to write that it was he, Cafiero, Costa and Covelli who took up the idea of anarchist communism and got it accepted by the Tosi Congress of 1876, and through it by the Italian Federation of the International (p.2).

It was in three months at Naples, between July and October 1876, that Cafiero, Covelli and Malatesta took walks along the seashore. Covelli's interest in economic matters may have initiated their consideration of the problem of collectivism. If the worker was to receive the full product of his/her labour how was this to be determined? This would imply a general standard which would have to be enforced. In addition, there were the problems of physical strength, skill and so forth. The weaker and less able would be a victim of such a system. This would bring about inequality and new economic privilege. The solution therefore was that in addition to the collectivisation of property, that all products of labour should be equally collectivised and accessible to all in the measure of their wants. This was communism. Thus this trio arrived independently from Dumartheray and Reclus at the idea of anarchist communism. Because the concept of communism was discredited by the authoritarian systems of Cabet et al, then the prefix of anarchist needed to be added to rehabilitate it.

It would appear that Costa, Cafiero and the others had reached the same conclusions independently, a view espoused by the Italian historian A. Romano.

The Tosi Congress, attended by Cafiero, Malatesta and Covelli (and, as we have seen, with the unfortunate non-attendance of Costa) confirmed the move towards anarchist communism. The Italian federation became the first national section of the Anti-Authoritarian International to formally adopt anarchist communism.

After the Congress of the First International at Berne in Switzerland on 26th-29th October 1876, Cafiero and Malatesta made a public announcement to clarify the views of the Italian section of the First International.

"The Italian Federation considers the collective property of the products of labour as the necessary complement to the collectivist programme, the aid of all for the satisfaction of the needs of each being the only rule of production and consumption which corresponds to the principle of solidarity." The two militants had thus publicly made a statement enunciating anarchist communism, without explicitly mentioning it by name. At the same time they signalled in their statement an espousal of Propaganda by the Deed, which was to have profound repercussions on the anarchist movement." The Italian Federation believes that the insurrectionary deed, destined to affirm socialist principles by means of action, is the most effective means of propaganda and the only one which, without tricking and corrupting the masses, can penetrate to the deepest social strata and draw the living forces of humanity into the struggle sustained by the International".

Despite this move, many Italian anarchists still clung to the term collectivism to define their politics, still equating communism with statist, authoritarian ideas. Costa still felt inhibited from using the term, and at the Ghent congress of the Anti-Authoritarian International still referred to himself as a collectivist. It seems from his presentation at the Congress that his conception of 'collectivism' was in fact really a conception of communism.

Covelli broke with this prevarication by using the term openly in drafting the Manifesto for the Puglian Federation in early 1878. This was followed by Cafiero's and Malatesta's exposition of anarchist communism in their speeches to the court during the Benevento trial of August 1878. The idea of anarchist communism came to be adopted by the majority of Italian anarchists within the next two years. As Malatesta later remarked, "We were Kropotkinians before Kropotkin".

At the same time as the Italian developments, things were proceeding apace in Switzerland.

A letter signed by 'P.R.' appeared in the May 1876 issue of the Bulletin, the official organ of the Jura Federation, calling for the collectivisation of the fruits of labour.

In October anarchist communism was adopted by the Italian Federation at its Florence congress. Mentions of it appear from time to time in the pages of the Bulletin, including a report written by Malatesta and Cafiero and the Arbeiter-Zeitung of Paul Brousse. Cafiero and Malatesta wrote: "The Italian Federation considers collective ownership of the products of labour a necessary component of the collectivist programme, the cooperation of all the needs of each being the sole rule of production and consumption that corresponds to the principle of solidarity". 3rd December 1876 (quoted in Fleming, 1988, p.110.).

Varlaam Cherkesov, active in the anarchist movement in Switzerland in the 1870s, wrote that by 1877, a year after the death of Bakunin, everybody in the Swiss movement had accepted the concepts of anarchist communism without wanting to use the label.

That year saw the Verviers Congress of the International. Here Paul Brousse and Andrea Costa both strongly defended the new concept, whilst Vinas and Morago, the Spanish delegates, stuck to the old tenets of the collectivism of Bakunin. Guillaume, always ready to promote unity where possible, and defending the federalist notions that he and Bakunin had supported within the First International, put forward the resolution that it was up to each section to adopt, or not to adopt, anarchist communism. This resolution seems to have been passed with an amendment by Brousse that the adoption of anarchist communism should only be regarded as the second stage in the Revolution and that "we must split up the question: immediate and far off".

Chapter Nine
Elisée Reclus

As already mention the young Frenchman Elisée Reclus had developed anarchist ideas independently from those of Bakunin. At the age of twenty one he had written the essay Development of Liberty in the World (Developpement de la liberté dans le monde) in 1851. This remained unpublished until discovered among his papers by his sister Louise much later. Here he expresses his concerns about how a communistic society can be established without threatening the individual. Communism for him meant the guarantee of wellbeing for all whilst freeing the individual, and in this he was highly critical of the various "utopian" communist currents. Each member of a communist society must" develop freely according to his means and his faculties, without being hindered in any way by the mass of his brothers". This should be counterbalanced by the work of each member contributing to the welfare of all. He went on to say that "Our destiny is to live in an ideal state where nations no longer need to be under the tutelage of a government or another nation. It is the absence of government; it is anarchy, the highest expression of order" (quoted in Fleming p. 36). This expression of Reclus was to be often repeated by anarchists in the course of the next two centuries and even appeared on Makhnovist banners during the Revolution in the Ukraine.

Reclus had visited Germany as a young student prior to writing the above essay. He had registered as a student at Berlin University in January 1851. It was there that he was influenced by the geographer Carl Ritter to become a geographer himself. He also became interested in socialist and communist ideas that were circulating in the city. It may have been that he had become acquainted with the thoughts of the Young Hegelian Arnold Ruge. In 1849 Ruge had advocated the self-government of the people, and indeed the abolition of all government which he defined as a social order which in reality was an "ordered anarchy".

After his involvement in the Paris Commune his first two years of exile in Switzerland had been ones of political inactivity. Reclus had been estranged from Bakunin from at least 1869. Bakunin had, with some justification, been concerned about Reclus's accommodation with bourgeois politics. Reclus's involvement in the events of the Commune had broken him irrevocably with such tendencies. After 1874 Reclus became more involved with the International in Switzerland and within the Jura Federation, he was to be one of the major articulators of a developing anarchist theory. Bakunin had withdrawn from political activity in 1873 in profound disgust and despair and it was not until after his death in 1876 that a clear anarchist theory was to be enunciated.

Reclus had stood distant from the split in the International between Marx and Bakunin, (incidentally, he had met Marx in 1869 and it had been suggested that he become the French translator of Das Kapital in collaboration with Moses Hess. This faltered when Reclus and Hess suggested a shortened and modified version suitable for the French public). Reclus's evolution had, as already noted, been enabled by the Commune and the lessons that he drew from it. Any form of government established by revolutionaries would cease to be revolutionary and would divorce itself from the masses it sought to defend. In the process such a government would itself become an oppressive force. Revolutionaries needed to stay among the masses and resist the pretext of serving them.

Reclus apparently called himself an anarchist for the first time in public in March 1876 at Lausanne where he gave a talk on anarchist communism to a meeting of Internationalists, which impressed Dumartheray and others. The following year on the 3rd March he delivered a lecture "Anarchy and the State" at St Imier. By 1878 he was defending the words "anarchy" and "anarchist" as positive terms on a practical and logical basis. This was opposed to Guillaume's belief that what he regarded as negative and ambiguous terms should not be used with a preferred emphasis on the positive aspects of collectivist theory as formulated at Congresses of the International.

Reclus was one of the first to develop ideas of anarchist communism. Dumartheray was to tell Max Nettlau in 1927 that Reclus's 1876 speech at Lausanne had been "a completely anarchist speech (Elisée Reclus p.189, cited in Fleming, p.110) and Reclus may have contributed anonymously to Dumartheray's initial pamphlet. If not a progenitor of anarchist communism, he was certainly one of the first to take up the idea.

Thus, it can be seen that the idea of anarchist communism emerged in several places at the same time through Covelli, with his knowledge of communist ideas and through Dumartheray with his experience of Cabetianism, and again through Reclus.

Le Révolté's propagation of libertarian communism, by Kropotkin, Herzig and Dumartheray led to it being adopted by the Jura Federation at its Congress of 9th and 10th October 1880. This was the first occasion at which Kropotkin publicly discussed anarchist communism. He presented his The Anarchist Idea from the Point of View of its Practical Realisation under the pseudonym of Levashov. It was later printed in Le Révolté, which became an important mouthpiece for the diffusion of anarchist communist ideas.

References

Fleming, Marie. The Geography of Freedom: the Odyssey of Elisée Reclus (1988) Black Rose Books.

Graham, Robert. We Do Not Fear Anarchy We Invoke It; The First International and the Origins of the Anarchist Movement (2015) AK Press.

Chapter Ten
James Guillaume

"...Small, thin, with the stiff appearance and resoluteness of Robespierre, and with a truly golden heart which only opened in the intimacy of friendship". (Kropotkin, *Memoirs of a Revolutionist*, 1988, p 197)

James Guillaume has often been seen as the closest comrade to Bakunin, who carried on his ideas within the International and beyond. But there were differences between Bakunin and Guillaume that came to be expressed and these differences, and those between Brousse and Guillaume marked the emerging movement and still leave their traces to this day.

A schoolteacher from Locle in Switzerland, Guillaume served as a close ally to Bakunin and had immense influence within the Jura Federation of the First International, an influence in the main exerted via the Bulletin de la Federation Jurassienne which he edited from February 1872 onwards. He shared Bakunin's concepts of collectivism. It was he who in many ways initiated the discussion within the Jura Federation as regards defining the credo of the anti-authoritarians beyond the need for collective property, rejection of the State, and Bakuninist concepts of revolution. In the 1871 Almanach du Peuple he wrote a clearly delineated plan for a "commune sociale", a term which also appeared in the statutes of the Jura Federation.

Guillaume's ideas on collectivism appear to have evolved as can be seen by his important pamphlet of 1876 'Idées Sur L'Organisation Sociale', which he wrote with the encouragement of Cafiero, where he erred somewhat from the collectivist position on work as the arbiter of distribution and consumption, in admitting that this was not strictly so, and that after the Revolution there would be a general sharing of wealth.

However, always in a moderating role, when it came to the Verviers Congress of the International in 1877, where the newly evolved communist positions of Brousse and Costa were at odds with the strictly Bakuninist collectivism of the Spanish militants Morago and Vinas, he put forward a resolution that Anarchist Communism as a concept was for each section of the International to adopt or reject.

The failure of the Jura Federation to grow among the working class in Switzerland as well as Brousse's influence within it, turned Guillaume towards France, with much writing of reviews and magazine articles and he departed for Paris in May 1878.

Guillaume was to retreat from political activity for twenty years, involving himself in pedagogical research and the development of the secular school. He naturalised as a Frenchman in 1889. His meeting with the historian Max Nettlau led him to produce the Collected Works of Bakunin in six volumes and then L'Internationale, documents et souvenirs, 1864-1878 (Paris, 1905-1910). Responding to the emergence of the French syndicalist movement, he considered it as the continuation of the First International as influenced by Bakuninism. He now collaborated enthusiastically with Pierre Monatte and his paper Vie Ouvrière in the syndicalist movement. Unfortunately, like Kropotkin and Grave, he took the side of the Allies in the First World War, dying of a nervous disease in Switzerland in 1916.

But, as Nettlau wrote: "he considered Communist Anarchism, the work of Reclus, Kropotkin, Malatesta etc., as an aberration, a period of time lost (1878-94)". Nettlau goes on to point out that "he was at the bottom of the new dogma of syndicalist 'automatism' (1913-14) which misused certain writings of Bakunin (mainly of 1869-1870). By this dogma, by merely becoming an organised worker, a worker is expected to become automatically a revolutionary syndicalist, a social revolutionist." He can thus be seen, with Monatte, as the founder of revolutionary syndicalism, which sought a clear split with anarchism.

Chapter Eleven
Gustave Lefrançais: A Link to The Past

Gustave Adolphe Lefrançais was born in 1826 in Angers. He became a teacher, was sacked for his progressive views in 1847 and took part in the 1848 events in France. He was subsequently sentenced to several months' imprisonment for his activities with two different sentences. A communist influenced by Fourier and Pierre Leroux, he fled to England with the coup d'état by Louis Napoleon in 1851. Here he met with Déjacque "an old acquaintance of the 1848 clubs" who showed him around the London of the French exiles. This encounter was to radicalise his ideas considerably. Together with Déjacque and a dozen other exiles he set up a mutual aid association, La Sociale. As he wrote: 'All in the same precarious situation, with so thin resources, so thin that remaining isolated, we would surely die of hunger, and by associating our miseries, perhaps they will be less insupportable for each one'. He lived in poverty, teaching when he could, but also weaving baskets and selling tobacco at theatres during the Christmas season.

Returning to Paris in 1853, he associated with Proudhonists like Alfred Darimon and Georges Duchene and took part in militant activity with Alfred Briosne who advanced a theory of collectivism as a synthesis of individualism and communism. Lefrançais was critical of the mystical communists like Cabet and his followers, and the latter day Babouvists and Blanquists. According to police reports, he developed his ideas on collective property and the suppression of inheritance, as well as attacking marriage and advocating free union.

An active participant in the Paris Commune of 1871, he fought on some of the last barricades at the Bastille and Arsenal. He managed to escape and was condemned to death in his absence.

In exile in Switzerland, he immediately joined the Central Section of the International in Geneva, and found himself in the midst of a war between the Marxists and Bakuninists there. It did not take long for him to take sides. He attended the Sonvillier congress and took part in the "anti-authoritarian International. He chaired the Internal Congress of the Anti-Authoritarian International at St Imier on

September 15th, 1872. He contributed to various anti-authoritarian Swiss papers and helped Reclus with his geographical work.

Returning to France with the amnesty, he stayed outside of the different political groupings, whilst speaking at many political meetings. He consistently criticised universal suffrage, and when he ran as a candidate in the 1889 elections this was just a protest against Boulangism and not a move towards electoralism.

Speaking of himself in the third person, he wrote: "He is very convinced that the future is with communism, that is to say with the complete disappearance of any individual property as instrument of production... Only, while admitting as exact the communist formula: 'To each according to his needs and each according to his abilities', he recognises that the applications proposed by Gracchus Babeuf, Étienne Cabet and Louis Blanc do not respond sufficiently to the legitimate demands of individual liberty" (Memoirs, 1988, p.318-19).

In an article written in the paper La Commune in 1874 he wrote that the revolution" can be nothing else than the incessant demand for the individual of his autonomy, that is to say, the absolute government of his faculties." In order for this to come about, it was necessary for "The suppression of government – of power – in the political order; that of wage labour, in the economic order. Now this double suppression can only be accomplished by the triumph of the communalist idea which is incarnated in the social revolution – the only legitimate one, the only one that interests us".

Nettlau, in his Bibliography of Anarchy, describes the text by Lefrançais "Where are The Anarchists Going" of 1887, as one of the authoritarian critiques of anarchism. But in fact, Lefrançais, like Saverio Merlino after him in his Individualism in Anarchism, criticises both selfish individualism, in terms of anti-organisationalism and the dangers of illegalism and individual propaganda by deed. He remained a libertarian communist, who defended the ideas of the Paris Commune to the end, and who rejected "the evolution of a movement which privileged both philosophical individualism and ideological communism to the detriment of revolutionary anti-authoritarian socialism which had been its origin" (Frejaville).

References

Biographical notice on Lefrançais: http://maitron-en-ligne.univ-paris1.fr/spip.php?article33693

Frejaville, Claude. Gustave Lefrançais et les malentendues de l'histoire. In Le Monde Libertaire, 30th May-5th June 2013.

Chapter Twelve
Estrangement

The break between the supporters of Marx and the "anti-authoritarians" led to the eventual estrangement of the Anarchists from the other elements of the International. Four Congresses took place after the split: Geneva (1873) Brussels (1874) Berne (1876) and finally Verviers (1877) where the composition was completely Anarchist. Immediately afterwards the Universal Socialist Congress was held in the vicinity, at Ghent. This had been proposed by the Belgian De Paepe in an effort to heal the rifts between those in the International in favour of parliamentary activity and State socialism, and those who had a revolutionary outlook. Far from doing this, the Ghent Congress exacerbated those differences. Only eleven anarchists went from Verviers to Ghent, with the Germans, Dutch, Belgians and English enthusiastically supporting electoral activity. The irreconcilable differences meant that the old International was effectively dead.

For its part, the St Imier International fell apart in a short period of time. The Jura Federation lost its vitality. James Guillaume, one of the closest confidantes of Bakunin, was disappointed by the failure of the Congresses to achieve unity, and had grave doubts about the way the Anarchist movement was going. Moving to Paris in 1878, he dropped out of political activity for 20 years.

Any effort to coordinate the International was assimilated to Marxist authoritarianism. The Jura Federation was at the forefront of blocking any move to greater coordination and effectiveness. The 1873 Congress blocked the creation of a central commission. It was just as much these anti-organisational positions as the clashes with the parliamentarian socialists that led to the collapse of the St Imier International.

At the same time, the strategy of "propaganda by the deed" was actioned. An improvised insurrection at Benevento in 1876 led to a fiasco.

The anti-organisational impetus meant that no International Congresses were convened. The Jura Federation congresses, which brought together an assortment of foreign observers, replaced them. It was at the 1880 Congress at La Chaux-de-Fonds that anarchist communism was proclaimed as the goal of revolutionary socialist workers.

New divisions were to open up between those who were enthusiastic disciples of propaganda by the deed and those who had reservations about the strategy. At the same time, repression from the State and the bosses was to impact heavily. The Jura Federation was reduced to a few dozen from its beginnings with hundreds of members. Indeed, this was one of the reasons for Guillaume's move to Paris, closing down the Bulletin de la Federation at the same time.

The amnesty granted in France to the Communards accelerated the differences in the ranks of the St Imier International. Jules Guesde, who had been a staunch Bakuninist, played a key role in blocking any moves to greater coordination. He now founded the Parti Ouvrier Français, alongside Brousse.

The period that began with 1880 saw a boom time for capitalism. Concessions were offered to the working class, without whom the capitalists could not have achieved their increases in production. After the period of reaction that had begun in 1848 and culminated in the bloodbath of 1871 with the repression of the Commune, the working class saw the possibility of the bettering of conditions.

Reformist socialists were able to exploit these hopes. The intelligentsia found an ideal means of getting their particular talents recognised, turning away from revolutionary positions. In consequence, whilst appearing to still support the working class, they now acquired a sort of legitimacy and were ready to toss aside their earlier anarchist convictions in order to further their careers.

Kropotkin and the Jura Congress of 1880

The career of the Russian anarchist has been covered enough times in other books. What is important here is his undoubtedly huge contribution to the ideas of anarchist communism. Whilst certainly not its originator, Kropotkin was one of those who developed the idea and popularised it on a wide scale, and again was one of those who certainly had a key role in it becoming the mainstream current within the body of anarchist thought.

Kropotkin first became acquainted with libertarian ideas within the International when he started extensively reading Swiss internationalist literature in Zurich in spring 1872. He returned to Russia in the same year, involving himself in the activities of the Chaikovskii Circle in St. Petersburg. He wrote the essay 'Must We Occupy Ourselves with an Examination of the Ideal of a Future System?' in November 1873 aimed at the readership of the Circle. It was seized during the clampdown on the Circle, which also led to Kropotkin's arrest, and consequently not published until 1921 and not in a complete form until 1964. It clearly adopts a Bakuninist position on the need for social change, arguing against the gradualist positions of Petr Lavrov. It also owes much to Bakunin and indeed to Proudhon in its espousal of collectivism and its call for remuneration notes and the payment of labour value as for example: "In each city a committee should be named for the purchase of all these provisions the peasants bring to the marketplace. For a certain time the distribution should be free, but subsequently this committee should make the transaction with hour-receipts" (Miller, p.75). It alludes to Proudhon and the idea of anarchy, going at some length into the "harmfulness of any central authority," and how such ideas lead "consequently, to anarchy" (op.cit. p.63).

Kropotkin presages the position he himself was to arrive at later when he writes: "For several decades the learned representatives of socialism could find no other alternative for realising their ideals than by means of a strong centralised government, a strong government which would have fixed and regulated all social relations, which would have interfered with all the details of people's private lives. These conceptions were particularly developed among the writers of France and Germany. But this caused a natural aversion to other, correct, principles of communism, both among the masses and among especially sincere socialists.

It is clear, however, that all this is the consequence of a simple misunderstanding. Freed of the always dangerous idea of an all-powerful government, communism quickly began to spread even in Western Europe – in an altered and limited form – under the name of collectivism." (Miller p. 59)

Kropotkin puts forward ideas for the re-organisation of society, in the countryside by the peasants through the obshchiny (the peasant communities) and in the towns by the workers through the artels.

Apart from these features, another key note of what was virtually a manifesto for the Chaikovskii Circle was its recognition for the need for mass propaganda (as this would be among a mass of mainly illiterate peasants and workers in Russia, this would be predominantly oral). Kropotkin also recognises the need to face away from the radical intelligentsia and youth and "unquestionably" towards the masses of workers and peasants. Preparation for the coming social revolution must lead inevitably to an insurrection, as an initial phase in the social revolution itself. He makes it clear that "no handful of people, however energetic and talented, can evoke a popular insurrection, if the people themselves, in their own best representatives, do not achieve the realisation that they have no other way out of the position with which they are dissatisfied except insurrection" and that consequently the task of a revolutionary grouping is not to call for the insurrection on its own, but to pave the way for its success. He posits the need for a specific revolutionary organisation – "a friendly, closely united organisation" – and clearly delineates the form such a revolutionary organisation should take as well as detailing what its activities must be. "...we absolutely reject the introduction into the revolutionary organisation of a hierarchy of ranks which enslaves many people to one or several persons; mutual deception and coercion for the attainment of our goals." (Miller, 1970, p.82) He clearly specifies that such a grouping must be organised within the masses of the oppressed themselves: "But no less necessary for the success of the insurrection is the existence among the very insurrectionists of a strong, friendly, active group of people who, serving as a bond between the separate localities and having clearly determined how to formulate the demands of the people, how to avoid various traps, how to secure its victory, are agreed on the means of action. It is clear, moreover, that such a party must not stand outside the people but among them, must serve not as a champion of some alien opinions worked out in isolation, but only as a more distinct, more complete expression of the demands of the people themselves; in short, it is clear that such a party cannot be a group of people alien to the peasantry and workers, but must be the focus of the most conscious and decisive forces of those peasants and urban workers". (op. cit. p.86)

After his escape from a Russian prison in 1876 Kropotkin returned to Western Europe. He realised that it would be impossible for him to go back to Russia unless it were illegally. In addition, he was in disagreement with the way in which the Russian revolutionary movement was developing with a shift in focus from organising among peasants and workers to direct assaults on the Tsarist system. As he said: "I always believed that revolutionary agitation ought to be carried out mainly among the peasants for the preparation of a peasant uprising...I could not convince myself that even the successful assassination of the Tsar could have any significant direct results even in the sense of political freedom". (Memoirs of a Revolutionist, 1988, p.327)

Kropotkin attended the International Congress at Verviers in Belgium in September 1877, where delegates of the "anti-authoritarian" International met, and went on to attend the International Socialist Congress in Ghent the following week. This brought him to the attention of the international movement. But Verviers was to be the final chapter for the International. Brousse, along with the Spaniards Garcia Vinas and the Italian Costa took an intransigent anarchist stand causing a rift between reformist socialists and those wanting a revolutionary change. Guillaume and his associates for their part attempted to reach a conciliatory position but were foiled. The ensuing Congress at Ghent led to a further rift with former allies against the Marx coterie, as the English, the Dutch, the Belgians and the Germans at the instigation of Caesar De Paepe, took a stand clearly in favour of intervention in elections. Here Kropotkin aligned himself with the group around Paul Brousse within the Jura Federation.

Kropotkin was at first apprehensive about adopting the ideas of anarchist communism. He was concerned about the problems of scarcity after the revolution that he expected to see in a few years. He changed his position somewhat at a congress of the Jura Federation in 1879 when he put forward anarchist communism as the aim, with collectivism in a transitional period. Reclus seems to have had some influence in changing Kropotkin's views for the following year at the Congress at Chaux des Fonds, he was an advocate of the adoption of anarchist communism as an aim.

At this Congress held on 9th and 10th October Kropotkin gave a report where he suggested that the term collectivism was now open to misinterpretation. The "anti-authoritarian" International had originally opted for the term collectivism "with due consideration for the prejudices then existing in France against communism, which was understood to signify a monastic order walled up in a convent or barracks". Now however some French reformist socialists had adopted the term collectivism to signify the taking of the instruments of labour into common ownership through peaceful and parliamentary means. "Today, an attempt is underway to imply that the word collectivism means something else: according to evolutionists, it means, not the taking of the instruments of labour into common ownership, but rather individual enjoyment of products. Others go further still and seek to restrict even the social capital which would have to be taken into common ownership: supposedly, this would extend only to land, mines, forests and means of communication. Furthermore, collectivists of this stripe would be ready to defend it at gunpoint against those who would presume to lay hands upon it in order to turn it into collective property". Kropotkin went on to say that it was time to discard the term collectivism and make an open declaration of communism "pointing up the difference between our concept of anarchist communism and the one peddled by the mystical and authoritarian schools of communism prior to 1848."

References

Kropotkin, P. The conquest of bread. Chapman and Hall, 1906.

Miller, Martin A. Selected writings on anarchism and revolution, MIT Press, 1970.

Nettlau, M. A short history of anarchism, Freedom Press, 1996.

Chapter Thirteen
Paul Brousse

"...a young doctor, full of mental activity, uproarious, sharp, lively, ready to develop any idea with a geometric logic to its utmost consequences; powerful in his criticisms of the State and State organisation; finding enough time to edit two papers, in French and in German, to write scores of voluminous letters, to be the soul of a workmen's evening party; constantly active in organising men with the subtle mind of a true southerner". (Kropotkin, *Memoirs of a Revolutionist* Vol 1, 1988, p.200)

Born into a well-off family Brousse had first become active within republican opposition groups in Montpellier towards the end of Napoleon III's reign in 1869. The Paris Commune and the ensuing massacre greatly radicalised Brousse. However, the International was not immediately banned and the worker Emile Digeon, who had himself taken a leading role in the aborted Narbonne Commune, toured southern France and attempted to develop a regional organisation of the International. At a meeting in Beziers a provisional committee was set up on 17th December 1871 to create a radical newspaper to counter monarchism. Digeon served as its president with Brousse as its secretary. This led on to Brousse joining the International sometime in 1872.

Brousse took the side of the anti-authoritarians against the General Council controlled by Marx and his coterie, allying himself with Jules Guesde. When repression fell on the southern French sections of the International from December 1872 Brousse was sentenced to four months imprisonment in absentia at a major trial of Internationalists in Toulouse. He had gone into hiding and had fled to Barcelona in early 1873. He now allied himself more firmly with the anti-authoritarian wing and joined the Jura Federation. This was almost certainly because of his expulsion from the Montpellier section by followers of Marx. He never forgot his treatment by the Marxist coterie.

The anti-authoritarians blamed the centralisation pushed by Marx and the General Council for the collapse of the sections in the Midi. As Guesde was to say in a letter to the Jura Bulletin of 15th April, 1873:

"What comes out of the Toulouse trial, is not solely the infamous role of the authorised powers of Marx and the General Council, but a condemnation of the authoritarian system which Marx and the General Council support". This had permitted Dentraygues, as a representative of the Council, and seen as a police informer by Guesde and co, to hand over the organisers of the International to the police on a plate. He went on to say: "Let the working class, in every country, organise themselves anarchically, in its best interests and Dentraygues are no longer possible" because workers in each locality would not be exposed to someone who could betray them, and if there was a betrayal, only that section would be implicated. "The autonomy of the sections, of the federations, is not solely the spirit of the International but its security".

Brousse met up with the French workers Camille Camet and Charles Alerini in Barcelona. These two were very much in the Bakunin camp and Brousse himself became influenced by Bakunin, but never simply a "Bakuninist". When Pi y Margall was appointed head of the Spanish government in 1873 he was unable to push through his cantonalist programme due to Carlist opposition. This led to a number of insurrections throughout Spain in summer 1873. These all failed due to lack of coordination and popular support.

Brousse and others Internationalists seized the Town Hall in Barcelona on 20th June. However, like the previous attempt with Bakunin and the aborted Lyons Commune it turned into a debacle. The Internationalists were simply ignored and had to vacate the town hall. An attempted general strike a month later also collapsed.

The unstable situation in Spain had given the anti-authoritarian Internationalists high hopes of revolution there, which would be a spark for a conflagration that would spread to France and Italy. The failures in Spain and with the Communes in France led to much disillusionment in their ranks. Bakunin himself was to remark that "The events of France and Spain have given our hopes, our attempts a terrible blow" (Memoire Justificatif (1874) in Nettlau, L'Internationale en Espagne, p. 101, note 42).

It was these failures and the turmoil within the International itself, which inclined Bakunin and others to advocate exaggerated deeds to act as a goad to arouse the somnolent masses. Propaganda by the deed was what this became known as, a misunderstood expression that is often wrongly thought to mean individual acts of assassination and bombings rather than attempts by a small number of revolutionaries to act decisively within a social context seen as ripe for insurrection. The term has been attributed to the Italian revolutionary Errico Malatesta who first used it in a letter to Carlo Cafiero in 1876, following the failed insurrection in Bologna two years before. But it was Brousse who first developed the theory in the pages of La Solidarité Révolutionnaire, the Internationalist French-language paper in Barcelona. "Revolutionary propaganda is not made only by the pen and the word, by books, pamphlets, public meetings and newspapers; revolutionary propaganda is made above all on the public square, among the cobblestones piled up in barricades, the days when the exasperated people give battle to the mercenary forces of reaction".

The article went on to outline the nature of this propaganda, firstly the distribution of easily understood propaganda, and then following on from that the establishment of an active minority whose task was to help overcome the powerlessness and apathy of the masses through a third phase, what could be nowadays labelled as direct action. What was implied was that a revolution with a successful outcome was not at that moment possible but that a conscious grouping of activists had to maintain such a hope through exemplary actions.

Brousse, like many French members of the International, looked back to Proudhon for the concept of federalism, and saw a future society based on the autonomy of the individual, the autonomy of the Commune and the autonomy of the industrial grouping or trades. However, Brousse rejected the mutualism of Proudhon, looking towards collectivism like Bakunin and other Internationalists. Strangely enough, the concept of the general strike was not included in this theoretical elaboration as Brousse had been much disillusioned by the failure of the Barcelona strike in 1873. Instead, looking at recent examples in France, Brousse advocated the Commune as a "vehicle of revolution".

The commune is the basic municipal unit of French governance, although the Commune of Paris during the French Revolution, controlled by the sans-culottes, also has a certain significance. For those who were to develop the ideas of anarchism, the Commune was increasingly seen as the basic political unit, the building block, for the new society. If the advanced sections of the working class could form a revolutionary majority within such a unit, read a locality, they were in a position to bring about the Revolution. Brousse saw these Communes as being based in large cities. As soon as the revolutionary majority has seized control: "All that is in the commune, the army, finances, properties, would become ours, we would apply our principles and experience would inform the details". This would only be the beginning: "The autonomous Commune, there you have the means, but not the end".

Brousse saw workers combinations and organisations as merely spheres of influence where workers could begin to realise their own strength but could not take the place of revolutionary action within the Commune.

After the fall of Pi y Margall Barcelona was no longer a haven for revolutionaries and Brousse eventually ended up in Switzerland, along with Alerini and Camet. Here he became a leading light in the Jura Federation. Unlike other French exiles active in the Federation, he had not been involved in any of the Communes of 1871 and thus not in the subsequent recrimination over who was to blame for their failures.

The French exiles were organised as a section of the International, the Section de Propagande et D'Action Révolutionnaire Socialiste with Guesde and Nikolai Zhukovsky as its leading lights. The latter had had a key role in spreading the ideas of Bakunin in Switzerland. Others who joined them were the Communards Benoit Malon and Gustave Lefrançais, Jules Montels et al. It sent delegates to the Sonvillier Congress of November 1871 where the Jura Federation was officially established. Malon and Lefrançais had attempted to reconcile the "anti-authoritarians" with the General Council section but were expelled from the Geneva section controlled by the General Council in December of 1871.

At the Congress of Geneva of the International in September 1873 Brousse argued strongly against the idea of the General Strike which was being advanced as a means to social revolution: "If the general strike is a practical means in certain countries, elsewhere, in Italy and in France for example this means cannot be employed. Why not, in France, where the general strike is impossible, make the revolution under the form of a communalist movement?"

In doing so Brousse came up against both Guillaume and Cesar de Paepe but also those who were closest to him in other respects, Alerini and Costa, who supported the general strike as a tactic.

This disagreement appeared slight at the time but was later to take on far more important proportions, with Guillaume representing one wing of the movement on one hand and Brousse the other.

Brousse further elaborated his ideas in a pamphlet which appeared after the Geneva Congress. L'Etat a Versailles et dans L'Association Internationale des Travailleurs. Here Brousse attacked both the State and electoralism. "Thus then, by official Education is prepared the electoral body in respect of authority; by the exercise of the suffrage principle it is given itself an authority, maker of laws; a magistrature which judges it, a public force which beats it. It is this All which crushes under the pretext of civilising, this All which kills it, if it revolts, this cortege of institutions that one calls the State". Brousse looked back in this pamphlet to Saint Simon's idea on administration replacing authority and on Proudhon's an-archie where industrial organisation replaces political organisation. Brousse reiterated his argument that society had to be based on the worker, the organisation of the workers and on the Commune. All the basic functions of society could be fulfilled through the workers organisations with production and the Commune with consumption and exchange. He affirmed Bakunin's call for the destruction of the State. He went on to castigate the General Council controlled by the Marx coterie. He described the imposition of what he described as a governmental apparatus at the 1871 Congress of the International by a sect which tried to force an official line upon the organisation.

"...one does not declare a Revolution like one declares war, and when by good luck it breaks out, one cannot direct it in the same fashion. Serious movements are not born on command, in other terms one does not make a revolution. No General Council, no revolutionary committee can attain an end as unreasonable... A revolution is prepared lengthily in the collective intelligence of the masses and the most often its explosion is due to secondary circumstances. It is always any way autonomous by nature, borrowing from the country, from ideas and from circumstances, a special character which is the gauge of its success. One can by socialist propaganda unite with a long hand the aspirations of the masses, give to efforts at the moment of struggle a practical direction and a form to the results, but there ends the action of human activity on these collective phenomena of social life".

It can be seen that Brousse became an Anarchist Communist at least by 1877. In that year with Andrea Costa, he pushed the concept at the Congress of the International at Verviers. However, he was willing to compromise with Morago and Garcia Vinas, who still supported old-style Bakuninist collectivism, moving an amendment that "we must split the question, immediate and far off" and that Anarchist Communism should only be seen as the second stage of Revolution.

Brousse was key in spreading anarchist ideas to the German-speaking workers in Switzerland. As a result, fifty of the five hundred copies of the Socialdemokratischer Bulletin went clandestinely into Germany, the first anarchist propaganda to be spread there. In September 1876 the Socialdemocratischer Verein (Socialdemocratic Society) which had emerged as a result of the bulletin, and in which Brousse had a strong influence, joined the Jura Federation. Subsequent to this was the appearance of Die Arbeiter-Zeitung, a paper edited by Brousse with the assistance of the Germans Emil Werner, Otto Rinke, and August Reinsdorf. This was committed to Anarchist Communism and propaganda by the deed.

Brousse built up a successful organisation of both French-speaking and German-speaking workers in Berne. On the other hand, he was firmly opposed, as were Costa and Montels, to conciliation with non-anarchist components of the European socialist movement.

This came to a head with his clash with Guillaume, the leading Jura activist. The advocacy of propaganda by deed advanced by Cafiero and Malatesta at the Berne Congress of 1876 reinforced Brousse's views on the subject, views that he had already developed three years before in Barcelona. Brousse pushed for a demonstration in Berne on 18th March 1877, much against the advice of Guillaume, who regarded this as a make-believe parade which would have damaging results, with the red flag being captured and torn to shreds as had happened at a previous demonstration in Berne the previous year, or with a bloody victory, which would have detrimental results. Kropotkin for his part, who had only arrived in Switzerland the month before, was an enthusiastic supporter of the demonstration. "As to me", he wrote to

Paul Robin in London, "I approve entirely of this mode of acting... this will be the propaganda with blows of casse-tetes (head-breakers) and revolvers if necessary".

The demonstration numbering a few hundreds was attacked by the police. They met stiff resistance, and the demonstration, reinforced by a large crowd, was able to gain the release of two arrested demonstrators. The result was a massive amount of publicity, albeit overwhelmingly hostile. A subsequent inquiry led to the trial of 29 participants in August. Guillaume, who had taken part reluctantly in the demonstration, was now to admit that his scepticism had been partly misplaced, but as he wrote to Kropotkin, he felt the overall impression produced was bad rather than good. Robin took the side of Guillaume, raising grave concerns about the unity between activists in the Federation.

Brousse waxed lyrical about the effects of the demonstration and became the leading protagonist of propaganda by deed outside of Italy. He was reinforced by Costa, who had fled to Switzerland after the Benevento affair. In July 1877 Guillaume had to take sick leave from editing the Bulletin of the Jura Federation. On 5th August an article appeared on 'Propaganda by The Deed', most likely written by Brousse but with Kropotkin's cooperation which argued that if the worker was too tired or apathetic to read propaganda, then deeds must illuminate. What had popularised the idea of the Commune most was the Paris Commune itself. "The men who have taken part in these movements, do they hope for a revolution? Do they have illusions in believing in success? No, obviously. To say that that was their thought would be to know them badly, or, knowing them, to calumniate them. The deeds of Kazan, of Benevento, of Berne, are, completely simply, acts of propaganda".

Unlike Malatesta, Cafiero and co., who had believed they were operating in a potentially revolutionary situation when they took action at Benevento, Brousse believed that such actions were propaganda solely, with the acceptance that a revolutionary situation did not exist.

Brousse, as we have seen, took an increasingly intransigent attitude to non-anarchist elements within the broad socialist movement, in contrast to the conciliatory outlook of Guillaume and de Paepe. As a result, the International began to be transformed more and more into a purely anarchist organisation, distant from the original aim of uniting the mass of the working class, or at least its advanced sections, on an international level. As Brousse was to admit much later, but without mentioning his own role: "The Marxists were defeated... but we, anarchists, who we find among the victors, we loyally committed a comparable error. We tried to encase all of the International in the narrow frame of our doctrine: we defeated, at the Geneva Congress, the governmentalism of Eccarius, of John Hales: at that of Berne, the statism of de Paepe; we stayed masters in the International, yes, masters, but isolated and impotent, in the face of the bourgeois masses in coalition against the working class that the spirit of the sects had so unfortunately divided. Dating from this day, the International was dead." (Le Marxisme dans L'Internationale, p.15)

Just before the annual congress of the Jura Federation in July 1877, Brousse argued against conciliation with other currents like the Belgians, who whilst not adopting an anarchist outlook, had rebelled against the Marxist coterie. He argued that now anarchist groups had been set up in Germany, how could there be conciliation with the already existing Social Democrats there? It seemed to him that there was no such spirit of conciliation amongst Social Democrats either in Germany, and from his own direct experience, in Switzerland. The establishment of the Volksstaat (People's State) or Etat Ouvrier put forward by Social Democrats and other socialists would be bound to end in discord with the anarchists.

The Congress of the International at Verviers in Belgium on 6th September was later described by Guillaume in 1910 as the beginning of a split between what he called the "extreme left" and the Jura Federation, a split which he felt was in the main provoked by Brousse.

Brousse brought out the newspaper L'Avant-Garde which first appeared on 2nd June 1877, with an international column written by Kropotkin. It was sold in Switzerland with underground sales in France, as well as among the French exiles in London, Belgium, Spain and Germany. In 1878 it merged with Le Travailleur of Geneva, to replace the Bulletin of the Jura Federation. From the first the paper was noticeably for violent insurrection. In its third issue an article, La Commune par L'Insurrection (The Commune through Insurrection) stated: "The ballot boxes must be deserted and the barricades peopled, and for that, one must organise... Throughout history, the Commune has always been first of all the means of realising in the city, that intellectual foyer so favourable to the blossoming of the idea, the material form of the new idea: it has been after that the insurgent who has struggled to generalise this idea, to make it exit the walls that surround its cradle, and to generalise it throughout the territory". However, what at first seems eminently revolutionary in the pages of L'Avant-Garde metamorphoses into a concern for socialist control of municipalities where the benefits of such administrations can be contrasted with clerical domination and poverty in the countryside. After two years such examples would win the working class and the peasantry away from reactionary parties.

The Jura Federation was now in crisis. The investigations over the Red Flag demonstration in Berne had meant that thirty demonstrators now came to trial, leading to terms of sixty days for two, forty days for the unfortunate Guillaume, thirty days for Brousse and ten days for others. On top of this were crippling costs and damages, whilst foreign militants were banished from the Berne Canton for three years.

The prison sentence, where Brousse had insisted on sharing a cell with common criminals, had a serious effect on his health. He now began to adapt his ideas. In a speech at Berne on 24h December 1877, whilst still calling for electoral abstention and against an International uniting different currents, Brousse began to hedge his bets in relation to propaganda by the deed, saying that such tactics should only be employed "in serious conditions". He also called for the establishment of socialist parties. By this he did not mean political parties but more effective organisation within the anarchist movement, a concern that was being taken up by others.

Brousse went on from this to question abstention from all electoral activity at the meeting of anarchist sections at Neuchatel on 9th June 178. He couched this in terms of intermediate stages between the present society and the desired future society. Parts of the anarchist programme had to be made immediately possible. The full Anarchist-Communist programme could not be immediately implemented, it was necessary to be occupied with the autonomy of the Commune, the collectivisation of land and the instruments of labour. Whilst agreeing that the vote was "nearly always dangerous" he suggested that it could be used as a form of propaganda. Rudolf Kahn strongly contradicted Brousse in the general discussion that followed, rejecting the stages theory of the adoption of the Anarchist Communist programme. Brousse countered by citing the example of Blanqui's candidature to the French Chamber of Deputies, which was linked to the amnesty campaign for Communards. When Blanqui was elected, he argued, the Chamber would almost certainly invalidate the ballot and reveal the true nature of the French State. "The use of the vote can also sometimes be useful. One should not then through abstentionist orthodoxy proscribe this means of action in an absolute fashion". It was interesting that the majority of delegates supported Brousse on this, with its reformist conclusions, but came to no decision because of Kahn's opposition.

Strangely enough, it was the question of assassinations that were to lead to Brousse's departure from Switzerland. A wave of assassinations and attempted assassinations had broken out throughout Europe, on various monarchs and police chiefs. The populist Vera Zasulich had shot the chief of the St Petersburg police on 5th February 1878, and there had been two attempts on the Kaiser, one on Alfonso of Spain and one on the King of Italy. L'Avant-Garde was suppressed because of its supposed support of these attentats. In actual fact the paper was level-headed in it approach. It refused to join the general press outrage and denounced the attitude of the German Social Democrat Liebknecht vis a vis the attempts by Hodel and Nobiling on the Kaiser's life (Liebknecht had called Hodel a madman).

The paper stated that certain forms of murder were justified such as regicide, or the killing of a factory owner by a worker in conditions of severe industrial oppression. However how valuable were the acts to the social struggle? Hodel's attempt was deemed valueless: "as to the anarchist party the death of the Emperor furnishes no advantage to it". It was NOT propaganda by the deed, which was described by Brousse as being a collective effort. Far better as propaganda by the deed was the Paris Commune itself. These acts were of limited value, reflecting a "republican" rather than a socialist attitude, although under certain circumstances assassinations could possibly bring about a revolutionary situation.

Two years later writing in the Paris paper Le Citoyen, Brousse wrote that: "In the France of our period the moment of the attentat seems to give place to a larger action, the raising of the shields of an entire class".

Writing later, Max Nettlau was to state: "Kropotkin, who at that time knew Brousse more intimately, asserted that Brousse was also weary and was looking towards France, and that especially when the attentats began believed he saw the beginning of a struggle of which he did not wish to become the victim. His rhetoric continued, but his faith had gone. In addition, Brousse and Kropotkin were very much involved with the beginning of the French workers' movement and began to devote their propaganda activities to it... Brousse, whose revolutionary will exhausted itself in words, was genuinely pleased to be able to participate in the working class movement in a less exposed way".

L'Avant-Garde was suppressed in December 1878 as a result of the articles. Brousse was tried in Neuchatel on 15th-16th April. He was found guilty on only one charge concerning the article on assassination, thanks to his spirited defence. He was sentenced to two months imprisonment, ten years' banishment and a 200 franc fine and costs. At the end of his sentence he went to Belgium, and from there to London. By now Brousse was drastically revising his ideas. By June 1880 he had made a decisive break with revolutionary anarchism. His return to France that year thanks to the political amnesty saw him completely abandoning anti-electoralism. In 1883 he wrote: "the ideal should be divided into several practical stages; our aims should, as it were, be immediatised, so as to render them possible". Brousse had evolved the doctrine of Possibilism, where gradual reforms could be won through control of the municipalities, a reformist adaptation of his revolutionary theory of the Commune as a vehicle of revolution, as David Stafford says a move from the Commune as a vehicle of revolution to the Commune as a lever of pragmatic reform. In fact, the Possibilist current became for a while an important current in France, co-existing for some time with the current led by another erstwhile anarchist, Jules Guesde, within the new French Socialist Party. Unlike Guesde, Brousse remained resolutely anti-Marxist.

For Brousse, socialism in the municipality would spread to socialism throughout society. In many ways he prefigured the ideology of libertarian municipalism that was evolved by followers of Murray

Bookchin, like Janet Biehl, et al. Brousse's subsequent career graphically illustrates the fallacy of this long march through the institutions, which would lead to a new socialist society. This reformist trend has now manifested itself at least twice in relation to Anarchist Communism.

In 1899 the Socialist Auguste Millerand entered the centre-left government of Waldeck-Rousseau. Not only did he take a seat alongside General Gallifet, one of the militarists responsible for the massacres of many Communards, but he broke with the idea that compromise could never be parleyed with bourgeois administrations. This produced one of the first great rifts within the parliamentary socialist movement. Jean Jaures took the side of Millerand, whilst the Guesdists maintained Marxist purity and the Blanquists followed suit, the semi-syndicalist Allemanists split down the middle, whilst of course Brousse and the Possibilists supported Millerand. After all, Millerand's outlook was more or less the same on the national scale as Brousse's at the municipal level. Brousse provided frequent contributions to Millerand's paper.

In 1905 as President of the Paris Municipal Council he was part of the municipal delegation to the London County. He was present at the official opening of Kingsway and the Aldwych by Edward VII and was received at Buckingham Palace and Mansion House. On Alfonso XIII's visit to Paris in the same year he provided municipal hostility. This was the last straw for James Guillaume, who had maintained some contacts with his erstwhile comrade.

Possibilism very shortly became a current that was played out within the French socialist movement and Brousse a forgotten figure. Far from bringing about profound change within two years, as Brousse had asserted in 1877, a fiery revolutionary had been reduced to a purveyor of piecemeal and ineffectual reforms, and to craven complicity with some of the worst enemies of the working class.

Chapter Fourteen
The Idea of the Commune and its Effect on Anarchist Communism

The communes of the next revolution will not only break down the state and substitute free federation for parliamentary rule; they will part with parliamentary rule within the commune itself. They will trust the free organisation of food supply and production to free groups of workers which will federate with like groups in other cities and villages not through the medium of a communal parliament but directly, to accomplish their aim (Kropotkin, The Paris Commune, 1880).

The Paris Commune meant different things to Marx and his followers than to the current that had begun to define itself as anarchist. To the first current it meant the worker's state and the dictatorship of the proletariat, to the latter it meant free federation of a system of communes and the abolition of State and Government. Kropotkin was well aware of the shortcomings of the Paris Commune, writing: "The Commune of 1871 could not be any more than a first sketch. Born at the end of a war, surrounded by two armies ready to give a hand in crushing the people, it dared not declare itself openly socialist, and proceeded neither to the expropriation of capital nor to the organisation of work, nor even to a general inventory of the city's resources. Nor did it break with the tradition of the State, of representative government, and it did not attempt to achieve within the Commune that organisation from the simple to the complex it adumbrated by proclaiming the independence and free federation of Communes. But it is certain that if the Commune of Paris had lived a few months longer, the strength of events would have forced it towards these two revolutions." (Words of a Rebel, 1885)

In the article he wrote on the Paris Commune in 1880, Kropotkin expands on the concept of the commune as the essential and basic unit of the social revolution, in a characteristically optimistic fashion:

"The next rising of communes will not be merely a "communal" movement. Those who still think that independent, local self-governing bodies must be first established and that these must try to make economic reforms within their own localities are being carried along by the further development of the popular spirit, at least in France. The communes of the next revolution will proclaim and establish their independence by direct socialist revolutionary action, abolishing private property. When the revolutionary situation ripens, which may happen any day, and governments are swept away by the people, when the bourgeois camp, which only exists by state protection, is thus thrown into disorder, the insurgent people will not wait until some new government decrees, in its marvellous wisdom, a few economic reforms.

They will not wait to expropriate the holders of social capital by a decree which necessarily would remain a dead letter if not accomplished in fact by the workers themselves. They will take possession on the spot and establish their rights by utilising it without delay. They will organise themselves in the workshops to continue the work, but what they will produce will be what is wanted by the masses, not what gives the highest profit to employers. They will exchange their hovels for healthy dwellings in the houses of the rich; they will organise themselves to turn to immediate use the wealth stored up in the towns; they will take possession of it as if it had never been stolen from them by the bourgeoisie".

Paul Brousse had dwelt on the ideas of the Commune as the essential unit of the revolution in an earlier number of articles in 1873, called Le Socialisme Pratique (Practical Socialism). He saw the Commune as the "vehicle of revolution". The Commune, of course, was already the basic unit of French governmental administration but increasingly became to be used in a different sense by anarchists. So the Communes on a local level would be seized through revolution involving the majority of the working class, according to Brousse. "The autonomous Commune, there you have the means, but not the ends", that being a far sweeping revolution.

At the annual Congress of the Jura Federation in 1875, the anarchist Schwitzguebel advanced the idea of the Federation of Communes, contrasting it with the idea of the workers' State. With these ideas Brousse, Schwitzguebel and Kropotkin were expanding on the statement of Bakunin who in his writing on the Paris Commune proclaimed: "I believe that equality must be established in the world by the spontaneous organisation of labour and the collective ownership of property by freely organised producers' associations, and by the equally spontaneous federation of communes, to replace the domineering paternalistic State," (The Paris Commune and the Idea of the State, 1871).

Thus, whilst the organisation of workers within the workplaces always remained a major concern of the anarchists, certainly from it developing as a current within the First international, and carrying on with the establishment of libertarian workers' organisation in Spain and other countries as a direct consequence of developments within the International, the idea of the Commune as the revolutionary vehicle was the central concern of those anarchists.

This communal idea was seen as the most viable way of organising the whole of the oppressed and not just in the workplaces. It would be the means of expression of the mass of the oppressed, whether workers in large or small factories, women, the unemployed, the youth, the old and it would as be as efficacious in the countryside among the peasantry and the agrarian workers as it would be among the urban masses. The organisation of workers in the workplace was seen as an extremely valuable adjunct to that, but it was not as yet seen as a substitute for the idea of the Commune. The idea of the Commune meant obviously a communal organisation of life which would unite the interests of the mass of the working class, not just those sections actually employed in factories and workshops. In his Ideas on Social Organisation written in 1876, the close friend of Bakunin, James Guillaume expanded on the nature of communal organisation in both countryside and city. The idea of the Commune met with approval at the 1880 congress of the Jura Federation which drafted a statement including the following: "The ideas set out regarding the Commune are open to the interpretation that it is a matter of replacing the current form of State with a more restricted form, to wit, the Commune. We seek the elimination of every form of State, general or restricted, and the Commune is, as far as we are concerned, only the synthetic expression of the organic form of free human associations."

In another document drafted at the same congress the functions of the Commune were defined: "What are to be the powers of the Commune? Upkeep of all social wealth; monitoring usage of various capital elements – sub-soil, land, buildings, tools and raw materials – by the trades bodies; oversight of labour organisation, insofar as general interests are concerned; organising exchange and, eventually, distribution and consumption of products; maintenance of highways, buildings, thoroughfares and public gardens; organising insurance against all accidents; health service; security service; local statistics; organising the maintenance , training and education of children; sponsoring the arts, sciences, discoveries and applications. We also want this local life in these different spheres of activity to be free, like the organisation of a trade; free organisation of individuals, groups and neighbourhoods alike, to meet the various local services we have enumerated."

Whilst the idea of anarchist communism and the Federation of Communes as the principal revolutionary vehicle remained central to anarchist ideas in the 1880s, in other ways the anarchist movement made a number of serious mistakes, not least those originally advanced by those like Kropotkin and others from the days of the First International. These erroneous ideas were engendered by the following:

1. The climate of repression reigning throughout Europe and the United States
2. The bullying tactics used by social democrats like Jaures, Hyndman, Millerand, Bebel, Liebknecht and Eleanor Marx to physically exclude anarchists and libertarian socialists from the Socialist Congresses of the 1880s.
3. An increasingly narrow interpretation of the idea and tactic of Propaganda by the Deed. Originally used to mean exemplary action by a small group of revolutionaries to illustrate tactics of direct action and/or spark revolutionary movements in a situation that was ripe for revolution (as seen by anarchists in southern Italy for example) it soon came to mean attentats and assassinations of individual members of the ruling classes, whether they be from the monarchy or from government. It had developed in reaction to the mass apathy and demobilisation reigning in the working class after the division of the First International and the defeat of the Paris Commune and the international climate of repression that had delayed the expectations of all European socialists.

4. A move away from the organisation developed in the International towards small and sometimes secret groups organised through affinity of friendship and political conviction.

This created isolation from the mass of the working class (though it should be emphasised that the bulk of the anarchist movement at that time was composed of advanced workers). Thus Kropotkin could say in 1880: "Permanent revolt in speech, writing, by the dagger and the gun, or by dynamite... anything suits us that is alien to legality" (in his paper Le Révolté), though he always dissociated himself from the extremely narrow definition by Brousse of the idea of propaganda by the deed as defined as individual acts of terrorism. In addition, he is referring not just to the conditions prevailing in Western Europe but those within the autocratic regime of Tsarist Russia where different tactics might be called for. Whatever, in the long run these concepts brought down further repression on the anarchist movement with the execution and imprisonment and exile of many of the most courageous militants. Kropotkin was able to see the dead end of isolation that the anarchist movement was marching into and had the presence of mind to make various corrective statements, as witness what he said in 1890 when he affirmed "that one must be with the people who no longer want isolated acts, but want men of action inside their ranks," (quoted by Daniel Guérin, Anarchism: From Theory to Practice, 1970, p.78). He warned against the "illusion that one can defeat the coalition of exploiters with a few pounds of explosives".

Flight from Sanity

The crushing of the Paris Commune in 1871 and the killing of thousands of Communards, and the imprisonment and exile of many other thousands, brought a long period of reaction and repression throughout Europe. The anarchist groups turned in on themselves, partly as a result of repression and partly from ideological convictions that made them look askance at the idea of effective organisation, and praised the development of loosely organised groups of affinity. At one anarchist congress in Geneva, in August 1882) a delegate from Cette (now Sete) in France received massive applause when he stated "we are united because we are divided".

In the period 1891-94 a series of bomb explosions culminated in the killing of Sadi Carnot, President of the Republic. Those who carried out these attacks, were not, in the main, individualist anarchists, but professed anarchist communists (Ravachol and Vaillant) who were courageous and full of generous feelings for their fellow sufferers under capitalism. They maintained a revolutionary outlook without concessions, rebelling against apathy and resignation, and as Fontenis writes, "against a narrow determinist conception, an excuse for reformism and capitulation, for acceptance of domination (p.23. Fontenis, L'autre Communisme.)

But the deeds of Ravachol, Vaillant, Henry and the assassin of President Carnot, Caserio, were too separate from the actual class struggle. These actions inevitably led to defeat. It is true that the period of bombs coincided with an increasing unpopularity of parliamentarism among the masses (the Panama Scandal of 1893, etc.) and some of these acts were regarded with a certain sympathy. As the syndicalist Robert Louzon has suggested, these acts may have helped in the awakening of organisation among the exploited.

Writing at the beginning of this period, Kropotkin wrote in his paper La Revolte: "That was the error of the anarchists in 1881. When the Russian revolutionaries killed the Tsar... the European Anarchists imagined that a handful of ardent revolutionaries, armed with a few bombs, were sufficient to make a social revolution... an edifice based on centuries of history cannot be destroyed with a few kilos of explosives". (La Revolte, No.32, 18-24th March, 1891).

Alongside these genuine acts of revolt were numerous provocations carried out by police agents, designed to target Anarchists as scapegoats and to bring down repression on the Anarchist movement.

Chapter Fifteen
Anarchist Communism and Anarchosyndicalism

The term syndicalism derives from the French word for union, 'syndicat'. It was the mass syndicat (or union) in France, the Confederation Generale du Travail (CGT), which gave "syndicalism" the meaning it has today. When such tactics developed in other countries, militants consciously used the term syndicalism to differentiate themselves from the openly reformist, social democratic Trade Unions. Syndicalist unions began to become a significant factor in the decade before the First World War, as both a reflection of the ongoing class struggle and as the result of the efforts of consciously 'political' minorities critical of 'socialist' parliamentarism. The early syndicalist movement was far from homogenous, politically or organisationally. In many countries the syndicalist movement developed through deliberate attempts to organise those workers who had been ignored by the established social democratic unions, particularly the unskilled and immigrant workforces whilst in other countries, syndicalist unions were craft or trade based and organised highly skilled artisans (e.g. the CGT in France).

In France, Fernand Pelloutier moved from radical republicanism through a lukewarm support of Guesdist socialism to a fully committed adherence to anarchist communism in 1893. He was one of those to reject the tactics of Ravacholism and to look towards a reconnection with the working class on a mass scale, and away from the world of the affinity groups. He was involved in the founding of the Bourses du Travail, which had the functions of being self-organised cooperative labour exchanges, as well as acting as workers' clubs and cultural centres, and local federations of unions. He became secretary of the Fédération des Bourses du Travail (FBT) in 1895. Because he realised that he would eventually die of tuberculosis, he threw himself into building the FBT, with the result that by the time of his death in 1901 the number of bourses had increased from 34 to 57. As Alan Spitzer notes: "During Pelloutier's tenure the Bourses expanded their range of action far beyond that of the labour exchange which was their original function. Each Bourse was a federation of all the trade unions in a locality willing to co-operate across craft or industrial lines. The heart of each Bourse was, wherever possible, some permanent location – a union hall which was to be the centre of working class existence, and to provide a great variety of services including a mutual benefit society, a job information and placement bureau, a system of financial assistance for travelling workers, a strike chest, a programme of propaganda for organising the unorganised, a sort of bureau of labour statistics, and education courses, periodic conferences, and a library".

Pelloutier saw the bourses as the embryos of the Communes as advocated by the theorists of anarchist communism. He wrote in Anarchism and the Workers Union (1895) that: "In Saint-Etienne, for example, ...the members of the trade unions venerate Ravachol: none of them, however, dares declare himself an anarchist, for fear that he might appear to be turning away from working towards collective rebellion and opting for isolated rebellion in its place. Elsewhere, by contrast, in Paris, Amiens, Marseilles, Roanne and a hundred other towns, anarchists admire the new spirit by which the trade unions have been moved these past two years, yet do not dare to venture into that revolutionary field to ensure that the good seed sown by harsh experience germinates. And, between these men, emancipated almost to the same extent, intellectually connected by a shared objective and by a perception here and a conviction there, regarding the necessity of a violent uprising, there is a lingering mistrust which keeps the former distant from comrades held to be systematically hostile to all concerted action, and the latter from a form of combination in which, they persist in believing, alienation of the freedom of the individual is still obligatory." For Pelloutier, anarchist communism must approach the masses both to propagate anarchist ideas and to save the unions from the narrow corporatism in which it had bogged down. As a laboratory of economic struggle detached from electoral competition were not unions the only libertarian and revolutionary organisation which could counterbalance and destroy the evil influence of the social-democratic politicians, Pelloutier asked. He linked them to the libertarian communist society which remained the ultimate aim of the anarchists. He argued that on the day when the revolution breaks out, would they not be an almost libertarian organisation ready to succeed the existing order, thus effectively abolishing all political authority?

The Bourses represented a grassroots form of organisation closer to the anarchist communist method of organising than the new syndicalism that emerged with the CGT. They were to be instruments of self-education and self-emancipation for the working class. The Confédération Générale de Travail (CGT) founded in 1895 in Limoges was at first a rather somnolent organisation. Emile Pouget was to write, "During the following five years, the CGT remained in an embryonic state. Its actions amounted to almost nothing and its greatest efforts were employed in an unfortunate conflict which had arisen between the CGT and the Federation of the Bourses du Travail. The latter organisation, which was then autonomous, concentrated all the revolutionary life of the trade unions, while the CGT assiduously vegetated, since at that time it only included corporativist federations. During this period, the driving force for the orientation of the Confederation was provided by elements which were subsequently to be classified as reformist...." Between 1897 and 1900, revolutionary elements, anarchists and Alemannists, moved into the CGT and began to transform it. This could be seen at the Paris congress of 1900, where revolutionaries were in the ascendant and attempted to replicate the outlook and structures of the First International. This was reflected in its statutes, drafted by Pouget and Griffuelhes, at its congress in Amiens in 1906, which proclaimed that it "groups, outside all political schools, all workers conscious of the struggle to lead for the disappearance of the wage-earning class and of the bosses. As a consequence, with regard to individuals, Congress affirms the entire freedom for the union member to participate, outside the corporate grouping, in such forms of struggle corresponding to their philosophical or political conception, limiting itself to asking them, in reciprocity, not to introduce into the union the opinions they profess outside." This meant that the CGT would discuss neither taking of positions on electoral candidates, nor, on the other hand, anti-electoral struggle. Thus, the CGT was neutral politically, concentrating its activities on class struggle through direct economic action.

The transformation of the CGT was the work of anarchist communist militants like Emile Pouget, Paul Delesalle, and Georges Yvetot, as well as Victor Griffuelhes with a Blanquist background, and revolutionary socialists like Jean Allemane. Unfortunately, the Bourses quickly ran out of steam after they were deprived of the animating spirit of Pelloutier by his death. Pelloutier had been wary of the CGT, not least because of its early hostility to the Bourses. The oft repeated claims that Pelloutier was either a founder or transformer of the CGT are spurious. As Pierre Monatte noted "After the death of Pelloutier in 1901, the Fédération des Bourses du Travail was nothing more than a great wounded tree, from which every year a withered branch fell to the ground." They ended up merging with the CGT in 1902. There were reservations amongst some in relation to the CGT. For example, the metal worker, Benoit Liothier, later secretary of the Saint Etienne branch of the Fédération Communiste Anarchiste Révolutionnaire (FCAR), was to comment: "Syndicalism cannot be revolutionary if it cannot be political...whether we like it or not the economic struggle is tied to the political struggle." However, he, like many others, was to join the CGT. The Bourses finally merged with the CGT in 1902 though militants like Yvetot were opposed to this fusion on the same grounds as Pelloutier, that they fulfilled different and distinct roles.

Jean Grave and his paper Temps Nouveaux were supportive of the CGT, whilst Sebastien Faure and his paper Le Libertaire were sceptical eventually adopting a neutral stance, thus reflecting different stances among anarchist communists.

In fact, whilst the CGT was perceived publicly as a revolutionary syndicalist union, and as an antechamber of anarchist-communism, the later entry of many members of the social-democratic formation, the French Section of the Workers' International (SFIO) led to an evolution.

The neutrality of the CGT meant that whole sections of it relinquished the generalised dimensions of the struggle, its political character, in the broader sense of the term, and not the narrow understanding of the meaning of politics as parliamentary action. Thus, Louis Niel, who moved from revolutionary politics to a more reformist approach, and was a standard bearer of the reformist wing of the CGT, was to justify his position by saying:" There are reforms which have a profound revolutionary virtue: they are all those which pass part of the economic or moral power of the employers into the hands of the proletariat. For example the trade union law, the law on weekly rest, the law of ten hours...So therefore, all trade unionists who pursue any reform are reformists. And since the trade union reforms are of revolutionary quality, all these reformists are revolutionaries," (Les réformes révolutionnaires, in La Revue Syndicaliste, May, 1909). He was to call on the anarchists to stop their war against the socialists, that is, stop their criticisms of electoralism and its proponents.

Pierre Monatte, on the syndicalist left of the CGT, was to second this when he commented: "in the union the differences of opinion, often so subtle, so artificial, take a back seat", and he was to go on to state that these differences could be overcome by class struggle. Pouget was to echo this, writing in his paper, Le Pere Peinard that: "The union's object is to wage war on the bosses and not concern itself with politics." But the cold hard facts of real life showed the weaknesses of these arguments when first the First World War and then the Russian Revolution arrived, splintering the French union movement.

The Malatesta-Monatte debate at the International Anarchist Congress, Amsterdam, 1907

Monatte had become an anarchist communist through his encounters with Pelloutier and Pouget in Paris. Both Monatte and Malatesta defended union unity and independence from political parties, from different perspectives. Debating together at the International Anarchist Congress in Amsterdam in 1907, their different positions became apparent.

Malatesta, it has to be reiterated, was not in the least opposed to the entry of anarchists into the unions, stating that " I recognise all the usefulness, the necessity even, of the active participation of anarchists in the workers' movement, and I have no need to insist to be believed, because I have been of the first to regret the attitude of haughty isolation that anarchists took after the dissolving of the old International, and to push comrades into the path that Monatte, forgetting history, calls new." However, this position was qualified by the belief that the unions were irreparably reformist, and thus entry into them was to be without illusions. He further illuminated his position, "Today, as yesterday, I am a syndicalist in the sense that I am an upholder of the syndicates. I do not ask for anarchist syndicates, which would immediately give legitimacy to social-democratic, republican, royalist and all other kinds of syndicates, and which would divide the working class more than ever against itself. I do not even want to see red syndicates, because I do not want to see yellow syndicates. I would like far more to see syndicates wide open to all workers without regard for opinions, syndicates that are absolutely neutral."

In an article written later in 1922, Syndicalism and Anarchism, he was to further clarify his position on the unions: "In a word, the worker's union is by its nature reformist and not revolutionary".

For Monatte revolutionary syndicalism was sufficient unto itself. It had little philosophy and was defined above all by action. "Just as there is only one working class, there must be, in each profession and in each city, only one workers' organisation… On this condition alone, the class struggle (ceasing to be hampered at all times by the bickering of schools and rival sects) will be able to develop to its full extent…"

Monatte, whilst remaining active in the CGT began to distance himself from anarchism, further developing his ideas of a self-sufficient syndicalism, not attached to any ideology, anarchist or otherwise. He held to internationalist positions with the outbreak of the First World War, resigning publicly from the Federal Committee of the CGT in December 1914 over its capitulation over the War. Appalled by the stance of Kropotkin, Grave and Malato etc., in favour of the Allies, which distanced him further from anarchism, and effected by the outbreak of the Russian Revolution, and looking towards effective action, he ended up joining the French Communist Party (PCF) in 1923. He was expelled the following year, and continued defending revolutionary syndicalism in the pages of the journal La Révolution Prolétarienne until his death in 1960. It should be noted that, despite their differences, Monatte maintained an enduring friendship with Malatesta, whom he judged as someone whose words and deeds matched. The anarchist Louis Lecoin was to be harsher towards Monatte, who he believed pulled a large number of anarchist militants into the PCF in his wake. "It is beyond doubt that the partisans of the so-called dictatorship of the proletariat would never have caused so much damage among us if integral revolutionaries of the Monatte type had not acted for them and had not put them in the saddle". In particular, this refers to the split from the CGT, now in the hands of the social democrats, which regrouped anarchists, revolutionary syndicalists and PCF members within the CGT Unitaire (CGT-U) in 1922.Monatte and the group around his paper Vie Ouvriere formed an alliance with the PCF, leading to the increasing grip of the Communists over the new confederation. It led to the scission of a number of anarcho-syndicalists around Pierre Besnard, which formed the CGT-Syndicaliste Révolutionnaire (CGT-SR).

It was only at the founding congress of the CGT-U at St. Etienne in 1922, that the term "anarcho-syndicalism" began to be used. Up until then, syndicalism or revolutionary syndicalism were the preferred terms. Indeed, it was first used in a pejorative sense. When affiliation to the Bolshevik controlled Red International of Labour Unions (RILU) was discussed at the congress, Alexander Lozovski, the general secretary of the RILU described those opposed to affiliation as 'anarcho-syndicalists', also using another term 'anarcho-reformism' to describe the opposing position (the Russian Daniil Novomirskii first used the term 'anarcho-syndicalism' in his writings in 1907. Paul Avrich noted: Novomirskii's group in Odessa adopted the name "Anarcho-Syndicalists" rather than the French term "revolutionary syndicalists" partly to emphasise their distinctly Russian character, partly to indicate that their members were all anarchists (many of the revolutionary syndicalists in France had Marxist, Blanquist, and other radical affiliations), and partly to distinguish themselves from the Anarchist-Communists, who were not as exclusively concerned with the labour movement as they were," (The Russian Anarchists, p.77) But it was only when Besnard became secretary of the syndicalist international, The International Workers Association, which had been created in opposition to the RILU, that the term was reclaimed and was used to describe the unions affiliated to the IWA and achieved common currency.

"The relationship between the anarcho-syndicalists and the 'revolutionary' syndicalists varied from country to country. Many 'revolutionary' syndicalists rejected even the 'anti-political' politics of the anarchists and saw in syndicalism the form and the content of revolution. They created a syndicalist ideology, at the pinnacle of which was the union organised General Strike which would usher in the new society. For some syndicalists the General Strike assumed an almost mythical significance and replaced the idea of violent revolution, which was considered unrealistic. For 'revolutionary' syndicalist ideologues the union replaced the party and was identified with the class as a whole. A desire to organise all workers, regardless of political or religious belief, led to 'revolutionary' syndicalists attempting to marginalise anarcho-syndicalists in order to appeal to workers who actually remained tied to social democracy. Whilst this anti-politicism led many of the 'revolutionary' syndicalists to a pronounced anti-statism, it did not stop others from entering into alliances with 'revolutionary' parties and politicians. Although politics were unwelcome in the syndical organisation itself this did not mean that 'revolutionary' syndicalism was not involved in politics. Whilst the Italian 'revolutionary' syndicalists flirting with extreme nationalism from 1914 onwards, demanding that Italy join the imperialist bloodbath (a demand totally opposed, to their great credit, by the anarcho-syndicalists of the Union Sindicale Italiana) is probably the most graphic example of syndicalist political alliances, many others existed. In Norway the pre-war 'Revolutionary' syndicalist "fagopposition" (union opposition), for example, was closely identified with the left wing of social democracy whilst in the United States the industrial unionist (the North American equivalent of syndicalist) Industrial Workers of the World were for the first three years of their existence (1905-1908) riven with open political rivalry between the Socialist Party of America and the Socialist Labour Party. In Ireland the syndicalistic Irish Transport and General Workers Union was led by people who had been or still were active members of socialist parties and Irish syndicalism, despite its militancy, rarely exhibited the anti-statism and anti-party sentiment of other syndicalist movements". The Union Makes Us Strong? (Syndicalism, a critical analysis, from Organise! Issues 46-48, magazine of the Anarchist Communist Federation, 1997-1998).

The view of neutral syndicalism was questioned in the 1920s by a new generation of militants. Diego Abad de Santillan of the Argentinian FORA stated that "Malatesta defends, a metaphysical conception of the workers' movement by advocating its unity in the abstract, according to which there exists "a pure workers' movement without any particular social tendency, the aim of which would be only to organise itself into unions... If such an ideal movement, open to all tendencies, were possible, if history could show that it had never existed, then it would be possible to discuss the advisability of introducing [anarchist] tactics into it... But, a pure movement never existed, does not exist, will never exist. The reality is that the labour movement is divided into several tendencies, from fascism to anarchism... What to do? Malatesta advises us to respect the unity of the class. We reject this illusion and call on Malatesta to help us build a revolutionary trade union force, that is to say anarchist, in every country. With such labour union strength, we will be able to resist the invasion of political currents and tendencies that are opposed to the revolution. Without such force, we will passively wait for history to one day turn in our direction..." (El movimiento obrero puro, in El Productor, January 29th, 1926)

The Spanish response to the Monatte-Malatesta dilemma was to be mass syndicalism, not in industrial federations as with the French CGT, but in local unions organised by municipality and region. They would be based on aversion to parliamentary action and advocacy of direct action, with the final aim of libertarian communism. But it should be remembered that at its beginnings the CNT was not an exclusively anarchist organisation. It was an umbrella organisation, including anarchists, syndicalists, socialists and republicans. When it was founded in 1910, it was seen as an organisation that was politically neutral. It only later evolved into an organisation where anarchism was predominant. This was caused by the economic and political situation in Spain, the radicalising effect of several hard fought strikes, as for example the Canadiense strike of 1911, and repression of the unions by the government. This radicalisation was strengthened by the Russian Revolution of 1917 and the economic depression of the interwar period.

The CNT was illegalised during the Primo de Rivera dictatorship of 1923-24 and this allowed the reformist tendencies that were always there in the CNT to come forward. Thus Angel Pestaña was able to advocate participation in the arbitration committees, the comités paritarios, which were being used by the socialist union central, the UGT, which along with the right-wing sindicatos libres, was going ground over the CNT in this period. It was precisely moves like this that caused the establishment of the Federacion Anarquista Iberica

(FAI, Iberian Anarchist Federation) in 1927. Originally founded at the initiative of Portuguese militants, its main aim in Spain was to ensure that the CNT was not lured by the sirens of reformist compromise. The FAI sought to create an organic bond, a "trabazõ, between the FAI and the CNT. Thanks to its decentralised nature, this meant that Faistas could gain control of the CNT apparatus and direct the union central. With the coming of the Second Republic in 1931, the FAI engaged in revolutionary gymnastics, ultra-revolutionary tactics that juxtaposed FAI tactics against those within the CNT it considered as its enemies. The FAI also increased its educational and propaganda efforts within the ateneos and the centros obreros (centres for self-education, mutual aid and culture developed by the libertarian movement). But the FAI cannot be described as a specific anarchist communist organisation. It was the result of the particular situation of anarchism in Spain. It was impossible to disentangle its existence from that of the CNT, to which it was linked quasi-organisationally, acting as its defence corps and as the clandestine organisation of the conscious militant anarchist minority within it.

The CGT-SR in France

The CGT-SR around the militant Pierre Besnard had positions analogous to those of the Federación Obrera Regional Argentina (FORA) in Argentina, in that they advocated the creation of a syndicalist union central that was explicitly anarchist. As we have noted, it resulted from the establishment of PCF hegemony over the CGT-U. This was to be further aggravated by the murder of anarchist militant by Communist thugs at the Maison des Syndicats in Paris on 11th January 1924. The founding conference of the CGT-SR took place in November 1926, and it made a decision to affiliate to the International Workers International at this conference. It never went beyond the figure of a membership of 10,000 though it often punched significantly above its weight. From 1930 it explicitly rejected the neutrality of syndicalism, affirming that syndicalism had to develop not just outside the political parties, but against them. As the exiled Russian anarchist Alexander Schapiro, then active in the CGT-SR wrote:" To counter the policy of subordinating the workers' movement to the conveniences of the so-called "workers'" political parties, a new movement founded upon mass direct action, outside of and against all political parties, rose from the still smoking embers of the 1914-1918 war" (from introduction to Besnard's pamphlet Anarcho-syndicalism and anarchism).

In the pamphlet, written for the extraordinary congress of the IWA in 1937, Besnard develops the concept of anarcho-syndicalism as getting "its doctrine from anarchism and its form of organisation from revolutionary syndicalism". He wrote: "Of necessity, agreement between anarcho-syndicalists and anarcho-communists on libertarian communism as the objective is complete, permanent and absolute. So it is clear and self-evident that the place of the workers, the exploited of whatever sort, whose ideal is anarcho-communism, cannot be other than in the anarcho-syndicalist unions and nowhere else. Their doctrine makes this an imperious, specific and ineluctable duty. Moreover, it is their best practical means of actually achieving that unity of action so necessary for the modern revolutionary anarchist movement. All of the above leads naturally and logically to consideration of the role of the anarchist groups and the trade unions. Anarcho-syndicalists completely admit that the anarcho-communist groups, being more flexible than the union organisations, can more readily comb the toiling masses; that they should seek out recruits and temper militants; that they should carry out active propaganda and intensive pioneering work with an eye to winning the greatest possible number of workers hitherto deceived and gulled by all the political parties, without exception, over to their side and thus to the anarcho-syndicalist trade unions. This wholly ideological undertaking, this psychological-type propaganda drive falls, without question, within the purview of the anarcho-communist groups, on the express condition that they identify with the work of the anarcho-syndicalist trade unions which they complement and reinforce, for the greater good of libertarian communism. But let me state bluntly that the decision-making responsibility, action and supervision of the latter should reside in the here-and-now with the trade unions as the executive agents and operatives carrying out revolutionary tasks." He goes on to say "that the anarcho-communist movement should concern itself primarily with propaganda and education tasks: the study of society and the popularisation thereof." Thus, his view the anarchist groups and organisations is that they should be an ancillary to the anarcho-syndicalist movement, there just for propaganda and education, and not acting as a key tool of struggle. For Besnard, the work of the anarchist communist groups is in "the exclusively ideological field", whilst the anarcho-syndicalist unions fulfil the tasks of libertarian communism at a practical and constructive level.

In his work the Le Nouveau Monde (The New World) of 1934 he sums up his ideas in the slogan "All the economy to the unions! All social administration to the communes! thus developing a fusion of anarcho-syndicalist and anarchist communist ideas. The anarchist Eric Vilain remarks upon this work of Besnard that "Evil tongues said of Pierre Besnard that he had a station master's vision of revolutionary society. This was doubtless a treacherous allusion to the fact that he was a railway worker. However, it is not entirely false if, of the station master, we have the image of a man who insists that the trains arrive and leave on time and that everything is well organised. Besnard believed that one should not wait for the revolution to take place to begin to consider how things would be organised. Reading The New World can give the impression of a manic and picky vision of what the future society should be like, a vision that would fit into the countless utopian projects that Western thought has given us to read since Thomas More, the inventor of the word" (http://monde-nouveau.net/spip.php?article714). In this meticulously worked out new world, Besnard retreats from anarchist communism back to Bakuninist collectivism, positing the concept "From each according to their work", rather than "from each according to their means to each according to their needs". It is not the case that everyone has the same needs nor that they have the same means. An anarchist communist society must look towards meeting the needs of all. In fact, under Besnard's envisaged system, work vouchers replace money but in fact perform the same function as money. But how can one hour of work be the equivalent of another hour of work, whether harder work or less rewarding work? The number of working hours gives no indication of social usefulness. And in fact in Besnard's system, money is retained so that trade can be carried on with foreign countries (obviously countries still existing under capitalism) to buy raw materials and to sell surplus products!

Besnard also believes that in a new society unions will still exist, and that in fact, they will be indispensable for the functioning of a libertarian society. Rather than unions being transcended by workers' councils and workplace committees, the unions will continue to exist to carry on the economic functions of society.

Unfortunately Besnard's decision to create a pure anarcho-syndicalist union in the form of the CGT-SR separated from the mass of the workers condemned it to a cloistered existence. World War Two led to the end of the CGT-SR. After the war, Besnard called for the resurrection of a united CGT before his death in 1947.

As Philippe Pelletier notes: "Because let us not forget one thing. In the post-revolutionary society new structures would appear that necessarily transcend the existing splits of workers and unions. Even if, by their position and their heritage of struggle, the unions are the essential nuclei of this recomposition, they can be gone beyond, they will be gone beyond! For, until proven otherwise, the functioning of a hospital, of a railway station or a rolling mill will not be partitioned between x union sections but controlled by a common organism- council, committee, collectivity or whatever other name – for the benefit of the entire society, not that of a partisan interest. The commune, in particular, will be one of the key elements of this communist going beyond. To say it in a different way, the union must carry in it the seeds of its own dissolution, which is not necessarily the case of the specific organisation. Besides, this specific organisation, which must be the most active, the most dynamic and the most federative of the revolutionary worker-peasant movement… has not the pretension of being hegemonic".

Mass anarchist movements have characteristically been organised within and around anarcho-syndicalist unions, with the exception of groups like the FORA in Argentina and the All Japan Libertarian Federation of Labour Unions (Zenkoku Jiren in Japan). The relationship between anarchist communists and anarcho-syndicalist trade unions has been an often uneasy one, not least with the move away from the concept of the commune as a central building block of the new society. In addition, the concept that syndicalist unions should endure, and indeed replace the commune as the most important organism of management of a new society, has provoked disquiet within anarchist communist ranks. This uneasy relationship can be traced in the chapters in this book on movements within various countries.

On an international level, syndicalism in its anarchist and revolutionary forms spread out to Italy, Spain, England, Germany and the Latin American countries. In many of these places it gained a mass following, able to rally hundreds of thousands behind it. It was only the decimation of the First World War, the confusion engendered in syndicalist ranks, and finally the rise of Bolshevism as a seemingly credible revolutionary alternative, that anarcho-syndicalism and revolutionary syndicalism began to decline, reaching their lowest level with the crushing of the Spanish Revolution.

References

Alliance Syndicaliste. L'anarcho-syndicalisme. Aperçu historique et théorique (1976)

Bance, Pierre, Deschamps, Etienne. Nous sommes syndicalistes revolutionnaires. Editions CNT (1978).

Besnard, Pierre. Anarcho-syndicalisme et anarchisme (1937).

Damier, Vadim. Anarcho-syndicalism in the 20th century (2009).

Groupe Communiste-Anarchiste Errico Malatesta de la Federation Anarchiste. L'anarcho-syndicalisme est-il soluble dans le syndicalisme revolutionnaire? (1997)

Nettlau, Max. Fernand Pelloutier and syndicalism (1932).

Pelletier, Philippe. Anarchisme, syndicalisme, mouvement ouvrier, le debat Malatesta-Monatte toujours d'actualite. Le Monde Libertaire 1997, 27 Feb-4 March, no.1073.

Spitzer, Alan. Anarchy and culture – Fernand Pelloutier and the dilemma of revolutionary syndicalism. International Review of Social History (1963).

Chapter Sixteen
Kropotkin and his ideas

"Peter Kropotkin is without doubt one of those who have contributed perhaps most – perhaps even more than Bakunin or Élisée Reclus – to the elaboration and propagation of anarchist ideas" (Errico Malatesta, in *Studi Sociali*, April 1935, appearing three years after his death).

Whilst not originating anarchist communism, Petr Kropotkin was a key figure in its development. He wrote a large number of articles and pamphlets on the subject, as well as books like The Conquest of Bread (1892) and Fields, Factories, and Workshops (1899). The Conquest of Bread is heavily influenced by the experience of the Paris Commune of 1871 and posits a vision of a future anarchist communist society.

Kropotkin was harsh in his criticism of the mutualism of Proudhon and Benjamin Tucker and of individualist anarchism, as well as of Marxism. He thus advanced anarchist communism as the alternative to these currents. Equally Kropotkin rejected Tolstoyan pacifism, saying, "I am not in sympathy with Tolstoy's asceticism, nor with his doctrine of non-resistance to evil, nor with his New Testament literalism".

However, he believed that anarchist communism was a merger of radical liberalism and communism. As a member of the International, he should have realised that anarchist communism emerged from that body and the workers' movement in Europe in general, and was an evolution of communist ideas as developed by workers themselves and had nothing to do with the radical liberalism of sections of the bourgeoisie.

From 1890, Kropotkin stepped back from full scale activity within the movement, although his commitment still remained very high. Kropotkin became increasingly critical of the turn towards individual attentats and began to reconsider his positions. Whilst understanding that despair often led to these attentats, he refused to condemn them outright, counterposing the terrorism of the State itself. An eternal optimist, like many in the 19th century, he still believed that social revolution was around the corner. At the 1883 trial of anarchist at

Lyons, Kropotkin voiced the opinion that social revolution would break out within the decade, followed by an insurrectionary period that might last five years. He maintained these optimistic views in his Memoirs of a Revolutionist of 1899. By the early 1900s, he had tempered his views and in a letter to Max Nettlau from 1902 wrote, "the general situation is not as revolutionary as it was before 1894-95, and we have realised that one cannot begin a revolution with a handful of people. It was foolish to imagine that the strong effort of a few could succeed in inciting the revolution: things did not happen that way, and it was necessary to organise the preparatory movement which precedes all revolutions. It was necessary, in addition, to have an ideal for the revolution".

Kropotkin always connected science to anarchism and even insisted when writing to James Guillaume, that it was necessary that anarchists could write about history, political economy or even biology. He regarded anarchism and explicitly anarchist communism as the theory and philosophy of the current age and that science and anarchism should be as one. However he rejected the ideas of absolute knowledge and truth as developed by Hegelian dialectics. He believed that anarchism and science complemented each other, whilst rejecting Marxism as a scientific method. Recognising Capital as a "marvellous revolutionary pamphlet" he wrote that its "scientific significance is nil". Kropotkin rejected the dialectical and historical materialist analysis of Marx and Engels, regarding them as pseudo-science. He believed that the idea that capitalism would give birth to socialism was grossly determinist, and furthermore inhibited the actions of revolutionaries. He rejected the theory of surplus value as developed by Marx. This brought him into dispute with Carlo Cafiero who supported Marx's theory. He was harsh about Marx's supposition that capital tends to centralise, expand, and concentrate. He described it as the "fatality of a natural law", and felt that it contributed greatly to the social-democratic vision of a centralised socialism. He believed that Marx would have revised his views if allowed more experience. He concluded "Very probably he would have mitigated the absoluteness of his early formulae... As I have demonstrated, Marx's "formulae" of a tendency toward centralisation were not "absolute," (in Fields, Factories and Workshops, 1985, p.145).

He allowed that some small industries had disappeared but felt this was more to do with the need for profitability, leading on to tighter control of workforces, fewer expenses incurred through wholesale selling, cheap mass buying and the creation of mass markets rather than developments in productivity. This was really not at all against what Marx was saying. Kropotkin's belief that prices were affected not just by labour time but also by supply and demand and by the intervention of monopolies and the State was not really at odds with what Marx thought.

Kropotkin was very much under the sway of the concept of scientific progress, prevalent among thinkers in the 19th century. Malatesta was to address himself to the notion of 'scientific anarchism' as expressed by Kropotkin. He thought that this concept was neither science nor anarchism. Mechanical concepts of the universe could not be equated with human aspirations and the idea of anarchism. In addition Malatesta rejected Kropotkin's views on harmony in nature, which he saw as too optimistic. This in its turn would create too much optimism about the inevitability of anarchist communism. Rather for Malatesta, it was not the emphasis on harmony in nature but the struggle against disharmony in human society. Despite this, it was Kropotkin's linking of science and anarchism, with all of its faults, which won an audience throughout society and enabled anarchist communism to play a role in the international working class movement as well as in intellectual life.

Malatesta believed that Kropotkin's "concept of the Universe was rigorously mechanistic", and that he, 'who was very critical of the fatalism of the Marxists, was, himself the victim of mechanistic fatalism which is far more inhibiting.' Malatesta felt that, "Thus, after having said that "anarchy is a concept of the Universe based on the mechanical interpretation of phenomena which embrace the whole of nature including the life of societies" (I confess I have never succeeded in understanding what this might mean) Kropotkin would forget his mechanistic concept as a matter of no importance, and throw himself into the struggle with the fire, enthusiasm and confidence of one who believes in the efficacy of his Will and who hopes by his activity to obtain or contribute to the achievement of the things he wants." Kropotkin: Recollections and Criticisms of an Old Friend, 1931).

Kropotkin was very much influenced by Darwin in his theories on evolution. He felt that the advances made in science by Darwin, particularly in the fields of biology, zoology, and anthropology, cleared the way, not just for the study of organisms, but for that of human institutions. However, he was less convinced by Darwin's theory of natural selection, and believed that mutual aid was a decisive and progressive factor in evolution. He believed that in his later years Darwin himself recognised this and felt that it was more important than individual struggle within a species. Kropotkin thus opposed himself to the social Darwinists who believed in nature bloody in tooth and claw. In this he built on the ideas of the Russian biologist, Karl Kessler, who suggested that mutual aid was more important than struggle within a species. In his book Mutual Aid: A Factor in Evolution, Kropotkin concluded that those species which had developed mutual aid to the greatest extent were more successful and numerous than other species.

Turning to the human species, he believed that mutual aid had been an essential factor in ensuring its survival, despite everything else. Furthermore, for Kropotkin, mutual aid was the key ingredient in the development of morality in human society. It fostered ethical feeling, the concepts of right and wrong, which developed into 'those feelings of benevolence and of that partial identification of the individual with the group which were the starting point of all the higher ethical feelings.

As the German dissident communist Paul Mattick was to comment, to a degree somewhat unfairly, in a review of Mutual Aid (in Western Socialist, 1956), "Although it is good to know that there is just as much, or more, mutual aid as competition in nature and society, this is not enough to make men change their ways and to alter social relationships. For those who profit by conditions it does not matter whether it is "natural" or "unnatural," the "best" or the "worst" method for survival of the species. Mankind is none of their concern. For those who create the profits it may be nice to know that the mutual aid practised in their own circles attests to their high ethical concepts and natural behaviour, but it does not stop their exploitation. The whole controversy between Huxley and Kropotkin is somewhat beside the point – it does not touch upon the relevant issues of society, namely that "mutual aid" in human society presupposes the abolition of class relation".

Kropotkin has been criticised for juxtaposing mutual aid against class struggle. This was clearly not his aim. As he wrote in the above mentioned letter to Max Nettlau, "From the Jura Bulletin to La Revolte, I have always preached active participation in the workers' movement, in the revolutionary workers' movement". In Mutual Aid itself, he is aware of the limits of mutual aid. Writing about the mutual aid efforts of European peasants, he concludes, "From the point of view of social economics all these efforts of the peasants certainly are of little importance. They cannot substantially, and still less permanently, alleviate the misery to which the tillers of the soil are doomed all over Europe."

Kropotkin believed that what he saw as 'State socialism' (the social-democratic parties, etc.) as having their origins in the Jacobinism of the French Revolution. Whilst describing himself as a communist, he was critical of Babouvism, and of those he saw as its heirs, like Blanqui, Cabet and Weitling. On the other hand, he traced the origin of libertarian communism back to the Enragés, also active during the French Revolution. He believed that socialism and anarchism had emerged from the struggles of the masses, and must remain in contact with the masses. These struggles had given birth to first the First International and then the Paris Commune of 1871. He believed the latter had demonstrated the bankruptcy of state socialism. It was the task of anarchist communists to act within the masses to prevent the same mistakes being made again and to aid the working class to establish a new society under their control, and not mediated by state socialists.

He specifically wrote both the Conquest of Bread (1892) and Fields, Factories and Workshops (1898), to highlight the need to establish everyone's access to housing, food and clothing from the first day of the revolution. He did not believe that scarcity would impede the ending of the wages system and that any shortages incurred during the first days of the revolution as a result of the disruption of production, would be solved by rationing put in place by the revolutionary communes. He believed that production would be improved so that adults between twenty or twenty-two to forty-five or fifty would only have to work a five hour day in order to provide for all. In developing his ideas of revolution, he thus fell a victim to productivism, by encouraging post-revolutionary increase of production, and then increased consumption.

Kropotkin's views of state socialism led him to examine the history of the State, as outlined in his The State, Its Historical Role, of 1896. According to him, a process started in the fifteenth century, with the consolidation of feudal lords' power. This was at the expense of federalist tendencies within society, and the decline of the medieval cities. Kropotkin believed that the process of State consolidation had started in the 11th century, facilitated by the Church, and he always twinned Church and State as malignant twin institutions. He saw the sixteenth century as a time of full scale attack on the free cities, orchestrated by the feudal lords and Church and leading to the development of stronger centralised States. In the next three centuries, these States, according to Kropotkin, campaigned against federalist forms of organisation, whether in neighbourhoods, villages or guilds. Cooperative social relations were destroyed, and with the rise of capitalism, the State became 'the chief instrument for the few to monopolise the land, and the capitalists to appropriate a quite disproportionate share of the yearly accumulated surplus of production'.

Kropotkin regarded parliament as 'Built up by the middle classes to hold their own against royalty, sanctioning, and at the same time strengthening, their sway over the workers, parliamentary rule is pre-eminently a middle-class rule'. For him, serfdom related to feudalism and absolute monarchy, whilst bourgeois democracy was the political form characteristic of capitalism. So, "the political regime to which human societies are submitted is always the expression of the economic regime which exists within that society". Each new form of political organisation "corresponded to each new form of economic organisation".

Kropotkin believed that the State and capitalism were inseparable, each supporting the other. "They are bound together not by a mere coincidence of contemporaneous development, but by the bond of cause and effect, effect and cause". Thus the destruction of capitalism necessarily implied the destruction of the State, and vice versa.

Representative government meant the rule of capital, so therefore any call by workers for universal suffrage could achieve nothing in the long run as those who have control of the economic system manipulate the political system.

Kropotkin made a distinction between State and government, although he regarded them as equally abhorrent – "the State has also been confused with Government. Since there can be no State without government, it has sometimes been said that what one must aim at is the absence of government and not the abolition of the State. However, it seems to me that State and government are two concepts of a different order. The State idea means something quite different from the idea of government. It not only includes the existence of a power situated above society, but also of a territorial concentration as well as the concentration in the hands of a few of many functions in the life of societies. It implies some new relationships between members of society which did not exist before the formation of the State. A whole mechanism of legislation and of policing has to be developed in order to subject some classes to the domination of others" (The State – Its Historic Role, 1896).

Kropotkin concludes, "Either the State for ever, crushing individual and local life, taking over in all fields of human activity, bringing with it all its wars and domestic struggles for power, its palace revolutions which only replace one tyrant by another, and inevitably at the end of this development there is… death! Or the destruction of States, and new life starting again in thousands of centres on the principles of the lively initiative of the individual and groups and that of free agreement."

Kropotkin, like Déjacque and Bakunin before him, rejected the antifeminism and misogyny of Proudhon. Bakunin had openly called for gender equality and Kropotkin advanced from this towards a critique of housework as an instrument of the oppression of women, in Conquest of Bread, writing "To emancipate woman, is not only to open the gates of the university, the law courts, or the parliaments to her, for the "emancipated" woman will always throw her domestic toil on to another woman. To emancipate woman is to free her from the brutalising toil of kitchen and washhouse; it is to organise your household in such a way as to enable her to rear her children, if she be so minded, while still retaining sufficient leisure to take her share of social life. It will come. As we have said, things are already improving. Only let us fully understand that a revolution, intoxicated with the beautiful words, Liberty, Equality, Solidarity, would not be a revolution if it maintained slavery at home. Half humanity subjected to the slavery of the hearth would still have to rebel against the other half."

Kropotkin was unable to see that liberation from housework would need the sharing of domestic tasks by men, and could only posit the use of technology to solve this problem. Similarly, he still seems to think that the rearing and education of children would still be a main task of women.

Kropotkin was perceptive enough to see that gender and class could not be separated. He believed that reformist feminists only referred to the emancipation of one class of women, leaving their working class sisters in subjection, many compelled to act as domestic workers in the households of the upper classes. He was careful to replace the term "fraternity" with "solidarity".

Kropotkin's views on the First World War cannot be ignored. Enemies of anarchism have tried to draw the lesson that this failure to take an internationalist position and to instead side with the Allies must have somehow sprung from his anarchist communism, and hence this body of ideas must be flawed. When one considers that the overwhelming majority of anarchist communists took an internationalist position then this theory is shown to hold no water. Rather it was perhaps Kropotkin's blinkered views on France as the leading country of radical thought and revolution, which must be defended at all costs, with false comparisons with the Paris Commune of 1871, which may have swayed Kropotkin to adopt this mistaken position, a position disastrous for both his reputation and for the international movement.

Kropotkin was to write: "The causes of war must be attacked at the root. And we have a great hope that the present war will open the eyes of the masses of workers and of a number of men amid the educated middle classes. They will see the part that capital and state have played in bringing about the armed conflicts between nations.

But for the moment we must not lose sight of the main work of the day. The territories of both France and Belgium MUST be freed of the invaders. The German invasion must be repulsed – no matter how difficult this may be. All efforts must be directed that way" (Letter to Steffen, in Freedom, October 1914).

As Alexander Berkman remarked: "It is a most painful shock to us to realise that even Kropotkin, clear thinker that he is, has in this instance fallen a victim to the war psychology now dominating Europe. His arguments are weak and superficial. In his letter to Gustav Steffen he has become so involved in the artificialities of 'high politics' that he lost sight of the most elemental fact of the situation, namely that the war in Europe is not a war of nations, but a war of capitalist governments for power and markets. Kropotkin argues as if the German people are at war with the French, the Russian, or English people, when as a matter of fact it is only the ruling and capitalist cliques of those countries that are responsible for the war and alone stand to gain by its result" (In Reply to Kropotkin, November 1914).

Malatesta, devastated by his friend and comrade's betrayal of internationalism, wrote: "there was never serious disagreement between us until that day in 1914 when we were faced with a question of practical conduct of capital importance to both of us: that of the attitude to be adopted by anarchists to the War. On that occasion Kropotkin's old preferences for all that which is Russian and French were reawakened and exacerbated in him, and he declared himself an enthusiastic supporter of the Entente. He seemed to forget that he was an Internationalist, a socialist and an anarchist; he forgot what he himself had written only a short time before about the war that the Capitalists were preparing, and began expressing admiration for the worst Allied statesmen and Generals, and at the same time treated as cowards the anarchists who refused to join the Union Sacre, regretting that his age and his poor health prevented him from taking up rifle and marching against the Germans. It was impossible therefore to see eye to eye: for me he was a truly pathological case. All the same it was one of the saddest, most painful moments of my life (and, I dare to suggest, for him too) when, after a more than acrimonious discussion, we parted like adversaries, almost as enemies."

In fact Kropotkin had held a pro-French position from early on. He wrote in 1882 that: 'Bismarck knows, that on the day on which the alliance of people of the Latin race take place, German supremacy will be at an end. He understands that the principle of the almighty State will also be done away with whose faithful expression and final vanguard at this moment is Germany – the monarchical as well as the republican, and the republican as well as social democrat. An almighty State, even if it wore republican colours can satisfy neither France, nor Italy, and even less Spain. Therefore, the alliance of the Latin peoples is the nightmare which presses on Germany against which Bismarck works' He repeated these ideas in 1899: 'The triumph of Germany was the triumph of militarism in Europe, of militarism and political despotism, and at the same time the worship of the State, of authority and State socialism, which is in reality nothing but State capitalism triumphant in the ideas of a whole generation.' Malatesta was not surprised by Kropotkin's stance on the war. Writing to the British anarchist paper Freedom in 1914 he confessed 'that we were in the wrong not giving importance to his Franco-Russian patriotism, and not foreseeing where his anti-German prejudices would land him.'

Let's leave the last word to Malatesta: "In any case anarchists will always find in his writings a treasury of fertile ideas".

Chapter Seventeen
Malatesta: the pragmatist

Malatesta described himself as an anarchist communist throughout most of his life. However he was not loath to alter his ideas throughout his lifetime. Writing in the paper Il Risveglio in 1929, he said of Galleani's The End of Anarchism, that "the Kropotkinian conception… was a conception which I personally find too optimistic, too easy-going, too trusting in natural harmonies…". He wrote in 1931 that, "Kropotkin adhered to the materialist philosophy that prevailed among scientists in the second half of the 19th century, the philosophy of Moleschott, Buchner, Vogt and others; and consequently his concept of the Universe was rigorously mechanistic. According to his system, Will (a creative power whose source and nature we cannot comprehend, just as, likewise, we do not understand the nature and source of "matter" or of any of the other "first principles") – I was saying, Will which contributed much or little in determining the conduct of individuals – and of society, does not exist and is a mere illusion. All that has been, that is and will be, from the path of the stars to the birth and decline of a civilisation, from the perfume of a rose to the smile on a mother's lips, from an earthquake to the thoughts of a Newton, from a tyrant's cruelty to a saint's goodness, everything had to, must, and will occur as a result of an inevitable sequence of causes and effects of mechanical origin, which leaves no possibility of variety. The illusion of Will is itself a mechanical fact. Naturally if Will has no power, if everything is necessary and cannot be otherwise, then ideas of freedom, justice and responsibility have no meaning, and have no bearing on reality. Thus logically all we can do is to contemplate what is happening in the world, with indifference, pleasure or pain, depending on one's personal feelings, without hope and without the possibility of changing anything. So Kropotkin, who was very critical of the fatalism of the Marxists, was, himself the victim of mechanistic fatalism which is far more inhibiting".

Like Kropotkin, Malatesta was critical of theories of economic determinism. Under the influence of Merlino, he came to believe that transition to a new post-capitalist society is not inevitable.

Furthermore, he warned that any communism that was imposed, "Would be the most detestable tyranny that the human mind could conceive." His predictions were certainly proved right by history.

Like Marx, Malatesta believed that it would not be possible to immediately install a fully formed communism on the day after the Revolution. Whereas Marx referred to lower phases of communism, through a historical process, Malatesta preferred to sketch out how the revolutionary process could develop. What he was convinced of, unlike Marx, was that no form of the State should be used in this process. He was far from being opposed to manifestoes and programmes, but felt that these should be presented with a due modesty, and altered and moderated with the unfolding of circumstances. He was conscious that, "In order to abolish the police and all the harmful social institutions we must know what to put in their place, not in a more or less distant future but immediately, the very day we start demolishing. One only destroys, effectively and permanently, that which one replaces by something else; and to put off to a later date the solution of problems which present themselves with the urgency of necessity, would be to give time to the institutions one is intending to abolish to recover from the shock and reassert themselves, perhaps under other names, but certainly with the same structure" (The Anarchist Revolution, 1922, p.10).

However his views on anarchist communism were moderated by false ideas that somehow anarchist communists could cooperate with the individualists and mutualists. Malatesta believed in effective action, and this sometimes led him into alliances with these elements and indeed with other radicals and socialists.

Thus he was able to say that "Free and voluntary communism is ironical if one has not the right and the possibility to live in a different regime, collectivist, mutualist, individualist – as one wishes, always on condition that there is no oppression or exploitation of others.", going on to say that "One may, therefore, prefer communism, or individualism, or collectivism, or any other system, and work by example and propaganda for the achievement of one's personal preferences, but one must beware, at the risk of certain disaster, of supposing that one's system is the only, and infallible, one, good for all men, everywhere and for all times, and that its success must be assured at all costs, by means other than those which depend on persuasion, which spring from the evidence of facts."

Malatesta was searching for a united front against fascism, and in the pages of his paper Pensiero e Volonta (Thought and Will, 1924-1926), he stated that differences between the individualists and the communists were not fundamental. This was an about-turn from his previously hostile attitude towards individualists, as the result of previous experience. Now he sought to involve them in the anti-fascist struggle, making many concessions along the way, and saying that controversies over economic and social organisation could be dealt after fascism was defeated.

The disappointments of the Russian Revolution and the rise of fascism in Italy were to colour his attitude towards anarchist communism. He tinkered with the idea of dropping communism altogether as a descriptor, moving closer to the concept of 'anarchism without adjectives', writing in 1924 that, "I use the word 'associationist' as an alternative to the word ' 'communist', not because I like pointless new jargon, but because I foresee the possibility that the communist anarchists will gradually abandon the term 'communist'; it is growing in ambivalence and falling into disrepute as a result of Russian 'communist' despotism. If the term is eventually abandoned this will be a repetition of what happened with the word 'socialist'. We who, in Italy at least, were the first champions of socialism and maintained and still maintain that we are the true socialists in the broad and human sense of the word, ended by abandoning the term to avoid confusion with the many and various authoritarian and bourgeois deviations of socialism. Thus too we may have to abandon the term 'communist' for fear that our ideal of free human solidarity will be confused with the avaricious despotism which has for some while triumphed in Russia and which one party, inspired by the Russian example, seeks to impose worldwide . Then perhaps we would need another adjective to distinguish us from the rest – and this could well be associationist or societist or such like, although it seems to me that simply to use the term 'anarchist' would suffice." Thus, instead of defending and reaffirming anarchist communism in face of its appropriation by the Bolsheviks, he was willing to host the idea of relinquishing it altogether. Perhaps he was thinking out loud, because in the same article he concludes by saying,

Communism is our ideal. We are communists because communism seems to us to be the best way in which people can live together, in which people can best demonstrate their love for one another and at the same time render more productive human attempts to conquer natural resources. For this reason we must preach it; and as soon as circumstances allow we must apply it through example and experiment, in all those places and in all those branches of activity where it is possible so to do. For the rest we must trust in freedom, which ever remains our aim and the means of all human progress."

Whilst Kropotkin believed that the State and government were not the same, Malatesta thought the opposite writing in his essay Anarchy, in 1891, "Anarchists, including this writer, have used the word State, and still do, to mean the sum total of the political, legislative, judiciary, military and financial institutions through which the management of their own affairs, the control over their personal behaviour, the responsibility for their personal safety, are taken away from the people and entrusted to others who, by usurpation or delegation, are vested with the powers to make the laws for everything and everybody, and to oblige the people to observe them, if need be, by the use of collective force. In this sense the word State means government, or to put it another way, it is the impersonal, abstract expression of that state of affairs, personified by government: and therefore the term abolition of the State, Society without the State, etc., describe exactly the concept which anarchists seek to express of the destruction of all political order based on authority."

Malatesta was always a fervent partisan of organisation, and often incurred the wrath of anti-organisationalists in the ranks of the movement. His polemics with the authors of the Platform in the late 1920s were hindered by his house arrest under Mussolini, but it seems in his latter correspondence with them, that some consensus was being arrived at. He was always aware that anarchists would be an active and conscious minority in capitalist society and during revolutions, and that as such a conscious minority it had "to profit from every situation to change the environment in a way that will make possible the education of the whole people" (The Anarchist Revolution, 1922, p.1).

Malatesta was a convinced internationalist, as above all illustrated by his attitude towards the First World War. Whereas Kropotkin,

Grave, Malato, Pindy, Cherkesov, Wintsch et al. capitulated to the War hysteria, and supported the Allies, whilst Nettlau took the side of the Austro-Hungarians, Malatesta remained committed to a rejection of all the States. He counterposed class war to the slaughter in the trenches: "More than ever we must avoid compromise; deepen the chasm between capitalists and wage slaves, between rulers and ruled; preach expropriation of private property and the destruction of States as the only means of guaranteeing fraternity between the peoples and Justice and Liberty for all; and we must prepare to accomplish these things" (Malatesta, Anarchists have forgotten their principles, in Freedom [London] 28, no. 307, November 1914).

As a pragmatist, he believed both in anarchists organising effectively together in groups and organisations, and in anarchists making propaganda wherever they could, among the organisations of the masses, saying,, "We must immerse ourselves in the life of the people as fully as we can; encourage and egg on all stirrings that carry a seed of material or moral revolt and get the people used to handling their affairs for themselves and relying on only their own resources; but without ever losing sight of the fact that revolution, by means of the expropriation and taking of property into common ownership, plus the demolition of authority, represents the only salvation for the prolétariat and for Mankind, in which case a thing is good or bad depending on whether it brings forward or postpones, eases or creates difficulties for that revolution" (article in the French paper La Révolté, October 1890).

Malatesta exhorted anarchist communists to involve themselves in the lives and activities of the masses, to get their hands dirty. "Popular movements begin how they can; nearly always they spring from some idea already transcended by contemporary thought. It is absurd to hope that in the present condition of the proletariat the great mass are capable before they stir of conceiving and accepting a programme formulated by a small number to whom circumstances have given exceptional means of development, a programme which can only come to be consciously accepted by the great number through the action of moral and material conditions which the movement itself must supply. If we wait to plunge into the fray until the people mount the Anarchist Communist colours, we shall run great risk of remaining eternal dreamers; we shall see the tide of history flow at our feet while scarcely contributing anything toward determining its course, leaving a free field meanwhile to our adversaries who are the enemies, conscious or unconscious, of the true interests of the people" (in The Commonweal, 1893, online at https://theanarchistlibrary.org/library/errico-malatesta-the-first-of-may).

Malatesta's position on class was finely honed by his experiences with the Italian factory councils of 1920-1921. He was ready to admit that, "It is a truth that history has made the proletariat the main instrument of the next social change, and that those fighting for the establishment of a society where all human beings are free and endowed with all the means to exercise their freedom, must rely mainly on the proletariat" (About My Trial; Class Struggle or Class

Hatred, Umanita Nova, 1921). However this did not mean that the proletariat should be idealised. For Malatesta it was natural for those who have nothing, and therefore are more directly and clearly interested in sharing the means of production, to be the main agents of the necessary expropriation. This was why anarchist propaganda was aimed at proletarians, whose conditions of life, on the other hand, make it often impossible for them to rise and conceive a superior ideal. However, proletarians should not be fetishised, just because they are impoverished, or to encourage a sense of intrinsic superiority.

Malatesta, whilst acknowledging that capitalist production engendered class antagonism, was not convinced that the development of capitalism developed the conditions for its own destruction. Active participation of a revolutionary minority was crucial in acting upon circumstances to aid this destruction.

For Malatesta, the conscious anarchist minority had the task of pushing unrest and uprisings as far as they could go. "The revolution is the creation of new living institutions, new groupings, new social relationships; it is the destruction of privileges and monopolies; it is the new spirit of justice, of brotherhood, of freedom which must renew the whole of social life, raise the moral level and the material conditions of the masses by calling on them to provide, through their direct and conscientious action, for their own futures. Revolution is the organisation of all public services by those who work in them in their own interest as well as the public's; Revolution is the destruction of all coercive ties; it is the autonomy of groups, of communes, of regions; Revolution is the free federation brought about by desire for brotherhood, by individual and collective interests, by the needs of production and defence; Revolution is the constitution of innumerable free groupings based on ideas, wishes, and tastes of all kinds that exist among the people; Revolution is the forming and disbanding of thousands of representative, district, communal, regional, national bodies which, without having any legislative power, serve to make known and to coordinate the desires and interests of people near and far and which act through information, advice and example. Revolution is freedom proved in the crucible of facts – and lasts so long as freedom lasts, that is until others, taking advantage of the weariness that overtakes the masses, of the inevitable disappointments that follow exaggerated hopes, of the probable errors and human faults, succeed in constituting a power, which supported by an army of conscripts or mercenaries, lays down the law, arrests the movement at the point it has reached, and then begins the reaction" (The Anarchist Revolution, 1922, p.11).

Chapter Eighteen
The Yellow Fever of Disorganisation: Individualist anarchism

"The anarchists have been tormented and rendered powerless by the conflict, which has never ceased to rage among them, between individualists and communists. They are poles apart and agree on only one thing – their abhorrence of parliamentarism" (Saverio Merlino, in Number 1 of *Pensiero e Volonta*, 1924).

"Like yellow fever, this disease of disorganisation introduced itself into the organism of the anarchist movement and has shaken it for dozens of years. It is nevertheless beyond doubt that this disorganisation derives from some defects of theory: notably from a false interpretation of the principle of individuality in anarchism: this theory being too often confused with the absence of all responsibility. The lovers of assertion of 'self,' solely with a view to personal pleasure obstinately cling to the chaotic state of the anarchist movement and refer in its defence to the immutable principles of anarchism and its teachers," Organisational Platform of the Libertarian Communists.

"My motto is: Me, me, me... and then the others!" (Hynan Croiset at the International Anarchist Congress, Amsterdam, 1907).

The end result of the trend among self-avowed anarchist communists towards all but the most improvised affinity groups, a fear verging on paranoia at any attempt at effective organisation, and a narrow interpretation of propaganda by the deed was the emergence of individualism within the anarchist movement between 1880 to 1900.

The various strands that come together to create the individualist anarchist current came about through various defeats of the workers' movement. In Italy this was first experienced with a mutation out of the anti-organisational tendency, which had emerged after the defection to the parliamentary socialists of the important anarchist militant Andrea Costa in 1880-1881. In reaction some anarchists "began to preach and to practice disorganisation; they wanted to elevate isolation, disdain for obligations, and lack of solidarity into a principle, as if these were a function of the anarchist programme, while instead they are its complete negation... They wanted to prevent betrayals and deception, permit free rein to individual initiative, ensure against spies and attacks from the government – and they brought isolation and impotence to the fore" (Malatesta, Organisation, 1889). Unfortunately, against the counsel of Malatesta, a strong advocate of effective organisation, the anti-organisational current became strong within the Italian movement. One example was the anarchist-communist paper Il Paria (The Pariah) founded at Ancona between 1885 and 1887. It was at best ambivalent about organisation, and had an aversion to economic strikes and workers' organisation, in contrast to Malatesta, who was firmly in favour. Fortunately, Il Paria was succeeded in Ancona by Il Libero Patta (Free Pact) in 1889, which grouped together pro-organisationists who were later to become Malatesta's closest associates, like Emidio Recchioni and Luigi Fabbri.

The individualist current in Italy developed out of anti-organisationism. They had nothing to do with the individualist theorists Stirner, Tucker, John Henry Mackay, or indeed Nietzsche, who were unknown in Italy until the twentieth century. Whilst they often described themselves as anarchist communists, they "were amoralists who embodied the worst attitudes and propensities of the antiorganisationist current: egoistic preoccupation with individual autonomy and free initiative; unwavering rejection of organisation in any form; isolation from and contempt for the masses; and, in some cases, a strong tendency toward individual acts of violence" (Pernicone, p.239).

Leading lights were the Gruppo Intransigente, which numbered Vittorio Pini and Luigi Parmeggiani in its ranks. Wedded to expropriation and a lauding of bombs and dynamite, this group was firmly against organisation and the development of a movement through propaganda and education. Pini ended up spending the rest of his life in the French penal colony at Cayenne. Parmeggiani moved to London, where he was a bane to the organisationists there, Malatesta among them. A decidedly dubious character, who might have been an agent provocateur, his speciality was forging antiques. He ended up as a wealthy antiquarian back in Italy.

Another disruptive individualist was Paolo Schicchi. Bitterly opposed to the organisationists Malatesta and Merlino, he and other individualists sought to disrupt any constructive moves within Italian anarchism. He was opposed to the idea of convening congresses, which were, according to him, "absolutely contrary to the spirit of anarchist ideas... formulating dogmas, dictating laws, creating gospels, making commitments and falling into authoritarianism." and of any collective action. For him, structured organisation "always led to intolerance, exclusivism, blind obedience" (quoted in Nunzio Pernicone, Italian Anarchism, 1864-1892. 1993). Schicchi ended up incarcerated in 1893 after various bomb attacks.

Another individualist, Attilio Curzii, denounced the idea of organising demonstrations on May Days. He regarded this as a "masquerade" organised by the bourgeoisie. Anyone who supported a mobilisation around May 1st was either an "opportunist" or a "spy". He believed that organisation and collective action only brought about State repression, and that turning up to May Day marches only led to the police gaining a list of militants. For him, rather than engaging in agitation among the masses, propaganda should only be carried out within the family and among relatives and friends.

The individualists waged a fierce war against Malatesta and Merlino throughout 1892. The former became convinced that cooperation was now completely out of the question. By January 1897, Merlino, in part angry and frustrated by the continued undermining by the individualists, moved over to the legalitarian socialists.

A significant number of individualists took the side of the Western Allies during the First World War. In fact one of them, Libero Tancredi, was to become a leading fascist. After the war, Carlo Molaschi updated Italian individualism by taking on the ideas of Stirner and Nietzsche. Together with Leda Raffanelli and Giuseppe Monnanni, he was a leading light in individualist circles in post-World War One Italy. He eventually abandoned individualism to adopt a more social anarchist position, whilst Raffanelli became enmeshed in lifestylism and Sufi mysticism.

The most damaging action of the individualists was the bomb at the Diana Theatre in Milan, in 1921, which killed 21 people and injured hundreds. This was meant to be an attack on a police chief, Gasti, as a response to the arrest of Malatesta and other editors of the anarchist paper Umanita Nova, and of Armando Borghi, a leading light in the syndicalist Union Sindicale Italiana (USI) on the grounds of conspiracy against the State.

The consequences of the bomb attack included the ending of a hunger strike by Malatesta. "Not one of the bombers' intended aims was achieved: the bourgeoisie was not cowed, but rather became even more determined in its fight against the "red rabble"; the fascists seized the chance to carry out further, more savage actions such as the destruction of the offices of Umanitá Nova and the socialist Avanti! Malatesta and his colleagues remained behind bars, burdened even further by what had been done in their names; hundreds of completely innocent people were killed or maimed; Gasti plumbed even lower depths and grew more powerful; the anarchist movement was isolated and came in for savage repression; anarchism's ideals of solidarity and emancipation were obscured, yet again, by the bloody nature of an atrocity carried out in its name..." (Massimo Ortalli, A Rivista Anarchica, No 279, March 2002). In events similar to the later Reichstag fire, the fascists were able to increase their influence in urban centres thanks to the imprisonment or flight of many anarchists. This was a deadly blow to the whole of Italian anarchism.

In France, individualist anarchism developed as the result of working class defeat and the institutionalisation of the CGT. Dubious that a working class revolution was possible, the individualists favoured the fostering of a lifestyle approach, where each individual carried out transformations in their own lives. Whilst in the main involving working class members, it looked towards the establishment of colonies in the countryside, naturism, vegetarianism and veganism, the development of birth control methods – "a revolution of minds". It was propagated in the pages of Autonomie Individuelle in the late 1880s, and then in L'Anarchie from 1905, where Albert Libertad, Andre Lorulot, Paraf-Javal, Emile Armand and Victor Serge developed individualist ideas. Strongly under the influence of Stirner and the American Benjamin Tucker, unlike their counterparts in Italy, the individualists excoriated the anarchist communists and the syndicalists. This was accompanied by a profound contempt for the masses and for "wage slaves". Disillusioned by the lack of reception of anarchist ideas among the masses, the individualists turned in on themselves. They denied the existence of social classes and recognised only individuals – conscious individuals and the passive and 'unconscious'. Indeed L'Anarchie declared in 1905 that workers were inferior to sheep "because in a sheepfold, when one wants to shear a sheep, it tries to escape, one has got to tie it up. For the worker, that is superfluous". For Lorulot the proletarian "bows before the rich exploiter, licking his boots with servility. Turn and turn about: criminal soldier, spineless worker, collaborator of the police, mainstay of every despotism, the people cannot overnight acquire the capacity to live out its fate with pride, logic and solidarity".

An extension of the lifestyle revolution they advocated was the adoption of 'extralegal' activities in order to survive. This included counterfeiting, burglaries, "individual recuperation" or "illegalism" as it was designated. Whilst originally employed by Duval and Pini and later Alexandre Jacob for selfless reasons, and often to fund anarchist propaganda efforts, this illegalism soon degenerated into crime for personal profit, as we have seen with Parmeggiani. It meant mixing with the underworld and inevitable contact with informers and provocateurs.

This climaxed in the affair of the Bonnot Gang. Whilst Lorulot paid lip service to the concept of communism as a means of developing the individual, Armand and Serge purveyed the cult of the Ego and its Own, and were cheerleaders for the illegalists. Jules Bonnot, a car mechanic, made the acquaintance of a group of individualists and they carried out a series of armed robberies in 1911, famous for a pioneering use of the motor car. In the course of their rather inept exploits, they succeeded in killing several civilians who got in their way, including two bank clerks. Bonnot shot another member of the gang dead, in murky circumstances that could have been either as a result of an accident or deliberate murder. Bonnot and two other members of the gang died in police sieges. Subsequently, three other members of the gang were guillotined, whilst others, including innocent anarchists falsely accused, spent many years in prison.

The authorities used these events to come down heavily on the anarchist movement. A large number of raids took place, and the press screamed out for more repressive laws. It was little wonder that the Fédération Communiste Anarchiste denounced the illegalist venture and that later the Organisational Platform was harsh in its criticisms of these disorganisers.

The individualist current in Russia was minor compared to those of anarchist communism and anarcho-syndicalism. Again it was influenced by Stirner and Tucker. Its chief advocates were the university professor Alexei Borovoi, who later moved over to Platformist anarchist communism, and Lev Chernyi, who described his form of individualism as 'associational anarchism'. Whilst rejecting Kropotkin's anarchist communism, he called for the free association of individuals, and he made some effort to connect with the masses. As a leading light of the Moscow Federation of Anarchist Groups, he was involved in the mass circulation of propaganda in 1918, including the daily paper Anarkhiia. He was shot by the Bolsheviks in 1921.

As Murray Bookchin remarks: "Hardly any anarcho-individualists exercised an influence on the emerging working class. They expressed their opposition in uniquely personal forms, especially in fiery tracts, outrageous behaviour, and aberrant lifestyles in the cultural ghettos of fin de siècle New York, Paris, and London. As a credo, individualist anarchism remained largely a bohemian lifestyle, most conspicuous in its demands for sexual freedom ('free love') and enamoured of innovations in art, behaviour, and clothing. It was in times of severe social repression and deadening social quiescence that individualist anarchists came to the foreground of libertarian activity – and then primarily as terrorists. In France, Spain, and the United States, individualistic anarchists committed acts of terrorism that gave anarchism its reputation as a violently sinister conspiracy. Those who became terrorists were less often libertarian socialists or communists than desperate men and women who used weapons and explosives to protest the injustices and philistinism of their time, putatively in the name of 'propaganda of the deed'. Most often, however, individualist anarchism expressed itself in culturally defiant behaviour. It came to prominence in anarchism precisely to the degree that anarchists lost their connection with a viable public sphere," (in Social Anarchism or Lifestyle Anarchism, 1995, online at https://libcom.org/library/socanlifean2).

Like Proudhon, some individualists regarded property as a guarantee of liberty. As some German individualists wrote: "Contrary to the 'anarchist communists' the individualist anarchists do not consider private property as the cause of poverty and oppression, being convinced that, by 'private property' it should be understood the possession of the means of subsistence, of clothing, of tools, of machinery, of the soil, sub-soil and their dependants, on condition that they are exploited by the individuals or associations of individuals which hold them. They consider a struggle against private property without object. Much more, they are of the opinion that property is indispensible to liberty and to the independence of the individual. They declare that those who attribute to private property the same share as the State in servitude which overpowers men, are not anarchists, even though they take the title, such as the anarchist communists" (Declaration of the German individualist anarchists, 12th August, 1910, Berlin, Vereinigung Individualistischer Anarchisten – Union of Individualist Anarchists).

The individualists rejected class struggle, organisation and revolution, plumping instead for individual revolt and egoism. Whilst some evolved to illegalism, others moved over to complete reformism. Emile Armand, a one-time advocate of illegalism, attacked the Spanish anarchist Durruti for using coercive methods against the Spanish fascists.

The transformation of sections of anarchism from working class groupings founded on the class struggle, to a form of extreme liberalism and humanism, reflected more the advanced ideas of the liberal bourgeoisie than a truly revolutionary movement. It was at the same period that the frantic search for forebears to anarchism began. As Fontenis notes"To trace anarchism to Antiquity or the Renaissance and forget its birth in the heart of class society of the 19th century, must lead to a purely philosophical or literary anarchism, detached from proletarian struggles and magnifying the great deeds of an illegalism which forbade any future to the movement" (in Changer le monde: Histoire du mouvement communiste libertaire 1945-1997, 2000).

Chapter Nineteen
Johann Most, Peukert and the German exile movement

Johann Most was born in 1846, in Augsburg in Bavaria. He had a harsh upbringing, aggravated by an infection of the jaw, which led to a disfiguring operation. His rebellious nature was apparent from early on, when he organised a school strike at the age of twelve against a particularly sadistic teacher. For this he faced expulsion from school and then had to learn a trade as an apprentice bookbinder. Receiving his diploma at the age of seventeen he then had to take to the road in the traditional way required of all German skilled workers until the end of the nineteenth century.

This roaming life took him through Germany, Austria, Switzerland and parts of northern Italy. Getting employment was difficult enough for these roaming workers, but Most had the extra impediment of a disfigured face. He began to educate himself and in La Chaux-de-Fonds in Switzerland joined a branch of the First International. This lost him his job and he went on the tramp again, ending up in Zurich. There he continued to work with the First International, and completed his apprenticeship. In autumn 1868, he moved to Vienna and became active in the workers' movement there. His activity won him a month in prison. The suppression of the Viennese workers' movement in late 1869 led to the arrest of the local socialist leaders, including Most. He ended up with a five year sentence on the charges of treason. However, an amnesty a year later led to his release.

His reputation as a socialist agitator was now considerably enhanced by his persecution and imprisonment. He embarked upon an extensive propaganda tour throughout Austria. But on his return to Vienna he was arrested and told that he would be expelled from Austria forever.

Most now became active within the German Social Democratic Party, and was elected to the Reichstag in 1874. The previous year he had written a summary of Marx's Capital, whilst serving a short sentence in prison, which both Marx and Engels felt did not satisfactorily explain the ideas within it. As a result, it was not reprinted. Most was again arrested for a speech in support of the Paris Commune on its third anniversary in April 1874.

His reputation was again enhanced by his spell of two years in jail and he was welcomed jubilantly by Berlin workers upon his release. Marx was to sneeringly comment in 1877 that "the workers who, like Herr Most and company, give up work and become professional litterateurs, always cause trouble in matters of 'theory'" (quoted in Max Nomad, Apostles of Revolution, 1939).

After two attempts upon the life of Kaiser Wilhelm, Chancellor Bismarck used this as an excuse to close down the Social Democratic Party in 1878. The Reichstag was dissolved and in the subsequent elections, Most was among those who lost their seats. He was subsequently expelled from Berlin. The laws promulgated by Bismarck closed down practically all socialist and anarchist activity in Germany. If Most wished to continue with propaganda work, then he was obliged to emigrate. He did so, and moved to London, where he established contact with the Communist Workers' Educational Association (CABV). There, he produced the first issue of the paper Freiheit (Freedom) on January 3rd, 1879.

At first, Freiheit adhered to the Social Democratic party line. The lily-livered response of the Social Democratic leaders including Wilhelm Liebknecht was that the tone of Freiheit was too revolutionary, and were scared that this would be used as an excuse to bring down more repression on the Party, which had announced its own dissolution and disbanding. Liebknecht was to announce that "many of the most influential party members disapproved of the founding of the Freiheit." To their credit, both Marx and Engels disapproved of this spineless attitude.

When finally, the official Social Democrats set up the paper Sozialdemokrat in Zurich, it launched scurrilous attacks on Most and his paper. In the end, Most was expelled from the Party at a conference held in Switzerland in 1880, after Freiheit began to evolve towards increasingly social revolutionary positions via an interest in Blanquism and admiration for the actions of the Russian People's Will. In fact, Most's journey away from the ideas of Blanqui was slow at first, even though German anarchists had gathered round Freiheit and helped with its distribution.

However, Most's joyful welcoming of the assassination of Tsar Alexander II resulted in his arrest by the British authorities and his sentencing to eighteen months of hard labour. Whilst in jail, Freiheit had further excited the British authorities by expressing support for the Irish rebels, resulting in a raid on the Freiheit offices. It was forced to move to Switzerland. When Most came out of jail, he moved to the United States. He was welcomed by thousands of German workers in New York on December 18th, 1882.

The large number of German workers in the States had become increasingly radicalised with the depression that had hit America and grouped around the Revolutionary Socialist Party, breaking with the staid and plodding Socialist Labor Party. Active in this grouping were Albert Parsons and August Spies, later to be among the Chicago anarchist martyrs.

Most's arrival in the USA strengthened this current. Most still held to views much influenced by Blanquism, representing the "social-revolutionary" wing of German social democracy. Also now added to this mix was the increasing influence of Bakunin's anarchist collectivism.

Most and others pushed for a massive organisational drive leading to the conference in Pittsburgh in October 1883 where the American Federation of the International Working People's Association was founded. In the following two years it grew to an organisation of eighty groups, comprising 7,000-8,000 members. Most re-founded Freiheit in the USA, and in addition to this, Albert Parsons edited an English language paper and Chicago boasted a German language daily paper. However, the American Federation still adhered to collectivism, calling for "Free exchange of products of equal value through the producers' organisations themselves and without middlemen and profit-making." The need for armed struggle was also heavily emphasised. Indeed, in the pages of Freiheit, individual acts of violence against the ruling class were lauded and instructions on the production of explosives were given in its pages.

Meanwhile developments were taking place within the German-speaking world. Josef Peukert, an Austrian born in northern Bohemia at Albrechtsdorf, moved to Paris in 1877 where he began to absorb anarchist communist ideas. Like Most, Peukert had suffered a harsh childhood and came from a similar working class background. In Paris, Peukert met Otto Rinke, who as we have seen, was a close associate of Paul Brousse and one of the first German anarchist communists. Rinke had produced the first issue of his paper, Der Rebell, in Geneva in 1881.

In the early 1880s Peukert became editor of Die Zukunft (The Future) which had been founded by Austrian radicals in 1879. He had initially helped distribute Freiheit but became increasingly critical of its social-revolutionary approach.

In 1883 both Rinke and Peukert were in London. The second issue of Der Rebell, appeared in October 1883, followed by the third and fourth In November and December of the same year. Rinke printed Der Rebell in his London flat with the support of the Swiss Moritz Schulze and the Czech E. Mily, both compositors. Peukert carried out most of the editorial duties. It proclaimed itself the organ of all German-speaking anarchists. In all 17 issues appeared, the last one appearing in October 1886.

By 1884 differences between the two currents in the German movement had crystallised. Freiheit came out openly for Bakuninist collectivism in April of that year whilst Der Rebell had already nailed the colours of anarchist communism to its masthead.

Most now published a pamphlet Der Freie Gesellschaft (The Free Society) subtitled Treatise on Principles and Tactics of the Communist Anarchists. In fact, it was no such thing, as Most continued to defend collectivist ideas. Peukert immediately denounced the text as a misrepresentation of anarchist communism.

Together with Peukert, Rinke set up the paper Die Autonomie in opposition to Freiheit) in November 1886. It was much better written than Der Rebell with far more news of the movement. In an editorial written by Peukert, it was stated that the paper would promote "the ideas of anarchist-communism with energy and consequence". This further solidified the anarchist communist current around Peukert and Rinke.

Animosity grew between Most and Peukert. This was aggravated by the arrest of the leading anarchist militant Johann Neve by the Belgian authorities in 1887. Neve was subsequently handed over to the German authorities. Peukert was attacked by both the Social Democrats and the followers of Most of having caused the arrest of

Neve by taking a suspected informer and provocateur, Reuss, to a meeting with Neve.

The arrest and imprisonment of Neve intensified the strife within the German movement. As Andrew R. Carlson says in his Anarchism in Germany Vol 1: "Neve was loved and admired by all of the German-speaking anarchists and his loss to the movement, both as a worker and as a personal friend, was deeply felt by all. Perhaps this more than anything else explains the long period of bitter recriminations which followed his capture".

Peukert was certainly naïve, but undoubtedly not a State asset. But the resulting controversy had a damaging effect on his reputation, one from which he did not fully recover. The Bruderkrieg (Brothers' War) broke out and did a considerable amount of damage to the movement.

Rinke's reputation suffered badly during the Bruderkrieg. In March 1882 Rinke and fellow anarchist Balthasar Grün had gone on a propaganda tour of Germany. However, they were soon arrested at Darmstadt. Grün committed suicide in Hanau prison in September of that year. Rinke served a sentence for desertion in Ulm prison and was then released. Old matters were raked up around the death of Grün. Victor Dave accused Rinke of persuading Grün to kill himself in order to save himself, and of being involved in the "champagne bottle murder" and robbery of a rich French woman in which Grün appears to have been implicated. However, police files do not bear this out. Grün committed suicide in remorse, after breaking under questioning and revealing Rinke's real identity. Johann Most later brought the matter up again during the height of the Bruderkrieg. Max Nettlau, it seems more through hearsay than anything else, appears to have agreed with Dave and Most, referring to the Janus face of Rinke. Kropotkin, on the other hand always had the highest regard for Rinke. Otto Rinke had devoted all of his short adult life to the cause of anarchist communism but in the end was left sidelined and discredited. Rinke had moved to St Louis where he worked as a foreman in a factory producing electric motors. He died in 1899 at the age of 46, "choking to death on a piece of meat which he was eating in haste in order to get to an anarchist meeting" (Carlsen).

Meanwhile those around Parsons had developed their own take, starting to organise around the campaign for an eight hour day. Most had never prioritised workplace struggles, and condemned such campaigns as reformist.

Most was arrested one week before May Day 1886 for his encouragement at a public meeting for workers to arm themselves. As a result, he served a year's imprisonment on Blackwell's Island. He stayed true to form and denounced the eight hour campaign at the same meeting, characterising it as "a little more butter" on the workers' bread. This stance caused Emma Goldman, up to then an enthusiastic supporter of Most, to break with him.

As late as 1887, Kropotkin had detected traces of Blanquism in Freiheit and Max Nettlau believed that Most's connection to and understanding of anarchism were for a long time tenuous, and maturing slowly.

Most's imprisonment had given him time to reflect and, on his release, he called for unity and tolerance. He also finally moved to an anarchist communist position. He brought out his pamphlet Der Kommunistische Anarchismus in December 1889, which reflected a general acceptance of the tenets of anarchist communism over collectivism within the German language movement and within the movement internationally, with the exception of Spain.

As Tom Goyens noted: "By 1888, Most had embraced communist-anarchism and spent more time on constructive ideas about an anarchist society than focusing on rifles and drills. Individual terrorist actions were immature, ineffective, and almost cultish. He refused to republish his explosives manual despite requests. In November 1889, he even fancied a genuine rapprochement between socialists and anarchists. Anarchists, Most felt, should refocus on propaganda through print and oratory and reject the proposition that "any act of violence against some representative or guardian of the ruling classes" would invariably have a positive effect. "Propaganda by deed has by no means become for us an exclusive hobby-horse that we ride constantly and forget all other propaganda. We work by the printed word wherever and whenever we can" (Johann Most and Anarchist Violence, 2012).

Peukert and Rinke moved to the States in 1890 and settled in New York. The old antagonisms flared up once more, and Goldman and Alexander Berkman took the side of Peukert and Autonomie.

Most served another sentence in 1891 after a speech about the Chicago martyrs. Meanwhile a strike of steel workers of the Carnegie Steel Company in Homestead, Pennsylvania, flared up. The steel boss Henry Clay Frick brought in Pinkerton private police and an armed confrontation led to the death of a dozen workers, with many others wounded.

Berkman attempted to assassinate Frick, and in the aftermath, Most to the surprise of many, condemned the act. In subsequent articles, Most stated that propaganda by the deed as expressed in individual acts was harmful to the movement, and only brought down repression. For this Goldman vehemently denounced Most, and there was a further split in the movement. It should be stated that Most had just served his ninth prison year, and this had awakened him to the uselessness of such acts. Ten years were to pass before his views on the matter became generally accepted within the movement.

Peukert still sought exoneration for the charges brought against him over Neve and Reuss. In addition, he wished to heal the rift with Most, who had now accepted the ideas of anarchist communism. In September 1893 he travelled to Chicago to attend the International Anarchist Conference as a delegate of the autonomist groups. A year later, an investigative committee set up by anarchist groups found that the charges against Peukert were slander based on lies. Most and his followers refused to accept these findings. Furthermore, Most refused to publish the findings in the pages of Freiheit. Nevertheless, these circumstances took the heat out of the controversy.

Most also changed his tack in relation to the workers' movement and Most reprinted texts from the emerging French syndicalist movement. Later, and shortly before his death, he was to welcome the founding of the Industrial Workers of the World. With the killing of President McKinley by Leon Czolgosz, Most received another year in prison. Ironically, he had now taken against such acts for a long period of time. The period of repression that began after Czolgosz's act caused further damage to the movement, with a falling away of militants intimidated by the force of state repression.

Most doggedly continued with his propaganda, dying suddenly during a speaking tour in 1906. Peukert was to die in poverty and obscurity four years later in 1910.

The anarchist communists assembled around Die Autonomie, the autonomists, had a similar outlook to anarchist communists in other countries at the time, like France and Spain. They were characterised by their distrust of formal organisation, and regarded Most and Spies's IWPA as too centralised and party like. They vaunted extreme decentralisation and discounted the need for long term work within the working class. They loosely federated in the Autonome Gruppen Amerikas (Autonomous Groups of America).

The autonomist groups in the USA were strengthened by the economic depression of 1893 which brought mass unemployment. Most and Freiheit ignored the many activities of the autonomists. As a result, the autonomists began to produce newspapers of their own, chiefly Der Anarchist in New York. The autonomists were heavily involved in agitation and mobilisation during this period.

Some of the younger German anarchist communists like Claus Timmermann became dissatisfied with the sequestered club life of both autonomists and Mostians. Both groupings, in particular that of the Mostians, had ignored propaganda in English, regarding such propaganda among Anglophone workers as a waste of time and money. Timmermann was one of those who now began to produce English-language propaganda, reflecting changes in the German immigrant community, and the new layer of increasingly Americanised young Germans.

However, by the late 1890s German-American anarchism was in decline. The old divisions between the autonomists and the Mostians disappeared. Anarchist communism had now been accepted as the main current within the movement, and young German-Americans united with other young Jewish and American anarchists.

The often vitriolic exchanges between the Mostians and the autonomists had undoubtedly damaged the movement. Most had an intransigent and sectarian attitude whilst Peukert was seen as cold and humourless. Nevertheless, whilst Most was not a deep or original thinker, he was a determined propagandist, writing in lurid and attractive fashion. He continued with his propaganda to the end, despite persecution and many prison sentences. It was unfortunate that the rift in the movement could not have been patched up, and the conflicting personalities of Most and Peukert could not be reconciled. Peukert "lacked the vivid personality of (Most), his genius and fascinating spontaneity. Peukert was grave, pedantic, utterly devoid of humour. At first I believed that his sombreness was due to the persecution he had suffered, the accusation of traitor cast against him, which had made him a pariah. But soon I came to understand that his inferiority was conditioned in himself, and that, in fact, it was the dominant force in his hatred of Most. Still our sympathies went out to Peukert. We felt that the feud between the two anarchistic camps – between the followers of Most and those of Peukert – was to a large extent the result of personal vanities" (Emma Goldman, Living My Life, 1931, p.75).

Chapter Twenty
German Anarchist Communism from the 1890s to the 1930s: the AFD and the FKAD

German anarchist communists influenced by the ideas of Johann Most or by the Autonomie Group around Peukert gravitated at first to Der Sozialist set up by Gustav Landauer in 1891. However, they soon found Landauer's approach too intellectualised and his role in the paper too dominant. They were critical of his attitude to cooperatives which they regarded as reformist and they thought that whilst Landauer had broken with social-democracy he had not sufficiently made a break with Marxism. These arbeiteranarchisten (worker anarchists) as they were called split with Landauer in 1897. As a result, they abandoned Der Sozialist and regrouped around Neues Leben (New Life). Neues Leben was edited by the metalworker Paul Pawlowitsch (born 1864 in Berlin). Pawlowitsch was described by Rudolf Rocker as "at best an acceptable propagandist" and "unscrupulous and authoritarian".

Pioneering efforts to create a new organisation were first initiated by Wilhelm Hugo Klink, a brush maker living in Bietigheim in Baden-Württemberg. In 1899 he pushed the idea of organising a coordination of anarchists throughout Germany in conjunction with other parties and trade unions. A year later, he realised that he should focus solely on the setting up of a specific anarchist organisation. He wrote: "To action! Out there, out to the public and so involved that we come closer to our ideal. First, misconceived individualism must be dropped and the comrades must organise themselves and shape the organisation so that it does not run counter to our views. The task of this free association must be to provide for agitation, education and education among the comrades and to bring them to a higher spiritual culture. Economic combat organisations must be created and organised locally; with it, rigid union centralism, which is a drag on the movement, must be broken" (1899).

Wilhelm Klink suggested the setting up of four federations to cover the whole of the German Empire, covering southern Germany, Rhineland-Westphalia, Silesia and northern Germany (including

Berlin). However, anarchists in Berlin rejected the need for organisation so Klink devoted himself to setting up a south German federation. At an anarchist meeting in Württemberg in summer 1900, comprising ten anarchists from four cities, the Süddeutsche Föderation (South German Federation) was founded. In addition, an agitation committee was set up in Bietigheim to work towards the development of a movement of free unions and cooperatives. By the end of 1900 group from ten cities had joined the Süddeutsche Föderation. In addition, a free trade union association was set up in which Klink served as chair for a time.

The Federation kept up its connections with anarchists in Berlin and Silesia. It formalised a process of setting up local groups and connecting them through contact persons to the Federation as well as supra-regional structures. This growth resulted in the first conference of the German Federation of Revolutionary Workers (Deutschen Föderation Revolutionärer Arbeiter-DFRA) on 7th-8th April 1901 in Bietigheim and Gablenberg. This was attended by 21 delegates from Bietigheim, Stuttgart, Heilbronn, Mainz, Wiesbaden, Cologne, Munich, Görlitz, Rixdorf, Berlin, Leipzig, Halle, and Hirschberg in Silesia. Sympathy subscriptions came from Mannheim, Dusseldorf, Solingen, Reutlingen, Graz and Basel. There was fierce argument about where the DFRA should be centred, whether Bietigheim or Berlin. Pawlowitsch in particular was adept at creating enemies and the DFRA split into two different federations the following year. There was rivalry over which was to be the organ of the DFRA, Neues Leben or Freiheit, edited at first in Bietigheim by Klink, then subsequently by him in Stuttgart and then Amsterdam). Pawlowitsch continued to snipe at Freiheit saying "Freiheit as an organ of the Federation has not done what they should do. Instead of explaining the basic ideas of federalism systematically and explaining the federalist form of organisation historically and theoretically they propagate rather polemical articles in the columns of Freiheit and often in the ugliest forms".

Parallel to the development of specific anarchist organisations was the founding of an umbrella organisation of 'localist' unions opposed to the increasingly centralised trade unions at a conference in Halle in May 1897 which in 1901 took on the name Freie Vereinigung Deutscher Gewerkschaften (Free Association of German Unions

FVdG). At first this grouping saw itself as being on the left of social-democracy but turned rapidly in the direction of revolutionary syndicalism. Thus, there were discussions in anarchist circles whether they should work within anarchist unions or within syndicalist unions, as for example at a meeting in Ludwigsburg in 1909 which produced a statement noting that "Syndicalism must not weaken anarchism, as is unfortunately to be noticed in some cities".

In March 1901 Pawlowitsch founded the Verein Freiheitlicher Sozialisten Berlins und Umgegend (VFSB, Association of Libertarian Socialists of Berlin and the surrounding area) along with Rudolf Lange and Albert Dräger, a mechanic and metalworker born in 1868. Lange, who from time to time had edited Neues Leben, now founded Der Anarchist. Lange had at first been under the influence of Landauer but disagreed with his orientation, whilst continuing to recognise his qualities as a human being and as a thinker, looking to create a movement oriented to the working class, He had become unhappy with the possibility of Neues Leben being able to accomplish this task. Rocker wrote that putting that paper in the hands of Pawlowitsch was a "colossal mistake" and that "many comrades in Germany understood it immediately" and tried after Lange returned from abroad to entrust him with its direction. Pawlowitsch resisted this and he and his supporters tried to remove Lange from the movement in 1902, using "the most dishonest and meanest means" (Rocker) to achieve this. Lange was denounced in the pages of Neues Leben as an individual harmful to the movement, and then accused of financial irregularities during Lange's agitation tours of Germany. Another collaborator with Neues Leben, Richard Klose, was also included in these accusations. Lange and Klose responded to these accusations with a hectographed circular which was reprinted in the pages of Klink's Freiheit.

Lange had some influence in the Elberfeld anarchist federation and one of its leading militants Ernst Schwab suggested that Lange edit a new newspaper to replace Freiheit after Klink was charged with crimes against morality, the sexual abuse of a twelve-year-old girl and then fled to Amsterdam. The paper was first scheduled to be printed in Dusseldorf according to a circular put out in mid-February 1903, but there were difficulties about obtaining a printer and finally in March 1903 Der Anarchist appeared initially edited by Richard Klose. Rocker described it as "certainly one of the best German sheets". Its subheading read: "Anarchy is order, freedom and prosperity for all". After a raid Klose moved abroad in July 1903 and Lange edited the paper which ran until 1907. Meanwhile Klink had issued a statement saying that police had framed him and that really, he was being prosecuted for lèse-majesté. The editors of Neues Leben dissociated themselves from Klink and their supporters.

Meanwhile Klink had been handed over to the German police by the Dutch authorities in 1903 shortly after publishing the last copy of Freiheit on the 1st May 1903. In the meantime, Pawlowitsch had obtained a salaried position with the labour exchange of the metalworkers' union in 1902 and shortly after left the editorial board of Neues Leben, gradually dissociating himself from the anarchist movement and joining the SPD in 1907. "But the unfortunate controversy created in the new movement by those odious facts continued to have consequences for a long time and prevented any fruitful activity" (Rocker, on Lange in Max Nettlau collection, International Institute of Social History, 1932).

In 1903 Paul Frauböse (born 1869-?) and Lange pushed for the founding of the organisation Anarchistische Föderation Deutschlands-Anarchist Federation AFD). They tried to counter the sectarian character of the movement and move towards mass agitation and a mobilisation for the Social General Strike. The first issue of Der Freie Arbeiter, which succeeded Neues Leben, spoke for the AFD and was edited in Berlin, appearing first in January 1904. Forty groups were involved in the Federation, with a total membership of between 400-500. "In January 1904 the Der Freie Arbeiter (The Free Worker) started being published in Berlin, its editors put themselves entirely in the field of the revolutionary movement of the masses, and it defended direct action and the general strike. A strong case for those tactics had already been made by Rudolf Lange and other comrades, which is why they published the Anarchist. But, at the time to place oneself in the mass revolutionary movement, the subject of organisation came up once again and, in fact, Lange was one of the strongest supporters of large scale anarchist organisation, and his staunch defence of this position frequently stirred up opposition among his German comrades. When the German Anarchist Federation's Mannheim

Conference (1907) established lines of conduct in that regard, it, as expected, caused several people to protest against it, in these complaints the autocratic absolute autonomy of the individual played a big role" (Rocker, Anarchism and Organisation, 1920).

However, Frauböse began to criticise Der Freie Arbeiter and in 1905 founded Der Revolutionär (The Revolutionary) which also spoke for the Federation with a circulation of 2000 copies. It was a failure and Frauböse left to join Landauer's Sozialistische Bund in 1908. Der Freie Arbeiter thus won the argument with a circulation of about 5,000 copies at its peak in 1910.

Lange continued to push for greater organisation within the AFD. He prepared a new constitution, addressing itself to a statute of membership, autonomy of groups and a management commission at the 6th congress of the AFD in Leipzig in 1909 which was accepted in 1910. Lange said that the anarchist movement "must shed its sectarian character" and transform itself into a "freely chosen but firmly binding association that is not opposed to anarchist principles" .... We are part of the proletarian movement and must take the organisational consequences". This was followed up at the 9th Congress in 1912. Landauer, who had set up the Sozialistischer Bund four years earlier and tried unsuccessfully to attract most anarchists into his grouping, strongly criticised this move. He argued against the class positions of the AFD, counterposing the idea of "community" to class.

Extremely active in the AFD in Hamburg was the activist Paul Schreyer who built up an anarchist influence among the dockers there.

But the First World War was to play havoc with all the anarchist and socialist groupings in Germany. On the outbreak of war Lange committed suicide in despair. His "death left a void that could not easily be filled" (Rocker), whilst Schreyer died after a harsh prison term in 1918. The AFD and the Freie Arbeiter were banned by the German state. The AFD activists were disoriented by the war. Only in April 1919 did an old member of the AFD, Rudolf Oestreich, begin to resurrect anarchist communist organisation, with the foundation of the Föderation Kommunistischer Anarchisten Deutschlands (Federation of Communist Anarchists of Germany-FKAD) as the successor to the AFD. The Freie Arbeiter was revived as the organ of the FKAD running until it was closed down by the Nazis in 1933. It reached a peak print run of 7,200 in 1923.

However, in the aftermath of the war, many old AFD activists decided to join the FAUD (Freie Arbeiter Union Deutschlands) itself the successor of the FVdG. These included Oskar Kohl in Dresden, Arthur Holke in Leipzig, Richard Klose in Magdeburg, Heinrich Drowes in Elberfeld, Georg Hepp in Frankfurt, Frank Künstler in Stuttgart, August Kettenbach in Wiesbaden, Fritz Oerter in Fürth, Emil Scheurer in Heilbronn, Wilhelm Wehner in Schweinfurt, Max Metzner in Halle.

In addition, Oestreich was an extremely sectarian and argumentative personality. He sued Rudolf Rocker and Helmut Rüdiger in 1928 in the bourgeois courts over the ownership of the contents of the London German anarchist library, as a result of which they received fines of 100 marks each and narrowly avoided a prison sentence.

As a result, the FKAD at its height had no more than 700 members and 35 groups whereas the FAUD at its peak had a membership of 112,000. Other active members of the FKAD included the Jewish anarchist Berthold Cahn who perished in the concentration camps and Clara Ellrich-Siemß (1869-1946) who had passed through the USPD and KPD before joining the FKAD in 1921.Erich Mühsam had initially been a member too.

The FKAD claimed to have "higher tasks" than just the economic struggle so there was a tense relationship between the FAUD and the FKAD (thought there were cases of joint membership). The FKAD's main activity was the production and distribution of propaganda, including leaflets and posters and the distribution of Freie Arbeiter. The average post-war circulation of Freie Arbeiter was 4,600 which compared unfavourably with a circulation three times that amount before the war.

In Berlin the Neukölln group left the FKAD and founded the Anarchistische Verein Neukölln (Neukölln Anarchist Alliance). However, this only had a membership of 36 with Mühsam joining it after a prison term in 1924.Up until then he had worked closely with Oestreich and the FKAD but his work with the Rote Hilfe (Red Aid) prisoner support organisation controlled by the KPD ended with his expulsion from the FKAD on 15th October 1925.

The toxic atmosphere generated by the trial of Rocker and Rüdiger worsened when Oestreich launched an attack on the FAUD at the FKAD conference in 1928.Here he called for active participation in all economic organisations rather than the specific syndicalist organisations. He was contradicted at the next FKAD conference by Cahn who called for cooperation between the FAUD and the FKAD. This was fiercely resisted by Oestreich.

When the Organisational Platform of the Libertarian Communists written by Arshinov, Makhno, Mett et al appeared in 1926 Oestreich agreed with them that the international anarchist movement was in a poor way. However, he disagreed with the need for tactical and theoretical unity and the need for a programme.

In the end the 1931 conference of the FKAD decided to change its name to the Anarchist Federation against the arguments of Oestreich. The Nazi rise to power in 1933 was to end any further developments.

In this often sorry tale of vicious disputes and splits it would be worthwhile to remember the words of Rudolf Rocker reflecting on this situation. "The vast majority of old comrades had passed through the social-democratic stage and had assimilated an inheritance that was not easy to eradicate. The claim to infallibility and a strict discipline, which did not allow the birth of free thought, are a bad school for development of mutual tolerance and understanding....to this add another circumstance: the movement was unfortunately so weak that any divergence of opinion had to lead to serious internal conflicts. In a broad field of action, each one finds at the end a place for his activity. But in one limited movement, where men (sic) are forced to meet in very small circles, there is a much greater possibility of clashes and internal conflicts".

Autobiographical Notes

Wilhelm Hugo Klink. Born in Affaltrach in 1875. Member of the Jungen (Youth) opposition within the Social Democratic Party. Moved to an anarchist communist position in 1896 like many members of the Jungen. A shop clerk. Published six issues of Freiheit from 1896. Before 1910 lived in Böckingen and in 1911 there founded the Association for social welfare Heilbronn, the nucleus of today's housing association GEWO. Wrote in May 1912 a play in four acts about Margarete Renner, the revolutionary of the Peasants' Wars.

Karl Rudolf Heinrich Lange, born 18th March 1873 in Lübeck. Spoke fluent Swedish, Danish, English, French, Spanish and Italian. A shop clerk. Son of a miller and described as very tall and strong by

Rocker who also complemented him as the most "remarkable brain" within the German anarchist movement, a good writer and a "capable and effective speaker, who was unlikely to be dominated by an opponent". Member of the Social Democrats, joined the Jungen and then under the influence of Landauer, moved to an anarchist position. Had a deep knowledge of Marxist literature. Oriented towards agitation within the working class, which Escaped to London in 1896 to avoid a prison sentence. Often accompanied Rocker on his visits to the East End of London. Some Jewish anarchists taught him shoemaking and he persisted with this work for five to six weeks but was not good at the job, and unable to gain employment elsewhere, he returned to Germany to serve his sentence. Settled in Berlin after this, where he remained until his death. Later visited Leeds, where he met with Rocker, Billy MacQueen and Toni Petersen, a former editor of the anarchist paper Proletaren in Copenhagen who had jointly set up a system for smuggling German language anarchist literature, printed by Petersen in Leeds, into Germany. Attended International Anarchist Congress in Amsterdam in 1907.

Rudolf Oestreich was born in 1873. A metalworker. Served four years for anti-militarist activities before WW1. After WW2 co-edited a reincarnation of the Freie Arbeiter with Willi Huppertz. Died in 1963.

References

Mendes-Flohr, P, Mali, A. (eds.) Gustav Landauer: Anarchist and Jew (2014).

https://blackcatcollective.files.wordpress.com/2013/02/anarchisms-appeal-to-german-workers-1878-19143.pdf

http://www.centrostudilibertari.it/sites/default/files/materiali/Rocker%202%20Nella%20tormenta_sito_0.pdf

http://www.centrostudilibertari.it/sites/default/files/materiali/Rocker_Rivoluzione_Involuzione.pdf

https://fda-ifa.org/ausstellungstext-geschichte-des-anarchismus-in-ludwigsburg-und-umgebung/

http://www.fau-duesseldorf.org/downloads/anarchosyndikalismus-geschichte-dt/anarchistische_frauenbewegung_vor_33_m_oulios.pdf

http://cira.marseille.free.fr/includes/textes/bios.php?ordre=8

https://anarchistischebibliothek.org/library/ulrich-linse-die-transformation-der-gesellschaft-durch-die-anarchistische-weltanschauung.html

https://de.wikipedia.org/wiki/Paul_Pawlowitsch

Chapter Twenty One
Erich Mühsam

"He could not fully embrace the syndicalists because he considered revolutionary councils more important than union organising. He was separated from the individualists by his proletarian sympathies. And he was alienated from the FKAD because of his hostility toward frozen dogmatism and because of personal differences" (Augustin Souchy, *Erich Mühsam: sein Leben, sein Werk, sein Martyrium*, 1984).

The third child of a pharmacist, Mühsam was born in Berlin in 1868, but spent most of his childhood and young adulthood in Lübeck in northern Germany. Rebelling against school discipline, he gravitated towards socialism on his move to Berlin in 1900, where he had decided to start a career in literature. Writing later about his early years of political activism, in his 1927 autobiography, Mühsam stated: "Even at a young age, I realised that the state apparatus determined the injustice of all social institutions. To fight the state and the forms in which it expresses itself – capitalism, imperialism, militarism, class domination, political judiciary, and oppression of any kind – has always been the motivation for my actions. I was an anarchist before I knew what anarchism was. I became a socialist and communist when I began to understand the origins of injustice in the social fabric" (Autobiography, 1927).

He became involved in the group Neue Gemeinschaft (New Society) which mixed socialism with communal living and a dose of religion. Here Mühsam met Gustav Landauer and influenced his evolution towards a form of anarchist communism. Leaving the group in 1904, he relocated to the artists' colony of Monte Verita at Ascona in Italian Switzerland (the writer Herman Hesse, the dance theorist Laban, the psychotherapist Otto Gross and many Dadaists and Expressionists lived there at one time or other).

He began writing plays there, the first of which, The Con Men, mixed new political theory with traditional dramatic forms. He also continued contributing to many anarchist papers, which drew the attention of the German authorities. He was considered one of the most dangerous anarchist agitators. He moved to Munich in 1908 and took part in the cabaret movement. He did not care much for writing cabaret songs, but he achieved much notice because of them.

In 1911 he founded the paper Kain which advocated anarchist communism, choosing the title after the biblical figure Cain, not because of his murder of his brother Abel, but because he saw him as the "first rebel of mankind". He castigated and ridiculed the German state, fighting capital punishment and theatre censorship, and prophetically analysing international affairs. The World War that he had predicted led to the suspension of Kain.

At first Erich publicly supported the war, but by the end of 1914 was persuaded that he had been wrong, saying that, "I will probably have to bear the sin of betraying my ideals for the rest of my life". He threw himself into anti-war activity taking part in various actions. He supported the strikes that were beginning to break out. As these became more widespread and began to take on a revolutionary nature, Erich was among those arrested and imprisoned in April 1918, and then freed in November.

With the fall of the Kaiser and King Ludwig of Bavaria, Munich burst into revolt. Mühsam and Landauer as well as Ret Marut (later known as the novelist B.Traven) were among those agitating for the setting up of Workers Councils which led on to the founding of the Bavarian Council Republic. This lasted only a week.

The Social Democrats, terrified by the thought of revolution, allied with the right. The Freikorps, a reactionary militia utilised by the socialist minister Noske and composed of right-wing military and students, crushed the Council Republic. Landauer died under the blows of rifle butts and boots on May 2nd 1919.

Mühsam escaped but was later captured and sent to prison for 15 years. In prison, Erich continued with his writing, composing many poems and the play Judas. Released in the amnesty of 1924, he returned to a Munich in the grip of apathy. He joined the Anarchist Communist Federation of Germany (FKAD). He restarted Kain but this failed after a few issues. He then brought out Fanal (The Torch) where he attacked both the Communists and the far right. His openly revolutionary tone and his attempts to stop the rise of the right made him a hate figure among conservatives and Nazis.

He used satire to ridicule the Nazis with short stories and poems. This came to the personal attention of Hitler and Goebbels, arousing their anger. He agitated for the freeing of the revolutionary Max Hoelz and wrote a play, Staatsraeson (For reasons of State) in defence of Sacco and Vanzetti, in 1928. In 1930 he completed his last play Alle Wetter (All Hang) which called for mass revolution as the only way to stop the seizure of power by the radical Right.

A few hours after Marius Van der Lubbe had set fire to the Reichstag in February 1933, Mühsam was arrested and subsequently spent the last 17 months of his life in the concentration camps of Sonnenburg, Brandenburg and Oranienburg.

Mühsam was hospitalised after his teeth were smashed in with rifle butts, and his scalp was branded with a swastika from a red-hot iron. He was forced to dig his own grave for a mock execution, and his body became a mass of bruises and wounds. His tormentors tried to force him to sing the Nazi song the Horst Wessel Lied. He refused to give in and sang the Internationale. "Thanks to his will power he resisted all attempts to humiliate him" (Augustin Souchy).

Despite these tortures Erich remained intransigent to the end. Finally, he was tortured and murdered on the night of 9th July 1934. After beatings, a Stormtrooper leader administered a lethal injection and then a suicide by hanging was faked.

Mühsam's greatest writing, where he most clearly stated his anarchist communist viewpoint, was Die Befreiung der Gesellschaft vom Staat Was ist kommunistischer Anarchismus? (The Liberation of Society from the State: What is Communist Anarchism?) This was written as a pamphlet in 1931 after Fanal was banned by the Berlin chief of police, the Social-Democrat Grzesinski. Mühsam clearly spells out that anarchist communism must be based on class struggle: "The struggle against property rights must be carried out by those who have been prevented from owning anything; the struggle against exploitation and oppression by the exploited and the oppressed; the struggle against the rights of the master by the slaves and the disinherited.... The liberation of society from the State must therefore be carried out, principally, by the class whose repression by the capitalist system requires the State, whose docility is engendered by the authority of church and school, by the fomentation of national and racial vanities, by laws, punishments, taxes, unemployment, hunger, poverty, unhappiness, and by having been treated like children and deprived of their dignity. To be liberated from the State is to be liberated from class slavery; the enslaved class must be the vehicle of the emancipatory struggle. The struggle for communist anarchism must therefore be fought during the period of revolutionary preparation as a class struggle."

He further developed his criticism of all States in the pamphlet: "Speaking of a Class State is like speaking of iron steel. The State is nothing else, it can be nothing but an executive centralist service of a separate class of the people for the domination of the disinherited and subjugated class of the people. The administrative state procedures therefore divide human society into a class society in order to protect the land and the means of production created by men as the private property of the privileged class. Only where the right of the masters exists in opposition to the right of the slaves, does the State make sense, does it find work to do. Only when the development of personal property reaches the stage where men are exploited, does the State appear. With the development of capitalism, which made the material principles of exploitation the centre of man's whole life, the State constantly expanded the net of the laws, of coercive and surveillance measures, by means of which the proletariat is maintained in obedience to the privileged class. But, once again, it is the Marxist socialists who want to use, in addition to the materialist view of the world, the centralist form of organisation, that typical sign of the capitalist State, as foundation for the construction of a society emancipated from capitalism."

Mühsam also stressed the need for preparedness among anarchist communists, sourcing his own experiences within the Munich Council Republic. "Anarchists must try to create institutions in the present, plans for the federalist structure of the economy in the social order that is maturing for the revolution. Because the people's need for food during the revolutionary upheaval must be the concern of voluntarily associated men, the anarchists will have to set themselves the task of imagining the details of the economic organisation of the future society and carrying out the preliminary work for the transformation of the capitalist into the socialist economy. The childish fancy, according to which the possession of the factories by the workers and their simple continuing operation under the control of the workers will in itself signify the passage of the revolution into socialism, is as absurd as it is dangerous. The possession of the factories is certainly a magnificent means of struggle of direct intervention, but one that is suitable for the period before and during the period of overthrow of capitalism. After the revolution what is required is the complete transformation of the economy. The preparation for this transformation is the immediate practical affair of the libertarian revolutionaries. The anarchists should take advantage of this opportunity to investigate the possibilities of social reconstruction and to study how to provide healthy accommodations for all the workers, the elderly, the sick, the women and children; to study which bastions of State servitude, the palaces and the prisons, the courthouses and public buildings will prove useful for this purpose; to study which establishments of art and knowledge can be transformed into establishments of general instruction; which churches can be converted into meeting halls, community centres and schools for education against authority and the family, or into focal points of proselytism for freedom. The anarchists do not deliver their painstakingly calculated and detailed proposals to government departments, but to the responsible working class as a whole, which will examine them, improve them, oversee their execution by its own institutions, without ever forgetting for a moment the active community of all. These institutions will embody the impulsive social energy of the revolution, they will from the very moment of victory guarantee and safeguard the order of freedom, the economy and the administration of the community in the hands of the socialist working class social formations, they will create communist anarchy and will be the vehicles of the federation of the human and working class associations in the anarchist community. These institutions are the free workers and peasants Councils."

Mühsam, again referencing the experiences of the German Revolution, accentuated the need for anarchist communism to be based on the council form. "Concerning the essence, the meaning and the tasks of the council system, the most ambiguous ideas coexist, and even in the libertarian working class associations there is toleration for the most contradictory interpretations, with regard to the question of whether and to what extent councils must be created and how they are to function.... Even where the workers and peasants emerged victorious from the revolution under the slogan of, 'All power to the Councils', the councils were transformed into servants of the State and the party and, instead of determining public activity and orienting it in a socialist spirit, they were reduced to mere tools of authority. When, as frequently occurs, the anarchists conclude from this state of affairs that the whole idea of the councils has demonstrated its anti-libertarian character, they commit the same intellectual error that is committed by a person who wants to deduce from the conduct of the State's justice system that social rights cannot exist. Such falsification of thought can never refute the idea of the councils. In times of revolution it is the special task of the councils to carry out the coercive measures of the proletarian class which are necessary to crush counter-revolutionary plots and to prevent new governmental institutions from arising which, apparently supporting council power in order to fortify their own power behind the councils, under the pretext of countering the threats to the revolution, call for a dictatorship of the proletariat in order to make themselves dictators."

For Mühsam "Communist anarchism is revolutionary in its world view and its objective. Since the principles of social freedom can find no means of realisation in the soil of capitalist legal and economic inequality, the complete re-ploughing of the soil, the reformation of all human relationships, the total reordering of all organising institutions for the regulation of labour and consumption, is the precondition for reorganisation in the sense of anarchist community. The complete transformation of everyone's living conditions, however, can never be achieved on the path of slow development, through which at most improvements within a social system are possible. Just as the emergence of mountains and islands occurs in nature, after a long developmental process of subterranean convolutions, through the sudden bursting of the parts of the ocean floor or inner earth which are hindering expansion, just as every birth occurs because a living being, enclosed during its preparatory growth within the womb, now ready for its own existence, wins entrance into the light by force, so too can the coming into being of new social conditions take place only after suitable preparation and prenatal development through outbreak of revolution. Should poor, rotten, unbearable conditions predominate, that is very far from sufficient to clear the road for revolution. The prenatal labour for the new society must be supported to the point that its fertilised seed frees itself from its enclosure and the revolutionaries' task is discharged in functioning as midwives, to whom later falls the far more difficult task of keeping the revolution alive and ensuring its growth, from which all pathogens of the previous society will be kept distant, and which guarantees the shaping of the imagined ideal into the reality of the living human community."

Mühsam defines anarchist communism thus: "By communism we understand social relations based on community of goods, which allows each to work according to his abilities and to consume according to his needs. We believe the fundamental socialist demand for the equal rights of all members of society to be more safely guaranteed in this form of economy than in collectivism or mutualism, which wish to relate one's share in the collective produce to work performed. Libertarian socialism grants sufficient latitude to these different possibilities which have all found their defenders among the anarchists. Also, only the attempts and experiences of the future can decide, for example, to what extent the satisfaction of needs demands the private possession of goods for individual use. An emphatic distinction must be made from the merely individualist anarchists, who only in the egoistic intensification and assertion of the individual perceive the means to negation of the state and authority and reject even socialism like every general organisation of society as already a suppression of the self-sufficient ego. They close their eyes to the fact of nature that man is a social life-form and humanity a species in which every individual depends upon the totality and the totality is dependent upon each individual. We dispute the possibility and also the desirability of the individual detached from the whole, whose supposed freedom could be nothing other than lonely isolation, resulting in ruin within a social vacuum. We claim: no one can be free as long as everyone is not free. The freedom of everyone, however, and thereby the freedom of each individual, requires community in socialism."

As Heinz Hug notes "The incorporation of the council system into the body of anarchist social philosophy was Mühsam's most original move. It marks the attempt to merge anarchist, anarcho-syndicalist, and Marxist beliefs." Erich Mühsam. Untersuchungen zu Leben und Werk)

References
Hug, Heinz. Erich Mühsam: Untersuchungen zu Leben und Werk (1974)
Mühsam , Erich. The Liberation of Society from the State: What is Communist Anarchism? (1932) Translated by CR Edmonston: https://theanarchistlibrary.org/library/erich-muhsam-the-liberation-of-society-from-the-state-what-is-communist-anarchism

Chapter Twenty Two
The movement within the Austro-Hungarian Empire

Born in Austria in 1882, Rudolf Grossmann was thrown out of high school in Vienna for spreading social-democratic propaganda.

He became drawn to the ideas of Johann Most and Emma Goldman and turned from social-democracy towards an orthodox anarchist communism around 1900. Already a journalist for American German language social-democratic papers, he now began to write for Most's paper Freiheit, and became a speaker at anarchist meetings.

During the Paterson strike of 1902 he was arrested along with Luigi Galleani and the English anarchist Billy MacQueen for "inciting to riot" following speeches they made to the strikers advocating a general strike. He jumped bail and fled to England, then Switzerland and then back to Vienna in 1907. In London he had frequented the circle around Kropotkin and published the anarchist monthly Die Freie Generation. In Vienna he operated under the pseudonym of Pierre Ramus, after the French humanist philosopher of the 16th century. In Vienna he published the anarchist paper Wohlstand für Alle – Prosperity for All (1907-14) – and continued publishing Die Freie Generation until 1908. He was now falling under the influence of Tolstoy and began to develop an anarchist communism heavily infused with an advocacy of non-violence. Shortly before the start of World War One, he refused the military draft and was arrested, and in 1915 arrested again and out under house arrest for his opposition to the war.

At the end of the war, Ramus's devotion to non-violence became even more pronounced. He also began to develop criticisms of Marxism, in both its Austrian social-democratic form and in its Bolshevik variation.

He created the Bund Herrschaftsfreier Sozialisten (BhS, League of Ruleless Socialists) in 1918, which acted as a platform for his ideas. He briefly took part in one of the workers' councils that sprang up in Vienna in 1918 but was not elected as a delegate and withdrew from it in 1919.

Also in 1918 he founded a new paper Erkenntnis und Befreiung, (Knowledge and Liberation), with the subtitle of Organ of Ruleless Anarchism. It is interesting to note that he adopted a hostile attitude towards the young anarchist militants Leo Rothziegel and Egon Erwin Kirsch, who whilst originally under Ramus's influences, adopted radical positions within the soldiers' and workers' councils and did not hesitate to resort to armed action. For this they were denounced as renegades by Ramus in the pages of Erkenntis und Befreiung, siding with Austrian social democracy over Rothziegel's and Kirsch's revolutionary positions. Rothziegel angrily replied in the pages of the German anarchist paper Freie Arbeiter. Rothziegel and Kirsch represented the radical currents within anarchism that adapted to the emergence of workers' councils in Europe and throughout the world, whereas Ramus was left behind. Ramus was to later adopt the same hostile attitude to Mühsam, who had also learnt much from the phenomenon of workers' councils, denouncing him as a Bolshevik. The latter was to write in his diary in 1920, about "anarchist priests, among which Rudolf Grossmann is the most disgusting in Vienna."

On 23rd February 1919 at an anti-militarist assembly in Vienna there was a public debate between Rothziegel and Ramus. The individualist anarchist Karl Franz Kocmata, who took Ramus's side, was to write "The Red Guardsman Leo Rothziegel polemicised especially against Grossmann's statements... calls for the arming of the proletariat and is refuted by Grossmann," (in Revolution! No 2. 1st March, 1919).

In the early 1920s Ramus increased his pacifist activity, in the form of lectures and rallies. His ideas had large currency among Austrian anarchists, and within both the FAUD and the FKAD in Germany, which contributed to Mühsam's break with that latter organisation. Ramus continued with his pacifist agitation into the thirties, his positions on non-violence becoming increasingly less popular in the anarchist movement with the growth of fascism.

After the annexation of Austria by Hitler, Ramus had to flee, beginning a long procession through various refugee camps in Switzerland, France, Spain and Morocco, dying of a heart attack on a boat bound for Mexico in 1941.

Social democracy dominated the workers' movement in Austria, and continues to do so. Anarchism was always a minority current within that workers' movement. Whilst Rothziegel attempted to relate to the unfolding revolutionary events, Ramus and the majority of Austrian anarchists signally failed to do so, and consigned themselves to continuing marginalisation. Whilst Ramus vehemently opposed social-democracy, his hybrid form of anarchist communism might be judged to have been very much under social-democratic influence, and as opposed to the power of the workers' councils as the social-democrats.

The Czech lands

In the Czech lands, Johann Most helped spread libertarian ideas via his paper Die Freiheit. Unfortunately, individualist ideas influenced the Czech movement, but understandably two spheres of influence, the miners in north Bohemia and the workers in the textile industry, rejected individualism and looked towards anarchist communism.

Important disseminators of anarchist communist ideas were the militants Johann Rissman and August Krčal, who influenced a radicalising group of social democrats, the Independents, who had broken with the mainstream social-democratic party. The miners' strike of 1896 in north Bohemia was led by anarchists, among them Tomáš Kaše. It was defeated after two weeks and this increased both the resentment against the Social Democratic Party, and the prestige of the anarchists. However, once again, the movement was crippled by its mistrust of organisation, though at the first congress called by the movement in 1896, it rejected individual terror and the manifesto published by the congress proclaimed anarchist communism. Shortly afterwards the youth movement around the magazine Omladina (The Youth) lent their support to the movement. Anarchist communist ideas were also publicised through the paper Hornik (The Miner) which published a portrait of Kropotkin in 1901.

Another important advocate of anarchist communism was Vilém Körber (1845-1899). At first involved in the Social Democratic Party he moved via Proudhonist mutualism and individualism to an anarchist communist position and was associated with Omladina. He lectured on Kropotkin's ideas in January 1899 and brought out pamphlets entitled On the Development of Mankind and the Aims of

Anarchist Communism and Anarchism and the Communist Colony. However, he was already seriously ill from tuberculosis and died in December of that year.

The Česka Anarchisticka Federace (ČAF, Czech Anarchist Federation) and the Česka Federace vsech Idboru (ČFVO, Czech Federation of All Unions) which was under strong anarchist influence, were both founded in 1904. The ČAF congress held on Christmas Day, was attended by 68 delegates representing a membership of 250, and had groups in Prague, North Bohemia, Hořice, Mladá Boleslav, etc. It held to anarchist communist positions. Among its important founders was Stanislav Kostka Neumann, who had moved from the individualist anarchism around the magazine Novy Kult to anarchist communism. The ČAF produced a fortnightly paper Práce (Labour) edited by the shoemaker Michael Kácha with a circulation of 2,000 (Práce was criticised by some in the movement for being too intellectual and artistic and not understanding that "anarchism is a movement only fighting for workers' liberation").

The ČAF worked closely with the ČFVO, and many of its members had joint membership, but eventually Neumann fell out with Karel Vohryzek, the general secretary of the latter organisation. Vohryzek was influenced by individualism and was something of a maverick. He wished to maintain the political neutrality of the ČFVO whereas Neumann was an advocate of anarchist unionism. This dispute led to Neumann dropping out of activity for a while. Vohryzek's illegalist activities, expropriations and smuggling, were used as a pretext to severely repress the movement in 1908. Neumann returned from seclusion to aid the movement.

Another defender of anarchist communism and anarchist unionism was the tailor Hynek Holub. At the third anarchist congress held on Christmas Day, 1906, there was controversy between those who supported "non-political" revolutionary syndicalism and those who defended anarchist unionism, with the result that there was no mutual agreement.

The movement recovered from the repressive wave of 1908, although the ČFVO was banned and never re-emerged.

The Czech anarchist communists had lived for thirty years in anticipation of an impending social revolution. When this failed to make an appearance, some of the militants among the youth became impatient. A sign of this impatience was the presentation by the dentist Bohuslav Vrbenský at a special meeting of CAF in Prague in November 1913 of Draft Programme of the Party of Czech Anarchist Communists. This was in some ways a precursor of the Organisational Platform, in that it argued for a specific organisation, the Party of Czech Anarchist Communists, with an anarchist communist programme and a strategy of facing towards the revolutionary syndicalist unions. It typified efficient organisation as a "specific political party", not involved in State institutions and aiming at the independent stateless organisation of Bohemia, prioritising struggle against the Austro-Hungarian State.

Michael Kácha replied with A Critique of the Draft Programme of the Party of Czech Anarchist Communists. He typified the idea of an anarchist political party as an oxymoron, said that it was the "germ of the next compromises" and went against the key anarchist maxim of internationalism. Both texts were discussed throughout the movement. An extraordinary congress of the ČAF was held in April 1914 in Prague. Most delegates approved of Vrbenský's proposals, but a compromise name of the Federation of Czech Anarchist Communists (FČAK) was arrived at. The programme of the FČAK was to be finalised by a commission. However, the cataclysmic event of the First World War was to overtake all of this in July of that year.

As a result, the FČAK was banned along with many of the anarchist papers and periodicals. Vrbenský spent the war in prison, as did other militants, including Kácha.

The outbreak of the Russian Revolution in 1917 enthused Czech radicals, and by spring 1918, there was confidence enough to mount several large demonstrations. The FČAK began to function illegally.

At the end of 1917 there were efforts to unite the national socialists (left nationalists, not Nazis!) the social democrats and the anarchist communists in a single party, pioneered by an ex-anarchist, František Modráček. This was rejected by the anarchist communists who had a deep-seated hatred of the social democrats. However, another group within the Czech National Socialist Party began to propose the creation of a revolutionary socialist party in early 1918, which would call for the secession of the Czechs from the Empire and the establishment of a social republic. Anarchist communists were less wary about the National Socialists, because they had engaged in joint anti-militarist activities before the war.

Almost unbelievably, a Unification Congress took place in Easter 1918, with the establishment of the Czechoslovak Socialist Party (ČSS) and the coming on board of the FČAK. The programme of the ČSS proclaimed that: "In order to prevent all the shortcomings of central state collectivism, the nation will entrust nationalised means of production in its possession and administration to the immediate producers (producers' unions)." This was a concession given to the anarchist communists.

The anarchist communists wished to maintain their ideological independence and formed their own radical wing, which included Vrbenský and SK Neumann. Some refused to join this new party, whilst Kácha, although put out by this change of circumstances, cooperated with the Vrbenský grouping on specific activities.

With the end of the war the Czechoslovak Republic was proclaimed on October 28th, 1918. Shockingly, Vrbenský served as Minister of Supply in the first Czechoslovak government, whilst Neumann worked as a member of the National Council, and then in the Lower House of Parliament! One year later on 1st-2nd February 1919, there was a convening of an independent anarchist congress. This was to assess the result of the merger. Kropotkin may have been quoted on numerous occasions, but Vrbenský rose to justify the participation of anarchist communists in state structures, making out that the programme of the Party was anarchist. Neumann and Jaroslav Štych, whilst proclaiming their hatred of the State, supported the establishment of the Czechoslovak State. Other anarchist communists were wary about what had happened and expressed these misgivings pre-congress. F. Lábner wrote: "It had to compromise on the program and on the ideals, which I think is wrong and unfair", whilst J. Laloušek commented: "The congress should encourage further activities as a separate unit… because we cannot deny that we are anarchists." However, the Congress concluded, "We consider the cooperation of all socialist parties to be necessary nowadays… we want to apply the principles of communist anarchism in its organisational framework, implement social, economic and cultural ideas, partly expressed in the program... We really want to work, not just criticise at the table in a small crowd... We wanted out of the darkness, out of the vain circles of conspiratorial flavour... The results will be approved or condemned our tactics condemned. So let the few dissidents go the other way – we will be judged by the results."

Worse was to come. Neumann called for the unification of all left socialists, and in spring 1920 created the Union of Communist Groups (SKS), which then broke away from the ČSS to form the Communist Party in May 1921. As the ČSS moved, inevitably, towards the centre, the anarchist communists became spare baggage. After refusing to vote for a law for the protection of the Republic in 1923, which increased censorship and police powers, they were expelled and set up the Independent Socialist Party. In 1925 they merged with the Communist Party. The promising emergence of Czech anarchist communism was thus to end in a complete shambles.

Those who had refused to join the ČSS, or who had left it in disgust, set up the Free Association of Anarchists (VSA) in January 1923, but this did not survive the year. Immediately after the Vrbenský group departed from the ČSS, the VSA offered merger, as long as there was a return to the core principles of anarchist communism. This was rejected by the Vrbenský group.

Attempts by the anarchosyndicalists to create new union centrals also petered out, and although there were a number of diehard militants who stuck to their guns among the northern Bohemian miners and the textile workers, the movement was now moribund. A sign of this was, in 1922, the cessation of activity by Michael Kácha, who devoted the rest of his life until his death in 1940, to literary activity.

There were to be no signs of libertarian life in Czechoslovakia until the Velvet Revolution of late 1989. The Anarchosyndicalist Federation that emerged from the Left Alternative, a group of dissidents that had had an important role in the Velvet Revolution, gave birth to the Organizace Revolucních Anarchistu (ORA-S, Organisation of Revolutionary Anarchists-Solidarita) which had argued within that grouping for more effective organisation. At first, they defined themselves as anarcho-syndicalists or libertarian socialists, but by the latter part of the 1990s they had discovered the Organisational

Platform and re-defined themselves as anarchist communists. According to one account, they played an important role in the mobilisation in Prague in 2000 against the meeting of the World Bank and the International Monetary Fund there, including the organisation of an independent anarchist mobilisation and the occupation and general assembly in one factory.

However, some within ORA-S were now turning towards left communism. In April 2003 members who were still inspired by platformist anarchist-communism departed to form the Anarchokomunistická Alternativa (AKA, Anarcho-Communist Alternative). They stated that "We are anarcho-communists and that is why we consider the revolutionary anarchist organisation important." They produced a manifesto in August of that year. In October 2005, the Uherskohradišťské anarchistické sdružení (Anarchist Association of Uherské Hradiště, in Moravia) merged with the AKA. However, the AKA now appears to have disappeared, reflecting the current fragmented and weakened state of Czech anarchism in general.

References

Funk, Andrej. Anarcho-syndicalism in Bohemia. http://followers.thcnet.cz/CyberNet/Punk-Rock%20Rebels%20Library/1.%20Anarchist%20Classics/CSAF%20knihowna/historia/Anarchosyndikalismus%20v%20Cechach.htm

Haumer, Peter. Die österreichische Revolution 1918/19 und der Anarchismus. https://anarchismusforschung.org/wp-content/uploads/2019/09/Die-%C3%B6sterreichische-Revolution-191819-und-der-Anarchismus.-Teil-1.pdf

http://dadaweb.de/wiki/Kácha,_Michael Heath, N. Rothziegel, Leo, 1892-1919: https://libcom.org/history/articles/1892-1919-leo-rothziegel

Rovna, Lenka Anna. Peter Kropotkin and His Influence on Czech Anarchism (2013).

Senft, Gerhard. Pierre Ramus und die oestereichische anarchismus: ramus.at/home/pierre-ramus-und-der-oesterreichische-anarchismus/

Chapter Twenty Three
Anarchist communism in the Low Countries

The Netherlands

In the Netherlands, there has been a long established aversion by libertarians towards permanent organisation and there is a preference for grouping around different magazines or interest groups. This has had a debilitating effect especially on the growth of anarchist communism there.

One of the pioneers was the upholstery worker Piet Honig (1866-1952). Breaking with the social democrats in 1888, he formed an anarchist group and during the important strike of harbour workers in Rotterdam the following year, published a local paper there. Soon he became an editor of De Anarchist, a national paper, which described itself as anarchist communist and which had been founded in 1888 in the Hague and was distributed free for a couple of years. Honig and his associate Hubert van Bloppoel established links with the Die Autonomie group of Peukert and Rinke in exile in London and smuggled Autonomie literature across the border into Germany. However, by 1893 Honig had moved to Paris and became an individualist anarchist.

Another important pioneer was the anarchist communist Johannes Methöfer, who also contributed to De Anarchist. He, however, rejected permanent organisation, and thus aligned himself with Domela Nieuwenhuis, in opposition to Christian Cornelissen, a proponent of organisationalism. Another who took part in the editing of De Anarchist was Bart van Ommeren, and Frans Drion, who joined De Anarchist under the influence of Methöfer and Van Ommeren.

Ferdinand Domela Nieuwenhuis (1846-1919) son of a Lutheran pastor, established the first socialist periodical, the weekly magazine Recht voor Allen (Justice for All) in 1879. He became a leading light within the Social Democratic League (SDB) which emerged from the merger of various socialist groups in 1881. The SDB carried out intense propaganda throughout Holland, distributing leaflets in factories, barracks and in the countryside. In the 1880s the SDB became a mass movement, partly due to Nieuwenhuis's efforts in the countryside in northern Holland. By 1893 he had rejected electoral activity and started moving in an anarchist direction. His putting forward of an anti-electoral motion within the SDB led to the scission of the Federal Social Democratic Labour Party (SDAP) which began to model itself on German social democracy.

The SDB renamed itself the Socialistenbond (Socialist League) (SB), and anarchist communists like Drion joined it, hoping that it would move in an explicitly anarchist direction. However, the premature split from the SDB by the SDAP meant there were still a large number within the SDB in favour of electoral activity. Eventually, in 1897, these mostly moved over to the SDAP whilst others moved over to the anarchists, leaving a rump of 200 members. The SB then dissolved and its members joined the SDAP.

Nieuwenhuis for his part left the SDB in 1897 and he closed down Recht voor Allen in 1898 producing a new magazine, De Vrije Socialist (The Free Socialist) which was explicitly libertarian in outlook. The newspaper was co-edited by Christian Cornelissen. The Federatie van Vrije Socialisten (Federation of Libertarian Socialists) (FVS), was also set up. In that year he also published the book Socialism in Danger (which only appeared in French) where he harshly criticised social-democracy and its accommodation to the State and capitalism and highlighted what he saw as the differences between authoritarian and libertarian socialism. Whilst Nieuwenhuis was close to Kropotkin, and shared much of the latter's anarchist communist outlook, he preferred to call himself a vrije socialist (free or libertarian socialist.) Nieuwenhuis, as noted, was an opponent of permanent organisation, and this anti-organisationalism contributed to the defeat of the Dutch general strike in 1903.

Nieuwenhuis was appalled when war broke out in 1914 and equally appalled by Kropotkin, Jean Grave and others support for the Allies. In fact, the betrayal of Kropotkin hit him very hard, as he had felt particularly close to him politically. He accused the 'governmental anarchists' of capitulating to anarchism. He was enthused when he heard of Malatesta's positions and signed his anti-war manifesto of 1915. He organised and participated in anti-war demonstrations in Amsterdam. On one occasion the police attacked a demonstration and he was protected by a group of women. He quite correctly saw the war as one that the working class could not support and should not take sides on. He saw no difference between the imperialism of Britain, France, Germany, Austria or Russia.

His health began to deteriorate in mid-1916 and he died in 1919, robbing the Dutch working class of one of its greatest champions.

Christiaan Cornelissen (1864-1942) was a strong advocate of permanent organisation and of practical work amongst the working class within the Socialistenbond and then the FVS. As such, he opposed himself to Nieuwenhuis, whose attitude to organisation he regarded as individualistic. He never called himself an anarchist, preferring to be defined as a libertarian communist and proponent of labour organisation. He was a founder of the syndicalist union the Nationaal Arbeids-Secretariaat (National Labour Secretariat) (NAS), in 1893. In his text Revolutionary Communism, written in 1896, he called for the unity of revolutionary socialists and social anarchists on an anti-parliamentary platform.

Johan Jacob Lodewijk, (1871-1942) was a leading advocate of anarchist communism. He was one of the founders of the Federatie van Vrijheidlievende Communisten (literally Federation of Freedom-Loving Communists but more often translated as Federation of Libertarian Communists), on April 23rd 1905, and editor of its paper De Vrije Communist (the Free Communist). Others active in the Federatie were Cornelissen, and Izak Israël Samson, a diamond worker who had become an anarchist communist in 1899. He became editor of the libertarian communist magazine, De Zweep (The Whip), from December 1, 1900 to November 22, 1902. A supporter of organisational anarchist communism, he was a prime mover in the foundation of the Federatie. The creation of this grouping was opposed from the start by Domela Niewenhuis and associates like Gerhard Rijnders. Cornelissen, who had been living in France since 1898, wrote a series of articles in the magazine Grond en Vrijheid (Land and Liberty) explaining the declaration of principles of the Federation, which, according to its formulation, fought against parliamentary reform to the right and against disorganisation to the left. The grouping changed its name to the National Federation of Libertarian Communists in 1907 but dissolved itself in 1909 due to lack of support. When De Vrije Communist closed down Samson wrote for De Vrije

Socialist. Other notable activists to join the Federatie were Adrianus Van Emmenes, Henriette Hoogebeen, and Pieter Marinus Wink. Wink had long been a supporter of permanent organisation and of Christiaan Cornelissen within the FVS, and as such he was one of those who joined the short lived Kommunistenbond (Communist League) set up in January 1902, editing its paper De Communist.

Samson, along with Methöfer, was to join the SDAP in subsequent years, and indeed, after the First World War, many working class militants joined the SDAP or the Communist Party. Other anarchist communist activists like Wink, became liberals, or like Henriette Hoogeveen, Catholics. As for Cornelissen, his support for the First World War was to alienate him from many anarchists and syndicalists.

As a term sociaal-anarchisme (social anarchism) began to take precedence over that of anarchist communism. In 1915 the Bernardus Lansink jr., chair of the NAS, together with a number of anarchist communists founded the Landelijke Federatie van Revolutionaire Socialisten (FRS, National Federation of Revolutionary Socialists). Its weekly paper, De Toekomst (The Future), devoted itself to the problems of workplace organisation and the establishment of workers' power. Lodewijk was one of its editors for many years. Lansink, like his father, had started out as a social anarchist but his increasingly pro-parliamentary views and the discovery that he had become a member of the SAPD, caused ructions with other members and the organisation was transformed into the National Federation of Social Anarchists in 1919.

The much weakened Dutch movement continued to be plagued by anti-organisationalism and individualism in the interwar years. The NAS was captured by the Communists in 1923, leading to the departure of the
Syndicalistische Vakverbond (NSV, Syndicalist Workers Association). At the time of this departure, the NAS had 14,000 members and the NSV 8,000.

The struggle between Communists and libertarians was fierce, with the latter sorely divided into different small groups. During the economic depression, things were complicated by the spread of individualist anarchism. The doctrine of non-violence as purveyed by Bart de Ligt and others also had a detrimental effect, with some libertarians ill at ease at reconciling their non-violent views with support for the Spanish Revolution in 1936. Also peculiar to Holland was the development of a Christian anarchist movement. The strong Lutheran culture of Holland accounts for this to a certain extent, after all Nieuwenhuis himself had been a Lutheran pastor before he turned to social radicalism, as had de Ligt. But there were many other socialist pastors, who unlike Nieuwenhuis did not break with their religion and adopt atheism. This must account for the appearance of the Bond van Religieuze Anarco-Communisten (BRAC, League of Religious Anarcho-Communists), which existed between 1920 and 1932. It had a limited membership of around a hundred, and produced a paper De Vrije Communist. Oddly, this membership included non-Christians, such as Clara Wichmann, a devout atheist and syndicalist! When the grouping stopped representing as religious and changed its name to the Bond van Anarcho-Socialisten (BAS), many of the religious anarchists departed.

The Second World War and the Nazi occupation of the Netherlands dealt a very severe blow to the libertarian movement. In the post war period there was some renewal, with the emergence of the counter-cultural Provo movement. Today class struggle libertarians are united in the Vrije Bond (Free League) which also has some representation in Belgium. It seems to be the most encouraging indication of a social anarchist renewal in the Netherlands.

Belgium

In the time of the First International, Belgium sported an important section of its 'anti-authoritarian' wing around César de Paepe. However libertarian ideas hardly took root in Belgium, in the aftermath of the collapse of the International. After the Verviers Congress, the Belgian (French speaking Walloon and Flemish) sections departed from the International and oriented towards Marxism.

Anarchist communism thereafter lost influence in Belgium, particularly in Flanders. Nevertheless, it remained for a long period the only credible movement to the left of the social-democrats.

Jacques Gillen of the Centre for History and Sociology of the Left at the Université Libre of Brussels wrote: "several factors have combined in Belgium so that anarchism can only ever succeed in bringing together a very limited number of people. Belgian anarchism has always been confronted with major organisational difficulties and an almost permanent absence of internal cohesion which have hampered its extension" (Les Anarchistes en Belgique, 2007). In addition, many of the French-speaking militants often moved to France for work and to avoid persecution.

One of the few times that libertarian ideas had any great influence in Belgium was with the Walloon insurrection of 1886 when the Groupe Anarchiste Révolutionnaire of Liège organised a commemorative meeting for the Paris Commune. This sparked off a series of insurrectionary strikes and the police and military were brought in to quell the uprising, leading to the deaths of dozens of workers.

One of the most important figures of Belgian anarchist communism was the print worker Georges Thonar (real name Gérard Debehognes) born in 1875 in Huy. Breaking with the social-democratic Parti Ouvrier Belge (POB) in 1895 he for many years carried out propaganda throughout Belgium. In October 1904 a text written by him was adopted at the Libertarian Communist Congress at Charleroi, and the Fédération Amicale des Anarchistes de Belgique was set up. Thonar had a key role in this grouping. The congress endorsed two orientations, firstly the structuring of the movement and secondly the launching of a revolutionary syndicalist confederation animated by Henri Fuss. However, the Federation never got anywhere, though there was more luck with the syndicalist union. Nevertheless, it was the embryo of a future credible organisation. Thonar initiated, on July 25, 1905, the creation of the Groupement Communiste which became, the following year, Groupement Communiste Libertaire (GCL). The group's goal was to propagate the ideas of libertarian communism through public meetings, the establishment of study circles, and the publication of newspapers and propaganda books. The GCL was also at the origin of an attempt to put libertarian communism into practice with the creation in 1905 by Émile Chapelier and his companion Valentine David of the Colonie L'Experience located until 1908 first in Stockel-Bois (Stokkel) , then in Boitsfort, and grouping about fifteen people At its second congress a year later, the GCL could count on a membership of one hundred with sections, at least on paper in Brussels, Liège, Namur, Charleroi, Verviers, Mechelen, Ghent and

Antwerp. However, Chapelier was accused of turning the GCL paper, L'Émancipateur which he had been put in charge of, into no more a mouthpiece of the Colonie L'Experience rather than that of the GCL. Thonar therefore took over the editorship.

The GCL was an ambitious move and put the Belgians at the head of the pro-organisational current among European anarchists. The GCL, together with the Federation of Libertarian Communists of Holland, were initiators of the International Anarchist Congress held in Amsterdam from 24th to 31st August 1907. But in the meantime, the GCL found itself unable to function and dissolved itself at its congress in Brussels on the 4th August. Too many Walloon anarchists were still wedded to the idea of loose networks of affinity groups, and regarded the GCL as too authoritarian. In fact, the GCL created a backlash against organisation that lasted a long time among the anarchists of Wallonie. The International Congress decided to create an International and Thonar tried to revive the GCL, but in vain.

In July 1908 the Fédération Anarchiste de Belgique, (FAB) was formed and Thonar joined it, but it was a loose grouping with too many divisions, "without statutes, without regulations and without a committee", with prosyndicalists and antisyndicalists, communists and individualists and Thonar looked away from this shipwreck to work with the revolutionary syndicalists around Fuss. This too was a failure. Thonar was now in favour of a revolutionary federation which united social anarchists, revolutionary socialists and syndicalists. He defended this position within the FAB, at its conference in August 1909, but found himself in the minority. Together with other militants from Charleroi, Brussels and Liège, he quit the FAB and formed the Fédération Révolutionnaire (FR), which was based on the revolutionary unity mentioned above. This too failed. Thonar was indefatigable, and together with Félix Springael, who had been a member of the L'Experience colony, launched the paper Le Communiste, in July 1911, followed by the establishment of the Groupe d'Action Directe in September, on the same bases as the FR. It requested membership of the POB, but that party, fearing the entry of an anarchist communist tendency, turned this down and the group fell apart.

Thonar continued to publish libertarian journals but by 1913, appeared to have left Belgium, and was active in Paris in the Fédération Communiste Anarchiste. He took the side of the Allies with the outbreak of the First World War, with grave misgivings. He died in the Gironde region of France in December 1918.

Meanwhile a Fédération Communiste Anarchiste was founded at Liège at a meeting at the beginning of 1913, with Julien Delville as its secretary. A special edition of its paper L'Émancipateur was devoted to criticising militarism and patriotism and an antimilitarist poster was produced, which resulted in prosecutions by the authorities and the partial cessation of the activities of the FCA.

As elsewhere, the First World War and its aftermath, and the repercussions of the Russian Revolution, had deleterious effects on the libertarian movement. However, in 1921, a Fédération Communiste Anarchiste Belge was set up, uniting groups in Brussels, Liège and in the Borinage. Active in this grouping were Ernestan (real name Ernest Tanrez), Camille Mattart, and Adamas (real name Jean Baptiste Schaut). L'Émancipateur reappeared again, with the subtitle Organe Communiste-Anarchiste Révolutionnaire from July 1921, edited by Mattart. It made way in December 1925 for the newspaper Le Combat. Camille Mattart then republished it episodically from 1928 to 1936.

In Flemish speaking Flanders the movement was even smaller. The Dutch paper De Anarchist (1888-1897) had a readership of 3,000 of which 500 were in Flanders and as has been seen, there were GCL sections in Antwerp, Ghent and Mechelen. Indeed, Mechelen became a libertarian stronghold, but could not compete in any great fashion against the social democrats.

The arrival of Italian exiles fleeing from fascism in the 1920s reinvigorated the movement in Belgium to a certain extent but it never regained its pre-WW1 vigour and it was plagued by individualism, pacifism, humanism and anti-organisationalism. The Second World War and the Occupation dealt it a heavy blow.

There were various attempts to revivify the movement after WW2, with the participation of Ernestan in the independent socialist magasine Cahiers Socialistes (Socialist Notebooks) and the founding of the propaganda group Pensée et Action Thought and Action, which functioned between 1945 to 1952. A new anarchist grouping was then set up in 1952 by the syndicalist Jean De Boé, Action Commune Libertaire (Common Libertarian Action). This attempted once more to unite incompatible political currents and the individualists soon fell out with the libertarian communists and the grouping collapsed in 1954.

Another attempt to create an organisation was the Fédération des Groupes Socialistes Libertaires in 1967. This was created by a new generation inspired by the mass general strike in Belgium in winter 1961-62. Chief among this new generation was François Destryker.

Destryker, born in 1944, was active from 1966 in the group Socialisme et Liberté, founded by young anarchists from the l'Université Libre of Brussels. It was in contact with the anarchist communist magazine Noir et Rouge in France and later with the Mouvement Communiste Libertaire (MCL) there. It explained its stance as opposition to the USSR and China, as supposedly socialist countries, the recognition of historical materialism to understand the evolution of capitalism, insistence on the working class factor as an element of revolutionary change, a questioning of the unions, and the need for political organisation as a hub for bringing together revolutionary elements.

Destryker and his comrades broke with the individualists and produced a new series of the paper L'Alliance (named after the Bakuninist Alliance) from 1972 which had previously also included individualists and anarcho-syndicalists. This functioned for seven issues from January to December 1972 first as the organ of the libertarian communist group close to the MCL and then from summer 1973 to the French Organisation Revolutionnaire Anarchiste (ORA). This led to the creation of a Belgian ORA with a newsletter, Le Libertaire and then a paper, Journal Libertaire, for fifteen issues from September 1973 until February 1974 From April 1974 this became Journal Libertaire des Luttes de Classes (Libertarian Journal of Class Struggle). However, the group evolved towards left communism and Destryker moved close to the Bordigist current.

In the present period the Belgian movement remains in a parlous state, aggravated by the escalating divisions between Walloons and Flemings, where there is no Belgian-wide bilingual territorial organisation, let alone one uniting French speakers or Flemish speakers. There exists a Brussels group of the mainly French Union Communiste Libertaire, which offers the only glimmer of hope for the renewal of libertarian communism in Belgium.

Chapter Twenty Four
Stormy Petrel: Anarchism within the Russian Empire and in exile

Despite the fact that two of the most important theoreticians of social anarchism, Mikhail Bakunin and Petr Kropotkin were Russian, anarchism never really developed within the Russian Empire until after the beginning of the 20th century.

As Peter Gooderham notes: "That it failed to make an appearance before the onset of the twentieth century was largely due to the inadequacies of the anarchist movement in Western Europe. Throughout the period leading up to the end of the century anarchists showed time and again their inability to unite and form an organisational base from which to launch a systematic propaganda campaign. As a result, before 1905 few people inside Russia had even heard of, let alone read the works of anarchism's major thinker, Kropotkin. This in turn meant that once the movement got off the ground in Russia, Kropotkin's influence on it, so great in the West, would be negligible" (The anarchist movement in Russia, 1905-1917 [1981] Ph.D. thesis: https://research-information.bris.ac.uk/ws/portalfiles/portal/34507649/591039.pdf)

Whilst Bakunin made strenuous efforts to recruit among Russian exiles, no credible organisation emerged in the home country during his lifetime. The Bakuninist Z. K. Ralli-Arbore, a Bessarabian living within the Russian Empire set up a small group in Geneva, the Revolutionary Commune of Russian Anarchists in 1873 but it was not until 1892 that the Armenian doctor Alexander Atabekian, an anarchist communist and associate of Kropotkin established a group called the Anarchist Library. This group smuggled literature into Russia with very few short-term results. At the end of the 1890s the Geneva Group of Anarchists took up this work again.

Unrest within the Russian Empire in 1903 led to the establishment of the first viable grouping in Bialystok. This group, Bor'ba (Struggle) was composed of mainly young Jewish workers and students, disillusioned with what they saw as the gradualism of the Bund, the

Jewish Social Democratic grouping, the Socialist Revolutionaries and the Polish Socialist Party. Meanwhile young anarchist communist associates of Kropotkin established the paper Khleb I Volya (Bread and Freedom) in Geneva in August 1903, and 2,000-3,000 copies were smuggled across the borders into the Empire by Shlomo Khaimovich Koganovich, a young Bialystok worker also known as Seidel. Leading lights in this group were Georgi Gogelia, a Georgian, his partner Lydia Ikkonikova, and the young student Maria Goldsmith, who often used the pseudonym Maria Korn. Kropotkin contributed many articles and editorials. Yiddish anarchist communist papers printed in London also began to circulate within the Jewish Pale.

Khleb I Volya was received with great enthusiasm in Bialystok. As a result, the group produced pamphlets which were also smuggled into the Russian empire, including works by Bakunin, Kropotkin, Grave, Malatesta, and Elisée Reclus, among others.

One of the principal architects of the developing anarchist communist movement was Nikolai Rogdaev. He was born Nikolai Ignatievich Muzil in 1880 in the village of Silkino near Klin to the north of Moscow, into a family of nobility with Austrian origins. In the 1890s he became active in the revolutionary movement, joining the Riazan group of Social-Revolutionaries and also contacting a circle of Social-Democrats. In May 1900 he came to the notice of the Tsarist police. In late January 1901 he was arrested for possession and distribution of illegal Social-Revolutionary propaganda. He was condemned to three months imprisonment. He was freed in April under conditions of police observation. In June 1901 he fled to Bulgaria where he became an anarchist-communist. He started distributing anarchist communist propaganda and took part in organising anarchist communist groups in Sofia and Varna. He was also active amongst workers and intellectuals who had emigrated from Russia.

Rogdaev was a trailblazer of anarchist communism in Russia and the Ukraine. He was a propagandist in Briansk, Nezhin and Ekaterinoslav in 1903, when the anarchist movement was re-born, after its destruction by the Tsarist regime in the 1880s. Known as Uncle Vanya, he helped set up many anarchist communist groups. In December 1904 he represented Khleb i Volya at the Congress of Russian Anarchist Communists in London. In March 1905 he went with his wife Olga

Malitskaya and Vladimir Zabrezhnev to Kiev and organised the South Russian Groups of Anarchist Communists there, as well as editing the paper Nabat (Alarm) which he hoped would be the mouthpiece of a united movement. He escaped arrest on 30th March but the press and all the publications of Nabat were seized and destroyed.

In 1903 there were 12 organisations in 11 towns, in 1904, 29 groups in 27 centres of the north-west, southwest, and south; in 1905, 125 groups and federations in 110 towns; in 1906, 221 groups in 155 towns; and in 1907, at the height of the movement, there were 255 groups in 180 localities. The most important centres of the movement were in Bialystok, Odessa, and Ekaterinoslav, but anarchist communist activity could be found in three quarters of the empire. Many new recruits to anarchist communism came from the ranks of the Social Democrats and the Socialist Revolutionaries.

In June 1905 Rogdaev went to Ekaterinoslav and organised regular meetings of workers and meetings about anarchism. These met with great success and in July the whole cell of the Social-Revolutionary Party declared itself anarchist and named itself the Ekaterinoslav Group of Anarchist Communist Workers. One of the groups that Rogdaev helped coalesce by delivering a lecture on anarchism was the Union of Poor Peasants at Gulyai Polye in Ukraine. It had fifty core members and a circle of 200 supporters and sympathisers known as "massists". It carried out the dissemination of illegal anarchist propaganda through word and leaflets, an education programme among the local population, the countering of the Black Hundreds style organisation the Union of the Archangel Gabriel, the expropriation of funds from local landowners, industrialists and banks, and the burning of the estates of various active reactionaries. This rural organisation of anarchist communists was one of the first in the Russian Empire. Whilst others were set up in the Kiev, Poltava, Kherson and Kharkov regions of the Ukraine, none proved as durable as that at Gulyai-Polye. One of its key members was one Nestor Ivanovich Makhno.

Rogdaev fought behind the barricades in the Moscow uprising of December 1905. Ignatii Muzil, his brother, was seized in woods near Nizhnii Novgorod with anarchist communist literature in his possession in 1905. He refused to recognise the court or stand up before questioners and was one of the many victims of the Tsarist clampdown of 1905-06.

In late September and early October 1905 Rogdaev moved from Ekaterinoslav to Geneva and worked for the paper Khleb i Volya until its closure in November.

In Moscow, the first propaganda group was set up by the staunch Kropotkinist Vladimir Zabrezhnev in early 1905. However, this group, formed mostly of students, was arrested wholesale after issuing only two proclamations. A new group along the same lines, Svoboda (Freedom), was set up later in the year and carried out intense propaganda there, as well as establishing communication and distribution of propaganda with groups in Tuka, Kazan, Penza and Nizhnii-Novgorod.

The anarchist communist movement was severely affected by the wave of struggle that began developing in 1904 culminating in the Revolution of 1905 which rumbled on into 1908. Many thousands of anarchist communists fell on the barricades, were subsequently shot or hanged, imprisoned or forced into exile. While there were still 108 groups within the empire in 1908, by 1914, only seven remained.

Whilst the majority of the developing anarchist movement in Russia were anarchist communists, there were also smaller numbers of anarcho-syndicalists and anarchist individualists. However, there were serious differences within the anarchist communist current.

Two new groupings emerged, Chernoe Znamia (Black Banner) and Beznachalie (Without Authority). They both advocated and practised terror against the Tsarist regime, whilst espousing anarchist communism. Chernoe Znamia's members, the Chernoznamentsy, were particularly strong in Bialystok. Its members were in the main workers and students, with a few peasants participating. Jews predominated, but there were also large numbers of Poles, Ukrainians and Russians.

In response to brutal repression of strikers, they responded with attacks on the police and on factory owners. These attacks intensified with the outbreak of the 1905 Revolution, with raids on gun shops, arsenals and police stations in order to obtain arms, and expropriations carried out on shops, banks, post offices, factories and the homes of the nobility and the bourgeoisie. Attacks were also carried out against factory owners. The Chernoznamentsy advocated "motiveless" terror, that is attacks on the ruling classes in general, rather than on targeted specific individuals.

The group around Beznachalie, the Beznachal'tsy, in the main located in St Petersburg, was composed mostly of students, with a small number of workers as members. They too espoused "motiveless" terror, and called for an alliance of workers, peasants, the unemployed and tramps to unite to overthrow the old order. Its leading light was A, Bidbei (real name Stepan Romanov). The Beznachalie group originated in exile in Paris in 1905, with Bidbei looking towards a more radicalised form of anarchist communism than Kropotkin's. Whilst Kropotkin looked towards the creation of a mass movement, Bidbei, despite calling himself an anarchist communist, began to propagate ideas closer to anarchist individualism with his idealisation of the tramp who cultivated leisure, as opposed to the worker who sold himself to his Mammon, his wages, the only thing he cared about.

Some of the anarchist communist groups that sprang up adhered to Kropotkin's tactics of propaganda distribution to workers and peasants in looking towards the creation of a mass movement, as in Moscow and Kiev, but others followed the examples of Chernoe Znamia and Beznachalie, in the use of the tactics of terror.

Chief among the Kropotkinites, the Khlebovol'tsy, were German Sandomirski and the above-mentioned Zabrezhnev. The latter compared the exploits of the terrorist groups to the period of Ravachol and Emile Henry in France in the early 1890s, saying "It stands to reason that such acts as attacking the first bourgeois or government agent one encounters, or arson or explosions in cafes, theatres, etc., in no sense represent a logical conclusion from the anarchist Weltanschauung; their explanation lies in the psychology of those who perpetrate them." Kropotkin and the Khlebovol'tsy strongly disapproved of the use of expropriations. They also looked towards the creation of an anarchist party, but this signally failed in a Russia where above ground activity was difficult. However, Moscow became the centre of Khlebovol'tsy activity, first with Svoboda and then with the Federal Group of Anarchist Communists, formed of students, who operated into 1907. Elsewhere, Gogelia's efforts in the Caucasus produced some results, with the first Georgian language anarchist communist daily, Nobati (The Call). Unfortunately, groups in the region turned to expropriations, and Gogelia decamped to France.

The severe repression unleashed by the Russian state smashed mass action by 1907. The defeat of the Revolution saw the Beznachal'tsy turn to the belief that they should not sell their labour power. An anarchist "must not, by his work in a factory or a shop, strengthen and enhance the position of the same bourgeoisie that is subject to merciless extermination. A 'true' anarchist ought to satisfy his material needs by means of robberies and the theft of possessions from the wealthy to be utilised for his personal needs". Thus the politics of Beznachalie had degenerated to the point where their outlook approximated that of the French individualists of the Bonnot gang. On the other hand, the Chernoznamentsy came to see that intervention within the working class was necessary and were willing to support and participate in strikes. Both groupings had the optimistic view that the masses in general were ready for revolutionary action, and only needed exemplary actions to goad them into taking such action.

There was a history of terrorism in Russia with the Narodnaya Volya (People's Will) movement from the 1879 to 1882, whose greatest accomplishment was the assassination of Tsar Alexander II, and the Socialist Revolutionary (SR) Party from 1901 onwards, which carried out hundreds of assassinations. The "maximalist" atmosphere that prevailed during the 1905 Revolution created "boevizm" (total militancy) and this effected not just the anarchist communists and to a certain extent the anarcho-syndicalists but the SRs and the Social Democrats with all such groupings being involved in armed actions and expropriation. In addition the repressive actions of the regime called forth a response. Many militants fell in this period, and the necessity of propaganda and organisation in the workplaces and in the countryside was neglected in favour of sacrificial acts.

Founded in exile in Paris Burevestnik (Stormy Petrel) was an anarchist communist paper edited by Rogdaev, Maxim Raevsky and Mendel Dainov (aka Maxim Dubinsky). It was named after Gorky's famous poem of the same name. The last line from the poem – "Let the storm burst forth more strongly" – appeared on the masthead. It was described by Paul Avrich as "the most important anarchist journal of the postrevolutionary period".

The Burevestnik comrades had learnt something from the failures of the movement during the 1905 Revolution. Dubinsky writing in the pages of the paper in August 1906 wrote: "We have made many blunders, many mistakes. But to confess to these mistakes is not shameful; to confess to these mistakes signifies a willingness to understand and correct them. And we must correct them. We must undertake broad theoretical propaganda and not organise ourselves solely for terrorist activity... And what is most important, we must organise our strength, we must unite all our groups into one mighty whole ...to create, in a word, a Russian anarchist party." This was followed in subsequent issues by the emphasising of anarchist organisation as being "essential" and "indispensable" and that the task of making this come about was of the utmost urgency. However, how this organisation would be structured remained vague.

On the subject of the unions, the Burevestnik comrades accepted some of the criticisms of the anarcho-syndicalists and in a 1907 editorial wrote: "that at the present moment in Russia the anarchists must organise the workers into illegal unions, along – professional lines". They also favoured the organisations that had emerged during the 1905 Revolution, the soviets. Raevsky wrote: "The short-lived but famous history of the soviets of workers' deputies showed that the Russian proletariat in the present stage of its development irrepressibly tried to unite for the struggle in a non-party class organisation..."

Another exile paper that appeared in August 1906 was Listki Khleb I Volya (Bread and Freedom Letters, a successor to Khleb I Volya, founded by Kropotkin). This was preceded by a conference organised by the Khlebovol'tsy in London. The conference criticised the tactics of terrorism practiced in Russia, whilst sympathising with the thirst for revenge by some comrades. This was followed by an editorial by Kropotkin in Listki Khleb I Volya, where he called for the end of the futile acts of reprisal carried out by anarchists, and for a more responsible attitude to be taken.

In January 1907 an abortive conference took place in Paris, attended by Kropotkin, Goldsmith, Gogelia and other Khlebovol'tsy. The supposed aim was to unite with the Chernoznamentsy and carry on unitary activity. Nothing came of this, due most likely to tactical differences.

A number of unitary conferences then took place, the first in Geneva in 1908 where Khleb I Volya and Burevestnik fused and formed the Union of Anarchist Communist Groups. At one of the last of these conferences (London, 28th December 1913 to 1st January 1914) the decision was taken to form a Federation of Anarchist Communist Groups in Exile and to adopt the Zurich paper, Rabochy Mir (Workers' World), as its mouthpiece. These moves were thwarted by the outbreak of war and the acrimonious splits that resulted from the decision of Kropotkin and others to support the Allies. Nonetheless, by 1915, the movement at home had begun to grow again to around 250-300, mostly in Moscow, St. Petersburg, and other urban centres, composed mostly of workers and a few students. The Moscow Group of Anarchist Communists formed in 1913, carrying out propaganda among factory workers, and establishing links with other groups in Tula, Briansk, and Ivanovo-Voznesensk.

However, by 1909 the Khlebovol'tsy had practically ceased to exist, with the main currents within Russian anarchism being the anarchosyndicalists and the anarchist communists who had descended from the Chernoznamentsy et al.

The February Revolution of 1917 led to the freeing of many hundreds of anarchists from prison, soon reinforced by many others returning from exile. This galvanised a movement that had already started re-emerging during the progress of the First World War. The events took the anarchist communists by surprise, as it did other political currents, but they responded quickly. They immediately called for a social revolution, the overthrow of the Provisional Government, and the end of the imperialist war. After the creation of Soviets of Workers 'and Soldiers' Deputies, they began to consider participation in them. For his part Kropotkin was to write: "The idea of the Soviets, first put forward during the revolution of 1905, and immediately implemented in February 1917, as soon as the tsarist regime fell, the idea of such bodies of power that control political and economic life is the greatest idea… It inevitably leads to the understanding that these Soviets must unite everyone who, in fact, by their own labour participates in the production of national wealth…" (The Russian Revolution and the Soviet government: letter to the workers of Western Europe, 1919).

February was a great disappointment to all the anarchists, who were now moving into a loose alliance with their main rivals, the Bolsheviks, first in the July Days in Petrograd, and then during the October Revolution, to overthrow Kerensky's provisional government. The July Days in which the anarchist communists took an active part, which were a failed attempt to overthrow the government, bringing a partial setback, and naturally provoked repression from the Kerensky regime. Anarchist communists like I.S. Bleikhman. Pavlov, Kolubushkin, and Nazumov, had an important influence on workers and soldiers in the machine gun regiment during these events and competed successfully with the Bolsheviks in popularity among workers, sailors and soldiers.

The Petrograd Anarchist Communist Federation was created and the mansion of Durnovo, which had been the property of a Tsarist minister, was occupied. The mansion was opened to the workers of the neighbourhood, providing a garden, a meeting place and library. The Federation had a strong following in the city. Outside of Petrograd, the movement began to develop. It was particularly powerful in Moscow where an Anarchist Communist Federation was set up. As at Petrograd, the anarchist communists occupied several large mansions, twenty six in total, and published two daily papers, creating sixty groups in the city and developing a well organised armed corps, the Black Guards, numbering some 2,000 militants. Anarchist activity also took place in Odessa, Tula, Ekaterinoslav and Kharkov. The anarchists derided the Constituent Assembly and called for a social revolution, and for immediate peace. The Petrograd Anarchist Communist Federation issued a leaflet saying: "We must show the people the uselessness and the absurdity of the tactic 'push the bourgeoisie to the left'. Our historic task is to push the proletariat to the left so that it can push the bourgeoisie into the precipice... Despite its revolutionary appearance, the Soviet of Workers and Soldiers Deputies will not liberate the workers if, in deeds, it does not realise an effectively maximalist anti-capitalist programme. The liberation of the workers can only be accomplished by a social revolution, and its realisation constitutes the most urgent task for the Russian workers... All Russia must be constituted into a network of revolutionary sovereign communes, which, in occupying the land and the factories, will expropriate the bourgeoisie, and thus suppress private property".

The treaty of Brest Litovsk and the consolidation of Bolshevik power in 1918 soon brought confrontation with the Bolsheviks taking armed action against the anarchist movement in Moscow and elsewhere, attacking their centres and closing down their papers.

In face of this, the anarchist movement split three different ways. Some accepted collaboration with the Bolshevik regime, others sought to carry on despite the repression with open propaganda and activity, whilst others began to organise an underground movement. The first option was supported by some anarcho-syndicalists, some anarchist communists and the Anarchist Universalists of the Gordin brothers. This group felt that the Bolsheviks had greater organisational clout in defending the Revolution, whilst still wishing to criticise its Statism. In spite of this, they too were repressed in 1921. Those who followed the second option quickly collapsed with mass arrests, confiscation of propaganda, closing down of meetings. Those who followed the third option suffered a similar fate.

Only in Ukraine was the anarchist movement able to operate effectively, allied as it was to the insurrectional movement around Makhno. There, Makhno organised an insurrection, first against the Austro-German invaders, and then against the White armies. Makhno had been released from prison with the Revolution in 1917, after having been convicted for actions against the local authorities carried out by the Gulyai-Polye anarchist communist group. As he remarked later in his Memoirs: "I was determined to jettison different tactical requirements assumed by the anarchists in the years 1905-07. During that period in fact, the principles of organisation were sacrificed to the principle of exclusiveness: the anarchists huddled in their circles which, removed from the masses, developed abnormally, were lulled into inactivity and thus lost the chance to intervene effectively in the event of popular uprisings and revolutions" (Makhno, The Russian Revolution in the Ukraine, 2007, pp.52-53). He helped organise the Group of Anarchist Communists in Gulyai-Polye, and took part in the activities of a trade union, and a peasant union, taking positions in various bodies in the village and practising an early form of what later became known as 'social insertion'.

Some anarchists from urban centres began to join this movement, partly because of Bolshevik repression in the urban areas to the north.

The Nabat (Alarm) Confederation of Anarchists was founded, working alongside the Makhnovist insurrectional army, and carrying out educational, cultural and propaganda activities. Both these movements soon clashed with Bolshevism, leading to their repression. The Kronstadt revolt of 1921 was to be the culminating point, with Kropotkin's funeral as the last main manifestation of anarchism for many years.

Those who did not become Soviet anarchists (either openly embracing the Bolsheviks or fellow travelling) were driven into exile, but many did not have this choice, and were either murdered or spent many years in prisons and gulags.

The poor organisational state of the movement on the day after the unfolding of the February Revolution, as well as the lack of unity, contributed to the failure of anarchist communists, and indeed other tendencies like the anarchosyndicalists, to take full advantage of the unfolding revolutionary situation. This was a lesson to be learned by the group that coalesced around Dielo Trouda in Paris in the 1920s.

The Russian Movement Abroad

The first anarchist communist organisation in the Unites States was Burevestnik, formed in New York in spring 1908 by immigrants and those who had escaped from prison or exile within the Russian Empire. It distributed newspapers like the eponymous Burevestnik and Listki Khleb I Volya and organised meetings and lectures, fund raising for the above-mentioned publications. The group lasted three years, but the propaganda carried out by this group laid the foundations for the developing Russian movement in the USA and Canada.

In 1911 the newspaper Golos Truda (The Voice of Labour) was founded in New York. It published weekly for more than three years, leading to the creation of various clubs and groups, which soon reorganised into Unions of Russian Workers, with Golos Truda as their "organisational and ideological mentor" (Lipotkin, p.71). This was followed by the founding congress of the Union of Russian Workers (URW) in July 1914 in Detroit. The Unions had been originally of an anarchist communist persuasion, but after the constitution of the URW had adopted an anarcho-syndicalist standpoint. With the outbreak of war, the URW took an anti-war position. However, anarchist communist opposition to the syndicalist view began to manifest itself, particularly around the militants of the Pittsburgh URW, Grigory Dvigomirov, Robert Erdman (real name Yevgeny Dolinin), and Petr Rubin-Zonov. They founded the New Federation of Unions of Russian Workers and a paper, Vostochnaya Zarya (Eastern Dawn) which lasted for two issues, folding in September 1916. The debate within the exile Russian anarchist community must have been rancorous as Aron Baron still remembered it when writing a letter from Siberian exile in 1925, referring to "the libellous Ermando-Dvigomirovsky Zarya", although he misremembers the names of the authors of the paper.

With the outbreak of the Revolution and the return of many Russian anarchists to their homeland, Golos Truda stopped publication in June 1917. During its existence between 1911 and 1917 it had organised thousands of workers, peasants and intellectuals, published a large amount of libertarian literature, and organised distribution of propaganda in Russia. The Palmer Raids organised by the U.S. government in 1918-19 had the URW as one of its main targets.

At the last congress of the URW in January 1919, it was decided to publish a weekly, Khleb I Volya, which appeared the following month. It published for nine months, with a print run of 6,000, and expired with a raid organised by the police and the deporting to Russia of most of its editorial board. From the start it took an intensely critical attitude to the Bolsheviks.

Despite the repression, a group of anarchist communists founded the underground paper Volna (The Wave) in early 1920. Following this, a Federation of Anarchist Communist Groups of the United States and Canada was set up in mid-April. In many ways it was the inheritor of the URW, and recommended that all of the URW property (books, literature, funds) be transferred to the new Federation. It adopted Volna as its organ.

Volna ended after five years, with its supporters coming to the conclusion that underground activity could not lead to the establishment of a broad movement through the work of small groups. Work now had to be carried out in the open, and had to include cultural activities. Those in favour of a legal approach had already started publishing a daily newspaper, Amerikanskiye Izvestiya (American

News) in early 1920. This paper, weekly after a few initial months of being a daily, became explicitly anarchist communist from 1921. Meanwhile some activists in New York, dissatisfied with Volna began to produce the short-lived journal Burevestnik from October 1921.

In 1923 the paper Anarkhichesky Vestnik (Anarchist Herald) appeared, speaking in favour of "united anarchism". It was edited by Petr Arshinov and Volin, and called for the unification of all the anarchist currents. However, differences over the question of organisation between the editors meant the end of the paper after seven issues, in May 1924.

The appearance of Dielo Trouda in Paris, led to Russian anarchist communists in the USA and Canada gathering around it, leading on to the creation of the Federation of Anarchist Communist Groups. Eventually, though, the ructions within the Russian movement coincided with the closing down of Dielo Trouda by the French government in 1929. The paper was thereafter published in the United States, from 1930 to 1939. However, Dielo Trouda was transformed from being the organ of Russian Anarchist Communists to that of the Organ of the Federation of Russian Workers' Organisations, and it moved from an anarchist communist orientation to one supporting anarcho-syndicalism, when Maximov became its editor in 1931. Another paper, Probuzhdenie (Awakening) was started in 1927 in North America partly in reaction to Dielo Trouda, and took an anti-Platformist line. The first few issues were edited by E. Z. Moravsky, whose mystical inclinations did not resonate with the intended readership. So he was replaced and the journal became more of a mainstream anarchist communist journal. Dielo Trouda, meanwhile, had to relocate to the USA where G. P. Maximoff, an intransigent anarcho-syndicalist, took over as editor in 1932 and the Platformists soon disappeared from its pages.

By the late 1930s, Dielo Trouda and Probuzhdenie were rather similar in content eventually leading to their merger in 1939 at the unification congress of Russian anarchist organisations in New York. The politics of the new merged paper was in many ways a lot different from the outlook of the original Dielo Trouda.

In Canada Russian anarchists in Montreal accepted the ideas expressed in the Organisational Platform in 1929. However, by 1939, they welcomed the unification of the different organisations at the congress in New York that year, and the merger of Dielo Trouda and Probuzhdenie. By 1959, the Russian movement in North America had disappeared, at least in organisational form, some of its militants dead, others disillusioned, and others only engaged in a low level distribution of propaganda.

Apollon Karelin, Solonovich and the Anarcho-Mystics

One personality who was an ongoing source of controversy within Russian anarchist communism was the intellectual and economist Apollon Karelin. Moving from a Socialist-Revolutionary position to anarchist communism whilst in exile in Paris in 1911, he began to write for the anarchist newspaper Golos Truda between 1912 to 1914. He organised the non-partisan anarchist group Free Socialists in 1912 which then transformed into the Brotherhood of Free Communists (Bratstvo Vol'nykh Obshchinnikov) the following year.

In 1913 he called for a congress of Russian anarchist communists. Now however, Rogdaev and his associates in the Zurich group of Russian anarchist communists around the paper Rabochy Mir began to accuse him of anti-Semitism, and the use of religious terms in pamphlets published by Karelin's group. Karelin had indeed joined a Masonic Grand Lodge in Paris. Karelin was further accused of dictatorial methods of organisation and the use of mystical rituals.

The congress was eventually held on 4th-11th October 1913 in Paris but only by Karelin and his associates. It was surrounded by rumours of agents provocateurs being present. In fact, evidence emerged in 1917 that two Okhrana agents were present at the Congress. On November 2nd 1913, the Rogdaev group accused Karelin of "covert tactics Jesuitism, demagogy and diplomacy, as well as the manifestation of the love of power and dictatorship and abuse of impure methods of struggle with the opposition-minded comrades" as well as "nonchalance, centralism and intrigue in the struggle for power, various hoaxes, religious phraseology and ritual procedures allowed during admission to groups". They designated this as Karelinism (karelinshchina). Later on December 7th, of that year, they announced evidence of "compromising evidence" against Karelin himself. This may have referred to Karelin's murky relationship with

Lieutenant Colonel Sudeikin, a leading light in the Okhrana, the Tsarist secret police, in 1882.

Karelin returned to Russia in June 1917 and started writing for the Petrograd anarchist papers Burevestnik and Trud i Volya. Moving to Moscow, he was one of the initiators of the All-Russian Federation of Anarchist-Communists, a pro-Soviet grouping with a grandiose and misleading name. Its purpose was to persuade the anti-Bolshevik, critical elements of the anarchist movement to cooperate with the new government. Karelin argued that the Bolshevik dictatorship was necessary to fight the forces of reaction, and that it was acceptable as a transitional phase towards the establishment of anarchist communism.

At the same time he continued his work to build conspiratorial circles of "Gnostic" anarchists. In addition he attended the 5th All-Russian Congress of Soviets in Moscow from 4th to 10th July 1918, and was elected to the All-Russian Central Executive Committee, in theory the supreme decision-making body of the Soviet Union, as head of the anarchist fraction there. In short, he became a 'Soviet anarchist' and acted as a legitimiser of the Bolsheviks. He was subsequently regarded by revolutionary anarchist communists as a renegade.

He furthered his work as leader of the "Gnostic" movement. This movement, often referred to as Anarcho-mysticism developed in the 1920s as a millenarian sect and indicated the profound crisis the libertarian movement was going through, with the defeat of any attempt at a Third Revolution and the marginalisation and repression of the anarchists. It turned away from political and social action into philosophical and spiritual considerations, combining individualism with theosophy and Gnosticism. This movement, understandably, was composed largely of the intelligentsia, with little or no representation from peasants or workers.

From February 1921, Karelin became a member of the All-Russian Public Committee for the Perpetuation of the Memory of Kropotkin, and between 1923-26 a member of the anarchist section of the Kropotkin Museum in Moscow. Worse than Karelin was his associate Alexei Solonovich, a mathematician. The Russian exile paper Dielo Trouda remarked on his "organisational mediocrity", his "string of ephemeral organisations... endless orders and fraternities: Light,

Spirit, Cross and Crescent, Sphinx, Mutual Aid, etc., a whole hierarchy of occult, political, 'cultural' organisations".

Solonovich published patriotic poems during the First World War, glorifying the Kingdom of Russia and the Serbian king, and characterising the Germans as the primordial enemies of the Slavs. It was only in 1917 that Karelin engaged Solonovich in his political activity. Karelin and Solonovich penetrated the Kropotkin Museum, and engaged in struggle with the revolutionary anarchist-communists there, excluding Rogdaev and arguing against the organisational moves inspired by the Platform of the Libertarian Communists. Solonovich slandered anarchists like Rogdaev and Pastukhov by calling them agents provocateurs. But in fact, the dubious antics of Karelin and Solonovich indicate the opposite, and at the very least, a manipulation of the situation by the Soviet authorities. It was partially because of the development of Karelinism that materialist anarchist communists began to look towards organisational solutions to the morass that had developed within Russia.

References

Avrich, P. The Anarchists in the Russian Revolution (1973)

Avrich, P. The Russian Anarchists (2005)

Author: Gooderham, P. The anarchist movement in Russia, 1905-1917. (doctoral thesis, University of Bristol) 1981: https://research-information.bris.ac.uk/ws/portalfiles/portal/34507649/591039.pdf

Lipotkin, Lazar. The Russian Anarchist Movement in North America (2019)

Rabinowitch, A. Prelude to Revolution (1991)

Rublev. D. I. The Russian anarchist movement during the First World War: https://www.katesharpleylibrary.net/qrfksw

Skirda, A. Les Anarchistes Russes les Soviets et la revolution de 1917 (2000).

Zverev, Vasily, and Sapon, Vladimir. Was Apollon Karelin a Provocateur?: https://rg.ru/2016/01/19/rodina-karelin.html

https://lib.sale/istoricheskaya-literatura-uchebnik/prilojenie-trubadur-misticheskogo-anarhizma-59556.html

Chapter Twenty Five
Anarchist Communism in the USA

Lucy Parsons

The working class African-American Lucy Parsons was one of the leading anarchist women activists in the USA. Alongside her partner Albert Parsons, she was heavily involved in the eight hour agitation in Chicago. After Albert's State murder in 1887 she continued her devotion to revolutionary ideas for the rest of her life.

From 1890 to 1892 she published Freedom: A Revolutionary Anarchist-Communist Monthly alongside her long time comrade Lizzie Swank Holmes, who was heavily involved in organising among women garment workers. She paid particular attention in the pages of Freedom to the large scale strikes rippling through the USA at that time, including at the Carnegie Steel Mills in Pennsylvania and at the silver mines in Coeur d' Alene, Idaho. At the same time, she used the pages of Freedom to denounce the lynching of black people in the South, and to attack the system of peonage of black sharecroppers there, as well as addressing the burning question of rape, including within marriage. She stated that women's place in the home was often that of a servant, an unwaged servant, and advocated the organisation of domestic workers and housewives. She called for the access of women to birth control and abortion, and the right to at-will divorce. However, whilst she herself practised free union with a number of partners, she was inconsistently no fan of the ideas of free love as advocated by Emma Goldman and others, writing that marriage and the family were "natural" in human relations. Similarly whilst she exposed the racism that was endemic in the United States, she wrote that black people were lynched, not because of racial hatred but because they were poor and working class.

A persistent critic of reformism within the workers' movement, she was a staunch defender of the organisation of the working class, against what she characterised as the middle class obsessions of some anarchists. She was an advocate of the revolutionary general strike and of class violence, saying "My conception of the strike of the future is not to strike and go out and starve, but to strike and remain in and take possession of the necessary property of production" (speech at the founding conference of the Industrial Workers of the World, 1905). She was also acutely aware of the need for propaganda and education amongst the working class, "There was never a time in the history of America when there was such urgent need for radical education as at the present moment. The rich are becoming more oppressive, domineering and arrogant each day; the people more depressed, despoiled and helpless. Every radical should try to reach them and educate them to a correct understanding of their condition in society; tell them why they are exploited, and the remedy." As such she became a founder member of the IWW.

However Parsons increasingly became alienated from the anarchist movement in America, writing in a letter to a friend, "Anarchism has not produced any organised ability in the present generation, only a few little loose, struggling groups, scattered over this vast country, that come together in 'conferences' occasionally, talk to each other, then go home... Anarchists are good at showing the shortcomings of others' organisations. But what have they done in the last fifty years... Nothing to build up a movement; they are mere pipe-dreamers dreaming... I, personally, have always held to the idea of organisation, together with an assumption of responsibility by the members, such as paying monthly dues and collecting funds for propaganda purposes. For holding these views, I have been called an 'old-school' Anarchist, etc... Anarchism, as taught in recent years, is too far away from the mental level of the masses". She supported the Bolshevik suppression of the Kronstadt uprising in 1921, and castigated Emma Goldman over her series of articles exposing the Bolshevik bureaucracy. She was to take part in the activities of Communist Party front organisations from 1925 onwards. It is disputed whether or not she actually joined the Communist Party in 1939, two years before her death.

Alexander Berkman and Emma Goldman

Alexander Berkman and Emma Goldman were important figures in the development and popularisation of anarchist communism in the USA.

Alexander Berkman, who had emigrated from Lithuania to the United States in 1888, soon became a member of the Yiddish anarchist group The Pioneers of Liberty, the first Jewish anarchist group in the

USA. Founded by a dozen workers the group soon attracted gifted militants like David Edelstadt, Moshe Katz, Hillel Solotaroff and Saul Yanovsky. This group carried out intensive propaganda in the Lower East Side, and published Varhayt (Truth), the first Yiddish language newspaper in the USA. Berkman was to reminisce: "It was about 1890, when the anarchist movement was still in its infancy in America. We were just a handful then, young men and women fired by the enthusiasms of a sublime ideal, and passionately spreading the new faith among the population of the New York Ghetto. We held our gatherings in an obscure hall in Orchard Street, but we regarded our efforts as highly successful. Every week greater numbers attended our meetings, much interest was manifested in the revolutionary teachings, and vital questions were discussed late into the night, with deep conviction and youthful vision. To most of us it seemed that capitalism had almost reached the limits of its fiendish possibilities, and that the Social Revolution was not far off" (The Bolshevik Myth, 1925).

Subsequently joining Johann Most's circle, Berkman was a dedicated anarchist communist. However, he broke with Most and aligned himself with the Die Autonomie group around Peukert. Like Timmermann, Berkman sought to take anarchist communist ideas outside the narrow German-speaking and Yiddish speaking circles in North America. An advocate of armed action against the ruling class, he became involved in an attempt on the life of Henry Clay Frick, manager of the Homestead steel plant in Pennsylvania. Frick had employed 300 thugs against striking workers in 1892and as a result, nine workers had been killed. Berkman wanted to avenge their deaths. The assassination attempt was unsuccessful and Berkman was sentenced to 21 years imprisonment. He served 14 years of the sentence and was released in 1906.

This must be understood by taking into account Berkman's youth within the Russian Empire, and his Nihilist and Narodnik influences, as well as the prevailing atmosphere of extreme class violence in the United States, where the employers quickly resorted to the use of murderous armed thugs and vigilantes against the workers' movement. At the same time Berkman always sought to relate to the workers' movement through his support for strikes. In 1913 he organised solidarity demonstrations for the striking miners in Ludlow, Colorado.

Berkman became editor of Emma Goldman's paper Mother Earth from 1907 until 1915. Mother Earth's circulation rose to 10,000 under his editorship and it became a leading libertarian publication in the USA. The journal published articles from Kropotkin, Grave, Malatesta and other anarchist communists and came out regularly for 12 years and helped develop the American movement. In addition Berkman published the short lived Blast from 1916 to 1917. Berkman used its pages to come to the support of Tom Mooney and Warren Billings, two members of the Socialist Party and the IWW, framed for the Preparedness Day bombing in San Francisco, for which they were eventually pardoned in 1961. Berkman travelled around the USA speaking at many meetings on their behalf and had a key role in spreading the protests on an international level. This led to the commutation of Mooney's death sentence. With Goldman, he was active in the No Conscription League during World War One, which was closed down by the authorities when the United States entered the war in 1917. Berkman served a further two years imprisonment for his anti-conscription work, and with Goldman and hundreds of other anarchists and socialists was deported from the USA in 1919.

Arriving in Russia, Berkman and Goldman witnessed the attacks on the revolution carried out by the Bolsheviks culminating in the crushing of the Kronstadt Commune in 1921. Escaping from Russia that year, they moved to Berlin. Berkman was in contact with the anarchosyndicalists of the FAUD there and he participated in its last congress in Erfurt in March 1932. During his sojourn in Berlin, Berkman also produced his books on the Russian Revolution, The Russian Tragedy, The Kronstadt Rebellion, The Russian Revolution and the Communist Party, as well as his Prison Memoirs. Much of the remainder of his time was spent in aid work for imprisoned Russian anarchists and he established the International Aid Fund and edited its Bulletin which provided information on the situation of comrades in the prisons and camps in Soviet Russia. Berkman then settled in Paris, writing for various radical publications and producing his famous Now and After: the ABC of Communist Anarchism in 1929.

However, he was deported from there, and only the intercession of influential friends made possible his return. Now unable to openly engage in political activities, he was forced to resign from the secretariat of the International Aid Fund.

Berkman began to suffer from cancer of the prostate, and unable to bear the pain after several operations, decided to take his own life on 28th June 1936. The suicide was botched, and he spent hours of agony before eventually dying, just days before the outbreak of the Spanish Revolution. As Goldman had inscribed on his tombstone "His dream was a new free and beautiful world. His whole life a ceaseless struggle. For the ultimate triumph of his ideal."

Apart from his books on the Russian Revolution, his What is Anarchist Communism, later abridged as The ABC of Anarchism has long remained a useful introduction to the ideas of anarchist communism, to what he described as "voluntary communism, the communism of free choice." As Paul Avrich remarked: "Berkman was not an original theorist. His ideas were drawn largely from Kropotkin and other founding fathers of the movement. But he was a lucid and gifted writer with a firm and fluent command of his subject... The result was a classic, ranking with Kropotkin's Conquest of Bread as the clearest exposition of communist anarchism in English or any other language."

However, in this book, he finds time to give an exposition of the individualist ideas of Spooner and Tucker, and repeats this in others of his writings, like The Anarchist Movement Today (1934), contributing to the erroneous ideas of 'big tent' anarchism that were developing during this period of defeat for the movement. Similarly, he was one of those still wedded to the idea of a loose network of affinity groups, first developed in the early years of anarchist communism, and vehemently opposed the proposals of the Organisational Platform (see his letter to Nettlau: http://dwardmac.pitzer.edu/Anarchist_Archives/bright/berkman/iish/ABtoMN11-17-32/ABtoMN11-17-32.html)

Emma Goldman

Like Berkman, Emma Goldman emigrated from the Russian Empire to New York. Radicalised by the Haymarket events of 1886, she became involved in the movement around Johann Most in 1889, but later moved over to the groups organised around Peukert and the periodical Die Autonomie. Involved in the attentat against Frick by Berkman, she was later sentenced to one year's imprisonment, after speaking to a crowd of nearly 3,000 in August 1893, when the USA was going through a severe economic crisis. Unemployment had soared to more than 20%. Goldman had said, "Demonstrate before the palaces of the rich; demand work. If they do not give you work, demand bread. If they deny you both, take bread." For this, she was charged with incitement to riot.

She began to carry out the first of a series of cross country lecture tours on anarchism in 1897. In 1903 she re-established these tours on a more ambitious scale, using her notoriety to attract audiences. This move to exploitation of celebrity had its dangers. In an interview in 1901 she remarked "It is not in the labouring man, the lowest classes, that I find my hope. It is the middle class and the professional people … to whom theories of life like mine appeal." Berkman became acutely aware of this move away from agitation amongst the working class on his release from prison in 1906, "The little Sailor, my companion of the days that thrilled with the approach of the Social Revolution, has become a woman of the world. Her mind has matured, but her wider interests antagonise my old revolutionary traditions that inspired every day and coloured our every act with the direct perception of the momentarily expected great upheaval I feel an instinctive disapproval of many things, though particular instances are intangible and elude my analysis. I sense a foreign element in the circle she has gathered about her, and feel myself a stranger among them. Her friends and admirers crowd her home, and turn it into a sort of salon; they talk art and literature; discuss science and philosophise over the disharmony of life. But the groans of the dungeon find no gripping echo there. The Girl is the most revolutionary of them all; but even she has been infected by the air of intellectual aloofness, false tolerance and everlasting pessimism." Much later, Albert Meltzer noted that "her desire to entertain the bourgeoisie heavily detracted from her propagandist credibility," (I Couldn't Paint Golden Angels: Sixty Years of Commonplace Life and Anarchist Agitation, 1996).

Whilst continuing to refer to anarchist communism, Goldman "symbolised a more individualist tradition through her projection of personal charisma and assumption of a privileged speaking role.

Unlike later communist leadership cults, she embodied neither organisation nor even a movement but an ideal, a worldview and an affirmation of selfhood." (Kevin Morgan, Heralds of the future? Emma Goldman, Friedrich Nietzsche and the anarchist as superman, 2009, p.6). Berkman was not convinced by the speaking tours, referring to them as a useless disturbance of the sleeping zoo. Berkman wrote to Goldman in 1905, "Touring is quite useless and a waste of money and effort where there are no groups or where the latter are inactive; in such a case the tourist-speaker must also be the organiser, for it is not at all sufficient to make a speech; after the speech, those interested must be organised into a group…." For her part Lucy Parsons criticised Goldman for "addressing large middle-class audiences". From 1909 she took on a road manager to assist her in the tours, and she made a career and living out of her celebrity.

Introduced to Nietzsche and Stirner by the first editor of Mother Earth, Max Baginski, she encouraged his printing of Nietzschean and Stirnerite texts in that paper. She herself gave 23 lectures on Nietzschean topics between 1913 and 1917. As Murray Bookchin remarked "despite their avowals of an anarchocommunist ideology, Nietzscheans like Emma Goldman remained cheek to jowl in spirit with individualists". She increasingly exploited her fame to relate to the educated middle class, and spoke disparagingly of local anarchist efforts to book her meeting places. Referring to her meetings in St. Louis, she caustically commented that, "Some people seem to be incapable of learning that Anarchism and dirty halls in squalid sections of the city are not synonymous. True, Anarchism does not exclude the poor, the dirty or the tramp any more than the sun excludes them, but it does not make a virtue of filth. It seems to me that so long as people remain satisfied with their present conditions, absolutely indifferent to cleanliness, air and beauty, they cannot possibly feel the burning shame of their lives, nor will they strive for anything that might lift them out of the ugliness of their existence. I do not censor anyone, for I am convinced that the boys of St. Louis tried their best; yet I am grieved that they should be satisfied with so little. True, the halls were cheap, but though the future of Mother Earth depends upon the success of this tour, I cannot even for her sake speak in dingy little halls, dark and gloomy, with the dust and smoke making it impossible to breathe." On the positive side, her ceaseless tours connected to her furtherance of Mother Earth, spread anarchist ideas throughout the USA like never before or since, and she invariably spoke to packed audiences which did include working people. Neither should her activities against conscription and militarism be underestimated, nor her efforts in favour of workers' struggles, particularly with the IWW. Her visits to France introduced her to the Bourses de Travail there, and she enthusiastically praised them.

Goldman's Nietzscheanism heavily influenced her attitude towards organisation. Speaking in response to Amédée Dunois's and Malatesta's calls for organisation at the international anarchist congress in Amsterdam in 1907, she riposted, "I, too, am in favour of organisation in principle. However, I fear that sooner or later this will fall into exclusivism. Dunois has spoken against the excesses of individualism. But these excesses have nothing to do with true individualism, as the excesses of communism have nothing to do with real communism... I, too, will accept anarchist organisation on just one condition: that it be based on the absolute respect for all individual initiatives and not obstruct their development or evolution. The essential principle of anarchy is individual autonomy. The International will not be anarchist unless it wholly respects this principle."

Both Berkman and Goldman were relatively slow in coming to realise the counter-revolutionary nature of the Bolshevik regime, the Kronstadt uprising jerking them into shocked and full understanding. Once Goldman had come to this realisation, she produced a number of useful texts including the book My Disillusionment in Russia. One of Goldman's greatest assets was her courage in the face of disapproval and repression, and she attempted to show the true nature of Bolshevik rule by mobilising campaigns against it. Despite her honesty and indomitability, this proved to be a failure. Whilst some were now under the thrall of Bolshevism, others, whilst more critical of what was happening in Russia, were unprepared to be seen to be siding with international reaction.

Goldman's most important contribution was her development of ideas on women's liberation and her linking of anarchism to women's liberation. She refused to call herself a feminist, as the term was at that time identified with the demand for universal suffrage. She was not against granting the vote to women, saying, "I am not opposed to woman suffrage on the conventional ground that she is not equal to it. I see neither physical, psychological, nor mental reasons why woman should not have the equal right to vote with man. But that can not possibly blind me to the absurd notion that woman will accomplish that wherein man has failed but believed that it was ludicrous to think that "woman will accomplish that wherein man has failed" to " I am not opposed to woman suffrage on the conventional ground that she is not equal to it. I see neither physical, psychological, nor mental reasons why woman should not have the equal right to vote with man. But that can not possibly blind me to the absurd notion that woman will accomplish that wherein man has failed." She advocated and practised free love and was a staunch advocate of birth control, and the control by women of their own bodies. She realised that the emancipation of women could only truly come about with a revolution that established anarchist communism. For Goldman Woman has been "for ages... on her knees before the altar of duty as imposed by God, by Capitalism, by the State, and by Morality".

The US Movement in the Doldrums

The 1920s and 1930s were bad years for anarchist communism in America. Not only had many important figures of the movement been deported in 1921, like Berkman and Goldman, but the continuing state of repression and the lure of the Communist Party also decimated the movement. In addition stricter immigration controls limited the number of foreign-born anarchists entering the United States. There were other factors at work that also weakened the movement. Sam Dolgoff described the movement he came to in New York in the 1920s. "A great many of them did not believe in organisation. Or didn't believe in the class struggle. Or didn't believe in immediate demands, like shorter hours. Or they didn't believe that anarchism could be a movement of the people, but only a movement of the elite, and they complemented themselves that they were among the elite who were able to understand what was going on. No rational approach to the problem social. They were worse than utopians (and I don't consider utopians so bad, by the way). But their anarchism began with their belly-button and ended with it. The sacred ego, and so forth. In other words, the most unsocial type of individualism, a type of bohemianism. And, naturally, among themselves, it was all right. But for us young fellows, it was no good. They wouldn't even tolerate a committee of relations between two groups."

Under the influence of Grigori Maximov in 1923-24, Dolgoff came to understand that anarchism was a social movement and a social theory.

At the end of 1931 Dolgoff formed an anarchist communist group with nine other young working class anarchists and with Mark Schmidt, a Russian-American in his thirties. Abe Bluestein was to join the group the following year. It was called Vanguard and produced a magazine of the same name in April 1932. It criticised the old guard for being 'cooped up within the confines of little national colonies'. It sought 'to revive here, in America, the great anarchist idea of a revolutionary Vanguard, the anarchist idea of the role and place of an active revolutionary minority in the great mass struggles of today and the near future'. This disturbed some anarchists, who labelled the Vanguard group as "anarcho-Bolsheviks. They emphasised organisation and rejected individualism. Vanguard had 3,000 subscribers in 1936 and its circulation doubled in 1938. Writing to Emma Goldman in that year, Vanguard member Roman Weinrebe stated that "Thousands of our magazines are being sold among the seamen, especially those on the Pacific coast, who, despite the theoretical slant of the magazine, show an avid interest in our ideas. There is no doubt that a renewed interest is being shown in the ideas of Libertarian Communism among people who two or three years ago were Marxists."

This failed to enthuse older anarchists, still trapped in apathy and lethargy. Vanguard members were also active in bringing out Spanish Revolution between 1936-1939, which was produced under the auspices of the United Libertarian Organisations (ULO), essentially an alliance of Vanguard, the Yiddish anarchist Freie Arbeiter Stimme and the Spanish Labor Press Bureau. As its name suggests, it reported on the unfolding Spanish Revolution. Like elsewhere, the Spanish Revolution and Civil War, acted as a galvaniser for the movement in the USA, with sales of the libertarian press moving from 25,000 in 1935 to 40,000 in 1938.

Also appearing in 1937 and running for a year was Challenge, edited by former Vanguard member Abe Bluestein, with a critical attitude towards the CNT-FAI leadership in Spain, whereas Spanish Revolution offered no criticism and toed the CNT-FAI line about entry into the Republican government, as did Dolgoff who became an abject apologist for the "circumstantialism" of the CNT-FAI. Dolgoff, along with Rudolf Rocker, compounded this with his support for the Allies in the Second World War, with his "lesser evil" arguments.

However the collapse of the Spanish Revolution meant the end of all these periodicals by the beginning of the Second World War. Some of those connected with Vanguard went on to establish Why? between 1942 and 1947 which transformed into Resistance from 1947 to 1954. But this periodical voiced the views of the youth group that had emerged as supporters of Vanguard, the Vanguard Juniors, and reflected the effects of the defeat of the Spanish Revolution. That defeat for them meant not the armed defence of the social revolution, but a turn towards "non-violent" action and pacifism.

Why? was initially founded by members of the youth group like Audrey Goodfriend and David Koven, who at first advocated revolutionary defeatism and then pacifism as well as by Sam and Esther Dolgoff and others who took the "lesser evil" position. Soon the Dolgoffs withdrew from the group, describing the younger members as "Village anarchists" (referring to the bohemian quarter of Greenwich Village in New York) and "professional bohemians". The Why? youth then established links with the Galleanist insurrectionists of L'Adunati dei Refrattari. At the same time they came under the influence of the Dutch proponent of non-violence, Bart de Ligt.

Why? and then Resistance purveyed this non-revolutionary, bohemian and essentially radical liberal stance which had a long term and deleterious effect on the development of American anarchism in the sixties onwards. The period between 1940 and 1960 marked an "osmosis between anarchists, pacifists and avant-garde artists... the analyses of nineteenth century thinkers and activists such as Pierre-Joseph Proudhon and Mikhail Bakunin started to seem outdated. Social revolution seemed very far away, and the state system threatened not only individual liberties but also the very survival of humanity". (from review of Andrew Cornell's Unruly Equality: US Anarchism in the 20th Century by Ioannis Papagaryfallou).

References
Brodie, Morris. Rebel Youths: English-language anarchist periodicals of the Great Depression, 1932-39 (2018).

Chapter Twenty Six
Murray Bookchin

Born in New York, Murray Bookchin took a trajectory from the Communist Party through Trotskyism to the Movement for a Democracy of Content, a group of post-Trotskyists by 1947, around the German exile Josef Weber. By 1958 he began calling himself an anarchist communist, as a result of attending meetings of the Libertarian League. This group, founded in New York City in July 1954, included Sam and Esther Dolgoff and Russell Blackwell. It stipulated that all members also had to be members of the IWW and combined anarchist-communist and anarcho-syndicalist ideas. The Libertarian League eventually ran out of steam in 1966.

Bookchin became profoundly influenced by the thought of Kropotkin, in particular his views on the idea of the Commune and on federalism and decentralisation. He took part in the New York Federation of Anarchists, a loose network set up in 1964. Within this, he was a driving force within the East Side Anarchist Group and then the magazine it published from winter 1967, Anarchos. In its pages, Bookchin developed his ideas of Post-Scarcity Anarchism. He had already written Ecology and Revolutionary Thought in 1964 where, based on Kropotkin, Bookchin argued for a decentralised and ecological society. Decision making at the local level would ascertain the basic material needs of all, at the same time ensuring that over production was ruled out.

In many ways this was a logical extension of Kropotkin's anarchist communism, bringing out the environmental concerns already to be discovered in that thinker's ideology. This essay reappeared in the pages of Anarchos. Bookchin had visited Europe in 1967, and had met with anarchists and Situationists in Paris, and Provos in Amsterdam. His meetings with Spanish anarchist veterans like Cipriano Mera, Pablo Ruiz and José Peirats was to bring about his later book The Spanish Anarchists in 1977.

Bookchin attended the Students for a Democratic Society convention in 1969. He had had high hopes for this radical movement, but was appalled by the growing influence of Leninist groups within it. This gave rise to the pamphlet Listen Marxist!, published that year and later anthologised in his book Post-Scarcity Anarchism in 1971, along with others of his articles. Whilst useful for its criticisms of the Leninist left, with "its 'class line,' its Bolshevik Party, its 'proletarian dictatorship,' its puritanical morality, and even its slogan, 'Soviet power'", the pamphlet explicitly rejects class politics. He identifies the proletariat as solely those who toil in factories, stating that they have been fully incorporated into the capitalist system, with "the worker dominated by the factory hierarchy, by the industrial routine, and by the work ethic. The point is that the divisions now cut across virtually all the traditional class lines and they raise a spectrum of problems that none of the Marxists, leaning on analogies with scarcity societies, could foresee... The question we must ask at this late date in history is whether a social revolution that seeks to achieve a classless society can emerge from a conflict between traditional classes in a class society, or whether such a social revolution can only emerge from the decomposition of the traditional classes, indeed from the emergence of an entirely new "class" whose very essence is that it is a non-class, a growing stratum of revolutionaries".

Bookchin helped established the Institute for Social Ecology in 1974, a think tank that had some influence on the emerging Green movement. By the eighties his ideas of libertarian municipalism were fully fledged and he was to establish the Left Green Network in 1988, based on these ideas. Along with the acceptance of electoralism at a municipal level, that is at the level of the local State, Bookchin embraced the term "democracy", saying to Duncan Rayside in 2002 that "democracy is not a dirty word."

By 1995, disturbed by the negative trends within US anarchism like individualism, life style politics, and primitivism, and a failure to reconstruct social movements, Bookchin produced his Social Anarchism or Lifestyle Anarchism. There is much there that hits home accurately, though he tends to generalise and caricature, for example condemning all those who evinced ideas of deep ecology as misanthropic, relying mainly on the statements of David Foreman of Earth First, who advocated a rapid decrease in the human population of the planet.

Whilst criticising these damaging trends, Bookchin equally launched attacks on class-based anarchism as in his The Ghost of

Anarcho-Syndicalism of 1992. By 1999 Bookchin broke with anarchism completely, stating that it was essentially an individualist philosophy based on the furthest extension of liberalism, and ignoring anarchism's development within the workers' movement of the nineteenth century.

Murray Bookchin has deeply flawed criticisms of anarcho-syndicalism, in the way he interpreted the proletariat in a narrow way as the industrial working class. He often hurled the accusation of "vulgar Marxism" at his opponents, when he was just as guilty of that offence in his understanding of what constitutes the proletariat. However sometimes his salvos hit home as can partially be seen in the following:

"The authentic locus of anarchists in the past was the commune or municipality, not the factory, which was generally conceived as only part of a broader communal structure, not its decisive component. Syndicalism, to the extent that it narrowed this broader outlook by singling out the proletariat and its industrial environment as its locus, also crucially narrowed the more sweeping social and moral landscape that traditional anarchism had created. In large part this ideological retreat reflected the rise of the factory system in the closing years of the last century in France and Spain, but it also echoed the ascendancy of a particularly vulgar form of economistic Marxism (Marx, to his credit, did not place much stock in trade unionism), to which many naive anarchists and non-political trade unionists succumbed. After the Revolution by Abad de Santillan, one of the movers and shakers of Spanish anarchosyndicalism, reflects this shift toward a pragmatic economism in such a way that makes his views almost indistinguishable from those of the Spanish socialists – and, of course, that brought him into collusion with the Catalan government, literally one of the grave-diggers of Spanish anarchism" (Deep Ecology, Anarcho-Syndicalism and the future of Anarchist Thought, 1993).

Bookchin goes on to make the sweeping and ludicrous statement that "Syndicalism – be it anarchosyndicalism or its less libertarian variants – has probably done more to denature the ethical content of anarchism than any other single factor in the history of the movement, apart from anarchism's largely marginal and ineffectual individualist tendencies." Bookchin's lack of judgement in conflating the class struggle anarchist politics of anarcho-syndicalism with the deeply destructive individualist anarchist current does him no favours. At a time when clarity of thought is what was needed in reconstructing a serious revolutionary anarchist politics, Bookchin's powers of reason failed. His adventures with libertarian municipalism, and then his renunciation of anarchism and his adoption of "communalism" tells against him on this score. Bookchin is correct in his understanding of the de-emphasising of the idea of the Commune, on much else he is off the mark. One of his more lucid works The Spanish Anarchists 1868-1936 deals with greater precision on syndicalism: "Syndicalism, to be sure, has many shortcomings, but its Marxian critics were in no position to point them out because they were shared by Socialist parties as well. In modelling themselves structurally on the bourgeois economy, the syndicalist unions tended to become the organisational counterparts of the very centralised apparatus they professed to oppose. By pleading the need to deal effectively with the tightly knit bourgeoisie and state machinery, reformist leaders in syndicalist unions often had little difficulty in shifting organisational control from the bottom to the top. Many older anarchists were mindful of these dangers and felt uncomfortable with syndicalist doctrines. Errico Malatesta, fearing the emergence of a bureaucracy in the new union movement, warned that 'the official is to the working class a danger only comparable to that provided by the parliamentarian; both lead to corruption and from corruption to death is but a short step'. These Anarchists saw in syndicalism a shift in focus from the commune to the trade union, from all of the oppressed to the industrial proletariat alone, from the streets to the factories, and, in emphasis at least, from insurrection to general strike."

Bookchin's greatest contribution to anarchist communism and social anarchism remains his introduction to it of environmentalism and ecology, prefigured by some of the writings of Kropotkin and Reclus.

Chapter Twenty Seven
Social anarchism re-emerges within the United States

In 1972 the Social Revolutionary Anarchist Federation (SRAF) was formed, which was a loose federation of various groups, with 18 groups in the USA and seven in Canada. It published the SRAF bulletin which was composed of letters and articles sent in by supporters, and a number of discussions were initiated within its pages. In addition a number of congresses took place. The SRAF was a synthesist grouping, gathering together both anarchist communists and anarcho-syndicalists alongside individualists and mutualists. It produced a magazine, Black Star and a number of duplicated pamphlets. Among these, Malatesta's Anarchist Communist Programme had an influence on some of the participants of SRAF and beyond. At a gathering in 1977, at Wildcat Mountain, the Anarchist Communist Tendency was formed. This would later become the Anarchist Communist Federation. As one of the members of the ACT wrote: "About a year or so prior to the Wildcat Mountain conference folks from Resurgence in Chicago began to circulate Sam Dolgoff's proposal for the 'Regeneration of the Labor Movement'. I believe Sam originally wrote it for distribution and for action inside the IWW. This document was to be studied, discussed, adopted and promoted by those inside SRAF who were pro-organisation, pro-anarcho-syndicalist and class struggle anarchist-communist. It was to be the basis for initial discussion of our tendency beginning to form around the 'Self-Management Newsletter'. It was under the auspices of this tendency that a workshop was held at Wildcat Mountain. This was the kick-off to a more organised tendency, the ACT... We were mainly working class kids from Ontario, W.Virginia, the mid-west (IL & MI) and, I think, myself representing the whole north-eastern US. In March of 1978, in Ypsilanti, Michigan the ACF of North America was formed. The founding conference was a wonderful adventure and experience. I was 23 years old and wide-open to the new world that laid at our collective finger-tips. I would say that most of us who were involved were in their 20s... For the most part we had few elders to turn to. The class struggle anarchist movement was near dormant for decades. Our two areas of collective agreement were Peter Kropotkin's Anarchist Communism: Its Basis and Principles .The other was the Basis for Affiliation & the Internal Organisation of the ACF. (1978)".

The ACF published a well produced newspaper, the North American Anarchist and a series of pamphlets. The ACF was quite heavily influenced by the British Organisation of Revolutionary Anarchists/Anarchist Workers Association whose press circulated in North America to a certain extent, as witness this section from the 1978 statement:

"As anarchists we organise in all areas of life to try to advance the revolutionary process. We believe a strong anarchist organisation is necessary to help us to this end... We recognise that the revolution can only be carried out directly by the working class. However, the revolution must be preceded by organisations able to convince people of the anarchist communist alternative and method."

The ACF initially consisted of three groups in Canada and eight in the USA. Unfortunately the ACF was made up of already established groups that didn't seem to be looking for a unitary and universal approach. This led to the collapse of the ACF in 1982.

Some former ACF members went on to form a network around the newspaper Strike! It was formed of class struggle anarchist communists and anarchosyndicalists who had worked together in the ACF. Eventually the anarchosyndicalists moved off in 1984 to found their own organisation, The Workers Solidarity Alliance (WSA) which exists to this day. The Strike! Network collapsed soon after this.

The process that started in the 1980s in North America with the flourishing of various small groups and collectives culminated in the founding of Love and Rage, at a congress in Chicago in November 1989. Some seventy five people assembled there included those from several anarchist groups from around the United States and Canada, as well as various individuals and twenty former members of the Revolutionary Socialist League, which had broken with Trotskyism in the late 1980s.

These new anarchist groups had developed around various movements like nuclear disarmament, South African and Central

American solidarity and the AIDS campaigning of ACT UP, within the context of the decay of the old left, in particular the Maoist and Trotskyist groups, brought on by the collapse of the Soviet Union, the Tienanmen Square massacre, and the collapse of the Sandinista venture in Nicaragua.

Most of those involved in the Chicago congress saw the establishment of a continental paper as a means to building an organisation on the same level. The newspaper acted as an organiser for various contingents on demonstrations, like Earth Day actions of 1990 and then the Washington anti-war march. The second congress in 1991 in Minneapolis resulted in the establishment of the Love and Rage Network (L&RN). Two tendencies began to emerge, one believing that the L&RN was too centralised and concentrating too much on building a continental structure than on local initiatives, and another that believed in theoretical unity, a common strategy and a set of aims and principles and a constitution. This came to a head at the third congress in San Diego where the Love and Rage Federation (L&RF) was set up.

Love and Rage collapsed in 1998 due to disagreements over race and class. Two years later a new organisation emerged based in the north east part of North America which was more explicitly anarchist communist and Platformist, the North Eastern Federation of Anarchist Communists (NEFAC), and for its French speaking members in Canada the Fédération des Communistes Libertaires du Nord-Est. It included some ex-members of Love and Rage and came together at a congress in Boston after months of discussion. It had groups in the north east of the United States, and in Canada in southern Ontario and in Quebec province.

NEFAC split up in 2008, the Francophones forming the Union Communiste Libertaire (UCL) in Quebec, whilst those in the USA held on to the name NEFAC, before changing its name to Common Struggle-Libertarian Communist Federation in 2011. There were no ideological differences over this parting, which was fuelled by the difficulty of operating within two different countries with two different languages. Canadian members of NEFAC in Ontario province had already set up their own Platformist organisation in September 2007 before the emergence of the UCL, which was named Common Cause.

Common Cause produced an agitational paper, Linchpin, and an excellent theoretical magazine, Mortar, which ran to three issues. However, Common Cause seems to have disappeared after 2010. UCL dissolved itself on March 1st 2014, "As the organisation no longer meets the needs and desires of the majority of its members", and there is currently no specific anarchist communist organisation in Canada.

Several years of discussion between different groups in the USA began in 2008 with a Class Struggle Conference held in New York City, followed by further such conferences. At the Class Struggle Anarchist Conference in November 2012 various groups which included Common Struggle, Miami Autonomy Solidarity, Four Star Anarchist Organisation of Chicago, Rochester Red and Black, and Wild Rose Collective in Iowa City, agreed to merge to form the Black Rose Anarchist Federation/Federacion Anarquista Rosa Negra (BRRN). The new organisation referred to its influences being "anarchist-communism, anarcho-syndicalism, especifismo, platformism, feminism, queer liberation, black liberation, abolitionism, anti-racism and their history of global struggle for liberation." As a result of the merger BRRN could count on hundreds of members with branches in over a dozen cities.

However, the BRRN, like Love and Rage, was dogged by controversies over "accountability, poor feminist praxis, tokenisation, and the abuse of soft power within the organisation." Fifty nine members quit the organisation from late 2019, with two thirds of these leaving in autumn 2020. It remains to be seen whether BRRN will recover from this scission, and whether the ongoing crisis in American anarchism, fuelled by identity politics, can be resolved.

Chapter Twenty Eight
The Organisational Platform of the Libertarian Communists and the Synthesis

The post-war years saw the anarchist movement in complete disarray, with the repercussions of the Manifesto of Sixteen, the death of many in the War, the withdrawal of many others, disillusioned by the chain of events, and the rallying of many, at least temporarily, to the Communist Parties. Alongside this was the bolshevising of the workers' movement; the anarchist movement, whilst retaining its proletarian character, was a minority within that movement.

Any discussion of the Organisational Platform of the Libertarian Communists has to take into account the ideas of the Synthesis, that appeared at the same time and were also derived in some measure from experiences of the Russian Revolution. It also has to take into account that the ideas contained within the Platform did not spring from nowhere. Not only were they results of the Russian Revolution but of the experiences of the Anarchist movement in general up to that time. As such, they did have a certain resonance within the movement.

Some anarchists managed to glean particular lessons from the defeats of the Russian Revolution. Nestor Makhno and Petr Arshinov with other exiled Russian and Ukrainian anarchists in Paris launched the excellent bimonthly Dielo Trouda (Workers' Cause) in 1925. It was an anarchist communist theoretical review of a high quality. Years before, when they had both been imprisoned in the Butirky prison in Moscow, they had hatched the idea of such a review. Now it was to be put into practice. Makhno wrote an article for nearly every issue during the course of three years.

It was apparent to them that the failures of the anarchist movement were due in no small way to the lack of a strong and structured organisation actively participating in struggle.

In August 1925 Arshinov penned Our Organisational Problem which appeared in Dielo Trouda. It noted: "No matter how much we criticise and expose Bolshevism, there is no denying the fact that it politically destroyed our ranks through the aggressiveness of its ideology and its preponderant influence in Russian life and in the international context (not to mention of course the physical liquidation of thousands of anarchist activists, to which it became particularly attached as soon as it no longer needed them to militarily overcome the white guardists). This obviously led to a heavy haemorrhaging of active activists in our movement, and introduced pessimism and discouragement in others. This is how this development accelerated the defeat of the Russian revolution and its fundamental aspirations, until it destroyed all the libertarian seeds of self-management among the working class.

"The workers' movement thus finds itself castrated in Russia and elsewhere, and can no longer as a result feed the anarchist ranks.

"However, apart from these causes of our current failure there is another, no less important, and that is in ourselves. While it is undeniable that anarchy is nourished and developed by the forces of the workers 'movement, it is no less true that in turn it must stimulate the workers' movement of vital currents.

"The theoretical and practical problems of the Revolution, the political demands of the moment, the tasks and agenda, in general everything that constitutes the ideological basis of labour in struggle, should find its full expression in anarchism.

"It is only through ceaseless ideological and organisational work that it is possible to maintain the indispensable link with the masses and to maintain the mutual process of nourishment and development.

"However, we have taken an unforgivable delay in this area. During these eight years of revolutionary life, we have often limited ourselves to positions that are fair, of course, but too general, acting simultaneously in dispersed order, in multiple small groups, often diverging on many tactical points. Despite this, life passed, it required participants in the social struggle, the exact knowledge of their objectives, a determined practical program, well-coordinated actions.

"During this period, we did not worry about our programme, the organisation of our forces, of a collective practice, and by this we facilitated elements foreign to the workers movement, which took the initiative and the direction of the events."

Alongside Arshinov's call for organisational effectiveness in the pages of the same issue of Dielo Trouda was that of Alexander

Cherniakov, who had been an active anarchist communist since 1904 and who had been one of those banished from the Soviet Union in 1921, ending up as a leading light in the Dielo Trouda group in Montevideo, Uruguay. He called for the creation of an anarchist party, based on the Jura Federation, insisting that such a conception was qualitatively different from the parties of the statist socialists.

In the following issue there was a response from Volin, who questioned the use of the term "Party", which he felt was too linked to authoritarian socialism. He offered the Nabat Confederation in the Ukraine as an organisational model, in which he himself had been involved for a time. Nabat (Alarm) had been created as an umbrella for anarchist communists, anarcho-syndicalists and individualists and Volin proposed combining what was compatible for each current and rejecting the rest. In many ways this was the seed of the future organisational idea of the Synthesis that he was to advance in tandem with Sebastien Faure.

The Dielo Trouda group (now reinforced by Ida Mett, who had recently fled from Russia) gave a collective reply to the idea of the Synthesis in March 1926. In The Organisational Problem and the Idea of the Synthesis they stated that: "Our view is that everything necessary for the construction of an organisation founded upon a given platform can be found in Anarchist Communism, which espouses the class struggle, the equality and liberty of every worker, and is realised in the anarchist Commune.

"Those comrades who champion the notion of a theoretical synthesis of anarchism's various currents have quite another approach to the organisational question. It is a pity that their view is so feebly spelled out and elaborated and that it is thus hard to devise a thoroughgoing critique of it. Essentially, their notion is as follows: Anarchism is divided into three strands – communist anarchism, anarcho-syndicalism and individualist anarchism. Although each of these strands has features particular to itself, all three are so akin and so close to one another that it is only thanks to an artificial misconception that they enjoy separate existences.

"In order to give rise to a strong, powerful anarchist movement, it is necessary that they should fuse completely. That fusion, in turn, implies a theoretical and philosophical synthesis of those teachings on which each of these three tendencies is based. Such then is the content of the synthesis thus conceived, as set out in the 'Declaration on Anarchists' Working Together', and a few other articles by comrade Voline carried by The Anarchist Messenger and Dielo Trouda. We are in total disagreement with this idea. Its inadequacy is glaringly obvious. For a start, why this arbitrary division of anarchism into three strands? There are others as well. We might mention, say, Christian anarchism, associationism, which, be it said in passing, is closer to communist anarchism than to individualist anarchism. Then again, what precisely is the consistency of the "theoretical and philosophical" discrepancies between the aforementioned three tendencies, if a synthesis between them is to be devised?

"For one thing, before we talk about a theoretical synthesis of communism, syndicalism and individualism, we would need to analyse these currents. Theoretical analysis would quickly show the extent to which the wish to synthesise these currents is hare-brained and absurd. Indeed, does not the talk of a 'synthesis between communism and syndicalism' signify some sort of contrast between them? Many anarchists have always regarded syndicalism as one of the forms of the proletarian revolutionary moment, as one of the fighting methods espoused by the working class in fighting for its emancipation.

"We regard communism as the goal of the labouring classes' liberation movement." They went on to say that: "In fact, what does the anarchism of individualists consist of? The notion of the freedom of the individual?

"But what is this 'individuality'? Is it the individuality in general or the oppressed 'individuality' of the toiler?

"There is no such thing as 'individuality in general' because, one way or another, every individual finds themselves objectively or subjectively in the realm of labour or else in the realm of capital. But isn't the idea implicit in anarchist communism? We might even say that the freedom of the individual toiler is realisable only in the context of an anarchist communist society that will take a scrupulous interest in social solidarity as well as in respect for the rights of the individual.

"The anarchist commune is the model of social and economic relations best suited to fostering the development of the freedom of the individual. Anarchist communism is not some rigid, unbending social framework which, once achieved, is set and sets a term to the development of the individual. On the contrary: its supple, elastic social organisation will develop by growing in complexity and constantly seeking improvements, so that the freedom of the individual may expand without hindrance... So what remains of individualist anarchism? Negation of the class struggle, of the principle of anarchist organisation having as its object the free society of equal workers; and, moreover, empty babble encouraging workers unhappy with their lot to look to their defences by means of recourse to the personal solutions allegedly open to them as liberated individuals.

"But what is there in all this that can be described as anarchist? Where are we to find the features in need of synthesis with communism? That whole philosophy [of individualism] has nothing to do with anarchist theory and or anarchist practice, and it is unlikely that an anarchist worker would be inclined to conform to this 'philosophy.'"

They went on to baldly state: "We have to choose between two options:

"Either the tendencies named remain independent tendencies, in which case, how are they going to prosecute their activities in some common organisation, the very purpose of which is precisely to attune anarchists' activities to a specific agreement?

"Or these tendencies should lose their distinguishing features and, by amalgamating, give rise to a new tendency that will be neither communist, syndicalist nor individualist... But in that case, what are the fundamental positions and features to be?

"By our reckoning the notion of synthesis is founded on a total aberration, a shoddy grasp of the basics of the three tendencies, which the supporters of synthesis seek to amalgamate into one."

They clarified that: "The above does not at all mean that we are against concerted endeavour by anarchists of varying persuasions. Quite the opposite: we can only salute anything that brings revolutionary anarchists closer together in practice.

"However, that can be achieved practically, concretely, by means of the establishment of liaison between ready-made, strengthened organisations. In which case, we would be dealing only with specific practical tasks, requiring no synthesis and indeed precluding one. But we think that the more that anarchists clarify the basics – the essence of anarchist communism – the more they will come to agreement on these principles and erect upon that basis a broad organisation that will provide a lead in socio-political matters as well as in the realm of trade union/professional matters.

"As a result, we do not in any way see a link between the organisational problem and the notion of synthesis. If it is to be resolved, there is no need to get carried away by vague theorisations and expect results from that. The baggage that anarchism has amassed over the years of its life process and social struggle is more than sufficient. We need only take proper account of it, applying it to the conditions and exigencies of life, in order to build an accountable organisation."

That year also saw the publication of the 'Organisational Platform for a General Union of Anarchists', known in Britain as the Organisational Platform of the Libertarian Communists. Its appearance needs to be placed in the context of the previous period of anarchist communist history. The first phase had been characterised by a distrust in permanent organisation and a belief in the loose liaison of small affinity groups. In France, Italy and Spain, this also involved a use of a narrow interpretation of propaganda by the deed, as seen in the actions of self-proclaimed anarchist communists like Ravachol. The second phase, at least in France, involved the period of 1895-1914 when the anarchists entered the unions and bourses de travail, and in Spain created workers organisations that became the CNT. Whilst now looking outwards to action within the wider working class, the rejection of the need for permanent organisation was maintained. Whilst the CGT was seen as a unifying structure on the union level, there was no political equivalent until the attempt at a specific organisation in France with the abortive creation of the Federation Communiste Revolutionnaire Anarchiste (see the chapters on France).

The Platform was an attempt to face the defeat of the Russian anarchist movement and the crushing of the Russian Revolution, signalled by the suppression of the Kronstadt revolt and the final extinguishing of peasant uprisings in 1921. It also looked towards the weakening of the anarchist movement and the creation of various

Communist Parties around the world, at the beck and call of the Soviet Union.

The Platform has long been designated as the Arshinov Platform, in other words the creation of one militant, when in fact it was the collective effort of the Dielo Trouda group which included Makhno and Mett. It should also be remembered that these exiles were in the main active within the French movement and that the formulation of the Platform did not just involve the heavy defeats inflicted during the Russian Revolution, but the impasse at which the French movement had arrived. The failure of the strike movement of 1920 in France had once again underlined the lack of efficacy of the anarchist movement.

Thus the propositions of the Platform were not just aimed at the Russian movement, but at the movement in France and elsewhere. This can be seen in the fact that as Malatesta noted, the text appeared in a French translation. Certainly one of the implications of the Platform was the marginalisation of the individualists, whose influence was seen as particularly pernicious as regards the creation of an efficacious structuring of the movement.

The publication of the 'Platform' was met with ferocity and indignation by many in the international anarchist movement. First to attack it was the Russian anarchist Volin, now also in France, and founder with Sebastian Faure of the 'Synthesis' which sought to justify a mish-mash of anarchist communism, anarcho-syndicalism and individualist anarchism. Together with Molly Steimer, Fleshin, and five others, he wrote a reply in April 1927 stating that to "maintain that anarchism is only a theory of classes is to limit it to a single viewpoint". Anarchism from this point of view was as much based on humanitarianism and the individual as on the class struggle. The weakness of the anarchist movement was explained by the vagueness of several key ideas of anarchism, the difficult assimilation of libertarian ideas by the present world, and the mental state of the contemporary masses who were fooled by all sorts of demagogues, the general repression of the movement from the moment it began to show serious progress, the intentional stance of anarchists in not resorting to demagoguery, and the renouncing by anarchists of all artificial organisation and all artificial discipline.

The propositions of the Platform were denounced as "a hidden revisionism towards Bolshevism and the recognition of a transitional period" which was unacceptable.

Indeed, in response to the Platform and its rejection of individualism, the Synthesis sought a broad organisation where individualists, anarchist communists and anarcho-syndicalists could co-exist. Volin had elaborated Associational Anarchism within the Nabat Anarchist Confederation in the Ukraine. He, like the Platformists, had been worried about the effectiveness of Anarchism, and sought to reconcile anarcho-syndicalism and anarchist communism, whilst at the same time hoping that Anarchist Individualists could be drawn in. In doing this, however, he created a fatal weakness in diluting the class struggle core of Anarchism. As a militant within the French movement, he was to have an influential role, blending his ideas with those of Sebastien Faure, who had similar views. Faure compared the Anarchist movement to a physical body composed of equal parts of Syndicalism, Communism and Individualism. Each group would fix its own method of recruitment and internal organisation. The flimsiness of this setup seems evident. There are no links between the groups in the vision of the anarchist organisation. The ideological problem is fudged, and action is limited to 'our dear propaganda'. In effect, under cover of unity, a Synthesist organisation could, and did, become a battleground between different tendencies. If a rapprochement between anarcho-syndicalism and anarchist communism is still possible, the differences with individualism are too large (as pointed out in the Organisational Problem and the Idea of the Synthesis, see above).

The idea of a General Union of Anarchists that was advocated in the Platform seemed to contradict what had been argued against the Synthesis, and overlooked the fact that different currents could not satisfactorily coexist in the same organisation and that organisation advanced by the Platform would have to be based on anarchist communism. This was implied, especially in criticisms of the Synthesis but never directly addressed head on. The authors did not spell out clearly what the relationship between the organisation and other anarchist groups outside it would be.

The Platform was unclear in its reaction to syndicalism. It fudged the issue of revolutionary syndicalism.

The Dielo Trouda group responded with Reply to the Confusionists of anarchism in August of that year. They stated that the severe repression unleashed by the Bolsheviks against the anarchist movement was an obstacle but not the only one. It was more the internal impotence of the movement that was one of the principal reasons for the defeat of the movement. More than twenty years of experience and revolutionary activity had convinced them of the need for a "new organisation general anarchist organisation of party, based on a homogeneous theory, politics and tactics.

"An old militant of the Nabat confederation (still in the Soviet Union, and in prisons and gulags since 1920 and thus anonymous in the pages of Dielo Trouda) responded to Volin over the question of Nabat as a model of anarchist organisation. He contradicted the assertion by Voline that Nabat had been a loose structure, stating that it had in fact applied organisational principles and collective responsibility, and not only that, struggled to impose them. According to this anonymous member of Nabat, the organisation was tending towards becoming a prototype of a structured organisation. "It was in fact an organisational Union, on the base of several general principles, with the aim of accomplishing a common organisational work of the best and healthiest representatives of different anarchist tendencies, of those who felt the need for this."

The Dielo Trouda group issued, on 5th February 1927, an invitation to an 'international conference' before which a preliminary meeting was to be held on the 12th of the same month. Present at this meeting, apart from the Dielo Trouda group, was a delegate from the French Anarchist Youth, Odeon; a Bulgarian, Pavel, in an individual capacity; a delegate of the Polish anarchist group, Ranko (real name Benjamin Goldberg aka Jerzy Boresja), and another Pole in an individual capacity (Aniela Wohlberg); several Spanish militants, among them Orobon Fernandez, Carbo, and Gibanel; an Italian, Ugo Fedeli; a Chinese, Chen (a pseudonym for Wu Ke Kang/ Wu Zhigang); and a Frenchman, Dauphin-Meunier; all in individual capacities. This first meeting was held in the small backroom of a Parisian cafe.

A provisional Commission was set up, composed of Makhno, Chen and Ranko. A circular was sent out to all anarchist groups on 22nd February. An international conference was called and took place on

2nd March 1927, at Hay-les-Roses near Paris, in the Cinema Les Roses.

As well as those who attended the first meeting was one Italian delegate who supported the 'Platform', Bifolchi, and another Italian delegation from the magazine 'Pensiero e Volonta', Luigi Fabbri, Camillo Berneri, and Ugo Fedeli. The French had two delegations, one of Odeon, favourable to the 'Platform' and another with Severin Ferandel.

A proposal was put forward to:
- Recognise the class struggle as the most important facet of the anarchist idea;
- Recognise Anarchist Communism as the basis of the movement;
- Recognise syndicalism as a principal method of struggle;
- Recognise the need for a 'General Union of Anarchists' based on ideological and tactical unity and collective responsibility;
- Recognise the need for a positive programme to realise the social revolution.

After a long discussion some modifications of the original proposal were put forward. However, nothing was achieved as the police broke up the meeting and arrested all those present. Makhno risked being deported and only a campaign led by the French anarchists stopped this. But the proposal to set up an 'International Federation of Revolutionary Anarchist Communists' had been thwarted, and some of those who had participated in the conference refused to sanction it any further.

Other attacks on the 'Platform' from Fabbri, Berneri, Max Nettlau, and Malatesta followed.

Luigi Fabbri took a less rabid position than others towards the Platformists, saying that it placed "in the arena of discussion a number of problems regarding the Anarchist movement, the place of Anarchists in the revolution, the organisation of Anarchism in the struggles, and so on, which need to be solved if Anarchist doctrine is to continue to respond to the growing needs of the struggle and of social life in the present-day world". As an organisationalist, Fabbri at first welcomed the initiative of the Platform, with which he shared many conclusions and the concern over the defeat of the movement, not just in Russia, but in Italy. Above all he was searching for the development of effective anarchist action in the light of these defeats.

However, in his responses he was exhibiting many of the disturbing tendencies of both he and Malatesta towards what was seen as an effective unity among the different anarchist currents, and further away from a class-based anarchist communism towards a humanist outlook. Writing in his essay on the subject, About a Project for Anarchist Organisation, he was to write:

"One part of the 'Platform' that I believe is wrong is the section which would have 'class struggle' as practically the main characteristic of anarchism, reducing to a minimum the human element and the humanitarian objective. The expression 'class struggle' includes a nucleus of theories which can of course be shared by anarchists but which are not necessarily anarchist. They are, in fact, common to certain other schools of socialism, in particular to Marxism and bolshevism. This is not the place to argue whether or not it is true that human history is determined by the class struggle – it is a scientific question or a question regarding the philosophy of history which does not impinge excessively on anarchism. Anarchism follows its own path whether that theory be true or false. The main characteristic of Anarchism is the refusal of all imposed authority, of all government; it is the affirmation of individual and social life, organised on a libertarian basis. But anarchism is above all human, inasmuch as it seeks to realise (to use Bakunin's expression) Humanity upon the destruction of class and state divisions, and to realise it in the individual as much as in society. The class struggle is a fact which can be denied neither by anarchists nor by anyone with a head on their shoulders, and in this struggle the anarchists will stand with the oppressed and exploited classes against the dominant and exploiting classes. For this reason, the workers' class war against capitalism corresponds with the methods and forms of revolutionary action of anarchism, having the aim of expropriating the capitalist class. This expropriation must be to the benefit of everyone, so that the exploited may cease being exploited and the exploiters may cease being exploiters, and everyone voluntarily agrees to produce in common and consume the fruits of their common labour together, according to their needs.

"In this sense it could be argued that anarchists are 'against the class struggle', given that they bring to this struggle of the workers against capitalism the objective of ending the class struggle in order to substitute it with human cooperation. It is better, too, not to clutter our propaganda with formulae that can lead to misunderstandings and could, given the use made of them today, be interpreted in a sense which is contrary to Anarchism. Historically speaking, it seems inexact to me to speak of Anarchism as a 'class ideal'. The working class more than anyone else has every interest in the triumph of liberty in the anarchist sense, and consequently we anarchists address ourselves especially to our brother workers, amongst whom we know we can find the most comrades. Indeed, most anarchists, we can even say almost all anarchists, are themselves workers. But neither does this mean that the aim of anarchism is exclusively workerist, or that the triumph of the working class should necessarily lead to Anarchy. We do well to persuade ourselves that, unless I am mistaken, there is among the proletariat even a tiny, unhealthy part which is prey to overbearing, authoritarian or servile ways such as can be found among the bourgeoisie. Unless our anarchist will is able to prevent it, the victory of these elements could end up in new forms of domination which would in no way be desirable. The example of Russia can teach us something.

"Anarchism is also a human idea, the idea of all those, without exception, who want to destroy every form of violent and coercive authority of one man over another. By subordinating this idea to any class bias whatsoever, be it the old bourgeois bias or the more recent workerist bias – we would diminish it and in fact prepare the way for a dangerous psychology which would facilitate the formation (through revolution) of a new class domination."

For the authors of the Platform, the worst rejection for them was that of Malatesta, who they had recognised as a long-term proponent of organisational anarchism and who they deemed would be won over to their side. But in fact Malatesta was to say in his A Project of Anarchist Organisation in 1927 that whilst he found that the authors of the Platform had "excellent" intentions, and that until now the anarchists did not have an influence on political and social events in proportion to the theoretical and practical value of their doctrines, and that he approved of a more united, more enduring organisation, he believed that the Platform did not reply adequately to certain essential demands. These were "the blending of the free action of individuals with the necessity and the joy of cooperation which serve to develop the awareness and initiative of their members and a means of education for the environment in which they operate and of a moral and material preparation for the future we desire."

He quite correctly pointed out one of the flaws of the Platform document, that all anarchists could be grouped together in the same General Union.

The authors of the Platform had themselves stated that any idea of creating an organisation that united all the different tendencies was "inept". He balked at the idea of collective responsibility as advanced in the Platform, counterposing the idea of moral responsibility of each militant. In his reply to Malatesta the following year Makhno took him up on this, stating that only collective responsibility could allow modern anarchism to eliminate the false idea that anarchism could not be a guide, either ideologically or practically, for the mass of workers in a revolutionary period and therefore could not have overall responsibility. In his reply to Makhno the following year (it should be remembered that Malatesta was under house arrest and close scrutiny in fascist Italy and thus correspondence was tardy). Malatesta stuck by his repudiation of collective responsibility, saying that if the General Union of Anarchists was responsible for what each member does, how could it leave to its individual members and to groups the freedom to apply the common programme as they saw fit, and that the Union and through it the Executive Committee would have to monitor individual members and that no one would be able to act without the go-ahead from the Committee. He did admit that he accepted that anyone who cooperates with others for a common purpose must act responsibly and respect agreements that had been made. If that is what the authors of the Platform meant, then he would be in accord. However, he objected to the use of the term Executive Committee to give ideological and organisational direction to the organisation, fearing that this would mean a central body not dissimilar to Bolshevik centralism and thus a danger to the Revolution. As Skirda noted (Autonomie individuelle et force collective: Les anarchistes et l'organisation de Proudhon à nos jours, 1987, p.180). "It is certainly isolation and a problem of language that must have created this incomprehension with the veteran of the movement".

The old Kropotkinian Maria Isidine (Maria Korn) had at first welcomed the work of the Dielo Trouda group in calling for effective organisation. She then in her Organisation and Party herself opposed the idea of moral responsibility to that of collective responsibility. She, like Malatesta, also questioned the principle of majority decision, which would mean that dissenting minorities would have to abide by such a decision.

Arshinov replied to Isidine in his New and Old Elements in Anarchism in the November-December 1928 issue of Dielo Trouda. He deemed that Isidine was returning to an outmoded form of organisation, where anarchists did not have any real organisation but agreed ends and means by a common understanding. He considered that the problem of majority decision making was not a problem as "nearly always and nearly everywhere" minorities preserved their opinions but did not contravene the majority, "generally and voluntarily" they made concessions. Splits only happened when differences were very acute. Certainly, the General Union would let the minority have its rights to explain its positions. To illustrate this, Arshinov turned to the example of the Makhnovists as originally cited by Isidine, where anarchists in Russia and the Ukraine had different attitudes towards that movement. In fact, according to Arshinov, it "would have been more useful for libertarian communism and for the Makhnovist movement" if a collective decision, informed by meticulous study, had been arrived at, rather than the chaotic and unorganised position that prevailed in actuality.

The 'Platform' failed to establish itself on an international level, but it did have an effect on several movements. It was translated into Bulgarian, Italian, French and Spanish.

The Platform had quite an effect on the Russian movement, both in exile and in the underground movement in the USSR. In Russia it was defended by the veteran anarchist communist Vladimir Khudolei. Other supporters of the Platform inside the Soviet Union included the veterans Nikolai Rogdaev, Vladimir Barmash, Ivan Kharkhardin, and Alexei Borovoi. The latter had broken with individualist anarchism to become an enthusiastic Platformist. Others who defended the Platform included Alexander Pastukhov who had also evolved from an individualist position. In 1929 Pastukhov, together with Olga Andreevna, Vladimir Kozhukov, David Edetkin (Skitalets) and Vladimir Makaryants set up the underground group Union of Anarchist Workers (Soyuz Rabochikh Anarkhistov), heavily influenced by the Platform. Soviet repression extinguished the Platformist current and many of its supporters were shot or otherwise perished in the gulags.

In the USA, the Platform was supported by Russian exiles like Lazar Lipotkin and in Latin America the group around Alexander Cherniakov and David Elak-Berman.

In France, the situation was marked by a series of splits and fusions, the 'Platformists' sometimes controlling the main anarchist organisation, at other times forced to leave and set up their own groupings (see the section on French anarchist communism). In Italy the supporters of the 'Platform' set up a small 'Unione Anarcocomunista Italiana' which soon collapsed. In Bulgaria, the discussion over organisation caused the reconstitution of the Anarchist Communist Federation of Bulgaria (F.A.C.B.) on a "concrete platform... for a permanent and structured anarchist specific organisation... built on the principles and tactics of libertarian communism". However, the hard-line 'Platformists' refused to recognise the new organisation and denounced it in their weekly Probuzhdane.

Similarly, in Poland, the Anarchist Federation of Poland (AFP) recognised the overthrow of capitalism and the state through class struggle and social revolution, and the creation of a new society based on workers and peasants' councils and a specific organisation built on theoretical unity but rejected the 'Platform' saying it had authoritarian tendencies. They rejected the notion of a "transitional period" as developed in the Platform and concluded that "The major task of the AFP within the framework of the present order was the intensification of class struggle, the enlargement of the area of conflict by direct economic actions on the part of the revolutionary trade union organisations, the struggle against the political parties, against militarism. This declaration was recognised as binding for all existing active groups; it provided the sole basis on which newly formed groups could be accepted into the organisation. In this way the theoretical and organisational consolidation of the movement was attained and any future intrusion of undesired elements whose relation to anarchism was unclear, now became impossible" (History of the Polish Anarchist Movement 1919-29, published April 1930, https://www.katesharpleylibrary.net/f4qswj.)

In Spain, as Juan Gomez Casas in his "Anarchist Organisation - The History of the F.A.I." says "Spanish anarchism was concerned with how to retain and increase the influence that it had since the International first arrived in Spain". The Spanish anarchists did not at that time have to worry about breaking out of isolation, and of competing with the Bolsheviks. In Spain the Bolshevik influence was still small. The Platform hardly affected the Spanish movement. When the anarchist organisation the Federación Anarquista Iberica was set up in 1927, the Platform could not be discussed, though it was on the agenda, because it had not yet been translated. As J. Manuel Molinas, Secretary at the time of the Spanish-language Anarchist Groups in France later wrote to Casas "The platform of Arshinov and other Russian anarchists had very little influence on the movement in exile or within the country… The 'Platform' was an attempt to renew, to give greater character and capacity to the international anarchist movement in light of the Russian Revolution. Today, after our own experience, it seems to me that their effort was not fully appreciated."

The Platform was indeed translated into Spanish at the end of 1927 or the beginning of 1928 by the Prisma group of Spanish exiles in the southern French town of Béziers. There was also a partial translation of the Platform which appeared in the pages of La Protesta in Buenos Aires, with hostile interjections. Frank Mintz noted that: "particular conditions of the Iberian movement made discussion very difficult, that is to say inexistent. In exile, after the participation of certain anarchists in a coup de main, with the Catalanists, at the Spanish frontier in 1926, then the mobilisation for Sacco and Vanzetti, and the freeing of Ascaso and Durruti, without counting activities for Spain, one finds no echoes of the debate on the Platform".

Arshinov was soured by the reaction to the Platform and returned to the USSR in 1933. He was charged with 'attempting to restore Anarchism in Russia' and executed in 1937, during Stalin's purges.

The World War interrupted the development of the anarchist organisations, but the controversy over the 'Platform' re-emerged with the founding of the Federation Communiste Libertaire in France, and the Gruppi Anarchici di Azione Proletaria in Italy in the early 1950s. Both used the 'Platform' as a reference point (there was also a small Federación Comunista Libertaria of Spanish exiles). This was to be followed in the late 1960s and early 1970s by the founding of such groups as the Organisation of Revolutionary Anarchists in Britain and the Organisation Revolutionnaire Anarchiste in France.

References

L'Organisation: plate-forme d'Archinoff, la synthese de Sebastien Faure et Reflexions des groupes d'Angers at Malatesta de la F.A. Edition du Groupe Fresnes-Antony de la Federation Anarchiste (1980).

About the Platform. Errico Malatesta and Nestor Makhno 1927-1929. Wessex Solidarity (2009).

Fabbri, Luigi. About a Project for Anarchist Organisation: https://ithanarquista.wordpress.com/about-a-project-for-anarchist-organization-luigi-fabbri/

Chapter Twenty Nine
Anarchist communism in Britain
Prehistory

Thomas Spence

In Britain there was a parallel figure to Babeuf in 1792 in London. This was Thomas Spence, who had developed advanced views in Newcastle upon Tyne inside the Newcastle Philosophical Society. Within this rather genteel group, the plebeian Spence began to develop ideas of land communism expressed in his Plan. He first lectured on these ideas within the Society at the age of 25. "The land or earth, in any country or neighbourhood, with everything in it or the same, or pertaining thereto, belongs at all times to the living inhabitants of the said country or neighbourhood in an equal manner". He believed that each parish should take the land back into their possession and form themselves into corporations. The land becomes the property of the parish.

Spence in no way envisages the end of the money system. He pictures people paying rent to the parish for usufruct rights to the land. This rent would be paid into a parish treasury to support the poor and unemployed, and for the maintenance of lands and highways etc. The government, a democratic assembly of representatives, and elected by secret ballot, was seen by Spence as having limited functions, and would not meddle in the functioning of the parishes.

Spence chose to go beyond the gentlemanly hobbies of the Philosophical Society by disseminating his ideas through the publication of a halfpenny ballad in 1775-76. For this he was expelled from the Society, and subsequently lost his job as a teacher. Spence eventually resolved to go to London, because his radical ideas had little audience in Newcastle.

Spence's arrival coincided with the founding of the London Corresponding Society, set up by the shoemaker Thomas Hardy, and which consisted of tradesmen, shopkeepers and mechanics. The Society's aims were the discussion of parliamentary reform, and put forward demands for universal suffrage and annual parliaments.

Spence influenced members of the Society, among whom was Thomas Evans. He gathered a small group around him and began to propagandise the ideas contained within his plan. This included method of propagation similar to those of the Babouvists: chalk and charcoal notices on walls and public places, debates and public meetings, and the sale or distribution of handbills, broadsheets, tracts and pamphlets.

Spence was jailed several times for steadfast adherence to his ideas. His greatest period of activity was between 1792 and 1801 and he continued with intermittent publication of his ideas until his death in 1814. Evans and Allen Davenport formed a Spencean Society to propagate his ideas around 1807. With the death of Davenport Evans founded the Society for Spencean Philanthropists which continued with the propagation of Spence's ideas. The Spenceans were at the forefront of the working class demonstrations in London between 1815 and 1820. Some Spenceans were implicated in the Cato Street conspiracy in 1820. The repression which followed led to the disappearance of the Society and the extinction of the Spencean current, although his continuing influence on British radicalism should not be ignored.

Spence's emphasis was on land communism, and he saw "Private Property in land" as the main evil within society. The abolition of private property in land would of course mean the suppression of the aristocracy and "Lordship". However, goods, merchandise and cattle would not face similar communalisation.

Spence symbolises a radical current within the great movement that was emerging around Chartism and the demands for universal suffrage and annual parliaments. Spence expressly came to London to propagate his ideas there because he sensed that his ideas might have a certain resonance within this movement. The fact that he was not able to move beyond land communism to general communism is a result of the limits imposed by the class of artisans and "mechanics", of which he was an advanced spokesman, which was yet to develop into the working class.

Alongside his advocacy of land communism was the concept of a federation of parishes administering the economic process and with a system of social welfare. In this Spence prefigures the notion of the commune or municipality as the basic unit of society as developed by anarchist communist thinkers. Spence sees the parishes as providing public grain stores, free schools, libraries, public baths and hospitals. Spence was very wary of centralised State solutions to economic inequality and he believed that a bottom-up revolution was necessary which might well involve the use of physical force to overthrow the old ruling class.

Anarchist anthropologist and historian, Brian Morris has been instrumental in rescuing the important figure of Spence from obscurity. As he notes: "Neither the sans-culottes nor the enragés nor that much-neglected socialist Thomas Spence fully and explicitly articulated anarchism as a political doctrine. What they had in common was that they stressed local and popular democracy and were hostile toward big capital, whether of the merchant class or of the capitalist landlords. Their social idea was that of an egalitarian society consisting of independent artisans and small peasant farmers. Even Spence, though he advocated communal property in land, parish democracy, and parish militias.... allowed for a structure of provincial and national assemblies. Even so, like the sans-culottes, he tended to see the parish or local commune as the fundamental unit of society and sought any means to limit the power of the central government." (The sans-culottes and the enragés: libertarian movements within the French Revolution in Ecology and Anarchism, 1996, pp.101-02).

Spence needs to take his rightful place as one of the precursors within Britain of the libertarian communist current that was to appear with the emergence of the working class.

William Thompson

"author of the second great British libertarian book...". Max Nettlau

William Thompson was born into a well-off Anglo-Irish family of land owners and merchants in Cork in Ireland in 1775. Left some trading ships and a landed estate by his father in 1814 he proceeded to help the estate tenants with agricultural innovations and education for their children. Heavily influenced by the ideas of the Enlightenment, he was an enthusiastic supporter of the French Revolution.

At first Thompson was influenced by the utilitarian ideas of Jeremy Bentham with whom he began a correspondence, extending his letter writing to other utilitarians like James Mill. He was also influenced by his reading of William Godwin and Thomas Malthus. He wanted to transcend the limitations of these latter two thinkers by combining the "scientific" materialism of political economy with rational morality. He called this "social Science" and was the first to use this term.

This led him on to researching the role of distribution in political economy and he carried out studies in London. As a result, he produced his first book, An Inquiry into The Principles of The Distribution of Wealth. In the meantime, he had encountered the ideas of Fourier, Saint-Simon and the economist Sismondi.

In his initial book, Thompson contested the idea of the labour theory of value as put forward by Adam Smith, characterising the appropriation of the majority of surplus value as exploitation, and rejecting the views of both Mill and Malthus that an increase in the wages of workers would only end in their further immiseration. From a "demand for the full product of labour", as well as the regulation of distribution, he ended up with his own conversion to communism, that is, unlimited distribution," as the anarchist historian Max Nettlau observed.

Thompson then took on the socialist Thomas Hodgskin who in his Labour Defended, whilst agreeing with Thompson that the robbing of surplus value by landlords and capitalists should be classed as exploitation, believed that the way forward was through a reform of the system of competition. Thompson replied in his second book Labour Rewarded and developing the ideas of cooperative communism in response to Hodgskin's unequal wages.

Thompson paired his developing communism with an advocacy of contraception and a critique of the position of women in society. He was much influenced by the ideas of his friend Anna Wheeler, an advocate of political rights for women, equal opportunities in education and access to contraception.

Thompson's engagement with the newly emerging Cooperative movement in Britain led to his criticisms of the accepted leader of that movement, Robert Owen. He distrusted Owen's authoritarianism and autocratic behaviour. He was suspicious of his courting of rich patrons as he believed that the rich would never support any move towards emancipation by the working class. As a result, he gained a large hearing on the left of the movement which to distinguish it from Owen began to refer to itself as "socialist or communionist" (letter to "The Cooperative Magazine", London, November 1827, cited by the Oxford English Dictionary as the first documented use of socialist although Owen himself used the term in private correspondence five years earlier in 1822).

The differences between Owen and Thompson came into the open at the Third Cooperative Congress in London in 1832. Owen advocated governmental and capitalist investment in large cooperative communities whilst Thompson called for independent small cooperative communities relying on their own resources.

As well as developing the theory of surplus value, and that exploitation was fundamental to capitalism, Thompson rejected the view that the end of exploitation could come under capitalism. He also viewed the State as "the aristocratic law-making committee of the Idle Classes" and that in a future egalitarian society "almost all the occasions for the exercise of the ordinary functions of government would have ceased."

Thompson can thus be deemed as a pioneer of libertarian communism in Britain. Always dogged by ill health the further development of his ideas was interrupted by his death at the age of fifty-eight, five months after his confrontation with Owen.

Karl Marx had read Thompson, probably first being sent his work by Engels. He first mentions Thompson by name in his Poverty of Philosophy in 1847. There are further mentions of him in Marx's Critique of Political Economy in 1859 and in the first volume of Capital in 1867. Certainly, Marx must have been influenced by Thompson as they both employ the term 'surplus value' in the same sense.

Barmby

John Goodwyn Barmby was a British Owenite socialist who visited France in 1840 at the age of twenty with a proposal to set up an International Association of Socialists. A provisional committee was set up which included the Humanitaire Jules Gay. Nothing came of the venture but the attempt prefigured the setting up of the First International. It was probably through Gay and others that Barmby first discovered communist ideas and he claimed to be the first to use the term "communist" in English. In fact, he claimed to have invented the word "communism" and to have helped in the organisation of the Communist Banquet! He regarded "Communist" and "communitarian" as interchangeable. He reported regularly in the Owenite press on the phenomenon of French communism and the progress of the banquet. He must therefore be considered as the first person to introduce the terms "communism" and "communist" into the English language. Returning to England Barmby founded a Communist Propaganda Society. He set up a paper, The Promethean or Communitarian Apostle, later renamed the Communist Chronicle.

Barmby's communism was even more soaked in the syrup of religiosity than that of Cabet. Indeed, Barmby's saviour complex was much more pronounced and noticeable from an early period than Cabet's. He proclaimed the Religion of Communism and called himself the Pontifarch of the Communist Church. His concept of such a communist society was extremely hierarchical, one ruled by a Communarch and a Communarchess (presumably himself and his wife Catherine). This society would be based on the establishment of communal settlements known as Communitariums.

Early on he recruited the support of a radical Chartist and Owenite printer and journalist Thomas Frost. His schemes became even more bizarre and grandiose and he dreamt of establishing Heaven on Earth in the Channel Islands. Frost broke with him and established a rival paper, the Communist Journal whilst Barmby moved on to what he called National Communism, then became a Unitarian minister and ended up in liberal politics. Frost for his part went on to join the Fraternal Democrats in 1847. This had been set up in 1843 as an alliance of radical Chartists like George Julian Harney and Ernest Jones and members of the League of Just, formed of German workers, as well as radicals of Polish and other nationalities.

Barmby's antics only succeeded, to a certain extent, in discrediting the idea of communism in Britain. Unlike Cabet, who had galvanised a mass movement in France, he had failed to popularise it among artisans and workers, turning it into a freak side-show.

The founding years
The working class activists Frank Kitz and Joe Lane provided a link between the old Chartist movement, Owenism, the British section of

the First International, the free speech fights of the 1870s and the newly emergent socialism of the 1880s. Lane developed anti-state ideas early on, even before he came to call himself a socialist in 1881. A real power-house of an activist, he set up the Homerton Social Democratic Club in that year and attended the international Social Revolutionary and Anarchist Congress as its delegate. Kitz also attended as delegate from the Rose Street Club. Kitz met the German Anarchists Johann Most and Victor Dave there and was deeply influenced by them. With the help of Ambrose Barker, who was based in Stratford in east London, Lane and Kitz launched the Labour Emancipation League (LEL). The LEL was in many ways an organisation that represented the transition of radical ideas from Chartism to revolutionary socialism. The demands for universal adult suffrage, freedom of speech, free administration of justice, etc, sat alongside the demand for the expropriation of the capitalist class. The main role of the LEL was that it was to offer a forum for discussion and education amongst advanced workers in London, with seven branches in East London and regular open-air meetings in Millwall, Clerkenwell, Stratford and on the Mile End Waste. Nevertheless, anti-parliamentarism was already developing in the LEL.

The LEL succeeded in moving the Democratic Federation of Hyndman over to more radical positions. The intellectual and artist William Morris had recently joined this group and Lane was to have an important influence on him for several years. The organisation changed its name to the Social Democratic Federation. The autocracy and authoritarianism of Hyndman repulsed many members and a split took place in 1884. Morris, Belfort Bax, Eleanor Marx (Karl Marx's daughter) Edward Aveling and most of the LEL left to form the Socialist League. The new League itself contained both anti-parliamentarians and supporters of parliamentary action, who had been united by their opposition to Hyndman. A draft parliamentarist constitution inspired by Engels was rejected, but the divisions continued. One of the results of this was Lane's Anti-Statist Communist Manifesto, which had originally been a policy statement that had been rejected by the parliamentarist majority on the policy subcommittee.

Anti-Statist

The Anti Statist Communist Manifesto is not a brilliantly written or particularly well-argued document. Nevertheless, it stands as probably the first English home grown libertarian communist statement. It spends too long talking about religion. It rejects reformism through parliament or the trade unions. It calls for mass revolutionary action. In the Manifesto, Lane describes his ideas as Revolutionary Socialist or Free Communist. He never publicly used the word Anarchist to describe his politics, feeling that the word put too many people off, and wishing to distinguish himself from individualists. In private he was sympathetic to openly declared Anarchists and remarked about the Manifesto: "I do not claim that I have expounded anarchy; it is for others to judge". Lane must be considered as one of the most important pioneers of libertarian communism in Britain.

Whilst Anarchism was self-developing within the League, and attempting to achieve coherence, other developments were taking place. The veteran Dan Chatterton, who had participated in the Chartist agitations of 1848, produced his own Anarchist paper Chatterton's Commune – the Atheist Communistic Scorcher. This ran for 42 issues from 1884, produced in conditions of extreme poverty. Meanwhile one of the pioneers of Anarchist Communism, the Russian Petr Kropotkin, had arrived in Britain. Kropotkin's lectures to many Socialist League branches reinforced the Anarchist tendencies among many of its members. Charles Mowbray, a tailor from Durham, active in the London Socialist League, was one of the first to specifically call himself an Anarchist Communist. Kropotkin also helped set up the paper Freedom which was specifically Anarchist Communist. The Freedom Group also undertook the organisation of large public meetings and open-air public speaking. As a result, a number of workers, especially from the Social Democratic Federation, were won to Anarchist Communism, like the compositors Charles Morton and W. Pearson, whilst Socialist League members like Alfred Marsh and John Turner joined the Freedom Group. Regrettably, whist Socialist League branches distributed Freedom around the country there was a certain antipathy between the Leaguers and the Freedomites. As the Anarchist historian Nettlau was to remark, Kropotkin's failure to work within the Socialist League was: "regrettable, for in 1886 and 1887 the

League contained the very best Socialist elements of the time, men (sic) who had deliberately rejected Parliamentarianism and reformism and who worked for the splendid free Communism of William Morris or for broadminded revolutionary Anarchism. If Kropotkin's experience and ardour had helped this movement we might say today Kropotkin and William Morris as we say Elisée Reclus and Kropotkin... There was a latent lack of sympathy between the Anarchists of the League and those of the Freedom Group in those early years; the latter were believed by the former to display some sense of superiority, being in possession of definitely elaborated Anarchist-Communist theories... if both efforts had been coordinated a much stronger movement would have been created".

Progress

By 1890 Anarchism had made considerable progress within the League. In London there were two specific Anarchist Communist groups, one in St Pancras mostly formed from Freedom Group members, the other in East London, members of the Clerkenwell Socialist League in different hats, which produced the free handout the Anarchist Labour Leaf.

1888 saw the withdrawal of the parliamentarians from the League. There was still tension between those who like Morris, did not describe themselves as Anarchists but as free communists. This tension was aggravated by a pedantic approach among some of the League Anarchists. The Anarchists insisted too much on philosophical principle and not enough on social practice. Morris wrote: "I am not pleading for any form of arbitrary or unreasonable authority, but for a public conscience as a rule of action: and by all means let us have the least possible exercise of authority. I suspect that many of our Communist-Anarchist friends do really mean that, when they pronounce against all authority". The Anarchists H. Davis and James Blackwell were too ready to take issue with Morris's phrase "the least possible exercise of authority", failing to see that the 'public conscience' he proposed as the basis of Communism was the culmination of the voluntary principle in a society where it had become custom and habit. If Morris chose to call that a situation where authority was exercised then the dispute was semantic. (John Quail, The Slow Burning Fuse, 1978).

Morris's tendency felt that far more propaganda and education needed to be done before the Revolution could come about. Many Anarchists felt that mass action was in itself educational, transforming those taking part. Both were right, but only partially so. There should have been a dynamic dialogue between these two positions. This was not to happen. The dead-end of the advocacy of individual acts of 'propaganda by the deed' couched in fiery language meant the departure of Morris, not to mention Kitz and Lane. It also meant the infiltration of the movement by police agents, and a resulting clamp-down by the State. Some Anarchist Communists like Samuels were ferocious advocates of 'propaganda by the deed' others like Tochatti, were just as ferociously opposed to such tactics. The loss of Morris, the withdrawal of Lane and the temporary withdrawal of Kitz were a disaster for the development of libertarian communism in Britain. The Socialist League collapsed nationally.

Ruins

A number of specific Anarchist groups emerged from the ruins of the League. In fact, despite the repression, in the period 1892-94 the movement had a massive growth. For example, Morris had estimated the membership of the League in London as 120 in 1891. In 1894, Quail estimates the Anarchist movement in London as up to 2,000. (see work cited above). The 'bomb' faction had lost out, and the 'revolutionist' tendency was reaffirming itself. As a veteran of the League, David Nicoll was to say in the Anarchist which he brought out in Sheffield in 1894: "We are Communists. We do not seek to establish an improved wages system like the Fabian Social Democrats. Our work for the present lies in spreading our ideas among the workers in their clubs and organisations as well as in the open street". The revival was not to last. An attempt to unite the fragmented groups by James Tochatti and Louisa Sarah Bevington in 1895 – the Anarchist Communist Alliance – was stillborn and the movement was in definite decline by the following year. A period of reaction and lack of struggle within the working class as well as bitter internal conflicts was sapping the movement.

There was to be no revival till mid-1903. The growing industrial unrest, the growth of syndicalism and industrial unionism, were to be contributory factors to the refound vigour of the Anarchist movement. Examples of the returning strength of the movement can be seen in the secession of a group from the Social Democratic Federation in Plymouth, the majority of whom set up an Anarchist Communist group in 1910, and a similar secession from the industrial unionist Industrialist League in Hull in 1913. That year was to see considerable agitation in the South Wales valleys, where small propaganda groups were set up, called Workers Freedom Groups. At a meeting in Ammonford with 120 present, a Communist club house was opened. It was reported that: "The Constitution and programme of the Workers Freedom Groups have been shaped upon the model of future society at which they aim, namely Anarchist-Communism". A Workers Freedom Group was established in the pit village of Chopwell in Durham, by among others Will Lawther (later to be a right-wing miners' leader.) The Chopwell Anarchists also set up a Communist Club. Anarchists set up a Communist Club in Stockport in the following year. In London groups mushroomed and agitation was intense.

Here Guy Aldred, a young man who had started out as a Christian preacher, moving through secularism and then the Social Democratic Federation to Anarchism, began to attempt to synthesise his earlier Marxism with his Anarchism in 1910. He had set up a Communist Propaganda Group in 1907 and he now revived this, and helped set up several Communist Groups in the London area, as well as travelling regularly to Glasgow and helping form the Glasgow Communist Group there. He had serious criticisms of trade unions and had fallen out with the Freedom Group because one of its members, John Turner, was a leading trade union official. As Aldred noted: "...I gradually fell out with the Freedom Anarchists... Their Anarchy was merely Trade Union activity which they miscalled Direct Action. Their anger knew no bounds when I insisted that Trades Unionism was the basis of Labour Parliamentarianism."

But now the First World War loomed and its outbreak and repercussions were to have cataclysmic effects on the whole revolutionary movement, not least the Anarchists.

The War and its aftermath

The Anarchist movement, not just in Britain, but worldwide was shaken to its foundations by the news that Kropotkin and others were supporting the Allies against Germany and Austria-Hungary. To their credit, the majority of Anarchists took a revolutionary abstentionist anti-war position, including Freedom and the Spur, edited by Aldred. A fiercely active anti-war propaganda took place within the North London Herald League, where Anarchists worked alongside socialists from different organisations. This joint activity was reflected right across Britain. Indeed, the Anarchists were beginning to have a growing influence among the latter.

Aldred was to remark on the growing number of "Marxian anarchists" within the movement, who accepted a Marxian analysis of the State and of the importance of class struggle. These activists were becoming impatient with those, who to quote Freda Cohen of the Glasgow Anarchist Group, were satisfied with "fine phrases or poetical visioning". Alongside this was the heritage of Morris and his associates within the broad socialist movement, which was asserting itself within the Socialist Labour Party, the British Socialist Party, (the successor of the SDF) and the Independent Labour Party. Antiparliamentary ideas were re-emerging within these organisations – for instance, within the Socialist Labour Party, members were questioning the pro-parliamentary ideas of DeLeon who had founded the Party. Some left to become Anarchists.

An attempt was made to unite the Anarchists around Freedom and the Spur, edited by Aldred, with the anti-parliamentary dissidents of the SLP. This initiative came from within the SLP and at a unity conference in March 1919 the Communist League was founded, with a paper the Communist. In it George Rose was to remark: "we know that there must develop the great working class anti-Statist movement, showing the way to Communist society. The Communist League is the standard bearer of the movement; and all the hosts of Communists in the various other Socialist organisations will in good time see that Parliamentary action will lead them, not to Communist but to bureaucratic Statism... Therefore, we identify ourselves with the Third International, with the Communism of Marx, and with that personification of the spirit of revolt, Bakunin, of whom the Third

International is but the natural and logical outcome." Rose shows himself under the influence of Aldred, who looked for a fusion between Bakuninism and Marxism, in the process glossing over some fundamental differences. Indeed, an initial report in Freedom on the conference, whilst noting that the League was not an Anarchist organisation, remarked that the "repudiation of Parliament is a long step in our direction", but on the other hand there was a sharp exchange between Anarchists and League members over the idea of the dictatorship of the proletariat and economic determinism. At a Conference of London Anarchists, it was remarked that, "The anti-parliamentary attitude of many Socialists and Communists was greatly due to our propaganda in the past, and good results would undoubtedly follow if we worked with them". A resulting conference was very friendly in tone, although controversy over the dictatorship of the proletariat was not absent. However, this initiative of cooperation between revolutionary anti-parliamentarians was to evaporate when the Communist League disappeared without trace at the end of 1919.

The attempts at cooperation and unity continued however, although the whole process was clouded by the issue of the Russian revolution and support for the Bolsheviks. Aldred himself was at first a staunch supporter of the Bolsheviks, hardly surprising considering the lack of any hard information about Lenin's Party in Britain. (This was reflected in general ignorance in the revolutionary movement throughout the world). A series of critical articles by the Austrian Anarchist Ramus which were printed in the Spur in September 1919 were lambasted by Aldred and others, although in time he came to the same conclusions as he gained more solid information. Most revolutionaries, however were the slaves of wishful thinking, despite evidence that all was not well in Russia. This attitude, the unity-at-all-costs syndrome and "loyalty to the world revolution" position (translation = slavishly carry out whatever Lenin and the Bolsheviks tell you to do) was to have disastrous consequences for the British revolutionary movement. As Bob Jones says in his pamphlet Left-Wing Communism in Britain 1917-21: "There was, as happens repeatedly in the history of British socialism in the twentieth century, a complete abdication of critical judgement when basic principles and beliefs are put to the test by supposed friends and allies".

Despite the continuing growth of anti-parliamentarianism in both the SLP and BSP, Lenin was to insist that: "British communists should participate in parliamentary action... from within Parliament help the masses of the workers to see the results of a Henderson and Snowden government in practice". In practical terms this meant affiliation to the Labour Party and the call for a Labour vote, despite the (yes, even then!) reactionary role and nature of Labour. This position, which Anarchist Communists have consistently argued against in the 20th Century, is still very much an obstacle to the creation of a revolutionary movement in this country.

Sylvia Pankhurst

Anti-parliamentary communism had also developed inside the Workers' Socialist Federation (WSF). This had evolved out of the Women's Suffrage Federation based around Sylvia Pankhurst in the East End of London, above all in the Bow and Bromley districts. With her mother Emmeline and sister Christabel she had led a vigorous and militant campaign for votes for women. But differences developed between her and them over a number of issues, including Sylvia's emphasis for activity among the working class, and for joint action between working class women and men for common demands. This gap was widened by the War, which Emmeline and Christabel fiercely supported, whilst Sylvia came out in opposition. During the war the WSF were very active among the East London working class, setting up free or cut-price restaurants, day nurseries for children of working mothers, and distributing free milk for babies. In this period, it dawned on Sylvia Pankhurst that capitalism could not be reformed, but must be destroyed and replaced by a free communist society. She saw in the Russian revolution the model for a revolution based on workers councils, where committees of recallable and mandated delegates would be elected and answerable to mass assemblies of the working class. She rejected parliamentary action and the domination of leaders, calling for the development of self-organisation and self-initiative through class struggle. Indeed, at the time of the 1923 General Election when eight women M.P.s were elected she remarked: "Women can no more put virtue into the decaying parliamentary institution than can men: it is past reform and must disappear... the woman professional politician is neither more nor less desirable than the man professional politician: the less the world has of either the better it is for it... To the women, as to men, the hope of the future lies not through Parliamentary reform, but free Communism and soviets".

Unfortunately, like Aldred, Pankhurst was a headstrong and egotistical individual. Like him, she often put the narrow interests of her own group before that of the revolutionary movement as a whole. So, she and the WSF rejected a merger with the Communist League because the two organisations were too similar for that to be necessary! The WSF then in June 1919 transformed itself into the Communist Party. Lenin put pressure on the Pankhurst group to arrange talks with other groups for a unity conference, at the same time fearing the establishment of a Communist Party that had pronounced anti-parliamentary positions. In his attack on left and council communists Left Wing Communism: An Infantile Disorder he singled out Pankhurst, along with the Council Communists Pannekoek and Gorter. Another singled out was Willie Gallagher, who had left the SDF to join the Glasgow Anarchist Group in 1912. Gallagher, an admirer of Bakunin, was now a member of the Scottish Workers Council, which promoted 'communes'. In his pamphlet Lenin quoted Gallagher: "The Council is definitely anti-parliamentarian, and has behind it the Left Wing of the various political bodies". For his staunch anti-parliamentarianism (not so staunch as it turned out) Gallagher was chosen to represent the Scottish Workers Councils at the second congress of the Third International in Moscow. Gallagher pleaded with the delegates not to force on the Scottish revolutionaries: "resolutions which they are not in a position to defend, being contradictory to all they have been standing for until now." Lenin singled Gallagher and his associates out at this Congress, winning him over completely to his positions. From then on Gallagher was a loyal servant to Lenin, (and then to Stalin) working towards the establishment of a Communist Party of Great Britain which appeared in January 1921. The manoeuvres of Lenin and Gallagher were sharply attacked by Aldred in his new paper the Spur and by Pankhurst in the paper of the re-established WSF the Workers Dreadnought.

Pankhurst continued with her criticisms of Leninism. In 1924 she condemned the new rulers of Russia as: "Prophets of centralised efficiency, trustification, State control, and the discipline of the proletariat in the interests of increased production... the Russian workers remain wage slaves, and very poor ones, working not from free will, but under compulsion of economic need, and kept in their subordinate position by State coercion." The WSF was very close to the positions of the Dutch and German council communists, evolving increasingly Anarchist Communist positions by 1924, when it disappeared.

The collapse of the revolutionary wave of 1917-21, the Bolshevisation of the movement, and the repression of 1921, during which time Pankhurst and Aldred were both jailed, had taken its toll. Many had been won to Bolshevik positions, whilst many others dropped out including Pankhurst herself, ending up as a supporter of Emperor Haile Selassie of Ethiopia, with a burial in Addis Ababa.

The Anti-Parliamentary Communist Federation

The anti-parliamentary opposition to Lenin's positions coalesced around the Glasgow Anarchist Group and Aldred. It was to express solidarity with the Russian Revolution that this changed its name to the Glasgow Communist Group in 1920. This became the nucleus of the Anti-Parliamentary Communist Federation (APCF) set up in January 1921.

In many ways the APCF was an unstable alliance of those who accepted Anarchist Communist views and those who took a Council Communist position. Aldred and Co. still maintained illusions in the Russian Revolution up until 1924, flirting with the newly emergent Trotskyism for a while and launching attacks on Anarchist individuals and groups. As one member of the APCF in Leicester remarked in a letter to the editor of Freedom in 1924, Aldred was "running with Communism and hunting with Anarchism". Aldred also insisted on what he called the Sinn Fein tactic of running as an anti-parliamentary candidate with the promise of refusing to take his seat upon 'victory'. This was opposed in the APCF by Henry Sara, who left to join the Pankhurst group, and Willie McDougall and Jane Patrick. Other differences were over the question of economic determinism, with economic development as the motor to social change, and over the need for a transitional workers state.

The APCF had branches in London, the Midlands and North of England, although its base was primarily Scotland. It published the monthly The Commune from 1923-29. The seething differences over the use of anti-parliamentary candidates erupted in 1933 when Aldred left over these differences to form the Workers Open Forum.

Aldred claimed that the APCF stagnated after his departure. However, this is not true as the activity of the APCF continued unabated. Further splits were to come with the Spanish Revolution and Civil War. The APCF uncritically supported the Spanish anarcho-syndicalists of the CNT-FAI, the notion of anti-fascism with its unity at all costs message, and the false ideas of democracy versus fascism. They published, without comment or criticism, a statement by Federica Montseny, one of the chief Anarchist advocates of anti-fascist unity and Anarchist participation in the Spanish Republican government. Jane Patrick was one of the first to question these positions after her visits to Spain. She was disowned by the APCF, and went off to join Aldred's group, now called the United Socialist Movement. The uncritical attitude continued in the APCF, though it published several articles in its new paper Solidarity including a statement from the dissident Friends of Durruti group. A split took place in the APCF in 1937 when some Anarchists left in 1937 to set up the Glasgow Anarchist Communist Federation, although the reasons for this remain obscure. This evolved into the Glasgow Group of the Anarchist Federation of Britain, active during the Second World War.

The APCF for its part redeemed itself during the War by adopting a revolutionary defeatist position, with opposition to both sides. However as was stated in the Wildcat pamphlet on the APCF (1986): "... the APCF was too tolerant in allowing views fundamentally opposed to their own to appear unchallenged in the paper. These included at various times, pacifism, trade unionism, and 'critical' support for Russia". Wildcat also noted that: "The APCF also seemed to suffer from a lack of proper organisation. It appeared to be content to remain a locally based group, with no interest in trying to form a national or international organisation. It is sometimes argued that revolutionaries should only organise informally in local groups, to avoid the dangers associated with larger organisations... These dangers have to be faced up to, not run away from". These comments should be taken seriously by revolutionaries at the present time.

The APCF with Willie McDougall as its leading light transformed itself into the Workers Revolutionary League in 1942, eventually becoming the Workers Open Forum and continuing into the 50s.

As for Aldred and Patrick, their United Socialist Movement had become a populist organisation, espousing things like World Government and fellow-travelling with Russia after Stalin's death. As Nicolas Walter notes in (Raven No1.), Aldred was an: "extraordinarily courageous but essentially solitary man whose vanity and oddity prevented him from taking the part which his ability and energy seemed to create for him in the revolutionary socialist movement". Like Pankhurst, Aldred's egotism contributed towards hindering the development of a libertarian communist movement in this country, as did the differences between Anarchist Communists and Council Communists which were at first swept under the carpet and then totally polarised with no attempt to work out a practical synthesis.

Despite all this, the contributions of these groups and individuals were important. They courageously pursued revolutionary politics at a time of great isolation. They must be recognised as the forebears of present-day libertarian communism in this country.

Post war libertarian communism

A specific libertarian communist current did not re-emerge in Britain until the sixties and seventies. Anarcho-syndicalism was to be the dominant current within the Anarchist movement, alongside the newly emerging 'liberal' anarchism that was developing through the likes of people like George Woodcock. In one part, this was a response to the major defeats of both revolutionary Anarchism and the working class movement as a whole, in another part it was an uncritical adaptation to the rise of the anti-war movement (Committee of 100 and Campaign for Nuclear Disarmament). It was, of course, correct for Anarchists to aim their propaganda at mass movements, putting a revolutionary case against capitalism and the State as the root causes of war. What was lacking however was a theoretical strength that allowed for the recruiting of activists from C100 and CND that fought against the dilution of ideas and transformed these activists into fully-fledged revolutionaries. This was not the case, however, and the revolutionary core of Anarchism, already deeply affected by the erroneous ideas of the Synthesis as devised by Voline and Faure (which sought a fusion between individualism, syndicalism and libertarian communism within the same organisation) was further diluted in Britain. The development of the hippy and counter-culture movements was to further dilute and confuse the movement, as once again the Anarchist movement showed itself wanting in ways of relating to these movements on a revolutionary basis without surrendering to pacifism and marginalisation.

Solidarity

One healthy development was the group of activists who had been expelled from the Trotskyist Socialist Labour League of Gerry Healy in 1959, many of whom had served on its Central Committee. Revolted by the authoritarianism of Healyism, this group began to develop libertarian socialist ideas, continuing to base themselves on class struggle and class analysis. They began to edit a journal, Solidarity, from October 1960, as well as a flurry of pamphlets, at first on a monthly basis! They developed trenchant analyses of the industrial struggle as well as the peace movement, and their analysis of the unions was a huge step forward, as was their critique of syndicalism. As time progressed Solidarity began to identify themselves more and more as libertarian communists. However, they had developed a distrust of organisation as such as a result of their experiences of Healyism. Their unflagging publishing programme and their perceptive analyses had gained a great deal of respect among many activists. Their wilful failure to translate this into the establishment of a national organisation was a disaster, as International Socialism (the precursor of the Socialist Workers Party) was able to build on this territory abandoned by Solidarity (and by the Anarchist Federation of Britain). They failed to engage as fully with the Anarchist movement as much as they could have, as their contributions at meetings and conferences could have considerably strengthened the class struggle current within it. Finally, there was their use of the ambiguous term self-management (which could be open to a number of interpretations, including one involving a market society) and their assertion that the main differences in society were not so much between classes as between order-givers and order-takers. In the end the contents of the magazine became less and less distinguishable from the contents of Freedom, with, for example, long articles on Gandhi. Solidarity magazine stopped appearing in the early 1990s and the group came to a standstill – failing to live up to its promises of the 1960s.

The Organisation of Revolutionary Anarchists (ORA)

The Anarchist Federation of Britain (AFB) had slowly emerged in the aftermath of the political dead-end and decline of the Committee of 100 and the growing new radicalism of the 1960s, holding its founding conference in Bristol in 1963. There was an impressive list of group and individual contacts featured in Freedom. National conferences began to be organised that were well attended. Ostensibly, things looked very good indeed, with the potential for an Anarchist movement to grow and once again have some influence as the pre-WWI movement had. In reality things were far from rosy. Anyone could attend conferences, often to make contributions and then never to be seen again. There was no structure of decision-making, and therefore no decisions made at conference. There was no paper controlled by the AFB, and often groups loosely affiliated within it contained all sorts of 'anarchists' from individualists, pacifists and gradualists, lifestylists and agrarian communards, through to syndicalists and anarchist communists. No clear analysis could be developed because of the huge array of differing and opposing ideas. Indeed, the AFB only had an internal bulletin from late 1969.

The AFB was unable to respond to the huge potential offered to it, and began to drift. There was a massive exodus of activists to International Socialism (IS) and the International Marxist Group (IMG). A group emerged in the AFB around Keith Nathan and Ro Atkins, the former who had been a driving force in the very active Harlow Anarchist Group. This group produced a document called Towards a History and Critique of the Anarchist Movement in Modern Times as a discussion paper for a conference of Northern Anarchists in November 1970. Militants in Lancaster and Swansea (including Ian Bone, the future founder of Class War) also had criticisms of the AFB. The people in Swansea dropped out of the fray after their open letter was published, but their action had encouraged people in Lancaster, Leeds, Manchester and York to put a motion to the AFB that it call a "reorganisation conference" to discuss the criticisms raised" (from The Newsletter, bulletin of the ORA May 1971). The Critique and a joint statement produced by all the critics were taken from the conference to the AFB conference in Liverpool the same month. It should be pointed out that this critical current was made up of both anarchist communists and anarcho-syndicalists as well as those who had no specific identification other than Anarchist.

The Critique was a trenchant and deeply honest document. It is worth quoting at length on the state of the Anarchist movement: "the omission of an attempt to link present short term action with the totality of capitalist society and with the totality of the future alternative society, means that when the short term issue dies, as it will, then so does the consciousness created by this short term action. … bitter personal disputes based upon spuriously advanced positions; battles for the soul of the revolution / movement / Individual / reified anything, fought in reams of paper attacking and defending positions long since overrun by time. This is our 'theory'. Usually it totally replaces even the pretence of activity".

Ginger group

Following on from the Liverpool Conference the group in York decided to set up the Organisation of Revolutionary Anarchists to act as a ginger group within the AFB. The intention at this time was not to leave the AFB. It wanted the AFB to open its doors to other libertarian tendencies e.g., Solidarity. "… The ORA people do not want to form another sect – we see our role as acting within and on the libertarian movement in general, as well as initiating our own work… we hope it can act as a link and a catalyst not only for ORA and the AFB but also to all libertarians". (ORA Newsletter, see above).

ORA's objections to the traditional anarchist movement then, were more on the level of organisation than of theory. Their advocacy of collective responsibility, the use of a Chair and voting to take decisions at meetings, formal membership and a paper under the control of its "writers, sellers and readers" while warmly greeted in some quarters for example the May 1971 Scottish Anarchist Federation Conference was viciously attacked by others.

But the ORA itself was a hotchpotch including all sorts of anarchists, including syndicalists and those who argued for a pacifist strategy. When the ORA decided to bring out a monthly paper, Libertarian Struggle, in February 1973, it proved to be a forcing house for the development of the group, and these elements fell away. Also significant were contacts with the Organisation Révolutionnaire Anarchiste in France which had developed along similar lines within the Federation Anarchiste. Through the French ORA the British discovered the pamphlet the Organisational Platform of the Libertarian Communists.

The ORA produced a number of pamphlets and a regular monthly paper. At first this was lacking in theoretical content, in the main consisting of short factual articles on various struggles. Quite correctly, Libertarian Struggle gave extensive coverage to both industrial struggles and struggles outside the workplace, including tenants' struggles, squatting, women's liberation and gay liberation. By issue 8 a greater analytical and theoretical content emerged. For example, in an article on the Spanish Revolution of 1936 in Libertarian Struggle 1973 we can read about: "The failure of the anarcho-syndicalists who make a far too ready identification of their union with the working class as a whole. The way forward in a revolutionary situation is the rapid building of workers councils... union committees are no substitute for direct workers power". These anarchist-communist criticisms of anarcho-syndicalism were to be further developed within the libertarian communist movement over the years.

Similarly, the analysis of Labour was to be a consistent feature of British anarchist-communism over the following years. For example, we can read in Libertarian Struggle November 1973: "Only by carefully explaining and exposing the role of the Labour Party to the working class can any progress be made to building a revolutionary anarchist alternative... It cannot be done by first insisting we vote Labour". The Labour Party was defined as a bourgeois party.

On the unions, however, the ORA was not so clear. The criticisms of the union bureaucracies were clear enough, and this included the 'left' NUM leadership. Also clear was the call to create workers action committees leading to the establishment of workers councils. However, this was mixed up with calls to democratise the unions (!) and to democratise the various Rank and Files (all of which were International Socialism fronts).

Standstill

The events of 1974, the Miners' Strike and the three-day week, led many to think (falsely) that revolution was just around the corner. This led to the formation of the Left Tendency inside the ORA. They concluded that it was in the nature of anarchism that the attempts to form a national organisation were bound to fail, and turned to Trotskyism. Most of this group ended up in the horrific authoritarian Healyite outfit, the Workers Revolutionary Party (WRP), whilst others joined IS. Nathan himself, whilst not a supporter of the Left Tendency, also left at this time to join the WRP.

The Left Tendency had called for an elected Editorial Board rather than a paper edited in rotation by each group and for a "more coherent position on Ireland" among other things. The organisation came to a virtual standstill, as these members had been among the most active, and many others, who were not prepared to take on the workload, dropped out. Amongst those who remained, some took the initiative to revive the organisation. A limited edition (1,000) Libertarian Struggle was put out in November 1974 and sold out in ten days. There followed a period of recruitment and consolidation, until May 1975 when the paper began to appear again on a regular monthly basis.

The Anarchist Workers Association

At the beginning of 1975 ORA changed its name to the Anarchist Workers Association (AWA), which it was felt implied more of a class commitment, although others criticised this change as a mistake, implying workerism, and a too narrow obsession with the workplace. It was true that most of the membership in this period were heavily involved in workplace activity.

By 1976 the AWA had 50 members, most of them active, with three groups in London, groups in Oxford, Yorkshire, Leicester, and Scotland. The paper now called itself Anarchist Worker, was a regular monthly with sales of 1,500-2,000, mostly street sales. It was to some extent 'a libertarian version of Socialist Worker' but the coverage was wider, for example covering the struggles of claimants and squatters and provocatively questioning the work ethic.

The organisation went through a vicious split between spring 1976 and spring 1977. The Towards a Programme (TAP) Tendency was founded primarily to change the 1976 Conference decision on Ireland, where the majority, had argued for an abstentionist, anti-Republican position on Ireland, and that "Troops Out" was only meaningful if they withdrew through united class action. The TAP kept to the classic 'Troops Out' formula as well as the leftist "Self-determination for the Irish people as a whole". The TAP also argued for a less "ultra-left "position on the unions that is for "democratisation of the unions", "extend unionisation" etc. This tendency included Nathan who had returned to the fold.

The AWA did not have a tradition of political debate. Much of the debate there was conducted at a puerile level. The TAP tendency accused their opponents of "traditional anarchism" and wishing to "lead the AWA back to the days of the AFB" whilst the TAP tendency was accused by its opponents of "Trotskyism". The debate was clouded by controversy over the issue of abortion with a leading opponent of the TAP tendency taking an anti-abortion position., as well as some of the opponents of TAP (though only a small minority) taking increasingly anti-organisational positions.

Eventually at a conference in May 1977, on a motion sprung from the floor expulsions against the opposition to the TAP tendency was carried by two votes, with no prior notice or discussion at previous meetings or in the Internal Bulletin. Others left the organisation in disgust at these manoeuvres.

The expelled comrades committed to organisational politics regrouped under the title 'Provisional AWA' which then changed its name to the Anarchist Communist Association, producing a paper Bread and Roses and an introductory pamphlet to the ACA. The internal disputes had proved debilitating, however, and the ACA disappeared in 1980.

As for the TAP tendency and those others who remained in the AWA, the coming period was to be one of complete capitulation to leftism. The name of the organisation was changed to the Libertarian

Communist Group (LCG), there were defections to the International Marxist Group, and then the LCG announced that it had moved from class struggle anarchism to a "libertarian, critical, Marxism". The LCG backed "United Front Work" which in practice meant working in the Socialist Teachers Alliance, and the Socialist Student Alliance, fronts dominated by the IMG. This United Front work which in practice meant collaboration with leftist political formations, led to the LCG committing one of their most heinous errors – entering an electoral front set up by IMG called Socialist Unity (SU) and backed by other groups like Big Flame. Socialist Unity put up candidates where it felt they had the strength, and advanced the slogan "Vote Labour but Build a Socialist Alternative" where it did not. The LCG was supposed to be "critically" supporting SU, but failed to make any serious criticisms of this support for Labour. The SWP for their part, peeved by the SU running candidates, and perceiving this as a threat, decided to stand their own candidates. The LCG endorsed these candidates as well, completely forgetting all the criticisms it had made of electoralism and of the nature of the Leninist groups. Finally, after the IMG, in their usual fashion, got bored with SU as a way of recruiting, it was wound up. The LCG failed to deliver any post-mortem on this.

The end was soon to come. The LCG compounded these errors by supporting a slate run by an anti-cuts group called Resistance (Keith Nathan and friends) for council elections in Leeds.

Relinquished

The LCG moved for fusion with the "libertarian Marxist" group Big Flame in 1980. This organisation had been previously described in Anarchist Worker as "schizophrenic libertarians/Leninists": "Big Flame leads in uncritical copying of Lotta Continua in Italy, from their spontaneism to softness on Stalinism". For its part Big Flame was unable to withstand the instabilities of its politics. The 'left' "victory" orchestrated by Tony Benn in the Labour Party resulted in the collapse of Big Flame as most of its members decided to enter the Labour Party, where they eventually wound up as apologists for Neil Kinnock. The LCG had argued that they were "too small to give us an acceptable forum for political discussion" and that there were "no serious political differences between the two organisations". The LCG had relinquished any idea of constructing a specific libertarian communist organisation as well as any serious political analysis. But in any case, the politics of the LCG had transformed so much that there really was little difference between their leftism and that of Big Flame.

The Anarchist Communist Federation

The Anarchist Communist Federation (ACF) emerged shortly after the last great miners' strike in 1985. It coalesced around a merger of the Libertarian Communist Discussion Group (LCDG) and the independent 'Anarcho-Socialist' magazine Virus. The LCDG had appeared shortly before and was keen on building a Platformist-style organisation in Britain; an organisation built on class struggle and anarchist communist politics. One of its members had been active in the ORA/AWA/LCG. Virus then became the mouthpiece of the new organisation. It succeeded in gathering other militants around it, and attracted a small split from the anarcho-syndicalist Direct Action Movement, Syndicalist Fight. It became heavily involved in the Poll Tax struggle of the late 1980s, and produced two influential pamphlets on that struggle.

The ACF quickly moved away from explicitly calling itself Platformist, and from thence onwards only mentioned the Platform as a reference point, stating that much else had happened since 1926. It was hailed by one member as "a dramatic move forward, a significant development in both the strengthening and elaboration of Anarchist Communist theory, as well as an ongoing practice".

In 1999 it changed its name to the Anarchist Federation (AF), whilst still describing itself as anarchist communist. It became a member of the International of Anarchist Federations (IAF/IFA) and thus worked in this International alongside the Spanish FA, the French FA, and the Italian FAI.

In December 2018, a number of members left the AF and formed the Anarchist Communist Group (ACG) in February of the following year. It included three of the remaining founder members of the ACF. It felt that the AF has lost its direction and had become more like a synthesis organisation that orientated towards the anarchist 'scene'. It remains to be seen whether the ACG can orientate itself towards involvement in social movements as it desires, and which way the AF develops.

Conclusion

This history of the ORA/AWA/LCG/ACF/AF/ACG with its history of splits, defections and gross political errors is far from inspiring. But these developments, sometimes as unedifying as they were, signal the first attempts of libertarian communism to re-emerge in the post-World War II period. These attempts to re-emerge were as one member of the ACF noted in 1991 bound to be affected by the "present comparatively weak state of anarchist communism". Two "magnetic poles of attraction" would be at work, he went on to say. One would be Leninism, which would exert its influence through comrades moving physically and ideologically over to Leninist organisations, or adopting Leninist style politics whilst still professing to be within the revolutionary anarchist movement as happened with the LCG, and later with short-lived Anarchist Workers Group in the 1990s.

The other pole of attraction would involve comrades committing some of the errors associated with parts of the left communist milieu – spontaneism, refusal to construct a revolutionary organisation, and where theoretical elaboration was divorced from effective practice and intervention, and seemed to involve finding as many differences as possible between comrades.

References

Morris, Brian. Thomas Spence The agrarian socialism of Thomas Spence in Ecology & Anarchism, Images Publishing, Malvern Wells (1996).

Rudkin, Olive D .Thomas Spence and his Connections (1927).

http://richardjohnbr.blogspot.co.uk/2007/07/chartist-lives-john-goodwyn-barmby.html

Pankhurst, Richard. William Thompson (1775-1883): Pioneer Socialist. Pluto Press, London (1991).

Quail, John. The Slow Burning Fuse, Picador, London (1978).

Organise issue 42, publication of the Anarchist Communist Federation.

Chapter Thirty
Spain: a flickering flame

Anarchist communism reached Spain quite late, in comparison with other European countries. Spain had long been a stronghold of the anarchist collectivists and when anarchist communism did appear there, it was infected with ideas of propaganda by the deed.

At the Verviers Congress of the International in 1877, the Spanish delegates cleaved to anarchist collectivism and spurned anarchist communism. They regarded anarchist communism as too closely connected with what they regarded as the German conception of communism. They declared that: "We want the common ownership of the instruments of labour as well as the land for the community. But this gives autonomy to each community of producers and each receives according to his production. This conception however is not that of the German communists. For them it is the state which, like Providence, distributes to each according to his needs. This is a big difference. We cannot say that we agree with the German communists about the community" (Cahm, p.59).

When Costa had responded by insisting that communism meant that each person should decide for himself what he needed, not the State, the Spanish delegate José Viñas countered that this only meant that those who did not produce would be included in this scheme:" To each according to his will that is the wish to do nothing. Everyone must work to eat." The Spanish remained committed to collectivism and reaffirmed this commitment at the Spanish Federation congress in Barcelona in 1881.

When anarchist communism did appear in Spain it began to have consequences within the labour organisation set up by anarchists, the Workers' Federation of the Spanish Region (FTRE) which had been established in Barcelona on September 24th, 1881. This would contribute to the collapse of the FTRE in 1888, although the repression of the anarchist movement in the south and the harsh economic situation throughout Spain should also be taken into account.

Already in 1882 at the second congress of the FTRE in Seville, there was open controversy between the collectivists represented by Jose

Llunas Pujols of Barcelona and the anarchist communists represented by Miguel Rubio, (1837 until after 1904) a shoemaker of Montejaque in Andalusia. 1500 delegates, mostly from southern Spain, attended the congress, and there was a clash between those in work, organised in unions, and the Andalusian group of anarchist communists, who suffered from unemployment and hunger. They accused the collectivists of having bourgeois ideas of property and of social organisation, and of concentrating exclusively on the workplace, thus ignoring the 30,000 unemployed in Andalusia. Rubio also strongly advocated propaganda by the deed in response to the situation, which did not go down well with the national leadership of the FTRE or with those Andalusian workers struggling to organise in the workplace. Leading anarchist communist militants in Andalusia believed that they were being marginalised by the FTRE which devoted itself solely to unionism at a time when so many unemployed were facing starvation. Rubio accused Llunas and other Catalan leaders of being petty bourgeois politicians. He opposed the policy of land being divided into small plots and for the land and workshops to be held collectively, whether they belonged to the big landowners or small producers. Another anarchist communist, Vicente Daza from Madrid, argued that community decisions took priority over union autonomy. Dissent burst to the surface in Andalusia, and Rubio, Francisco Gago, Manuel Pedrote and other anarchist communists organised a secret meeting in Seville in September 1883, known as the Congress of the Disinherited, following their expulsion from the FTRE. They met again the following year, but as Temma Kaplan writes: "...their commitment to decentralisation, to each community's right to decide what to do, meant that there was very little coordination... Anarcho-communists' policy of support of terrorists does not mean that they were responsible for even a part of the violence aimed at the elite. They merely accepted the validity of a popular tactic already being used by the poor against the rich" (p.143, Kaplan). By this Kaplan means such developments as El Mano Negra (The Black Hand) a clandestine group of agricultural workers which organised attacks on landowners.

Rubio, the first Spaniard to be identified as an anarchist communist, appears to have had a knowledge of the Italian language as he later appeared as the Barcelona correspondent for the paper run by Pietro Gori, Sempre Avanti! (Forever Forward!) in Livorno in 1892-23. It is possible he acquired his anarchist communism from reading of the development of anarchist thought by French and Italian Internationalists, and much less possible that he developed these ideas independently. He did later claim that he had concluded that anarchist communism was a logical development of collectivism, the 'all for one and one for all' in the Alliance's programme.

Meanwhile anarchist communism began to develop in Barcelona in 1883, due on one hand to publicity about the Lyon trial of anarchist communists and on the other to the activity of exiled Italian anarchist communists in the city. This was reinforced by the Swiss revolutionary journalist Georges Herzig arriving there the following year and propagandising for anarchist communism for some time. This led to the Grupos Comunistas Anarquistas de Barcelona issuing a manifesto in 1885.

The French anarchist communist paper, Le Forçat du Travail (Slave Labourer) – subtitled Organe Communiste-Anarchiste – lists a number of individuals and groups in Barcelona in 1885. Among these were probably Francesca Saperas and her companion the shoemaker Martin Borras, later well known as Spanish anarchist communists. There is also evidence of an intervention by anarchist communists at the Cosmopolitan Congress held there in that year. This congress was meant to break the isolation of Spanish anarchists and to strengthen the collectivist current through a debate with anarchist communists. It was virtually ignored by anarchist groups outside Spain, apart from a few foreign delegates. The Grupo Anarcocomunista of Barcelona, comprised of Italians, was recorded as being present.

In 1886 the anarchist communists were able to initiate their first large scale propaganda venture, with the appearance of the paper La Justicia Humana (Human Justice). Those involved included Francesco Labrador, Victoriano San José, Emilio Hugas, Martín Borràs Jover and Jaume Clarà – the so-called Gràcia Group after the Barcelona neighbourhood where they were active. The Italian anarchist communist Fortunato Serantoni, then in exile in Barcelona, also appears to have contributed to La Justicia Humana.

The paper vaunted "spontaneous organisation" and the promotion of affinity groups. Eight numbers came out, the last one on November 25, 1886. On June 2, 1888, its successor Tierra y Libertad would appear, which would have more luck in the diffusion of anarchist communist ideas. The paper was initiated by Martin Borras, who had been converted to anarchist communism from collectivism by a meeting with Malatesta, , and by Emilio Hugas. He was aided in this by his partner Francesca Saperas. The director was Sebastian Suñér and the paper appeared fortnightly for 23 issues, doing much to strengthen the anarchist communist affinity groups. Suñér was from a wealthy family and had moved from anarchist collectivism to anarchist communism. He later became a pacifist free-thinker, rejecting the class struggle and calling for peace between the classes. During the Spanish Revolution of 1936, he once more returned to supporting the libertarian workers' movement.

In 1887, Jaume Clarà, one of the leading figures of anarchist communism in Barcelona, wrote in the French anarchist communist paper La Révolte that the anarchist communists had decided, after the end of La Justicia Humana to create a new newspaper, and that they recognised that "many foreign comrades had demonstrated to us for a long time the desire to see in Spain anarchist communist propaganda rise to the level of other regions". As a result, it had been decided to found an organisation to defend these principles.

La Révolte had been attacking the FTRE since 1885 over what it regarded as its authoritarian trade union structure. This was echoed by the Gracia anarchist communists who used Tierra y Libertad as a vehicle for their attacks. They believed that the FTRE's commissions were redundant and that the formal procedures developed by the Federal Commission and the local federations acted to impede the revolutionary movement. They also insisted that the revolutionary spirit of Spanish workers would be wasted in strikes they regarded as reformist. The structure of the FTRE needed to be replaced by a new form of organisation that matched up with anarchist communist ideas.

In between the closure of La Justicia Humana and the appearance of Tierra y Libertad there was a project to produce pamphlets of translated texts on anarchist communism. In 1888 the Biblioteca Anarquico-Comunista based around the Gracia group, continued to produce such texts right up until 1896 with the publication in Spanish of Kropotkin's Conquest of Bread.

Nettlau describes these anarchist communists as being ferociously opposed to collectivism, initiating a similar response in the collectivist camp. In the resulting controversies the FTRE was replaced by a specific anarchist organisation, the Anarchist Organisation of the Spanish Region (OARE) set up at one of the last congresses of the FTRE in Valencia in September 1888. The OARE was meant to include all revolutionary anarchists 'without distinction between methods or economic schools' and to give the Workers Societies of Resistance to Capital (Sociedades Obreras de Resistencia al Capital) a revolutionary orientation and as such presaged the later role of the Federacion Anarquista Iberica (FAI) in relation to the Confederacion Nacional de Trabajo (CNT). As mentioned, the OARE was meant to be open to all anarchist tendencies, but in practice and indeed in theory the OARE was a communist organisation. The only structure of the FTRE that continued in the new organisation was the administrative council, the Centro de Relaciones y Estadisticas (Centre of Relations and Statistics) which had no executive powers and acted as a liaison between the various local and regional bodies. As a result of the end of the FTRE, anarchist communist ideas now began to triumph within the Spanish movement. This was not due to the increasing numerical strength of the anarchist communists, but to an alliance with the Catalan syndicalists, many of whom remained collectivist after the Valencia congress, but who were equally opposed to the existence of the FTRE, and who also shared the idea of the decentralisation of the anarchist movement. The OARE itself, which had no statutes or rules, disappeared the following year in 1889.

The propaganda of Kropotkin, Reclus, Grave and Malatesta was used to spread the influence of anarchist communism in Spain. Kropotkin himself seemed quite insensitive to the debilitating effects of the quarrels between the communists and the collectivists in Spain, but he came round to supporting the compromise arrived at in Valencia, even though he believed that anarchist communist ideas would triumph in the end. Malatesta, on the other hand, was concerned about these rifts in the Spanish movement. His aim was always unity between revolutionaries of different currents and he was troubled by the hardline attitudes that manifested themselves on both sides.

The anarchist communists formed many grupos de affinidad (affinity groups) or grupitos (little groups) which alongside other elements within the Spanish libertarian movement – workers circles, workers centres, choirs, singing groups, orchestras, etc., and the development of evening classes and free schools – was one of the mainstays of the Spanish movement. As one anarchist communist paper wrote: "when one wants to carry out a revolutionary act of propaganda etc., it is in the group that he will find others with whom he can easily establish the intimate relationships which are needed for its execution". The group also corresponded to their concept of free social organisation. The Spanish anarchist communists rejected the collectivist concept of formal union between the respective federations and vaunted the total autonomy of the groups. This led on to bombing attacks in the late 1880s and the 1890s being carried out by such groups. These acts jarred with the pragmatic activities of the other groups mentioned which sought to create a culture of resistance which would replace capitalism.

Anarchism Without Adjectives

Some anarchists attempted to resolve the disputes between the different tendencies. Some Barcelona printers produced a magazine called Acracia (Without Rule) which had a non-denominational outlook. This was rejected by Clara and others around Tierra y Libertad, saying that the term "acracia" was vague and confusing. When Acracia stop publication in 1888, this nondenominational anarchism was continued by various intellectuals grouped around the circle of Antonio Pellicer. They formulated the concept of anarquismo sin adjectivos (anarchism without adjectives – henceforth referred to in this book as AWA). One meaning of the term referred to an anarchism without any qualifiers like communism, collectivism, mutualism or individualism. Another meaning was simply a stance that looked favourably on the coexistence of the different currents. In some ways these concepts presaged the development of the idea of the Anarchist Synthesis as developed by Voline and Faure in the 1920s.

The engineer and professor of mathematics Fernando Tarrida del Marmol was the originator of the term anarquismo sin adjectivos. From a bourgeois background, Tarrida became involved in the working class movement in Barcelona and described himself as an anarchist collectivist. He accepted Antonio Pellicer's views that anarchism could be represented by different economic systems. He believed that there should be peace and accommodation between the collectivist and communist currents.

La Révolte responded strongly in a series of articles, saying that the Spanish movement had not broken with collectivism, and that this predisposed it to adopt authoritarian forms of organisation. Tarrida argued that it was impossible to predict what a new anarchist society would be like and that anarchism should be seen as an axiom, and that the economic question was only of secondary importance! He also argued that a foreign style of anarchism, meaning anarchist communism, was being imposed on the Spanish. He quite rightly emphasised the powerful traditions of association among Spanish workers, and that the circles, workers' centres and ateneos developed by them should not be denounced as authoritarian, as the anarchist communists were doing. Like the anarchist communists and indeed the Catalan syndicalists, Tarrida was opposed to the FTRE which become increasingly bureaucratic, but there was a need to distinguish between the FTRE and forms of organisation that were organic and based on the grassroots. Tarrida's Anarchism Without Adjectives at first only attracted a few disciples within the Spanish movement.

Ricardo Mella, on the other hand used AWA to attack the polarised debate between collectivists and communists. However, he remained a staunch collectivist and was strongly opposed to the anarchist communists, caricaturing to some extent their positions, by stating that there would be "no more peaceful or serious action; no more assemblies, meetings, literary contests, periodicals, journals, pamphlets, or books". Despite avowing that he wished to end the acrimonious debate between collectivists and communists, he contributed to it. He was never able to see that communism need not be authoritarian and reiterated the old collectivist arguments like: "Who will work to the fullest of his abilities once it is known that the remuneration of work, whether one works a great deal or just a little, will be proportional to one's needs, a ratio that could be either directly or inversely related to work?" Mella's attitude towards anarchist communism was to soften over the years, to the extent that he wrote a foreword to the Spanish translation of Kropotkin's Modern Science and Anarchism, but he was never fully convinced of the validity of anarchist communism.

Kropotkin was to reply to such collectivist criticisms of anarchist communism that "Collectivists begin by proclaiming a revolutionary principle – the abolition of private property – and then they deny it, no sooner than proclaimed, by upholding an organisation of production and consumption which originated in private property. They proclaim a revolutionary principle, and ignore the consequences that this principle will inevitably bring about. They forget that the very fact of abolishing individual property in the instruments of work – land, factories, road, capital – must launch society into absolutely new channels; must completely overthrow the present system of production, both in its aim as well as in its means; must modify daily relations between individuals, as soon as land, machinery, and all other instruments of production are considered common property." (The Conquest of Bread). Max Nettlau was to write in An Anarchist Manifesto (1895): "One of the stock objections against Anarchist Communism is that no one would work. We reply that today work is viewed with disfavour and neglected by all who can possibly exist without it because it has to be carried on under the most disadvantageous conditions and is, moreover, looked upon as degrading. The worker earning his food by hard labour and ceaseless toil is a pariah, the outcast of society, while the idler who never does an hour's work in his life is admired and glorified, and spends his days in luxurious ease amongst pleasant surroundings. We believe that under Anarchism everybody would be willing to work; work being freed from the badge of dishonour now associated with it will have become a labour of love, and the free man will feel ashamed to eat food he has not earned."

The theory of AWA was to influence the Spanish movement to a greater and greater extent, contributing to its failure to reach theoretical clarity and to the disasters of 1936 and the entry of some Spanish anarchists into government. It influenced people who saw themselves as part of the Spanish anarchist movement like Federico Urales (alias Juan Montseny) and his daughter Federica Montseny, essentially individualists and radical liberals. Outside of Spain it influenced people like Malatesta, Reclus and Nettlau who regarded themselves as anarchist communists but who turned towards the theory of AWA because they felt that the movement was harmed by sectarianism between the different currents. In the case of Nettlau it led him to advocate a compromise between communism and individualism, and to further theoretical confusion within the international anarchist movement.

After 1892 under the influence of the anarchist communist current, the Spanish movement turned away from labour organisation and increasingly towards propaganda by the deed, by now understood as individual attacks on members of the ruling class and to a period between 1892 and 1896 which saw an increasing intensity of these attacks and a corresponding government response of increasing repression. The anarchist communist paper El Eco de Ravachol was to declare: "Force is repelled by force, and that is why dynamite was invented". The anarchist communist grupitos enthusiastically followed this line of action.

The collectivists, whilst recognising that revolutionary violence was necessary, rejected the extreme use of propaganda by the deed. Some anarchist communists like Pedro Esteve also supported this view.

The Jerez uprising in 1892 originated in the repression of the anarchist and workers' movements in Andalucía. In response thousands of workers turned out on May Day in Cadiz. Shortly after, two bombs exploded in that city, killing one worker and injuring others. This served as an excuse for the authorities to arrest 157 anarchists, including the notable militant Fermin Salvochea, who insisted that the bombing had been the work of agents provocateurs. Despite this, he was linked to the events of 8th January 1892 in Jerez when several hundred workers marched through the city, with the slogans of "Viva la Revolucion! Viva la anarquia!". The crowd intended to open the city jail and free the prisoners there, many of them political prisoners. This they failed to do, and shortly the forces of order were reinforced by a cavalry regiment. Over the next week, many workers were arrested, including many leading anarchist militants in Andalucía. Four were garrotted on 10th February, whilst Salvochea, who had been in prison throughout, was sentenced to 12 years imprisonment for being the mastermind of the uprising.

The authorities pushed their version of the incident as a planned anarchist conspiracy, whilst the anarchists upheld the notion that it was a spontaneous uprising impelled by the appalling conditions that both urban and agrarian workers suffered in Andalucía.

The execution of the four anarchists brought on a wave of retaliatory attacks. The anarchist communist Paulino Pallas attempted to kill the capitan general of Catalonia, Arsenio Martinez de Campos, by throwing a bomb under his carriage. Martinez de Campos was only wounded, but two others were killed as well as serious injuries being inflicted on twelve soldiers and bystanders. Pallas was executed on 6th October 1893. Santiago Salvador French reacted by hurling two bombs into the audience of wealthy opera patrons at the Liceo theatre in Barcelona, resulting in fifteen deaths and many injuries. Salvador had acted alone, but the police refused to believe his avowals, and other anarchists were rounded up, confessing to involvement in the bombing under savage torture. As a result, six anarchists were executed, and four others sentenced to life. Salvador himself was executed on 2st November 1894. Martin Borras was one of those arrested, eventually killing himself in Montjuich prison on 9th May 1894.

The repression that followed included the closure of all anarchist papers, including those opposed to the line of propaganda by the deed like La Tramontana and El Productor. The repression also resulted in the exile of numerous anarchist militants, many of whom fled to the Americas, including Pedro Esteve. However, in 1895 Francesca Saperas and Luis Mas managed to found a new anarchist communist paper La Nueva Ideal.

As if the waves of repression after Jerez and the Pallas attentat were not enough, a bomb was thrown into the Corpus Christi religious procession in Barcelona on 7th June 1896, killing at least six and wounding forty five. Whether this was a State provocation or an act carried out by a lone anarchist remains obscure to this day. A ferocious wave of State repression followed. Not only anarchists were arrested but freethinkers and republicans and anyone deemed sympathetic towards anarchism. Around 300 anarchists were arrested and many in the end deported to horrendous prison camps in Africa without trial. Eighty seven were put on trial after having suffered horrendous tortures in Montjuich castle in Barcelona. One militant, Luis Mas, was driven insane under these torments. This resulted in an international campaign in solidarity with those imprisoned, then followed by a movement against these State atrocities in Spain itself. In the end five anarchists were executed, whilst of the remaining who were prosecuted, only twelve were acquitted, the rest receiving eight to twenty years of hard labour. Among those executed were Luis Mas and the new partner of Saperas, Tomas Ascheri Fossatti. No clear evidence ever appeared about who exactly had thrown the bomb.

This series of events seriously damaged the anarchist communist movement in Spain. Borras, Mas and Fossatti had been executed, many others imprisoned, and many more like Saperas were forced into exile. It also ended the wave of attentats carried out by anarchist communists in Spain. The anarchist movement in general was seriously affected with practically all their newspapers closed down, as well as many of the different types of associations set up by them.

The movement did not revive until the early years of the 20th century, with the release of those imprisoned as a result of the Jerez uprising. Anarchosyndicalism emerged as the main current within Spanish anarchism, and attentats and bomb attacks were increasingly seen as an outmoded and bankrupt tactic, with the general strike being now seen as the major weapon of the working class.

In 1899 Tierra y Libertad was revived in Madrid but this time under the control of Urales. In 1906 it was removed to Barcelona, after protestations about Urales' personalised editorship, where it came under the control of the anarchist communists Francisco Cardenal and Juan Bason (or Bassons) wrongly referred to as Baron in Bookchin's the Spanish Anarchists, and Antonio Loredo. They were associated with the Grupo 4 de Mayo and Tierra y Libertad thus became an organ of the anarchist communist affinity groups. This represented the remnants of the old anarchist communist movement, now depleted by deaths and exile. Due to lack of funds, they had had to abandon their centre and meet in the offices of the newspaper. They regarded the anarchosyndicalists as reformists. As Bookchin says, they "held faithfully to the communist doctrines that formed the basis of the old Anarchist Organisation of the Spanish Region. They were not disposed to trade union activism and stressed commitment to libertarian communist principles. It was not their goal to produce a large 'mass movement' of workers who wore lightly the trappings of libertarian ideals, but to help create dedicated anarchists in an authentically revolutionary movement, however small its size or influence."

Cardenal was from a wealthy family but, converted to anarchism, he had learnt a trade as a draughtsman and later was involved in setting up a rationalist school. He was associated with the Fourth of May Group in Barcelona, alongside militants like Mariano Castellote, Obispo, Magin and Roman. During the general strike of 1909 he was arrested for carrying out agitation in the Drassanes neighbourhood of Barcelona. He was again arrested in 1911 in Madrid for incitement to the general strike. Imprisoned under the Primo de Rivera dictatorship, his health was seriously affected and he died in Barcelona in 1925.

The anarchist communists viewed the 1907 founding of a new libertarian workers federation, Solidaridad Obrera (Workers' Solidarity), in Catalonia, with suspicion. Founded by anarcho-syndicalists and revolutionary syndicalists it would become the base of a new libertarian mass movement. At first it included the Catalan Socialists but an ideological combat inside Solidaridad Obrera led to their withdrawal. The events of the Tragic Week in Barcelona, sparked by the war in Morocco, in July and August 1909, led to the usual reprisals, the execution of five anarchist militants including the radical educationalist Francisco Ferrer, and the imprisonment of many others. The repression also caused the temporary numerical decline of Solidaridad Obrera, with the departure of many of the "moderate" leaders and a strengthening of revolutionary anarchism within it. On October 30th 1910, a decision was taken to set up a national labour confederation, the Confederacion Nacional de Trabajo (CNT). The old veteran Anselmo Lorenzo, "the grandfather of Spanish anarchism" made overtures to the anarchist communists to join this new organisation. As a result, the groupings around Tierra y Libertad felt a growing need to join a labour organisation that was taking on a mass character and to defend revolutionary ideas within it.

Despite a commitment to libertarian communism and great efforts to function in a libertarian way, the CNT was never a fully anarchist organisation. One of the more moderate syndicalist leaders, Angel Pestaña, was to, probably correctly, describe the CNT as having only a third of its membership which could be called anarchist, the rest being militant and class-conscious workers looking for an effective organisation or joining because it was the strongest labour organisation in their area or workplace.

The entry of the anarchist communists into the CNT as well as the pernicious influence of the antiadjectivistas (supporters of AWA) resulted in an interpenetration between anarchosyndicalism and anarchist communism. To the point where only the expressions "anarchist" or "libertarian" were employed.

This was further reinforced by the founding of the Federacion Anarquista Iberica in 1927. It was meant to unite the two currents. The anarchosyndicalists were mollified by the fact that members of the new organisation also had to be members of the CNT whilst the anarchist communists were gratified that they had created a new national organisation, ready to do combat with those in the CNT they regarded as reformists and to steer the CNT in a more libertarian direction. Tierra y Libertad became the voice of the network of FAI groups. The goal of libertarian communism was affirmed by the FAI, although there was a fudge over compatibility between anarchist individualism and anarchist communism, surprising since individualism was always a tiny and marginalised current within the Spanish libertarian movement. In many ways the FAI was the completion of a process that had started with the OARE. Like the OARE the FAI was a loose network of affinity groups, with no membership cards, no dues, no organisational discipline with each group doing what it thought fit with no reference to the other FAI groups. It could not in all truth be defined as a specific anarchist communist organisation, more a loose network of affinity groups. Nevertheless in Spanish anarchist parlance the FAI was referred to as the Especifico (the specific organisation).

The Faistas pushed the CNT into adopting libertarian communism as its goals. The country doctor Isaac Puente, a member of the Peninsular Committee of the FAI, was tasked by that Committee with producing a statement on 'comunismo libertario' which appeared in 1933. Puente had produced Apuntes sobre el communismo libertario shortly after the January 1932 rising which, although a failure, had re-enthused rank and file workers within the CNT. The pamphlet proved immensely popular and was republished in 1935 under the tile Finalidad de la CNT: el communismo (The goal of the CNT: libertarian communism). Puente correctly sees the working class as the motor of revolution and is not influenced by vague notions of 'humanity' like some Spanish anarchists like for example the Revista Blanca group around Urales. He sees the State and capitalism as the twin enemies of the proletariat. He attempts to synthesise anarcho-syndicalism and anarchist communism by stating that the union and the free municipality will be the joint building blocks of libertarian communism.

It was Puente's formulations, rather than the 'scientific' economic theories of Diego Abad de Santillan, that won the day at the Saragossa conference of the CNT in 1936 when libertarian communism was indeed adopted as the goal of the confederation. Santillan had moved to Spain from Argentina, and had renounced the politics of the FORA.

Whilst Abad de Santillan talked about an alliance between workers, scientists and intellectuals, Puente reaffirmed the creativity and intelligence of the working class, with a distrust of the "intellectual aristocracy". The pamphlet suffers from a lack of an internationalist outlook, with Puente's views that an autarchic libertarian communist society could be established in Spain, without the need for international revolution.

Puente rejects the idea of a revolutionary and post-revolutionary elite and of a transitional period. He follows in the anarchist communist current in positing the commune as the organism to create control of a new society, but believes that this is only possible in villages and small towns.

However, like Besnard in France, Puente believes in the survival of the unions after the social revolution and that these unions will organise economic life, in large cities. As the French Groupe Communiste-Anarchiste Errico Malatesta (1997) note: "The only instance of the management of production in a future society must be the consumers themselves. Production units cannot be managed by themselves. Their sole purpose is to meet the needs of consumers, of which the producers themselves are a part. The appropriation of the means of production even by a structure of workers would exclude from its management cogs an immense majority of people dependent on their needs. This state of affairs necessarily refers us to the idea that a society organised around the economy cannot dissociate itself from a certain centralism, where only a few well-placed individuals can determine the needs of all."

Santillan's proposals developed in his text The Economic Organism of the Revolution totally reject the concept of free communes on the grounds of economic localism. He criticises Kropotkin for this, and describes the commune idea as a "reactionary utopia". Like Besnard, he puts forward the idea of a society rigidly controlled by the structures of the syndicalist unions. He sees libertarian communism as a transitional stage towards full anarchy and communism, which permits a break with communist principles of distribution (to each according to their needs) towards collectivism (to each according to their work).

Puente's pamphlet was based on both experiences of the January 1932 uprising and on the ideas of Kropotkin. Indeed, Kropotkin's writings in translation were immensely popular among Spanish anarchist peasants and workers, so much so, that according to the German anarchist Augustin Souchy, some illiterates had learnt how to read in order to access Kropotkin.

Puente was to take part alongside Durruti and Cipriano Mera in the committee that organised the Aragon uprising in December 1933. As Miguel Foz, a participant in the uprising wrote: 'Comrades carried out their task of burning the property archives, the church and municipal records, etc... A public announcement abolished thenceforth the circulation of money... We lived for five days under libertarian communism, relying on the loyalty of the village and the apprehensiveness of the enemy. Some of our opponents came before the unions to ask, in full assembly, for explanations of the meaning of libertarian communism, and some of them came over spontaneously.'

The FAI successfully resisted the penetration of the newly formed Communist Party into the CNT and forced many of the reformist leaders to either quit the confederation or to lie low. But this had come at the price of a submersion within syndicalism. The intervention of the FAI within the confederal movement undoubtedly radically politicised many in the working class base of the CNT, but the reformists were never completely eradicated from it. As Peirats noted, the FAI was prepared to compromise with the reformist leaders within the CNT in order to maintain its control over the confederal organisation. This was to inevitably lead to the compromises that not only leading lights in the CNT but also in the FAI made during the Spanish Revolution and Civil War with bourgeois republicanism and the State, and their entry into government.

The Spanish Revolution and Libertarian Communism

Large numbers of workers had an advanced consciousness and had been brought into a state of preparedness by the CNT Defence Committees against the threat of a right wing coup by the fascist Falangists, the royalist Carlists, and reactionary generals in the Army like Franco, Mola and Sanjurjo. When this happened on July 19th 1936 the fightback against the coup unleashed the Spanish Revolution in Catalonia and Aragon where there were large numbers of libertarian workers and peasants. Distribution of food, maintenance of public services, requisitioning of buildings, organisation of militia columns, and the opening of collective restaurants were all undertaken by these new revolutionary bodies. The State seemed to have lost any relevance.

The strength of the revolution developed through the arming of the masses, with the organisation of watch committees and patrols and the militias. There were 18,000 organised within these militias ten days after the start of the revolution. In the cities the militias lived at home, wherever possible, not in barracks, this ensuring greater and continuing contact with the working class

Land was expropriated and collectivised, in the main by CNT members and the joint CNT-FAI, and in some cases by UGT militants. In Barcelona and elsewhere factories were collectivised. This included in woodworking, bakeries and rail transport. As large landowners, who had supported the right, fled, their estates were taken over. Those who stayed and appeared sympathetic to the Nationalist revolt were expelled from their estates whilst some landowners were invited to join the collectives. In total around three million people were involved in the collectives. The collectives attempted to introduce libertarian communism but more commonly collectivism was established where a 'family wage' was paid.They were most developed in Aragon, where a CNT organised congress of collectives drew delegates from 80,000 collectivists. Of 0.43 million inhabitants, 69.5% were involved in collectives, farming 70% of the land.

Communal cafeterias were organised by the CNT, where people could eat for free. In the working class quarters of Barcelona, food committees were organised to requisition food supplies from warehouses, and to establish the exchange of manufactured goods for food with agricultural workers. The food acquired was then distributed according to criteria established by the committees. Items in pawn shops were returned to those who had been forced to pawn them in order to survive. Many large buildings, both governmental and private, were requisitioned by the syndicates. On the land, in Catalonia, Aragon, Andalusia and Valencia, agricultural work on a collective level was established. New organisational structures were spontaneously created by the workers of both town and countryside. Mass assemblies elected revolutionary committees, workplace committees, and soldiers' and sailors' councils, to carry out administrative and coordinating tasks. This was repeated in the countryside where new revolutionary committees burned documents relating to private ownership, churches were converted into storage or social-cultural centres, the land was collectivised and volunteer militias were set up. Where money was done away with, distribution was made either by rationing by the use of credit notes issued by the collectives, or totally free. A few were able, despite war conditions, to make local improvements. Schools were set up in villages for the first time, and many collectives voluntarily sent food to the front.

In the towns socialisation of the economy was undertaken at a spontaneous level, as in Barcelona, where most large enterprises were collectivised in the first week of the revolution.

In an extremely macho society, the unfolding of the Revolution saw the creation of a libertarian women's organisation, Mujeres Libres (Free Women) that was 20,000 strong. Apart from a mass consciousness raising propaganda drive, the activists of Mujeres Libres established a nurses' school, an emergency medical clinic, maternity clinics and a maternity hospital with birth and postnatal care, as well as health education programmes. In both town and country, they established childcare centres. Addressing themselves to the problem of the high level of illiteracy among women in Spain, they established literacy programmes.

In many ways the Spanish Revolution was one of the most profound and far-reaching of the twentieth century.

However whilst the rank and file of the libertarian organisations were attempting to develop the revolution, the 'leadership' had from early on started making compromises. The CNT-FAI leaders agreed to cooperation with the regional government of Catalonia, led by Luis

Companys, rather than sweeping it aside. As a result the Central Committee of the Anti-Fascist Militias (CCMA) was set up which coordinated with the government. Companys and co. had been given breathing space. Abad de Santillan was instrumental in favour of participation in the CCMA, arguing that global capitalism would not allow libertarian communism in Spain, and calling for the deferring of libertarian communism to the future.

One leading anarchist militant, Garcia Oliver of the FAI stated that it was a choice between: "Libertarian Communism, which means the anarchist dictatorship, or democracy, which means collaboration." This was a false concept, as the working class could have maintained and expended its gains without an 'anarchist dictatorship' whilst destroying the State both regionally as in Catalonia and centrally in Madrid. Solidaridad Obrera was to contain articles like 'No libertarian communism – first crush the enemy where he is', (21st July 1936.)The compromises continued with representatives of the CNT joining the regional government in Catalonia, the Generalitat. This decision appears to have been made a week before by the National Committee of the CNT. The CNT had called for a Regional Defence Council, but when offered seats in a coalition in the Generalitat did not hesitate to participate. This opened the way for CNT-FAI representatives to enter the national government which was led by the socialist Largo Caballero two months later in 1936. Solidaridad Obrera was to write, "Circumstances have... changed the nature of the Spanish State and government. It has ceased at this moment to be an oppressive force against the working class".

Meanwhile the Communist Party, which had been a marginal force, profited from its backing by the Stalinist regime in the Soviet Union. They opposed anyone who threatened the bourgeois republic in the name of effectiveness in the war against the Francoists. They therefore recruited heavily from those opposed to collectivisation, small businessmen, landowners etc. At the same time they infiltrated the Socialist Party, and through the use of Russian 'military advisers' and their own political commissars took a grip of the Republican military out of all proportion to their size. It was the Communist Party that pushed the drive to militarisation, to integrate the CNT-FAI militias and those of the anti-Stalinist left socialist Workers Party of Marxist

Unification (POUM) into the 'Popular Army' of the Republic. This was resisted by the grassroots of the CNT-FAI and from the anarchist militias themselves. They were against the traditional hierarchical set up as reproduced in the Popular Army which took away any popular initiative and which could be controlled by the State. However pressure increased and militarisation began. The revolution was being transformed into a conventional war between opposing factions of the ruling class.

The crunch came in May 1937. Throughout April the Generalitat, with the complicity of the four CNT-FAI ministers, had been increasing attacks on those they referred to as 'uncontrollables' within the CNT, FAI, FIJL and POUM. This involved disarming workers patrol groups and raiding offices. On May 3rd the Stalinists and the Generalitat started a provocation. The Barcelona telephone exchange was under the control of its workers who were mostly members of the CNT. The police attempted to occupy the building but were resisted. As a result CNT, FAI and POUM members turned out in the streets and started building barricades. The CNT leadership called for calm, but fighting broke out with the forces of the State backed by the Stalinists. Instead of encouraging the rank and file members, the CNT called for them to lay down their arms. Anarchists and POUMists were executed by the Stalinists and their allies the Catalan Nationalists. Some anarchists were shot down not far from CNT headquarters on May 5th. Also murdered on that night were the Italian anarchists Camillo Berneri and Francesco Barbieri. These refugees from Italian fascism had come to Spain to support the revolution and Berneri had been an acute critic of CNT-FAI collaboration with the State.

The Friends of Durruti were a group that had developed among the CNT-FAI columns and the libertarian youth. They were opposed to militarisation and collaboration. They were heavily involved in the May Days fighting and issued a statement calling for the establishment of a Revolutionary Junta. By this they meant a council that would represent the revolutionary grassroots groups. They called for the inclusion of the POUM in this junta. However the POUM wavered and looked to the CNT-FAI leadership. That leadership called for "anti-fascist unity", for the laying down of arms, in other words capitulation to the State, to the Stalinists and the Catalan Nationalists. Despite calls from the

Friends of Durruti not to abandon the barricades, the CNT-FAI-FIJL grassroots complied. By May 7th the fighting was over. Both the Generalitat and the national governments saw this as a heavy defeat for the CNT who they saw would accept anything. The telephone exchange was occupied, and anarchist militants, including many foreign ones, were harassed and imprisoned. In June the POUM was outlawed, and its members imprisoned and murdered. In July the State moved again and excluded the CNT-FAI representatives from the Generalitat. From August onwards the State started to attack the collectives, breaking them up with physical force. The Revolution was dead. The leadership of the mass anarchist movement that had developed in Spain over many years was betrayed by its 'official leadership'. When it came to the crunch they entered the government in the name of unity (in other words class collaboration) and anti-fascism. Winning the war was placed above winning the revolution. Instead of sweeping the State aside and establishing libertarian communism in the part of Spain they controlled they instead accepted the dictatorship of the democratic, anti-Francoist ruling class. The grassroots of the movement failed to challenge the integration of their own mass organisation into the state apparatus.

The dissident CNT-FAI militants, the Friends of Durruti, summed it up by saying: 'democracy defeated the Spanish people, not fascism'. Whilst they criticised the failures of Spanish anarcho-syndicalism, they remained on its extreme left, still within its orbit. Given the hegemony of anarchosyndicalism within the Spanish movement by this time, this was, perhaps, inevitable. The value of the statements and practice of the Friends of Durruti group rests on their attempt to resolve the dilemma of war and revolution, their affirmation of a revolutionary position against the class collaboration of the CNT-FAI ministers, the importance they gave to class analysis, and their denunciation of lack of theory and of improvisation of practice rather than revolutionary strategies within the Spanish Anarchist movement. The Friends of Durruti's analyses thus link up with what could be described as the libertarian communist pole in the realisation of a need for a specific revolutionary organisation, developing a theory and programme.

References

Francisco Fernández Gómez. Origins of Communist Anarchism in Spain, 1882-1896

Esenwein, George R. Anarchist Ideology and the Working-Class Movement in Spain, 1868-1898.

Bookchin, Murray. The Spanish Anarchists: The Heroic Years 1868-1936

Christie, S. We, the Anarchists: A Study of the Iberian Anarchist Federation

Chapter Thirty One
Anarchist communism in Portugal

There had been some Proudhonist influences in Portuguese workers' associations from the 1850s onwards and the Partido Socialista Português (Portuguese Socialist Party) founded in 1875 was heavily influenced by Proudhonism, adopting an anti-Marxist line and rejecting class struggle. In 1878 , following its merger with various workers associations, it changed its name to the Partido dos Operários Socialistas Portugueses (PSOP, Portuguese Socialist Workers Party) under the influence of Guesdist ideas.

The appearance of anarchist communism in Portugal can first be traced to the activities of the doctor Eduardo Maia, initially a Proudhonian socialist, who in 1873 gave a meeting on the right to property based on statements of the First International. In 1879 he was profoundly influenced by Kropotkin's anarchist communism, breaking with the PSOP and publicly declaring himself an anarchist communist, which caused a furore in Portugal.

It was not until 1886, though, that a speaking tour of Portugal by Elisée Reclus further processed the development of anarchist communism there. Reclus was to write "The Ignorance in which the Portuguese lived in the mid-nineteenth century was similar to that of their Moroccan neighbours, south of the Algarve. In the northern districts, Viana do Castelo,

Braga and Bragança, a girl who could read was a real phenomenon."

As well as Maia, others he met included the clerical worker João Antônio Cardoso. As a result, the Grupo Comunista Anarquista-Communist Anarchist Group of Lisbon was founded in April of the following year, including Maia in its ranks. Soon after another Communist Anarchist Group emerged in Porto. In 1888, the paper A Revolução Social (The Social Revolution) subtitled Anarchist Communist Organ, published by Cardoso and edited by Gonçalves Viana, appeared on a weekly basis for 13 issues, exercising an enormous influence on the spreading of anarchist communist ideas throughout Portugal. The paper was in effect a Portuguese version of Le Révolté, the paper edited in France by Kropotkin and Reclus, which, incidentally, carried news in its pages of the development of the Portuguese movement. Soon another anarchist communist group, Os Vingadores (the Avengers) appeared in Lamego. A monthly paper A Centelha (The Spark) was also set up in 1886.

From this period, the number of groups increased greatly, at the rate of ten new groups per annum. The movement was predominantly libertarian communist, with a small and limited individualist fringe.

In the years 1908 to 1910, republicans and anarchists collaborated to bring about the fall of the monarchy. But from as early as 1911, the same republicans, now in government rounded on the anarchist movement. Many workers had been involved in working towards toppling the monarchy, and a substantial number of these moved towards anarchist communism. As a result, there was an exponential growth in the movement. Sixty one new groups were created in 1911, 50 in 1912, 44 in 1913, 57 in 1914 and 35 in 1915. This resulted in the creation of the Anarchist Federation of the South in 1911, followed by that of the Anarchist Federation of the North and the Anarchist Union of the Algarve in the following year.

Alongside these developments was the move by many anarchists into the trade unions, peasants' union and workers and peasant cooperatives, and a general engagement in class struggle.

Leading lights among the workers who moved to anarchist communist ideas were Bartolomeu Constantino, Bernardino dos Santos and Julia da Cruz. The former, the son of a single mother, a washerwoman, was born in 1863. A shoemaker, he educated himself and was involved in the agitation for the republic. The writer Abilio Gouveia describes his presence at the May Day events of 1893." For the first time in Portugal, statements of high moral greatness were made at proletarian rallies. The meeting at the Teatro da Alegria had been celebrated, and an eloquent anarchist, the shoemaker Bartolomeu Constantino, had made the working masses vibrate with his condemnations of society. He was bald, with a big beard... his voice touched all ranges and, raising it, furious and indignant, the craftsman resembled an apostle, like the precursors of Christianity, preaching, among the rags, aspirations to fraternity. He spoke to the stars, with his feet in the swamp; his ragged suit forgotten, before the ardour of his exhortations". He was instrumental in founding one of the first libertarian coordinations, the Libertarian Socialist Federation, in 1902. He was arrested 36 times throughout his life. Imprisoned in 1904, he was released the following year, due to a massive campaign of solidarity. He set up the paper Comuna Livre (Free Commune) subtitled organ of Communist Anarchism, in 1915 and was active in the União Anarquista Comunista (UAC, Anarchist Communist Union) becoming its general secretary in 1915. He died in extreme poverty the following year. The UAC represented the hard-line anarchist communists, suspicious of reformist tendencies within the syndicalist unions. Comuna Livre first appeared on 13th October 1915 in Porto, with at least seven issues appearing up to 19th March, 1916. One of the groups affiliated to the IUAC was Dinamite Cerebral (Cerebral Dynamite)!

Bernardino dos Santos was heavily involved in the fight to establish the republic and was one of the first to be wounded at the Rotunda in Lisbon, where the pro-republic demonstrators gathered on 4th and 5th October 1910. As a result of this, he received a state pension, but was constantly unemployed due to his conversion to anarchist communism with the proclamation of the Republic. A close friend of Constantino, he continued to bring out Comuna Livre after the latter's death. Like Constantino, he was active in the UAC.

Julia Cruz was a proponent of libertarian pedagogy and was involved in the A Florescente free school. Together with Margarida Paulo, she was one of the main animators of the União das Mulheres (Women's Union group) which promoted feminism whilst rejecting suffragism. Partner of Constantino, she was active in the UAC.

At the November 1911 anarchist congress in Lisbon, Constantino, dos Santos, the group around the paper A Revolta, and most of the members of the Anarchist Federation of the South, whilst supporting involvement in workers' organisations, had been highly critical of the strategy of the anarcho-syndicalists like Manuel Joaquim de Sousa and the Porto group.

In 1914, reformist elements within the Lisbon Workers' Federation, called for a national congress to set up a cross-Portugal workers' organisation. They had hoped to take advantage of the large number of libertarian militants then currently imprisoned by the government. But the collapse of that government meant the release of many of these prisoners. As a result, the União Operária Nacional (UON, National Workers Union) was set up, with anarchist dominance.

An important development was the emergence of the Juventudes Sindicalistas (Syndicalist Youth). The first group consisted of only seven young men, associated with the Casa Sindical in Lisbon, who came together in January 1913. This initiative at first had little support in the working class, but its magazine O Despertar (The Awakening) soon created nuclei around the country. The Syndicalist Youth rejected reformism within the workers' movement. It organised a whole range of cultural and educational activities, as well as physical education and sports activities, and counted young workers and students among its members.

During the First World War they rejected the push to militarism, saying that the war was nothing more than the logical and fatal consequence of capitalism. Thus, they aligned with the UAC militants, some of them becoming members of that short-lived attempt at organisation.

Like elsewhere in the world, the coming of the Russian Revolution brought profound disturbances to the anarchist and syndicalist movement in Portugal. This resulted in the appearance of the paper Bandeira Vermelha (Red Flag), followed by the founding of the Federação Maximalista Portuguesa, Portuguese Maximalist Federation (FMP). This was formed out of a coalition of the left of the PSP, revolutionary syndicalists and anarcho-syndicalists, as well as some elements of the UAC like Américo Mesquita, Alberto Júlio das Neves, José de Sousa, Ferreira Torres, Salvaterra Júnior and Alfredo Cruz. Bandeira Vermelha was set up by revolutionary syndicalists like José Carlos Rates and Manuel António Ribeiro who defended the independence of revolutionary syndicalism from anarchism, seeing it as sufficient unto itself. At the same time, the enthusiasm for the Russian Revolution and for Bolshevism spread among some anarchist communists, who regarded the need for a specific organisation, in addition to the unions, which would defend anarchist communism, in line with the ideas advocated by Malatesta. Thus, Joaquim Cardoso and Américo Mesquita joined the Social Propaganda Soviet, the embryo of the FMP. There were already several maximalist nuclei, including the one around the anarchist communist shoemaker Manuel Ferreira Torres, in Porto.

By the end of 1920 the FMP had created at least 39 nuclei, some with hundreds of members. The Maximalists believed that The Russian Soviets were an extension of their practice within the unions over the past decades and that Maximalism was a tool to hasten the revolution. In this process they advocated the dictatorship of the proletariat. For example, the carpenter Álvaro Santos Curado said that "passionate about the sublime anarchist ideal I am with heart and soul with the Portuguese Maximalist Federation", and that, after the "first revolutionary act" the anarchist communist society had no chance of success and that a dictatorship of the proletariat, preferable to the dictatorship of the bourgeoisie, was necessary to keep revolutionaries in power.

Another leading anarchist communist, Clemente Vieira dos Santos from Porto, and editor of the paper A Aurora (The Dawn) likened the dictatorship of the proletariat to Bakunin's concept of the "organisation of the revolutionary commune by permanent barricades" from the Programme of the International Brotherhood of 1869.

The FMP issued the statement that "All members of the Portuguese Maximalist Federation and their councils are basically anarchists and revolutionary-syndicalists… Everyone who, in Portugal, declares himself as a bolshevist is an anarchist or a revolutionary-syndicalist". A Bandeira Vermelha declared itself a "valuable instrument of libertarian and syndicalist propaganda". It made reference in its pages to Bakunin and Kropotkin, etc, as much as it did to Lenin. This ideological confusion (reflected in Brazil with the Partido Comunista do Brasil and in France with the first Parti Communiste Français/ Fédération Communiste des Soviets) was to be challenged by Emilio Costa who questioned the concept of the dictatorship of the proletariat and in the pages of the anarchist communist weekly A Comuna (The Commune) which began questioning the gradual bolshevisation of the PMF. In response to false accusations in Bandeira Vermelha that Porto libertarians were financed by a local industrialist, A Comuna riposted in relation to Bandeira Vermelha that "the pure propaganda of healthy anarchist principles disappeared from its columns, and in its place came the staunch defence of Marxist socialism". A Comuna then published a series of articles which sought to distinguish between maximalism and libertarian communism, also making reference to the treatment of the Makhnovists.

In September 1919 the UON had transformed itself into the Confederação Geral do Trabalho (CGT, General Confederation of Labour) with the anarchist Manuel Joaquim de Sousa as its general secretary. De Sousa was involved in the publishing of A Comuna and had little time for the bolshevising Maximalists.

On March 6th 1921 the FMP gave way to the Partido Comunista Portugues, (PCP) which retained fewer of the anarchist characteristics of its precursor, and experienced an accelerating process of bolshevisation. Old members of the UAC like dos Santos, Julia Cruz and Alfredo Cruz were among those who joined the PCP, which was at first a tiny party, with 50 militants in Lisbon and 20 in Porto. This should be compared with a membership of 100,000 in the rapidly expanding CGT. Nevertheless, through a process of establishing cells within the CGT, the PCP began to grow. The CGT rejected efforts by the Communist minority to affiliate to the Red International of Labour Unions in that year, though that minority persisted with its machinations in 1924 and 1925. The increasing Bolshevisation of the PCP can be gauged by the death of Manuel Maria, who had joined the PCP, but had second thoughts and decided to return to the libertarian movement. His murder by PCP members resulted in a letter signed by over fifty imprisoned syndicalists. Old militants like Clemente Vieira dos Santos and Francisco Viana, disgusted by the turn of events, returned to the libertarian movement from the PCP.

Also, in 1921 the Syndicalist Youth held its first congress, declaring that the social-economic model for a future society should be anarchist communism. This organisational and political gain was somewhat marred by the decision of the general secretary of the Syndicalist Youth to lead a Bolshevik fraction out of the organisation, shortly after the congress. Nevertheless, the Syndicalist Youth could count on 5,000 members in the following year.

In the aftermath of the war, the anarchist communist groups found themselves in a weakened position. This was partly because of the developments around both the First World War and the Russian Revolution, but primarily because most militants had immersed themselves in the UON/CGT, privileging action in the mass organisations, and neglecting construction of specific organisations. For example, in 1917 there were only 14 groups in the whole country.

Luz ao Povo (Light to the People) an anarchist communist monthly based in Coimbra, and supported by the groups Homens do Futuro" (Men of the Future) and "Os Rebeldes (The Rebels), among whom were important militants like Afonso de Moura and Arnaldo Simões Januário, noted in the first issue (March 1920) that, "In Portugal, anarchist communists were completely absorbed in union action, but they did it in such a way that today, due to the official situations they occupy, they have been halted and preoccupied with minimally reformist formulas".

In 1923 in the village of Alenquer, the União Anarquista Portuguesa (UAP, Portuguese Anarchist Union) was set up, with the aim of gathering all the groups and to boost propaganda and action. After a period of scepticism and antipathy towards this new attempt at organisation, it developed an importance within the libertarian movement. The military coup of 28th May 1926, which led on to the establishment of the Salazar dictatorship, was to have grave consequences for the movement, with many militants imprisoned in dreadful conditions in concentration camps on the Cape Verde islands off the coast of Africa, and in East Timor. There under a regime modelled on the Nazi concentration camps, many militants met their deaths. The long dictatorship only fell in 1974 and the Portuguese movement has never again developed a mass character, let alone a class struggle approach.

As can be seen, the Portuguese movement quickly took on an anarchist communist character from its inception. However, a failure to create a specific anarchist communist organisation at an early date led to problems, first of all in the desire of some for greater organisational efficiency, looking towards the Communists, and secondly in the immersion by many militants in the mass organisations to the detriment of the specific organisation, only partially answered by the creation of the UAP. Despite this the huge influence of anarchist communism in Portugal is expressed by Plínio de Góes Jr thus:

"The anarchist communist belief in the expropriation of wealth was so widely divulged in Portugal during the early twentieth century, that the idea of socialising production was represented in the organisation of labour unions. The CGT formed a Liga Operária de Expropriação Económica (Worker's League for Economic Expropriation) to attack the capitalist system via 'expropriação total e completa' (total and complete expropriation) of the means of production, organising workers to study how each industry functioned in preparation for a social revolution – ultimately, the Liga was organised as a federated group of councils in different industries with specific workplaces reporting directly to the CGT leadership (Sousa, O Sindicalismo em Portugal, pp122-26)".

References:

De Goes Jnr, Plinio. Ferreira de Castro's Emigrantes: An Anarchist Portuguese Novel Responds to the Myth of the 'Brasileiro' – Anarchist Studies Volume 26, issue 1, 2018

Chapter Thirty Two
Anarchist Communism in France Part One

Throughout the 1880s into the 1900s the French anarchist movement was organised in affinity groups around its newspapers and magazines, both territorial and local. Anarchist communism had become the dominant trend in anarchism from 1879-80 onwards thanks to the influence of Kropotkin. However, again because of the influence of Kropotkin (and others) this anarchist communism was organised through loosely affiliated groups based on affinity. The groups around Jean Grave, a close friend of Kropotkin, and the paper he edited, Les Temps Nouveaux (New Times) whilst accepting collective action, bridled at the thought of effective and disciplined organisation and Grave remained opposed until the end of his life to such ideas. If he accepted the term "anarchist party" it was only to mean "a category of individuals who, having a background of common ideas, have, as a result, a certain effective and moral solidarity against their adversary, bourgeois society" (Skirda. 1987, p.63). However, discussion of effective organisation began to be discussed within the Etudiants Socialistes Révolutionnaires Internationalistes (ESRI). This group of medical students included Russians like Maria Goldsmith (Maria Korn), who became a staunch Kropotkinian, and Romanians. It had been set up in France in December 1891 and by 1893, after a split, had moved towards anarchism. At an anti-parliamentary congress in 1900 it proposed the establishment of a Federation of International Revolutionary Communism. This would communicate through correspondence bureaus on an international level. Grave opposed this move, in a report entitled Organisation, initiative, cohesion, saying the idea was based on "centralising and authoritarian systems" although he then went on to say that he was in favour of an anarchist federation but one that was based on a slow agglomeration of groups that would emerge spontaneously. The ESRI held weekly congresses and the historian Jean Maitron was of the view that it was important in orienting French anarchism back towards the workers' movement. It developed advanced ideas on several issues, including on women, before its dissolution in 1903.

Many anarchist communists became convinced of the need for greater organisation, partly in reaction to the anti-organisational outlook of individualist anarchists. The International Anarchist Congress in Amsterdam in 1907 had also reinforced the desire for effective organisation. There had been two attempts to at least organise regionally, both of which came to nothing, the Fédération Anarchiste of the Seine and of the Seine-et-Oise in 1908 and then the Fédération Révolutionnaire, in 1909-10.

With the elections in spring 1910 an Anti-Parliamentary Committee was formed. This committee decided not to dissolve after the elections and transformed itself into the Alliance Communiste Anarchiste (ACA) whose aim was "a public agitation fed by circumstances and finding in these circumstances the intensity and magnitude of its own action". The ACA affirmed that it wanted "to fight against authority in all its forms, especially the state, to pursue the abolition of wage labour and to engage workers in organising production and distribution in a communist fashion." This was met with opposition from Jean Grave and from Marc Pierrot, (a physician and mainstay of the Temps Nouveaux group) the latter of whom was to say that the ACA was "much the same as a party. There is only the name that differs." (Interestingly, both of these, like Kropotkin, took the Allied side in the First World War).

The ACA was not to last very long but a new initiative began almost immediately. This was the founding of the Fédération Révolutionnaire Communiste on 13th November 1910. Originally based in the Paris region, it soon won the affiliation of provincial groups. The FRC had its origins in a group of militants who had parted ways with the paper run by Gustave Hervé, La Guerre Sociale, which spoke to and for the anarchising wing of the socialist party, the Section Française de L'Internationale Ouvrière (SFIO).

At a regional conference in Paris the following year it could count on 400 members. At a conference in July 1912 the FRC changed its name to the Fédération Communiste Anarchiste FCA) to openly affirm its allegiance to anarchist communism. The FCA began to fill the gap left by the rightwards shift of La Guerre Sociale and it had influence among the CGT unions in the Paris region, particularly among building and metal workers.

Looking to create an anarchist communist organisation beyond the Paris region, the FCA called for a national conference in 1913. This congress took place on 15th and 17th August in Paris. It was attended by 130 delegates, representing 60 groups not just from the FCA but from the Temps Nouveaux groups and other autonomous anarchist groups. Others who supported the congress were those around the paper Le Libertaire edited by Sébastien Faure, and favourable to work within the CGT, and the Réveil Anarchiste Ouvrier, edited by Louis Jakmin under the pseudonym of Eugène Jacquemin.

The individualist Mauricius, an apologist for the illegalism of the Bonnot Gang, was expelled from the congress. The main items for debate at the congress were, activity within the CGT, where concerns were raised about the drift towards reformism there, antimilitarism and the threat of war, and repudiation of individualist anarchism. The congress adopted an eight point manifesto which included 1. repudiation of individualism 2. foundation of a federal organisation 3. reaffirmation of antiparliamentarianism 4. reaffirmation of antimilitarism (but without adherence to the desertion slogan) 5. profession of revolutionary syndicalist faith and call to join the CGT 6. reaffirmation that the revolution will be brought about by the expropriating general strike 7. recognition of illegality only for propaganda purposes (challenging the acts of the Bonnot Gang) 8. definition of the terms "anarchist", "communist" and "revolutionary".

This was a flimsy basis for an anarchist communist organisation, now called the Fédération Communiste Anarchiste Révolutionnaire (FCAR). There were no aims and principles, no declaration of intent, no constitution. Faure, who had been one of those calling for the congress, was to remain a member of the FCAR for only three weeks, withdrawing because of accusations of his membership of a Masonic lodge.

It had taken French anarchist communists decades to establish a specific organisation, and unfortunately this foundation was on the eve of the First World War.

In fact, the outbreak of war in August 1914 was to lead to the collapse of the FCAR. The war was to reveal the organisational inadequacy of the anarchist movement which was incapable of mounting a serious large scale anti-militarist movement. Worse still was the support of anarchist communists like Kropotkin, Grave, Pierrot, Malato and Paul Reclus etc. for the War. Later on, there was a failure to profit from the unrest in the armed forces in 1917. As a result, the need for an effective political organisation came to the fore in the immediate post-war period.

At the end of the War the organisation was refounded in December 1918, with a new name of Fédération Anarchiste. Its paper Le Libertaire began to appear in January 1919. There was no refounding congress of the organisation until 14th and 15th November 1920 when the FA changed its name to the Union Anarchiste (UA). The anarchist militant Louis Lecoin was to remark in an article in Le Libertaire entitled Let's Organise Ourselves, "How much have we regretted this shortcoming of organisation", referring to the lack of effectiveness of the movement in 1914 and calling for a "well ordered cohesion". However, there were still the same old problems of those asserting the absolute autonomy of the individual. A militant of the UA, Georges Bastien, was to write in Le Libertaire in 1925 complaining about the antics of individualists:" One has to speak clearly… they are afraid of seeing their 'me' mutilated in an organisation. That is why they rejected it categorically or go about arguing over every tiny detail." An indefatigable militant, Bastien should be considered as among the most important partisans of anarchist organisation in the period between the two World Wars.

At the 1926 congress in Orleans, A manifesto appeared, which, whilst basing itself on traditional anarchism, attempted to reconcile the positions of communists and individualists, revolutionaries and educationists. It affirmed that "communism is the sole form of society assuring to all and each their equal share of the commonweal" but proclaimed at the same time that anarchists are individualists because communism "gives each one material possibilities to develop all the faculties and individuality". Far from creating unity this manifesto made the partisans of a structured organisation more sensitive about the incompatibility of the two positions.

The publication of the Organisational Platform in 1926 was to have a not inconsiderable effect on the French anarchist movement. Its authors were based in France and indeed some of them militated in the UA. France, as the classic 'land of exile' has harboured anarchists from all over the world, not least the Spanish, Italian, Russian and Bulgarian emigrés.

So it comes as no surprise that the country where the Organisational Platform was penned was to give birth to a series of Platformist organisations from 1926 onwards, all ephemeral, some of them living within the larger Anarchist Federation for awhile, then becoming autonomous, and then sometimes 'returning to the fold' once more.

In 1926 the UA changed its name to the Union Anarchiste Communiste (UAC) under pressure from the Platformists and in the following year the Platformists within the UA were in the ascendant at the Paris congress and as a result some of those opposed to these ideas, including Faure, left the UA and founded the Association des Federalistes Anarchistes (AFA, Association of Anarchist Federalists). From 1928 Faure developed the ideas of the Synthesis in the pages of the AFA paper, Le Voix Libertaire.

The UAC now changed its name to the Union Anarchiste Révolutionnaire (UACR) and established Platformist principles within the organisation, with a majority vote that was to be binding, no criticisms to be made by members of UACR positions in Le Libertaire and no criticism to be made of the UACR outside the organisation. Membership of the UACR had to come via applying to a UACR group or regional federation, rather than individual membership, and the system of subscriptions was strengthened and included membership cards. Nevertheless, some synthesists remained within the UACR, including Louis Lecoin opposed to the Platformist tendency around Bastien, Nicolas Faucier, Rene Fremont etc. However, the Platformist triumph was not long lasting and in 1930 the synthesists regained control of the UACR with the rescinding of the new organisational moves. The Platformists, now in a minority, produced six issues of a Bulletin between 1930 and 1931, which, according to Faucier, expired due to "quasi general indifference".

In 1931, the Federation of Languedoc, as a component of the UACR, and which had been won lock stock and barrel to Platformism, put forward a motion at the Toulouse Congress which referred to "a period of adaptation" after the initial phases of a revolution. This was interpreted as a reference to the Marxist transition period and the Languedoc Federation, along with the group of Livry-Gargan, were expelled from the organisation. This expulsion did not last long and the Orleans congress of 1933 reintegrated them.

The first Federation Communiste Libertaire (1934)

The UACR reverted to the UA in 1934, at the so-called unity congress of Paris, with the organisationalists departing to form the Federation Communiste Libertaire (FCL) only to return to the UA in 1936 as a tendency within it, brought on by the strike movement of May and June 1936. The FCL's leading militants were Charles Cortvrint, better known under the pseudonyms of Charles Ridel and then Louis Mercier-Vega, Charles Carpentier, Robert Léger, Louis Le Bot, Charles Patat and Félix Guyard.

Cortvrint/Ridel was an anarchist from Brussels who had moved to France to escape his military obligations. He became active with the UACR via the Jeunesse Anarchiste Communiste (JAC, Anarchist Communist Youth) and was a supporter of the Organisational Platform. He contributed many articles to Le Libertaire. He worked as a porter at Les Halles Market, as a leather worker, a peddler and a proofreader.

The Unity Congress in Paris had come about after the riots of the extreme right earlier in the year, which were seen as a grave danger throughout the workers' movement. As a result, the AFA, UACR and various local anarchist groups merged to reform as the Union Anarchiste. The left of the UACR around Ridel and company rejected this merger in the name of antifascist unity, saying that this imperilled the libertarian communist character of the organisation and that it pandered to an antifascist "frontism", pointing to an antifascist alliance that had been formed with socialists of the SFIO in the Paris region. In addition, the UACR had made many concessions in the name of libertarian unity, for example on the right not to pay membership dues, on localism and individualism.

In consequence the Fédération Communiste Libertaire (FCL) was formed. This small organisation was based around groups in Paris, Aubervilliers, Gennevilliers, Saint Denis and Toulon and numbered 40 militants. It remained small and isolated. Together with the UA it took part on in a large meeting at St Denis on August along with various Trotskyists, pacifists and revolutionary syndicalists denouncing the politics of the Popular Front. With this shift of the UA, and because of the limited size and effectiveness of the FCL, and the external and internal threat from fascism, there was a rapprochement at the UA congress of 12th and 13th April 1936. This congress decided to work with the non-anarchist left in a broad antifascist front, but with the aim of influencing it in a revolutionary direction.

This brought about a new scission the following August, with the individualists seeing Le Libertaire "as of a sectarian spirit, resolutely and uniquely communist...which cannot interest or satisfy the other tendencies" as Zisly wrote in Le Voix Libertaire. The new grouping, the Federation Anarchiste de Langue Française, (F.A.F) criticised the UA for its centralism and its concessions to the French left. These disagreements deepened during the Spanish Revolution, with the UA supporting the official CNT-FAI policies, and the F.A.F. taking a position against anarchist involvement in the Republican government, and the prioritising of antifascism and militarisation to the detriment of the social revolution. (Interestingly, Ridel, Carpentier and others on the left of the UA, and who had fought with Carpentier in the anarchist militia columns in Spain, disagreed with the orientation of the UA on this subject and left the organisation at the congress of 29th and 30th October 1937).

As a result, on the eve of the Second World War, there existed two anarchist organisations, both of a Synthesist hue, the UA with 2,000 members and the FAF with 500. As to the Platformists, they had lost the ideological battle. They ceased to exist as an autonomous grouping, although they still held important posts within the UA, where they exercised a significant influence (Fremont on the secretariat, Scheck on the board of Le Libertaire, Ridel – before his resignation – with the propaganda section, etc.)

The magazine Révision

A stimulating magazine which attempted to renovate anarchist communism was the magazine founded in 1938 by UA dissidents who had disagreed with the line on Spain and who emanated from among young workers in the Jeunesse Anarchiste Communiste, the aforementioned Ridel, Carpentier, as well as Lucien Feuillade. Subtitled Revue d'études Révolutionnaires, six issues appeared between 1938 and the following year, the last issue mostly in Spanish. Ridel under the pseudonym of Louis Mercier-Vega contributed heavily to the magazine. Among others who wrote for it were Marie-Louise Berneri and Suzanne Broido of the Libertarian Students, Lucien Feuillade (writing under the name Luc Daurat) René Dumont of the UA, the exiled Russian anarchosyndicalist Nicolas Lazarevitch, etc.

1938 was a depressing year for the French workers' and revolutionary movements. There was a decline of militancy and growing pessimism with the deterioration of the situation in Spain and the tightening grip of the Stalinists there, the Anschluss in Austria, disenchantment with the Popular Front government in France and the coming to power of the reactionary Daladier government, compounded by the failure of the November general strike.

It was this situation, and both in spite of and because of it, that it was decided to launch Révision. Those who contributed to it were in the main anarchist communists as mentioned above, but also included some contributors from the revolutionary left around Marceau Pivert and the Workers and Peasants Socialist Party (PSOP) and other left currents. It was the first time there had been such collaboration at the level of a theoretical magazine, but all its contributors appeared impelled by a need for renovation at both a far reaching ideological, strategic, and organisational level. There were sharp criticisms of the "governmental anarchists" in Spain, and neither were the inadequacies of French organisations spared. As the manifesto of the group was to state: "Inside or on the sidelines of official trends, sincere and honest revolutionaries reject old creeds and catechisms to seek an interpretation of facts and a method of action that would take into account the new factors that the events of our century have revealed."

Therefore, the role of the magazine was to fight for "free and human socialism, libertarian socialism". They went on to say that: "We mean by libertarians all the revolutionaries who refuse to neglect the human side of socialism and who conceive of the social struggle and the new society only on the basis of a true democracy." Communist Party and CGT leaders were castigated as traitors, as were both the Second and Third Internationals and the "opportunism and purism that are closely associated in certain anarchist tendencies".

Ridel had harsh criticisms of the anarchist milieu, as he says a term often used to distinguish it from the anarchist movement, and which as a designation is partly true as it describes "all that is vague and inconsistent in anarchism". He went on to describe "The lack of solid organisations, the absence of written programmes and statutes, the elasticity of the doctrine, its vagueness, the generalities and contradictions it contains, constitute so many obstacles of a special order that make overall assessments and sharp opinions difficult to formulate."

Chapter Thirty Three
The Second World War and Its Aftermath in France

On the outbreak of war, the French anarchist movement was divided between the Union Anarchiste, which had supported the CNT-FAI in government in Spain, and the synthesist Federation Anarchiste. It failed to respond collectively to the situation, with only Louis Lecoin and other antimilitarists releasing their statement Immediate Peace.

Anarchists now had a choice between dodging the draft, exile abroad or the abandonment of all political activity. Underground work proved to be impossible and it was not until the armistice of 1940 that anarchists slowly established clandestine networks, culminating in 1943 with the creation of the Fédération Libertaire Unifiée, soon to be renamed the Mouvement Fédéraliste. Several flyposting campaigns were carried out as well as the issuing of a leaflet calling for rebellion against authority in all its forms. This was followed by more flyposting campaigns and the distribution of leaflets calling for the restitution of freedom of expression, association and press.

On 31st December 1944 the first issue of a new run of Le Libertaire appeared. The Fédération Anarchiste was reconstituted at a congress on the 6th and 7th October 1945 in Paris, with Le Libertaire as its official paper. The FA grouped three tendencies together – the individualists, the synthesists, and anarchist communists and anarcho-syndicalists, only the last current believing in anything beyond a minimal organisation.

This last current consisted in the main of young militants new to the movement, who had emerged during the Occupation and in the various Resistance networks.

Some of these young people had joined the Communist Party whilst it was still underground or in the first months after Liberation. Disillusioned by their time in the PCF those who did not join the various Trotskyist groups gravitated towards the anarchist movement. Their understanding of anarchism was slight, mostly formed by acquaintance with Spanish anarchist militants operating in the

Resistance networks, and the FA offered no educational programme. They immediately came up against the friction between the three different tendencies within the FA and quickly saw the deficiencies in this organisation. Whilst having split with the Communist Party, they still admired the efficiency of its organisation and pushed for this within the FA, allying with the anarchist communists there. Under their influence the FA now took a militant line in terms of workplace struggles and the end of rationing, as well as with the anticolonial struggle, above all with the Indochinese war. As a result of this intense activity, circulation of Le Libertaire soared.

The FA benefitted as a result of growing workplace militancy among the working class, whilst the PCF was lukewarm in its support for a movement that seemed to be getting beyond its control. Unfortunately, the numerical weakness of the FA meant that its influence could not go beyond agitation through propaganda, particularly through the selling of its paper. The hegemony of the PCF over the working class in France (as in Italy) also played a role in the failure of the FA to expand. In addition, French anarchism was embarrassed by the pronouncements of various individualist and humanist personalities.

The young militants of the FA hoped for a relationship between their specific organisation and a mass movement, in the manner of the CNT and the FAI. This appeared to be happening in 1946 with the emergence of the Confederation National de Travail (CNT) made up mainly of Spanish exiles. The CNT was given a full page in Le Libertaire, which affirmed the importance of workplace activity: "An anarchist can be a syndicalist, if he intends giving to syndicalism not a reformist or corporatist attitude, but a revolutionary spirit and a direction having as an essential goal the suppression of capitalism and the State". (Le Libertaire, no.64 16th January 1947).

This concept of "a revolutionary direction" could be seen as the anarchists wishing to take charge of the syndicalist organisation. This conception would bring it into opposition with many anarcho-syndicalists and revolutionary syndicalists, who wished to preserve the autonomy of the syndicalist organisation from all political organisations, including anarchist ones. Thus, they would have been unhappy at the motion passed at a regional congress of the FA in 1949 which stated: "The structure of the FA does not permit it to draw in the entirety of the workers in a revolutionary action. It is to the CNT that this role has devolved. It is for this reason that the anarchists should orient to it and not hesitate to take in hand responsible posts".

This was in line with the role of the FAI within the CNT in Spain, but proved to be a divisive development, with a break between the FA and the CNT, as a result of CNT militants worried that their union would be taken over by the FA. Both of these organisations subsequently experienced a loss of influence in the working class, with many anarchists now moving to work with different union confederations.

When Le Libertaire first reappeared in 1945 it reached a print run of 80,000 copies but following the mass strikes of 1947, insurrectionary in aspect, circulation steadied at 30,000 copies (the events of 1947 began at the Renault factory at Boulogne-Billancourt, and then spread across the country, involving large numbers of workers and taking on an insurrectionary aspect). There was also a falloff in the amount of militant activity due to internal problems within the FA, above all a high turnover in membership. Concerns were expressed about the number of new members who joined the FA only to remain briefly.

As noted, this state of affairs was partly due to the hegemony of the PCF and the union central it controlled, the CGT, over the working class. But it was also due to the synthesism of the FA which allowed individualists and humanists to block moves to more militant activity. As Georges Fontenis, one of the new militants of the FA, noted in an article in Le Libertaire on 20th May 1949:

"When we debate with the Marxists, we pass for dreamers or naives, when we have to defend several nonsenses in the Libertaire produced by synthesism (cf. a campaign for Celine)". Celine was the French writer famous for his novel Journey to The End of The Night. A notorious anti-Semite, he had been a collaborator with Vichy and the Nazi occupiers during World War Two. He had fled to Denmark and did not return to France until 1951.Some members of the FA supported a campaign of rehabilitation.

Fontenis became general secretary of the FA from 1946 to 1951 and he and his associates among the young militants attempted to steer the organisation away from synthesist ideas. This failed. At the beginning of 1950 he and others who included Roger Caron, Serge Ninn, Robert Joulin, André Moine, and Louis Estève, created a secret organisation within the FA, the Organisation Pensée Bataille (OPB) (Organisation, Thought, Fight). This was a reference to the Italian anarchist Camillo Berneri's book, Pensieri I Battaglia, Thought and Fight (his daughter Giliane, was Ninn's partner and was herself active in the FA, although refusing to join the OPB). Both Caron, Estève and Joulin had been Platformists of long standing within the Union Anarchiste.

The OPB in many ways had its roots in the Self Defence group set up inside the FA in 1946 as the result of a congress decision to counter State, Stalinist and fascist infiltrators and to prepare underground resistance in the event of a right-wing coup or a third world war. It was directed by Fontenis.

The aim of the OPB was to form a libertarian communist action group, to occupy all the responsible posts within the FA and to combat the individualists and humanists. The FA would be turned into a well-structured organisation with a united approach, in line with the Organisational Platform. At first count the OPB only numbered 17 militants but grew through a system of co-opting new members and of occupying local, regional and national posts within the FA. Eighteen months after its foundation the OPB had absolute control of the Paris region. This was in part due to two reasons, one being the reluctance of other members of the FA to take on these posts, and the other due to the extremely well-disciplined structure of the OPB with its own constitution and dues. Co-option of new members of the OPB was only possible through two sponsors. OPB members had to show example to others through flyposting and the street selling of Le Libertaire and to look out for possible new recruits to the OPB.

The original voting system of per FA member was replaced by that of group mandate at the 6th Congress of 1950 at Lille, thus allowing the OPB to control any decisions made.

After the Bordeaux congress of the FA in 1952 the victory of the OPB was complete. The individualists were the first to be driven out of the FA in October of that year, to be followed by others who objected to the methods used; like the anarchist communists Maurice Fayolle and Maurice Joyeux. In fact in May 1952, Fontenis had demanded a meeting with Joyeux, a member of the largest group of the FA, the Groupe Louise Michel of the 18th arrondissement of Paris.

This was in a walkway in the Parisian park of Buttes Chaumont. The intention was to sound out the attitudes of Joyeux and the Groupe Louise Michel before the approaching conference. Without revealing to Joyeux the existence of the OPB, Fontenis suggested to him that there should be a double leadership of the FA, with Fontenis filling the role of intellectual leadership and Joyeux that of worker leadership. The latter responded with disbelief and derision. This may have contributed to Joyeux and the Groupe Louise Michel being forced out of the FA (ironically, Joyeux was not unsympathetic to the theses of the Organisational Platform). The Paris Congress of 1953 saw the exclusion of the Groupe Louise Michel, as well as that of Asnières and Bordeaux. At this Congress there were motions calling for the transformation of the FA into the Parti Communiste Anarchiste or the Parti Communiste Libertaire. This was a move by the OPB to break with what they thought of as traditional anarchism. Failing to get consensus on this, they then moved that the name of the organisation be changed to Mouvement Communiste Libertaire. This ended with 61 mandates to preserve the organisation as the FA and 71 mandates to change its name. Seeing that they did not have a clear majority, an internal referendum took place with the FA being transformed into the Fédération Communiste Libertaire (FCL).

The FCL came out of all this considerably weakened. It could now count on no more than 130 to 160 militants in sixteen groups. It retained the bookshop and offices, the weekly paper and the treasury of the FA. The paper now had its title printed in red rather than black, another symbolic move to differentiate itself from "traditional" anarchism.

The Manifesto of Libertarian Communism

The 'Manifesto of Libertarian Communism' was written in 1953 by Fontenis as the result of a congress decision of the FCL. It was based on articles that had already appeared in Le Libertaire during 1945-50 and on those that appeared under the column Essential Problems that appeared in that paper between September 1952 and February 1953. It was published just before the Paris congress in May 1953.

As the anarchist communist and anti-colonialist Guy Bourgeois noted: "The Manifesto of Libertarian Communism was necessary. It marked for the first time within the post-war libertarian movement a clear break with the humanist tendencies of conciliation".

Like the 'Platform' it pitted itself against the 'Synthesis' of Faure and Voline. Like the 'Platform' it reaffirmed the class struggle nature of anarchism and showed how it had sprung from the struggles of the oppressed. It had the experience of another thirty years of struggle and was a more developed document than the 'Platform'. However, it failed to take account of the role of women in capitalist society and offered no specific analysis of women's oppression. Whilst the FCL was very active in the struggle against French colonialism in North Africa, it failed to incorporate an analysis of racism into its Manifesto.

It rejected, rightly, the concept of the 'Dictatorship of the Proletariat' and the 'Transitional Period'. Where it made mistakes was in the use of the concepts of the 'party' and the 'vanguard'. To be fair the word 'party' had been used in the past by Malatesta to describe the anarchist movement, but the association with social-democrats and Leninists had given it connotations which can only be avoided by dropping the term. Similarly, 'vanguard' had been used extensively by anarchists in the past to describe, not the Leninist vanguard, but a group of workers with advanced ideas. The term was used, for example, in this respect in the Spanish movement (see Bookchin's writings on the subject), and also by anarchist-communists in the United States who named their paper 'Vanguard' (see the memoirs of Sam Dolgoff). However, it has too many unhappy associations with Leninism. Whilst it should be recognised that there exist advanced groups of workers, and that the anarchist movement has ideas in advance of most of the class, we must recognise fully the great creativity of the whole of the working class. There exist contradictions between advanced groups and the class as a whole, complex contradictions which cannot be explained in simple black and white terms, which could lead to the Leninist danger of substituting a group for the whole class. The anarchist-communist Organisation should be aware of these problems and attempt to minimalise these contradictions. True, the Manifesto sees this vanguard as internal to the class, rather than an external vanguard of professional revolutionaries as Lenin saw it. Nevertheless, the term should be regarded with great suspicion.

The Manifesto continued the arguments for effective libertarian Organisation and ideological and tactical unity, based on the class struggle. Like the 'Platform' the 'Manifesto' is marred by a number of errors, with the 'Platform it was the idea of the 'executive committee', with the 'Manifesto' it was the idea of the 'vanguard'.

As Alexandre Skirda was to remark: "Thus far, the Manifesto and Fontenis's plan have been construed as an attempt to 'Bolshevise' anarchism, for the belief was that they were both addressed to anarchists. On the other hand, if we were to take them as specially geared towards the labour militants of the day who were under the sway of Stalinism-Leninism, or even towards the sympathisers and dissidents of the PCF, then it is possible to decode the Manifesto in the opposite sense: as an attempt to 'anarchise' these. In which case the confusions, contradictions or, if one prefers, the 'obscurities' in the text suddenly become clear, when viewed through the lenses of such a readership. Subsequent events – the unbridled workerism, the outbidding of CGT and PCF slogans, the active commitment to the anticolonialist struggle (the Algerian war), to begin with, and then the running in the legislative elections of 1956 and the comeback by Andre Marty, excluded from the PCF – appear to validate this construction. It is plain that the mimicry of the Communist Party was part and parcel of an intention to overtake it on its left and on its stamping ground, the working class: but the FCL had neither the stomach nor the wherewithal for that task. That said, we cannot agree with Jean Maitron when he writes that it was a 'synthesis between anarchism and a measure of Leninism', and 'consonant with a platformist line but going further than Arshinov's theses'. In our view, it was rather an extreme attempt to promote social anarchism on the back of labour disputes, with the obsession with 'impact' overtaking respect for a certain libertarian tradition."

Meanwhile those who had been excluded or who had left the organisation regrouped in a new Fédération Anarchiste in 1953, the following year bringing out their paper Le Monde Libertaire. It reunited 56 groups, and based itself on the broadest possible synthesism. Its basic principles involved a compromise with the individualists, resulting in a mode of functioning that Maurice Joyeux, one of its principal founders, considered "impossible", with unanimous decision making with each individual member of the F.A. having a right of veto over any proposed policies. This has resulted in the problems within the F.A. up to the present day, with a series of splits over the years as a result. As Roland Biard was to write "On the structural plan, the F.A. is thus defined as a place of "the connivance of all the tendencies". Each group is autonomous, the centralising organs are suppressed and replaced by a "Committee of Relations" which takes note of the work undertaken by the various responsible officers. These, anyway, are not responsible other than to themselves (no collective responsibility, no control procedure), This type of organisation makes the participation of organisational currents (libertarian communists, anarchosyndicalists) illusory. The history of the F.A. is a series of splits and departures: each period brings its lot of revolutionary militants wanting to break out of the traditional straitjacket" (Histoire Du Mouvement Anarchiste, 1976, p.114).

Returning to the FCL we see that increasingly its groups talked about unity of action with Communist Party cells. Its activities became more frenetic as it became involved in many campaigns, tail ending the PCF and the CGT, forming alliances with leftist organisations and militants beyond the libertarian communist sphere, and evolving towards an electoralist position. As Christian Lagant, a militant in the FCL up until 1955 was to write: "The temperature is high, too high even...One militates at 100 per cent, it's the period of all for the movement, and one has the tendency to consider all progress of the organisation in which one militates as an advance of the anarchist idea in itself ...And one day, having suddenly taken note that the revolution had not broken out, because the day before, one had sold five papers, stuck up ten posters more or had 20 extra people at a meeting, the eyes opened brusquely, and the tireless militant, brutally sobered up, took account of the real situation" (in Noir et Rouge, 17, January/February 1961)

The FCL entered the anarchist international, the Commission des Relations Internationales Anarchistes (CRIA) which had been set up in 1948 but in a parallel move worked to set up its own international. Between the 5th and 7th June 1954 at Paris, the FCL convened a congress to found the Internationale Communiste Libertaire (ICL). Apart from the FCL, the Italians of the GAAP, some Spanish militants around the Ruta bulletin, Bulgarian exiles, British anarchists in the

Syndicalist Workers Federation, and some Belgians attended the founding congress. Later they were joined by the Algerians in the Mouvement Libertaire Nord-Africain (MLNA,) in mid-October. However, the ICL proved to be still-born and the CRIA took offence at this parallel attempt to found an international and the FCL was forced to withdraw.

The FCL published various bulletins aimed at factories and postal workers and adopted a "worker's programme" later considered by the Groupe Kronstadt (see below) to be a pale copy of the CGT programme. Attempts were made to detach PCF members and to integrate them into the FCL. This led on to the opening of the pages of Le Libertaire to Andre Marty, following his exclusion from the PCF. Marty had been an arch-Stalinist for many years within the Communist Party, and he was known as the "Butcher of Albacete" for his bloodthirsty behaviour during the Spanish Civil War (The historian Roland Biard called him "the principal artisan of Stalinist repression during the war in Spain"). After the legislative elections of 1955 the FCL considered the possibility of a joint PCF/FCL slate as a "popular Front". This was a complete about face from two years before when the FCL had called for a Third Front with the slogan of "Neither Truman Nor Stalin". According to Lagant this came about because of the failure of the abstentionist campaign at the municipal elections of 1953, where in fact the voting turnout was higher than usual. The Maisons-Alfort group of the FCL wrote in its motion for the 1955 congress:" In systematically abstaining, do we risk losing our influence among the working class. On the contrary, the electoral battle must become a form of class struggle, can we not envisage this question as a question of tactics linked to the circumstances and facts of the social combat?" This motion was discussed at the congress, leading to the departure of militants opposed to electoralism.

This was followed by the presentation of the FCL at the elections as a party. It was only able to run such a list in the first sector of Paris. Elsewhere it called for a vote for "workers' candidates the most susceptible to bar the road to reaction in the immediate" (Le Libertaire, 22nd December 1955).

The electoral results were derisory for the FCL, with 2,219 votes, and with debts to the sum of a million francs as a result. The FCL explained this defeat in an article in Le Libertaire on 12th January, 1956, entitled The Lessons of Our Participation: "We don't dissimulate that the result obtained was modest… The reasons of these limited results must be explained and interpreted. The fact of the useful vote against reaction, the FCL only touched the vanguard of the workers. The influence of the FCL must be grown in direct struggles". As for Marty, at the last moment he refused to call for a vote for the FCL. The FCL replied to this by stating that it had to be "explained to the friends of Marty that to create the great revolutionary party they had to join us to develop and ameliorate the base of this party that is today the FCL".

However, it was not these breaks with anti-parliamentarism and anti-electoralism that sounded the death knell of the FCL but its involvement in the anti-colonial struggle, even though the electoral adventure lost it practically all sympathy within the French libertarian movement.

The FCL had taken an active part in the movement against the war in Algeria between 1954 and 1958 and in fact one of its militants, Pierre Morain, had been the first to receive a prison sentence for his anti-colonial activities. However, the anti-colonialism of the FCL went beyond this towards a "critical" support first for the independentist Mouvement National Algérien (MNA) of Messali Hadj, and then for the Front de Libération Nationale (FLN) with the eclipse of the MNA. As a result of this position, Le Libertaire was banned in Algeria and Morocco, it was seized seven times from 1954, three of these directly at the printshop in June 1956, there were 200 charges against FCL militants with a total of 26 months prison sentences, and more than three million francs in fines. This brought about the collapse of the paper in July 1956 and the abandonment of their offices. Two issues of a magazine, Partisan, appeared with the eclipse of the FCL at the beginning of 1958.

This was partly because of the desertion of some anarchist communists, with others moving towards the PCF or the Socialists, and others dropping out of activity, at least for a while. But it was also down to the decision by the core of the FCL to enter into clandestinity, because of the repression that had fallen on them. At the meeting of the national committee of the FCL on 5th July 1956, Roger Caron and Robert Joulin, who had done so much to build first the FA and then the FCL in the post-war period, were part of the minority opposed to the majority around Georges Fontenis who proposed the closing down of the paper and the beginning of underground work. Caron himself proposed the temporary suspension of the paper, considering that articles in Le Libertaire that had brought on the prosecutions could have been couched in different, less provocative language. He felt that this would avoid further prosecutions. Joulin, for his part, wanted the continuation of Le Libertaire. As a result, Caron and Joulin ceased all political activity.

Despite this, Caron, Joulin and Fontenis had further charges presented against them in October 1956. Whilst the majority of FCL members continued to lead a normal life, Fontenis, Pierre Morain, Gilbert Simon and Paul Philippe, all of whom had heavy charges arraigned against them, entered into clandestinity. A duplicated newssheet La Volonté du Peuple (The People's Will, with an allusion to the Russian underground organisation of the 19th century) was produced secretly and hastily handed out outside factory gates without any arrests. Fontenis and Philippe also made several tours around France to meet up with sympathisers and FCLers and met with the Italian GAAP in Nice. However, by July 1957 both Fontenis and Philippe had been arrested.

By now the FCL was defunct and Fontenis and his associates set up a new group, Action Communiste. This established links with the Socialisme ou Barbarie group and with oppositionists in the Communist Party. This group only existed for a few months and then Fontenis entered La Voie Communiste, a grouping made up of Communist Party dissidents and various ex-Trotskyists who were breaking with the traditions of the Fourth International. Fontenis thus found himself alongside the likes of Félix Guattari and Denis Berger (later to become respectively, a noted psychoanalyst/ philosopher and noted sociologist). Philippe and Simon ended up in the PCF whilst other ex-FCLers joined the Union de la Gauche Socialiste (UGS) made up of dissidents from the French Section of the Workers International (SFIO) and Christian socialists. The adventure of the FCL was well and truly over.

Towards the end of its life the FCL had carried an appeal in the pages of Le Libertaire to: "Become militants. Join the FCL, the party which struggles for peace in Algeria, the triumph of workers' demands, the social revolution and real communism". There was little there to distinguish it from any other leftist outfit.

The FCL had attempted to break out of the anarchist ghetto and to establish a strong relationship with the French working class. They recognised the hegemony that the PCF had over it and so sought to break the base of that Party away and to relate to its dissidents. Unfortunately, this sincere desire to increase the relevance of anarchist communism led on to Fontenis and his associates using dubious means to purge their opponents within the FA/FCL, to take a disastrous electoralist turn and to get into bed with the likes of Stalinists such as Marty, not to mention the increasingly uncritical approach to Algerian national liberation and the "overheated" militantism. Perhaps the greatest lesson of the FCL experience was what one should not do in attempting to build an anarchist communist organisation. As Skirda notes it was "an extreme attempt to promote social anarchism". The FCL experience was to leave its mark on the libertarian movement for many decades.

The Groupes Anarchistes D'Action Révolutionnaire (GAAR)

Out of the wreckage of the FCL emerged the Groupes Anarchistes d'Action Révolutionnaire. It was created from a number of groups who had left or had been expelled from that organisation (Kronstadt, Maisons-Alfort, Macon, and Grenoble). The Kronstadt group contained several important militants who had been key in constructing both the OPB and the FCL, and had numerically been the largest in the FCL. They issued a memorandum of 67 pages on their departure, accusing Fontenis of dictatorial behaviour. Whilst continuing to define themselves as anarchist communists they saw themselves as the anarchist communist tendency of the libertarian movement. They defined this movement as the Federation Anarchiste, the Groupe Socialiste Libertaire of Gaston Leval, the Groupe Contre-Courant of Louis Louvet and various individualist magazines. The organisation was founded in November 1955.

The main activity of the GAAR was the publishing of a duplicated magazine Noir et Rouge (Black and Red), founded in April 1956. Like the FCL the GAAR took an anti-colonialist stance, although of a more critical character than that of the FCL. The GAAR became a subject of greater attention in May 1958 when they initiated the resistance to the Gaullist putsch. On the 16th May they distributed leaflets calling for a general strike and convoked a meeting to found a Comité de Coordination Libertaire which also included the FA, the CNT, and the Jeunes Libertaires (Young Libertarians), although the FA left shortly afterwards to join another committee which included the SFIO and the UGS.

Noir et Rouge was an important magazine for the development of anarchist communist ideas not just in France but internationally. It addressed itself to problems, little discussed within the anarchist movement, at least not for a long time: nationalism, elections, Parliament, Freemasonry, as well as contemporary problems, and historical ones like the Spanish Revolution of 1936.

"The anarchist communist perspective expects of us an organised collective work, based on an ideological unity which implies the study and the collective resolution of problems posed by the doctrinal and tactical adaptation of anarchism with the actual political, economic and psychological conjuncture". Winter 1956-57 issue no.3 of Noir et Rouge in the article Making the Point.

The GAAR now took the initiative to enlarge the committee which became the Comité d'Action Révolutionnaire (CAR) with the entry of the Parti Communiste Internationaliste, the Spanish CNT, Socialisme ou Barbarie, and a split from that organisation, Pouvoir Ouvrier, etc.

The CAR took part in the demonstration of 28th May with its own slogans – "Shoot the Generals"; "Down with The Army"; "Paras=SS". The consolidation of De Gaulle in power led to the dissolving of the CAR and to a crisis within the GAAR itself. Some of its militants believed that the publication of Noir et Rouge was not enough. May 1958 had shown that the GAAR could act as an important force. As a result, the organisation transformed itself into the Federation Anarchiste Communiste in 1960. A permanent liaison committee was set up between the FAC and the FA. Those who had doubts about this and who saw Noir et Rouge as a priority left in 1961, when the Kronstadt, Maisons-Alfort, Lille, Strasbourg, Macon and Grenoble groups joined the FA at the latter's congress at Montluçon on 21st May

1961 and regrouped as a tendency within it – the Union Des Groupes Anarchistes Communistes (UGAC).

The Union Des Groupes Anarchistes Communistes

The UGAC issued a statement at the Montluçon congress stating:
"Considering that the different philosophic anarchist expressions remain valid, we think that anarchist communists, libertarian socialists, anarcho-syndicalists and even anarchist individualists have their place in our Federation because they are linked by a common ethic.

Considering that inside the Federation Anarchiste each of these tendencies has the right to organise as it sees fit to militate with the greatest efficiency for the triumph of its ideas.

The anarchist communists who presently militate within the FA declare to all the comrades of the FA and to those of fraternal movements that this Congress marks the date of the creation of an organised anarchist communist tendency in the framework of the FA under the name of the Union Des Groupes Anarchistes Communistes. The fact even of reclaiming anarchist communism implies a pooling of forces and the creation of an organisation, the only tactical means as good as towards the exterior as for ourselves, to apply the principles of anarchist communism.

Enemies of manifestoes and persuaded that it is impossible to explain in ten points of a catechism all the complexity of the ideology of the anarchist communists and its updating, we propose to give access to the anarchist communist doctrine through studies in a magazine that we plan on launching soon.

The group is the living nucleus: it delegates a militant to a committee, a council of liaisons of Anarchist Communist Groups, which is charged with coordinating and stimulating the activities of the Union. It is intended that each group affiliated to the Union stays in direct contact with the different organs of the FA. to those of the Committee of Relations of the FA.

The delegates to the Council are interchangeable and responsible, as much before their group as before the entire organisation.

One of the leading lights of the GAAR and then the UGAC was Paul Zorkine. Born in Montenegro in 1921, Zorkine (whose real surname was Vrbica) only came to anarchist-communism after long years of struggle and thought. A member of the Young Communists of Yugoslavia in the years before World War II, he struggled against the process of Stalinisation. He was expelled at the instigation of Milovan Djilas, who was himself to later develop harsh criticisms of state socialism.

He volunteered to defend Czechoslovakia in 1939, then organised an anti-Ustashi resistance network in Zagreb, Croatia. He was arrested, escaped to Britain and joined the RAF which parachuted him into Yugoslavia on several occasions where he led resistance operations. The war over, and despite his determined opposition to Stalinism, he was offered several posts of responsibility by the Yugoslav Communist Party. He refused this, and turned towards the anarchist movement. He became a militant in the land in which he took refuge, France. Whilst staying in contact with exiled anarchists from the Balkans (with whom he founded an ephemeral Balkan Anarchist Federation in Exile, and then the Christo Botev group, named after the Bulgarian anarchist poet) he joined the Kronstadt group of the Federation Anarchiste. He was the leading light in libertarian communist resistance to the Fontenis adventure, and in the Memorandum of the Kronstadt Group which outlined its objections to the behaviour of Fontenis and his associates.

As his friend and comrade Roland Breton remarked: "Paul sees the anarchist communist movement as political above all, that is to say the transformation of society's structures. It never stops insisting on the need for organisation. Specifically libertarian revolutionary organisation, in the framework of the class struggle of the workers against the bourgeoisies and the bureaucracies, against State or private capitalism. Federal organisation of the world of work to prevent the appearance of a new ruling class issuing from revolutionaries, combatants or organisers themselves. Rational organisation of the economy, the full utilisation of the forces of production and a communist distribution".

Unfortunately, Zorkine died in a car accident in September 1962 and the anarchist communist movement was robbed of an outstanding militant. Other leading lights of the UGAC included Paul Denais and Guy Bourgeois.

Zorkine and his comrades concluded from the Fontenis experience that the key task of the UGAC was not to eliminate other tendencies in the FA, as Fontenis had done, but to take their head, through the constitution of an active and coherent nucleus, to supplant them in theory and practice. To bring this about, this nucleus had to be more active and homogeneous than other tendencies, whether they were constituted as such, or existed as informal tendencies, to prove its arguments by good practice and exposition of ideas. At the same time, any putschist strategy should be rejected.

By 1962, the UGAC had five groups, followed by the adhesion of other groups, principally in the Paris region. It did not escape the extreme fluidity of the anarchist movement, and after the death of Zorkine, its membership shrank. The activity of the UGAC within the FA was limited by suspicion of Fontenisism and FA militants like Maurice Joyeux and the Groupe Louise Michel questioned the right of the libertarian communists to organise as a tendency.

In March 1962 the UGAC issued a communiqué stating that once more the libertarian movement was facing a grave crisis, that "our Federation finds itself isolated in relation to the masses", and that this situation had to be ended. It criticised the attitude of too many anarchists compromising with political parties and reformist unions. "This state of things is due in large part to the weakness, at the individual level, of study and analysis of the disciplines which constitute the essence of anarchist doctrine, as well as the absence of a genuine organisation."

Through the Readership Commission, UGAC militants attempted to galvanise the FA paper, Le Monde Libertaire, with a design remake, with a monthly tabloid in two colours, and columns specifically devoted to life of the organisation, and the current political situation, in an attempt to keep up with political and social events. In addition, the centre spread was devoted to the development of ideas, in particular historic and sociological problems. The UGAC hoped to give the movement a press capable of understanding the whole range of problems that revolutionaries faced. But very soon, the old guard of the FA took back the paper, and the UGAC had to struggle to have itself heard in its pages. By 1963, some members of UGAC had left and others started to talk of pushing for a split with the FA. The UGAC abandoned the FA the following year.

Two years later, they issued a pamphlet, Letter to the International Anarchist Movement. Affirming that they were Platformists, they declared that they had reached the conclusion that it was impossible to regroup all the anarchist tendencies within one organisation, but that all anarchist communists should unite and take an active part within the revolutionary movement. The UGAC put forward the following positions:

That the Third World was "the essential terrain of revolutionary struggles"

2. Western revolutionaries must support them "unconditionally".
3. The anarchist communist movement could not and should not assume a leadership of this movement, and was one of several tendencies of the revolutionary movement.

From these erroneous positions, the UGAC established several fronts with Maoist and Pabloist-Trotskyist groups – support networks for the FLN, the national Vietnam Committee, and the Comité d'Initiative pour un Mouvement Révolutionnaire (CIMR). Each of these fronts was a failure, each of the partners of the UGAC preferring political hegemony to a sincere political front.

In UGAC's bizarre statements, the Western working class is assimilated to the bourgeoisie, "workers' control" in Algeria and Yugoslavia (how Zorkine would have winced!) are shining examples, with the addition further along the line of embryonic workers' control by the Vietnamese FLN.

In 1967 The UGAC set up their own magazine, Perspectives Anarchistes, appearing every three months. The thirty or forty UGAC members took an active part in the May and June events of 1968, the sixth issue of the magazine appearing during the events. The following year, their magazine changed its name to Tribune Anarchiste Communiste, and the group now functioned under the same name. They attempted to enact their new political positions within the Mouvement Révolutionnaire, along with ex-Communist Party militants, ex-FCLers like Fontenis, Pabloist Trotskyists of the ex-Jeunesse Communiste Révolutionnaire (JCR, Revolutionary Communist Youth) and assorted unaffiliated individuals. The MR fell apart over differences in approach, to be replaced by the Centre d'Initiative Communiste (CIC).

The TAC gradually disappeared, leaving only its magazine, which continued until its disappearance in the 1990s. By then the TAC group had been a mere handful of militants for a long time.

Noir et Rouge

The magazine of the GAAR, Noir et Rouge, was continued by those who refused to go with the UGAC into the Federation Anarchiste, a half dozen comrades including Christian Lagant and Frank Mintz. At the same time N&R was constituted as a group that declared that it had "neither ambition for representivity nor for organisational regroupment". By then 20 issues had been published and N&R continued to publish over the next nine years up to 1970, supplemented by duplicated or printed pamphlets.

The print run varied over these years, reaching 3,500 after May '68. From issue 20 to issue 30, N&R involved itself in discussing the internal problems of the anarchist movement, at the same taking an extensive look at workers' control/workers' self-management (autogestion). It attacked the influence of freemasonry within the movement, considering joint membership of these two movements as incompatible. It described Freemasonry as the specific organisation of the bourgeoisie within the 1789 Revolution and that as anarchists, the bourgeois and capitalist regime, class division and the bourgeois class itself, had to be struggled against. In addition, the presence of conscious Statists within freemasonry made involvement impossible.

N&R also launched an attack on individualist anarchism. It examined the problems of elections and electoralism, heavily criticising the Fontenis electoralist adventure.

N&R's look at autogestion involved an in-depth study of the Spanish anarchist collectives in issues 30 and 31 in 1965. In issues 32 and 33 in 1966, it examined workers' control in Yugoslavia, finally taking a look at workers' control in Algeria in issues 35 to 37. An important contributor to N&R was Todor Mitev (1926-2002) an exiled Bulgarian anarchist doctor, who contributed articles on workers' control in Yugoslavia, a critique of Marxism and a spirited defence of Bakunin, under the pseudonym of "Yvo".

Invited to the annual congress of the FA in Bordeaux in 1967, the N&R witnessed confrontations between the tendency around Joyeux and Maurice Laisant on one hand, the historic leadership of the FA, and what was left of the UGAC tendency and other young militants on the other. This resulted in the exit of a dozen groups from the FA, to various other libertarian organisations, including to N&R. Noir et Rouge had been respected in many quarters of the libertarian movement for its theoretical and historical studies, but the resulting criticism of bureaucratic practices in the FA in the pages of the magazine, and its support for those who had left the FA, gained it hostility from elements within that organisation.

At the same time the nature and composition of N&R changed with the entry of these new militants. The founding N&R members, despite their important theoretical illuminations, felt stale and welcomed the influx of dynamic new members. During the rest of that year and into the following, N&R moved away from being a group for theoretical elaboration and renewal, to one of activism, finally jettisoning the magazine in 1970, against the advice of Mitev, and becoming what was described as a "non-group group". Among those attracted to N&R were the Nanterre students Daniel Cohn-Bendit and Jean-Pierre Duteuil, both of whom were to have important roles in May and June 1968. Up to those events, N&R had a very limited audience.

In the June 1970 issue, no.46 in his article "On Neo-Anarchism" Lagant wrote that "we took a position on Marxism in saying that the split did not come between it and anarchism but between Leninism and the libertarian spirit or anti-centralism. For having enunciated this completely simple conception, which commenced nevertheless to make its way in the libertarian movement, as well as on the necessity for us to confront Marxism by normal spirit of openness, the orthodox called our tendency "anarcho-marxist"! Lagant went on to say that a critique of Marxism was as necessary as a critique of anarchism as they were presently constituted, and that these critiques were inseparable.

The CLJA

The Comité de Liaison des Jeunes Anarchistes (CLJA) was created in 1965, grouping together members of the Jeunes Libertaires (JL, Libertarian Youth) the FA, the UGAC, the exile Spanish Federation of Libertarian Youth (FIJL) and various autonomous groups. This group organised a European meeting in April 1966 in Paris, with groups from

Britain, France, Belgium, Spain, Holland, Italy and Sweden attending. This addressed itself to youth and depoliticisation in Europe, the insurrectional movements in the Third World, the anti-Francoist struggle, electoralism and syndicalism, organisation, and Vietnam. Cohn-Bendit and Duteuil made several interventions at this congress. In many ways the congress anticipated what was to happen two years later with the May/June events. This movement took an anti-organisational posture, refusing the establishment of committees. It was an ephemeral grouping, its two main developments being the Dutch Provo movement and the establishment of the Nanterre group around Duteuil and Cohn-Bendit. The other members of the CJLA grouped themselves around N&R and the Nanterre group. This led on to the establishment by CLJA members of the Liaison des Etudiants Anarchistes (LEA) which worked closely with the Nanterre group, with some effective actions in the student milieu from 1966 up until May 1968.

Another development was the short-lived Jeunesse Anarchiste Communiste (Anarchist Communist Youth) founded in January 1968. This group, organising a hundred students in the lycées (high schools), carried out an intense activity in the Latin Quarter of Paris during the early months of 1968 with mass flyposting, and then was another small but important participant in the May/June events. At first influenced by situationism, and then by councilism, it became a component of the Mouvement Communiste Libertaire (MCL) – see below.

Chapter Thirty Four
May 1968 and After in France

The events of May/June 1968 were a major test for the French anarchist movement. One can estimate perhaps a thousand militants organised in the FA, UGAC, N&R, JAC, and the anarcho-syndicalist CNT and various autonomous groups. The small number of militants and their lack of initiative meant that many were little more than spectators of the events. Some members of N&R, the JAC and the UGAC, as well as the Groupe Louise Michel of the FA, took part in the street fighting, and of course the Nanterre group had an important role in the first days of the events. May/June 1968 revealed the weakness of the movement and the months which followed were to prove one of scission and crisis. At the same time, social anarchism, as expressed through the large numbers of black flags on demonstrations, the slogans chanted and painted on walls of libertarian providence, and the visibility of people like Cohn-Bendit and Duteuil, rescued the anarchist idea from obscurity. This revival was reflected in the large number of pamphlets and leaflets relating to anarchism that began to appear during and after May and June.

After the split within the FA at Bordeaux in 1967, the FA seemed to have stabilised but was unable to take advantage of the situation. One anarchist communist militant within the FA, Maurice Fayolle, began to advance ideas of organisational efficacy. Maurice Fayolle was active before World War Two in the Amiens group of the Union Anarchiste. After the war, he settled in Versailles and took part in the rebuilding of the anarchist movement, which led to the founding of the FA. He served as its Secretary of External Relations in 1950 and was a member of the Versailles group. He was one of those expelled from the FA in 1953 after the OPB took control of it and forced its opponents out. Always a social anarchist, he was one of those who refounded the FA and was a member of the Association Pour L'étude Et La Diffusion Des Philosophies Rationalistes (AEDPR, Association for the Study and Diffusion of Rationalist Philosophies), which represented various tendencies within the FA and was set up to avoid a repeat performance of the OPB event. During the Algerian war he took a clear position in the paper of the FA, Le Monde Libertaire, writing many excellent articles on the need for anticolonialist struggle but warning against a "nationalist revolution" and the emergence of a new bourgeoisie.

At the FA Congress at Vichy in May 1956 he opened up the road to renewed dialogue and set in motion various debates over structure and organisation. He advanced ideas for the restructuring of the organisation. Remarking on the stagnation of anarchism due, according to him, to its inaptitude for organisation he called for a more structured functioning. Fayolle concretised his ideas in the long article Reflexions sur l'anarchisme published in Le Monde Libertaire in 1965. At the 1967 Congress he took up his theses again on the formation of a revolutionary anarchist organisation. This was rejected by the Congress. On the bases he advanced, a new tendency was created, which supported his theses and called itself "Paris-Banlieue-Sud". Fayolle then joined this tendency which began to call itself the Organisation Révolutionnaire Anarchiste (ORA), of which he was the leading animator. This drive towards efficient organisation provoked the ire of individualists within the FA, who argued for the loosest organisation possible.

Fayolle was one of the first within the FA to draw lessons from 1968 and to state that organisational lapses in the FA had allowed the leftists, Trotskyists and Maoists, to take advantage of the situation.

The dynamism of the ORA led it in March and April 1969 to opt for a Platformist style organisation and to move towards total autonomy from the FA. This process was catalysed by the May '68 events and the preparation for the forthcoming international Congress in Carrara. In the months before the Congress a tendency formed within the FA opposed to the setting up of an international of anarchist federations. Events and discussions before, during and after the Congress led to the secession of the ORA at the end of March 1970. But Fayolle was ill with lung cancer, and remained undecided about the clear break between the ORA and the FA, even though elected to its provisional national committee. He posited a confederation in which the ORA could still collaborate where possible with other anarchist tendencies. He died on 30th September 1970.

Joyeux and co. had accelerated the departure of the ORA comrades by forcing them out of positions of responsibility in the FA. In 1967, the ORA had brought out a paper, L'Insurgé (The Insurgent) which clearly spelt out its adhesion to class struggle and to specific anarchist communist organisation. The ORA broke with the FA and constituted itself as a separate organisation at a national meeting on 29th and 30th March 1970 at Limoges, changing the name of its paper to Front Libertaire des Luttes de Classe (Libertarian Front of Class Struggle). However, the number of groups which departed was small – five groups in the Paris region, five in south east France and two in central France – and certain of these, like the Bourg-la-Reine group, soon quit the ORA. An attempt to merge with another dissident group, the Union Federale Anarchiste, failed and in November 1969 other groups left the organisation. At its origins the ORA was essentially a Paris-based organisation and was directly inspired by the Organisational Platform.

Another anarchist communist organisational initiative was the meeting of several dozen militants on the 10th and 11th May 1969 at Paris. Among those attending were members of JAC, TAC, and ex-members of the FCL. Major initiators of this meeting were Fontenis, making a reappearance in the libertarian movement, and Daniel Guérin, as well as the rail worker Michel Desmars. As a result of this, the TAC decided to withdraw, preferring to continue to engage with the CIMR (see above). Other militants who attended this meeting failed to continue their involvement, because they wished to continue activity within the traditional movement.

Fontenis had been involved in a libertarian communist group at Tours, affiliated to the UGAC, but taking a firm line on specific anarchist communist organisation, at odds with other UGAC members affected by spontaneism. The meeting at Paris led to the foundation of the Mouvement Communiste Libertaire (MCL) with groups in Paris, Tours, Nancy, Blois, Angers, Nantes, Caen and Poitiers. It consisted of a mixture of students, teachers, and workers. It was able to bring out a paper Guerre de Classes (Class War) in 1971, edited by Guérin. Those militants involved had been active in the CIMR but were dissatisfied with the manipulations by the Pabloists within its ranks. It pronounced for the power of the workers councils and for generalised autogestion (self-management). In many ways it reincarnated the old FCL. The MCL published workers bulletins aimed at rail workers and postal workers (Action-cheminots, Action-PTT) and numbered around a hundred militants.

A rapprochement began between the ORA and the MCL, leading to several meetings to discuss unity. By 1971 there was talk of fusion of the two organisations. However, some ORA militants were distrustful of the presence of Fontenis, including of his involvement in freemasonry, and of the "Marxist" and "councilist" orientation of the MCL. In addition, the ORA was still bound to the idea of a common anarchism, which alongside anarchist communism still included individualism etc. The end result was that some groups – Marseille, St-Etienne, Dijon and a number of Parisian militants – left the ORA and merged with the MCL, leading to the founding of the first Organisation Communiste Libertaire (OCL) in July 1971. At the same time some other Parisian militants like Alexandre Skirda and Roland Biard left the MCL because they deemed it insufficiently Platformist, to join the ORA.

It should be noted that attempts at libertarian communist cohesion in this period were damaged by the virus of spontaneism as fostered by Cohn-Bendit and Duteuil at the time. This sprang from a distrust of organisation acquired as a result of not just the Fontenis adventure but various bureaucratic manoeuvres within the FA. It affected even those groups seeking effective organisation, as can be seen with the MCL and the first OCL. It carried on with the founding of Informations Correspondences Ouvrières (ICO), made up of former members of Socialisme ou Barbarie, the libertarian socialist group around Cornelius Castoriadis (Paul Cardan), of N&R, of the FA, etc and adopting increasingly spontaneist theses.

The MCL was very much under the influence of Luxemburgism and councilism and more and more turned against the idea of the specific organisation, opting instead for a coordination of workers groups. They generalised from the examples of the Rail workers Committee of Tours (animated by Desmars and others) and of Cahiers de Mai, a magazine founded in 1968 seeking to coordinate workers base groups in France, and animated by militants from various political persuasions. This clashed with the views of ORA on the need for specific organisation. The ORA shared the view that the revolutionary movement must be based on base organisations – strike committees, action committees – but saw the need for an organisation able to coordinate and theorise the lessons of these grassroots movements.

The First OCL (1971-76)

The first Organisation Communiste Libertaire was founded in Marseille in July 1971. Efforts were made to continue talks between the ORA and the OCL but these foundered, and the chief advocate of unity, Daniel Guérin, left soon after to join the ORA.

In their Libertarian Communist Platform of 1971 drafted at the Congress, with the active participation of Fontenis and Guérin, the OCL stated:

"I – The individual and collective revolts mark out a history of humanity which is a succession of societies of exploitation. At all times, thinkers have led to a reflection questioning society. But it was with the advent of modern capitalist society that the division of society into two fundamental antagonistic classes became clear, and it was through the class struggle, the engine of the evolution of capitalist society, that the path is taken which leads from revolt to revolutionary awareness.

"Today, because it has changed form, the class struggle is sometimes denied and we invoke either the gentrification or the integration of the working class, or the birth of a new working class which would, so to speak, naturally fit into the decision-making centres of capitalist society. In fact, the old social layers are disappearing, the polarisation of classes into two fundamental classes is increasing, and there is always somewhere in the world a point where the class war is reigniting.

"Whatever ideological forms it takes, the capitalist mode of production is globally one. Whether in the form which, part of 'liberalism', moves towards state monopoly capitalism, or in that of bureaucratic state capitalism, capitalism can only increase the exploitation of labour in an attempt to escape the deadly crisis that threatens him. The massacres, the general ruin of living conditions, as well as all the exploitations and alienations more specific to this or that human group (women, young people, racial or sexual minorities, etc.) are manifestations that cannot be separated. The division of society into two classes: that which disposes of wealth, of workers' lives and that creates or perpetuates superstructures (customs, moral values, law, culture in general), and that which produces wealth.

"Today the proletariat can be defined by the following broad notion: those who, at one level or another, create surplus value, or contribute to its realisation. The proletariat is joined by those who, belonging to non-proletarian strata, rally to the proletarian objectives (intellectuals, students...).

"II – The class struggle and the revolution are not purely objective processes, are not the results of mechanical necessities independent of the activity of the exploited. The class struggle is not a simple phenomenon that we observe, it is the engine that constantly changes the situation and the data of capitalist society. The revolution is the result. It is the taking in hand, by the exploited, of the instruments of production and exchange, of weapons, the destruction of the centres and means of state power.

"Of course, class war is punctuated with bloody difficulties, failures, defeats, but the action of the proletariat periodically re-emerges, more powerful and more extensive.

"1. It first manifests itself in terms of direct confrontation in the workplace; it also manifests itself in terms of problems of daily life, in terms of struggles against the oppression of women, young people, minorities, in terms of questioning school, culture, art, values, etc. But these struggles must never be separated from the class struggle. To attack the state, the superstructures, is also to attack capitalist domination. To fight for working conditions or for salary increases is to lead the same fight. But it is clear that to pose the problem of the kind of life more than the wage level can give to the fight a more radical pace when it means a setting in movement of the masses for a whole concept of life, rather than merely quantitative improvements.

"2. Historical analysis highlights a deep tendency, manifested by workers through their direct struggles against capital and the state, towards self-organisation, and in the forms taken by revolutionary action, appear from embryonic structures of classless society. During the most daily struggles, the tendency to autonomous action manifests itself: wildcat strikes, kidnappings, various forms of direct action opposing bureaucratic directions, action committees, basic committees, etc. With the demand for power at general assemblies of workers and the refusal of the permanence of delegates, it is a real self-management of struggles that is on the agenda.

"For us there is no historical and formal break between the emergence of the ruling proletariat and its struggles to achieve this emergence, but a continuous and dialectical development of self-management practices from the class struggle to the victory of the proletariat and the establishment of classless society.

"A specifically proletarian mode of organisation, the 'power of the councils', arose through revolutionary periods such as the Paris Commune (1871), the Makhnovist Ukraine (1918-21), the workers' councils of Italy (1918-22), the Bavarian Republic of Councils (1918-19), the Budapest Commune (1919), the Kronstadt Commune (1921), the Spanish Revolution (1936-37), the Hungarian (1956) and Czech (1968) revolts, May 1968.

"The power of councils realising generalised self-management in all areas of human activity, can only be specified in its organisational forms by historical practice itself, and any attempt to define the new world can only be a approach, a project, a research.

"The appearance and generalisation of direct forms of workers' power imply that the revolutionary process is already well advanced. However, it is to be presumed that at this level, bourgeois power is still far from being completely liquidated. There is therefore a temporary duality between the revolutionary and socialist structures put in place by the working class and the counter-revolutionary forces.

"At this period, the class struggle, far from being attenuated, reached its paroxysm, and it was there that the terms of class war took all their acuity; the future of the revolution depends on the outcome of this war. However, it would be dangerous to design the process according to well-defined standards. Indeed, the nature of state power, that is to say, counter-revolutionary, in the fight against councils, can take different forms.

"Power and society are no longer separated, the maximum conditions being achieved for the satisfaction of needs, trends, aspirations of individuals and social groups, man escaping his condition of object to become the creative subject of his own life.

"It is therefore obvious that the revolution cannot be made by intermediaries, it is the product of the spontaneous action of the movement of the masses and not of a staff of specialists, or of an avant-garde supposedly only conscious and responsible for the direction and orientation of the struggles. When the word 'spontaneous' is used here, its use should absolutely not be interpreted as an adherence to a so-called 'spontaneist' conception favouring the spontaneity of the masses at the expense of revolutionary consciousness which is its essential complement and overcoming. In other words, a misuse of the concept of spontaneity would consist in assimilating it to a 'disorderly', 'instinctual' activity, which would be incapable of generating revolutionary consciousness as Kautsky claimed and later by Lenin in his What Is to Be Done?

"It is no less obvious that the revolution cannot be a simple political and economic restructuring of the old society, but that it overturns all fields at the same time by breaking the capitalist relations of production, by breaking the state, it is not only political, economic, but cultural, at all times, and it is in this sense that we can use the concept of total revolution.

"3. The real vanguard, it is not this or that group which proclaims the historical conscience of the proletariat, it is indeed those of the workers in struggle who are at the forefront of offensive combats, or those who maintain a certain degree of consciousness even in periods of decline.

"The organisation of revolutionaries is the meeting place, of exchanges, of information, of reflections, allowing the development of theory and revolutionary practice which are only two aspects of the same movement. It brings together activists who recognise themselves on the same level of thought, activity, cohesion. In no case can it replace the proletarian movement itself, nor impose a leadership on it, nor pretend to be its complete consciousness.

"On the other hand, it must tend to synthesise the experiences of struggles, help in achieving maximum revolutionary awareness, seek the greatest possible coherence in the perspective of this awareness, considered not as a goal or existing in the abstract, but as a dynamic.

"In short, its role is to support the proletarian vanguard, to help the self-organisation of the proletariat by playing either collectively or through the intervention of militants, a role of disseminator, catalyst, revealer, and by allowing the revolutionaries who compose it to coordinate and converge interventions, in terms of information, propaganda, support for exemplary actions.

"A consequence of this conception of the organisation of revolutionaries is its vocation to disappear not by a mechanical decision, but when it no longer corresponds to the functions which justified it; it then dissolves in classless society.

"The practice of revolutionaries takes place among the masses, and theoretical development only makes sense if it is constantly linked to the struggles of the proletariat. Thus, revolutionary theory is the opposite of ideological repetitions covering the absence of any really proletarian practice.

"It follows that the organisation of revolutionaries gives itself the vocation of grouping the militants who are in agreement with the above and independently of any 'label' of Marxist, anarchist, councilist, libertarian communist, the label being able to cover in fact a dirigiste and elitist conception of the avant-garde that we find certainly among the Leninists, but also among so-called libertarians.

"It does not recommend itself exclusively to any particular theoretician, nor to any pre-existing organisation, while recognising the positive contributions of those who systematised, clarified, spread, the ideas drawn from the very movement of the masses, but it is situated as a continuation of the expressions of the anti-authoritarian workers' current of the First International, a current which, historically, is known as communist anarchism or libertarian communism, a current which so-called 'anarchist' organisations have often unfortunately grossly caricatured.

"The organisation of revolutionaries is self-managed. It must foreshadow in its structures and its functioning the non-bureaucratic society which sees the disappearance of the manager-operative distinction, and which establishes delegation only for technical tasks and with the corrective of permanent revocability.

"Technical knowledge and abilities of all kinds should be generalised to the maximum, so that effective task rotation is achieved. Discussion and development must therefore be the fact for all activists and more than the organisational standards essential and revisable at all times, it is the level of consistency and awareness of responsibilities achieved by each which is the best antidote to any bureaucratic deviation."

This text was important in coalescing the lessons of the previous two decades. It showed clearly the influences of Guérin with his attempts to reconcile Marxism and anarchism, something which the Noir et Rouge militants commented on in 1967 (N&R no 38, 1967): "We take position on Marxism to say that the split is not between it and anarchism, but between Leninism and the libertarian spirit or anti-centralism... All the same we have never wanted as Daniel Guérin proposes, a sort of mixture of the two ideologies, certain cocktails appearing indigestible to us".

The history of the first OCL was not a happy one. It weathered a number of crises. Some of its militants started negotiations with a councilist group, Gauche Marxiste (GM), which itself soon collapsed. They then joined various fragments of GM. In 1974 the OCL was joined by two groups which had left the ORA. A new magazine, Rupture, was set up in 1975 and the OCL became more and more Luxemburgist and councilist before finally imploding.

Daniel Guérin

Daniel Guérin was born in Paris on 19th May 1904. His family was well-off, with a liberal and Dreyfusard outlook. His family background was conducive to a vivid interest in the arts, letters and music. He distinguished himself at university. Reading Marx, Proudhon, Sorel, Lenin and Trotsky in 1930, Guérin broke with his bourgeois upbringing and began to be active on the left. Later, as he says in his own words: "the reading of Bakunin, in the six-volume edition of Max Nettlau and James Guillaume, immured me to any type of authoritarian socialism, whether it called itself Jacobin, Marxist, Leninist or Trotskyist. Under the effects of the commotion provoked by this reading, I was led to fundamentally revise the sentiments of admiration that the revolutionary strategy of Lenin had inspired in me... I concluded... that socialism must rid itself of the fake notion of the 'dictatorship of the proletariat' in order to rediscover its libertarian authenticity. This led me, when I revised my historic work on the French revolution to substitute 'revolutionary constraints' for 'dictatorship of the proletariat'" (Towards a Libertarian Communism, 1988).

In 1936 Daniel had been active with Marceau Pivert in the left wing of the SFIO (forerunner of the Socialist Party). By successive stages he moved in a libertarian direction. One of these stages was the Hungarian Revolution of 1956. He first of all took up "What I call classic anarchism, which I explained in 'The Youth of Libertarian Socialism' (1959) then 'Anarchism' (1965) and simultaneously 'Neither God nor Master', an anthology of anarchism, where at the side of Bakunin space was given to Stirner, Proudhon, Kropotkin and many others. Then distancing myself a little from classical anarchism and not turning my back so much on my previous Marxist readings, I published 'For a Libertarian Marxism', whose title, I admit, leant itself to confusion, and shocked my new libertarian friends".

After the 1968 events in France, in which he took an active part, marching at the side of Daniel Cohn-Bendit, the Nanterre University student activist made famous by those events, on many demonstrations, he helped set up the MCL. Following the collapse of the MCL, he was active in the OCL and then the ORA and then in the Union des Travailleurs Communistes Libertaires from 1980 up until his death in 1988.

The ORA again

The history of the ORA was marked by confusion and contradiction. Some of its members underlined the importance of a specific anarchist communist organisation, others saw the organisation as primarily a coordinating body between different base groups. There were also contradictions over the question of the unions. Some saw all the unions as being contradictory, others saw the union central of the Confédération Française Démocratique du Travail (CFDT) as a vehicle of struggle. There were contradictions over strategy, with some wanting the ORA to turn in on itself and develop its theoretical positions and some wanting to continue to engage in highly charged activism.

The ORA-MCL debacle caused a major crisis within the ORA, with the loss of its most dynamic militants, many of them founders of the organisation. The ORA reached a nadir with a dozen groups remaining at most, comprising 60 to 70 militants.

In response to this, the ORA decided to create a double structure to accommodate sympathisers. Cercles Front Libertaire (Front Libertaire Circles), made up of readers of the ORA paper, had existed since 1969 and were a gateway for membership of the organisation.

From July 1971, they were given an autonomous status. This resulted in contact with those engaged in activity in the high schools and the neighbourhoods. At the same time, "inter-professional" structures were set up, of building workers, postal workers and railway workers etc. Some of these structures quickly became autonomous, producing their own news sheets and taking an important role in struggles in their particular industries.

This effervescence was halted by a number of splits. Guy Malouvier, a key figure in the secession of the ORA from the FA, began producing the paper Occitania Libertaria in 1970, which soon became the bulletin of the Anarchist Communist Federation of Occitania (FACO) founded in 1971. As he said in 2007: "In parallel with the ORA, I had created the Fédération Anarchiste Communiste d'Occitanie (FACO). Post-68 saw the emergence of the question of nationalities, and more widely than in France. In fact, we were defending the idea of a socialist federation of regions, breaking with the current Jacobin order.... FACO counted fifteen groups and up to a hundred activists. The organisation tried to link libertarian communism to national and cultural emancipation."

Occitanie refers to the southern regions of France, where various variants of Occitan – Limousin, Gascon, Provençal, etc. – are spoken. This support for national liberation was greeted with disgust by many members of the ORA, and the Marseille group quit the organisation to join the MCL. Malouvier followed soon after, preferring to devote himself to the development of the FACO. This grouping collapsed in 1976. Soon after these departures, the Juvisy and 14th arrondissement of Paris groups also pulled out of the ORA.

These groups had not digested libertarian communist ideas in any profound way and discovering Marxist texts, proposed the winding up of ORA and the creation of circles of study of Marxist thought. They ended up in the most Stalinist of the Maoist sects, the Union des Communistes de France!!

So, by the end of 1971 all of the Parisian founders of the ORA, apart from Ramon Finster, had left the organisation, or in the case of Fayolle, had died. A new generation of militants was to carry on the work of the ORA.

But another crisis was to come in 1972 with the support of a minority of ORA members for an electoral front composed of groups like the Trotskyist Ligue Communiste, Revolution! etc. These were expelled from the ORA but posed as a split. A minority joined the Trotskyist group Lutte Ouvrière, whilst the rest moved to the Ligue Communiste. The Ligue made out that 25% of ORA membership had come over to them, when in reality it consisted of a dozen people, the ORA having considerably grown towards the end of 1971. Subsequently, the leader of these electoralists, one Marco, introduced fire arms into the headquarters of the Ligue, resulting in its prohibition by the French State. The whole affair from start to finish was almost certainly a police provocation.

This series of splits was completed by the groups of Grenoble, Lyon and Vitry taking on ultra-spontaneist positions, accusing the organisation of being too "dirigiste" and subsequently departing.

These splits liquidated the various ambiguities and contradictions within the ORA, making it a more united grouping. It integrated the Cercles Front Libertaire in 1973 and by now had a hundred groups throughout France. It began to engage in international relations with the British ORA, and with various groups throughout the world, including Hong Kong. It defined itself as Platformist and from this developed seven principles in 1974:

- Recognition and practice of class struggle;
- Objective and subjective necessity of a violent social revolution;
- Libertarian communism is the expression of those who aspire to the suppression of all exploitation and of all violence, as much against the individual as against the masses;
- The expression of class collaboration is Parliament and national representative government;
- The State is simultaneously the organised violence of the bourgeoisie towards the workers and the system of its executive organs;
- The State must perish, not 'one day' in future society, but straightaway. It must be destroyed by the workers, the first hour of their victory, and not be re-established under any form whatsoever;
- In the transitional period, the taking in hand of the productive and social functions by the workers will trace the clear demarcation between the Statist epoch and that of non-Statism.

Need for an organisation of globalisation and coordination of struggles: the libertarian communist organisation

This organisation in order not to know the 'temptations' of vanguardism must rest upon
a) Theoretical unity (so refusal of eventual syntheses, in particular those based on class alliances)
b) Tactical unity
c) Collective responsibility
d) Federalism (conceived as a contract defining the rights and duties of everyone)

These theoretical acquisitions appeared to solidify the organisation. Significantly, Guérin joined the ORA, obviously seeing the theoretical developments within ORA as a continuation of those developed in the first OCL. However, a further crisis was to shake the ORA.

At the Easter conference of the ORA in 1974 a decision was taken to support "Pour qu'une force s'assemble" which prioritised work around the workers and trade union left. This orientation was supported by young postal workers like Patrice Spadoni and Thierry Renard. In autumn of the same year these militants took part in the big postal strike. Following this, they deemed that the leading core of militants within the ORA on its national committee had an antipathy towards workplace organisation and proceeded to create an official tendency within the organisation, the Union des Travailleurs Communistes Libertaires (Union of Libertarian Communist Workers, UTCL) with other ORA militants in the post offices, building sites, banks and on the railways. This tendency numbered only 14 militants, most of them postal workers, the oldest being 22 years old.

At the ORA national meeting in November Spadoni defended a text inspired by the UTCL tendency, "Polarising our forces towards the workplaces". The text was adopted but the UTCL tendency saw a reluctance of the rest of the organisation to enact it, and an increasing orientation towards the autonomist movement, influenced by the similar movement in Italy, which was drawing large numbers of youth into street battles with the police.

The UTCL tendency was expelled from the ORA at a congress in 1976, where the ORA changed its name to the Organisation Communiste Libertaire. Others considered too close to the UTCL conceptions were expelled at the same time, including Guérin.

The OCL continued with its collaboration with the autonomists until breaking with them in 1980. The leading role of Gerard Mélinand, of the national committee of the OCL, within the autonomist movement, led to the departure of many OCL militants. Whilst the Parisian OCL threw itself enthusiastically into the autonomous movement, the OCL groups outside of Paris, numbering about a dozen, had their doubts.

In 1978 the OCL rejected Platformism and embraced movementism, that is to say, support for autonomous movements. It changed its structures and created an extremely decentralised network, controlled by assemblies of its militants. In that year, Jean-Pierre Dutueil joined the OCL, and has been its leading light up to the present day. In a 2008 self-critique, the OCL stated that it: "believes that militant effort must invest all fields of struggle of society, because the class struggle cannot be reduced to the only economic ground. It takes stock of the leftist faults of the ORA, and considers that the organisation as defined by Arshinov's platform (ideological unity, tactical unity, anarchist program) is an illusory structure. Because it is not the political or trade union organisations which transform a historical subject (the proletariat) into a revolutionary subject, but the fighting spirit in social struggles, by allowing people in movement to pass from a phase of revindication to a breaking point according to a process of awareness and empowerment.

But, although breaking with platformism, the OCL continued to live for a few years in a centralised mode, which is reflected in particular by a Paris-province dichotomy in the production of its newspaper Front Libertaire. This led to a major crisis in 1978-79, a period when the Parisian OCL was seduced by the sirens of "autonomy" imported from Italy. This "autonomous" phase was in fact only a resurgence of the workerism of previous years, with the "discovery" of a new revolutionary subject, the young rebel and urban proletarian, and the mythification of the riot as a place central to the class confrontation. This drift would cause a Paris-province rupture and the disappearance of the newspaper.

After 1979, the OCL was down to a dozen groups, and began working towards creating a new magazine, Courant Alternatif, which first appeared in November 1980 and has continued to appear up until the present day. Apart from its attitude towards organisation and rejection of Platformism, the OCL is distinguished by its support for national liberation struggles, including those of the Bretons and Basques within the French "hexagon".

The OCL define this as taking a class position in these national liberation struggles and "defend the idea that liberation does not pass through the installation of a national bourgeoisie but through a reorganisation of social life and production oriented towards the satisfaction of the needs expressed by the exploited classes and not according to "imperatives" of the market and profit". They "fight forms of claims or struggles that would tend to strengthen the weight of a future or current bourgeoisie", and "favour the weight of the basic popular structures to the detriment of the parties".

During the first half of the 1980s the OCL became an "anti-organisation organisation" like the "non-group group" of previous decades. It prioritised activity in the social movements rather than building the specific organisation. In 1986 with its publication of a book collectively produced by the OCL, L'Etat des lieux (The State of Play) it changed its positions on organisation and began to promote the development of an organisation conceived as an instrument to share experiences of struggle and stimulating activity and thought. It thus went on to participation in a national anti-fascist coordination, an anti-nuclear coordination, activity among the unemployed, etc. It was able to get a national distribution of Courant Alternatif in newsstands and kiosks, as well as producing pamphlets, stickers, posters and leaflets of a specific organisational nature.

The UTCL, Alternative Libertaire and UCL

After its expulsion from the OCL the UTCL tendency became the Collective for a UTCL and launched the monthly Tout le Pouvoir aux Travailleurs (TLPAT, All Power to the Workers) in May 1976. At its foundation, the Collectif consisted of four groups, Paris-Nord, Paris-Sud, and, in the provinces, Clermont-Ferrand and the Anarchist-Communist Group of Marseille. In March 1978, the UTCL became a fully-fledged organisation at a founding conference in February. In the meantime, the Marseille group had distanced itself and did not participate in the congress. On the other hand, the Groupe Communiste Libertaire of Nancy had developed close relations with the UTCL, particularly over anti-militarist activity. This important group had originally left the MCL. Other militants, from Angers, Nantes, the Sarthe region and the Mayenne region, also joined the UTCL at the end of the congress. Among those who subsequently joined it were Fontenis and Guérin. The following year, in June, the UTCL fused with the Organisation Combat Anarchiste (OCA) which had its origins in a split from the FA and in several groups of the Union Federal Anarchiste (see above) which had united between 1971 and 1975 around the paper Confrontation Anarchiste. This grouping had slowly evolved towards positions close to those of the UTCL.

At its third conference in June 1982 the UTCL began work on a collective document Projet Communiste Libertaire Pour Une Alternative (Libertarian Communist Project for An Alternative) which adopted the completed document at its fourth congress in 1986. It was decided to move towards the construction of a new libertarian communist organisation within a larger movement towards autogestion. UTCL militants had taken a key part in the strike movements on the railways in 1986, among teachers in 1987, and among postal workers in 1988. However, there was no noticeable increase in the strength of the UTCL as a result of these activities. The UTCL initiated joint work with the TAC and members of the Comité d'organisation des journées de réflexion anti-autoritaires (COJRA), animated by anarchist communists like Daniel Guerrier and the ex-Pabloist Michel Ravelli.

At the same time following the struggles in the universities and lycées in 1986, some young anarchists had formed the Collectif Jeunes Libertaires (CJL) around the magazine Clash. This gravitated towards these unity moves. So, from 1989 a process began involving the CJL, TAC, UTCL, COJRA, the magazine Noir et Rouge (second reincarnation), the Collectif de Lutte Anti-Capitaliste of Thann-Mulhouse, which included the notable sociologist Alain Bihr, the OCL, the Gauche Autogestionnaire (GA, a split from the PSU, Unified Socialist Party, closest British equivalent being the Independent Labour Party) and some anarchist communist groups of the FA. This led in 1990 to an Appel pour une Alternative Libertaire (Call for a Libertarian Alternative) with 150 signatories. Fifteen different Collectifs pour une Alternative Libertaire were set up and a calendar of meetings and debates began. But at the end of 24 months of debate the majority considered that the process had come to an end and should be terminated, whilst a minority around Guerrier, Mélinand, and Ravelli felt the discussions should continue.

As a result, a new organisation, Alternative Libertaire (AL) was set up in March 1991 with an eponymous magazine. However, the process only involved the fusion of the UTCL and the CJL, and various other individuals involved in the debates coming on board. It was far from the hoped-for results of the process. As for those groups which rejected fusion, the TAC disappeared in 1993, followed by Noir et Rouge in 1995.COJRA went into hibernation, whilst the GA and the Thann-Mulhouse group united to produce the magazine A Contre Courant (Against the Current) which existed up to 2014. Alain Bihr, its leading light, was later to join the UCL (see below).

Over the last few decades AL attempted to relate to the succeeding waves of struggle in France, without noticeably growing. Its attempts at creating an international also led to failures. The first of these was Solidarité Internationale Libertaire (2001-05) involving not just groups like the Federazione dei Comunisti Anarchici in Italy, the Workers Solidarity Movement in Ireland, the North East Federation of Anarchist Communists in North America, the Organisation Socialiste Libertaire in Switzerland etc but various syndicalist organisations like the Spanish Confederacion General del Trabajo and the Swedish Sveriges Arbetares Centralorganisation. It failed to be more than a network of support, its principal achievements being to finance various endeavours in Latin America. With its collapse some of the libertarian communist groups involved regrouped in the loose network Anarkismo which exists up to this day.

In the continued strategy of discourse with similar groups in France, AL entered into discussions with the Coordination des Groupes Anarchistes (CGA) in 2018. This latter grouping had left the FA in 2002 over its methods of decision making, which required complete unanimity and which led to political immobilisation. The CGA called for qualified majority decision making where consensus was not possible. After its departure from the FA, it began to define itself as libertarian communist.

On June 11th 2019 the fusion talks came to fruition and AL and

CGA united to form the Union Communiste Libertaire (UCL). It claims over 600 members and 40 groups. This fusion came at a time when the FA, despite its successes in the past in developing a radio channel, Radio Libertaire, a number of bookshops, and a continuing propaganda with a monthly magazine, appeared to be in difficulties. This is at a time of heightened struggle. History began to repeat itself with the growth of autonomous anarchist groupings involved in street actions, ill-disposed to specific organisation and repeating the many mistakes of the past.

If these chapters on French anarchist communism have occupied a substantial part of this book, this is because France has been a laboratory for libertarian communism over the last 150 years, involving different libertarian communist groupings and organisations. Any assessment of the libertarian communist current has to take account of what has happened in France, its successes and indeed its many failures and mistakes.

References

Biard, Roland. Histoire Du Mouvement Anarchiste 1945-1975. Editions Galilee. (1976)

Dubacq, Philippe. Anarchisme et Marxisme au travers de la Federation Communiste Libertaire (1945-1956) Collection Anarchisme et Mouvement Social. Noir et Rouge no.23 (1991)

Fontenis, Georges. L'autre Communisme: Histoire subversive du Mouvement Libertaire (1990)

Short biography of Todor Mitev: https://libcom.org/history/articles/1926-2002-todor-tocho-mitev

Maitron, Jean. Le Mouvement Anarchiste en France, Vol. 2. (1975)

Interview with Guy Malouvier and Rolf Dupuy in Alternative Libertaire (2007): https://www.unioncommunistelibertaire.org/?Dossier-68-Rolf-Dupuy-et-Guy-Malouvier-Chacun-de-ces-mots-comptait-organisation

The OCL, Forty Years of Revolutionary Anarchism: https://oclibertaire.lautre.net/spip.php?article4

Noir et Rouge: Anthologie 1956-1970. (1982)

Chapter Thirty Five
Anarchist Communism in Italy

After the Congress of the First International at Berne in Switzerland on 26th to 29th October 1876, Cafiero and Malatesta made a public announcement to clarify the views of the Italian section of the First International.

"The Italian Federation considers the collective property of the products of labour as the necessary complement to the collectivist programme, the aid of all for the satisfaction of the needs of each being the only rule of production and consumption which corresponds to the principle of solidarity." The two militants had thus publicly made a statement enunciating anarchist communism. At the same time they signalled in their statement an espousal of Propaganda by the Deed, which was to have profound repercussions on the anarchist movement. "The Italian Federation believes that the insurrectionary deed, destined to affirm socialist principles by means of action, is the most effective means of propaganda and the only one which, without tricking and corrupting the masses, can penetrate to the deepest social strata and draw the living forces of humanity into the struggle sustained by the International".

As we have seen the Italian section of the First International was the first to adopt the ideas of anarchist communism. This included the idea of propaganda by deed and the Internationalists were to soon put this into operation. Pietro Cesare Ceccarelli, one of the Internationalists, was to write "we wanted to carry out an act of propaganda; persuaded that revolution must be provoked, we carried out an act of provocation...We were a band of insurgents destined to provoke an insurrection that cannot and must not count on anything but the echo it may find in the population."

The events that followed – the Matese insurrection of 1877 – has often been portrayed by historians (bourgeois, Marxist, and even some anarchists) as a quixotic, madcap and ill thought-out venture. However, Carl Levy has shown in his writings that Italy had been affected by waves of unrest in the 1860s and early 1870s, riots, strikes and insurrections. This included the Turin riot of 1864, when the provisional capital was moved to Florence, an insurrection in Palermo, and a whole series of riots in the countryside throughout Italy as a result of the grist mill tax, as well as the creation of bandit formations, particularly in the Naples region. In fact, the Matese mountain region in the provinces of Caserta, Benevento, and Campobasso, was noted for its tradition of guerrilla warfare in the years after Italian unification. This was specifically why that region was chosen, with the hope that exemplary action there would spark a social conflagration, as conditions existed for such an occurrence. It was intended, said Ceccarelli, to carry out a mobile campaign, preaching class war, and inciting social brigandage, and occupying small towns for a short time to carry out propaganda and actions.

However, the Internationalists did not count on problems of communicating with the local rural labourers in their own dialect, the infiltration of spies, the small number of insurgents who in addition were poorly armed, as well as the weather. Whilst the symbolic actions were greeted with sympathy by the peasants, they failed to react in any significant way. In the end the insurgents, who included Malatesta and Cafiero, were surrounded and captured. The authorities used the events to move to crush the International and outlaw it by 1880.

The trial of the Matese insurgents began on 14th August 1878. The Internationalists were able to use the court room as a successful forum for anarchist communist propaganda. As a result, the jury, made up of middle class citizens, still imbued with the ideas of Garibaldi and Mazzini of the Risorgimento, and swayed by the defendants' eloquence, acquitted the insurgents. In fact, two thousand townsfolk turned out to cheer those acquitted. However, this was the last triumph of the Italian Internationalists. Cafiero and Malatesta realised that they could soon be re-arrested, and went into exile.

The new liberal government of Zanardelli and Cairoli that had come to power in Italy in March 1878 was prepared to tolerate middle-class republicans but not working class revolutionaries. They launched a crackdown, starting in Florence. Juries consistently acquitted anarchist internationalists, including Covelli, who himself fled into exile.

As a result, the government moved to designate the Internationalists as criminals rather than subversives. This led to the robbing of legal status of the anarchist revolutionaries, and a wave of mass arrests.

Andrea Costa, who had taken a reluctant part in preparations for the Matese uprising, a reluctance due to his conviction of the lack of preparedness, was amongst those arrested. His arrest in France in March 1878, appears to have galvanised his disillusionment with the International. Released from prison after an amnesty in June 1879, Costa published an open letter on July 27th, 1879, in the newspaper La Plebe, where he described the tactic of insurrection as a failure. Whilst acknowledging the need for a violent revolution, and anarchist communism as an ideal somewhere off in the distant future, Costa called for the establishment of a revolutionary socialist party. Thus, Costa broke with anarchist communism and became one of the founders of maximalist socialism. This meant the winning of reforms, and once these reforms were won, workers who would become class conscious as the result of the struggle for such reforms, would see that it was still necessary to overthrow capitalism through violent revolution.

Costa's defection threw the anarchist movement into shock. In response Cafiero called for the organising of "the party of social revolution" in response to Costa's legalitarian party. This would in fact be a secret and conspiratorial network with a rejection of organisation. This presaged what would come within the Italian anarchist movement and the development of an anti-organisational current.

The worst fears about Costa were realised when he stood for parliament in 1882 and decided to take his seat. As a result, the Italian anarchist communists went into crisis. Blaming the defection of Costa on the idea of organisation itself, they, according to Malatesta: "began to preach disorganisation, they wanted to elevate isolation, disdain for obligations, and lack of solidarity into a principle, as if these were the function of the anarchist programme, while instead they are its complete negation. That is what happened to those who, in order to fight authority, attacked the principle of organisation itself. They wanted to prevent betrayals and deception, permit free rein to individual initiative, ensure against spies and attacks from the government – and they brought isolation and impotence to the fore" (writing later in the London Italian paper L'Associazione on 7th December 1889).

Cafiero called for action by any means: "by the word, in writing, by the dagger, the rifle, dynamite, sometimes even by the ballot, when it comes to voting for Blanqui or Trinquet who are ineligible...Everything is good for us that is not legal". Alongside him Covelli called for similar illegalism, concentrating on "the declassed, the dangerous classes, the putrid precipitate of the other social classes, the malefactors, who for individual or social reasons fight and cannot but fight for the moral revolution", and similarly going down the road of irrelevance by his parody of some of the theories of Bakunin.

Cafiero and Covelli fell back on clandestine activity organised in small groups, and the use of bombs. Whilst Malatesta and another prominent anarchist, Saverio Merlino, always opposed these tactics, they remained silent on this in this period of 1880-81 and the tactic spread throughout Italy and other parts of Europe.

Malatesta was in London in 1881 and became involved in the organisation of an international revolutionary socialist congress. Always a strong advocate of effective organisation, he had to argue against the growing anti-organisational currents, like Felico in Naples, and Matteucci in Egypt. Matteucci envisioned a movement which would live in a bubble, remaining distant from the masses, and only communicating with other anarchists.

Malatesta began communicating with other prominent anarchists who constituted what was named the Intimate International. Before the Congress of Verviers in 1877, Kropotkin, Guillaume, Adhemar Schwitzguebel, Brousse, Costa, Pindy, Vinas and Morago had met at La Chaux de Fonds in August or September, to set up a "revolutionary community" known as the Intimate International. This would replicate Bakunin's inner group of dedicated revolutionaries of 1864. Cafiero and Errico Malatesta, in prison at the time, were also associated with this grouping. Now reduced to five by defections and retirement, it now consisted of, besides Malatesta, Cafiero, the Swiss Adhemar Schwitzguebel, the French Jean-Louis Pindy, and Kropotkin.

Kropotkin communicated that what was needed to be created at the forthcoming London congress was dual organisation on Bakuninist lines, a mass organisation that was open and public, but excluding the Marxists, co-existing with a clandestine organisation committed to direct action. To this Malatesta added the need for an international revolutionary league. This was supported by Schwitzguebel but given no assistance by him. For his part Pindy felt gloomy about the situation and consigned himself to wait for a spontaneous mass movement. Cafiero, who was beginning to show signs of mental collapse, wanted to disappear into complete clandestinity. He told the comrades, "In order to make ourselves impalpable and imponderable, we must become atomised. We must no longer write to each other except to say good day and good night... Do not count on me for your conspiracy. Do not write to me about it, and take note that, henceforth, I will be the apostle of the cell. My every dream is to find and create one in which I can immerse myself and disappear until the Last Judgement" (letter, 26th June 1881).

As a result, the Intimate International had no influence on the London congress.

The congress reflected the demoralisation and dejection of the movement. The defection of Brousse and Costa, the withdrawal of Guillaume had had their effects, as had the growth of reformist socialism to the detriment of the anarchist movement. Only in Spain was there any revolutionary élan. Disillusioned with the masses for failing to revolt, anarchist groups turned to the advocacy of bombings and assassinations.

As a result, and despite the efforts of Malatesta, Merlino and Kropotkin to continue the International as a revolutionary vehicle, the other delegates spoke for small group action and disorganisation. Kropotkin did indeed support the use of bombs as one form of action, but was worried about the development of a conspiratorial elite of small groups and urged wide scale propaganda among the masses. This was ignored and the London congress signalled the end of any hope for the continuation of the International. The suggested correspondence bureau never materialised and the proposed next Congress the following year never happened. It was not until 1907 that the next international anarchist congress was to take place. In the meantime a number of unsatisfactory meetings, sometimes billed as international meetings, took place, all of them reaching no decisions.

Merlino

Merlino returned to Italy with the aim of working within the workers' association and to counter the legalitarian socialists. Unfortunately, he had to contend with the anti-organisationalism of Felico and co.

Alongside this was the continual banning of anarchist papers. Merlino himself put up with arrests and imprisonment. Like Malatesta, Saverio Merlino was a strong advocate of effective organisation and continued determined propaganda, including a number of interventions at various international socialist congresses. In exile in London in the late 1880s, Merlino associated with Kropotkin. However by 1907 Merlino was disillusioned with the state of the movement, disgusted by individualism and anti-organisationalism, which he referred to as "atomism" and "amorphism" and he made a dramatic break.

In the meantime, the mental decay of Cafiero continued. In 1882 he announced his conversion to electoralism. This was followed by a suicide attempt. Following this episode, Cafiero made a temporary recovery, but soon total mental disintegration manifested itself the following year. He died of TB in an insane asylum in 1892. Covelli for his part suffered a mental breakdown in 1884 and started a long procession through mental institutions for the next 23 years, dying in 1915. On his gravestone are his own words: "I shall not sell myself either to any government or to any party... I have craved misery, persecution and slander. I have lost everything, there remains only what is me". The pressure of maintaining radical revolutionary positions in a repressive society, exile, poverty and the constant harassment of the State had been too much for Cafiero and Covelli, and they tragically broke.

Luigi Galleani

One of the new generation of notable anarchist communists after that of Cafiero, Costa, Malatesta and Merlino, Luigi Galleani was born in Vercelli near Turin in 1861.He took workers' struggles seriously and cofounded Gazzetta Operaia in Turin, and the Circolo Socialista Difesa del Lavora (Socialist Workers Defence Circle) and the Lega dei Lavoratori in Vercelli. He propagandised among factory workers in the Biella neighbourhood and took an active part in the strikes of mechanics and sand diggers in Turin and the button makers and cotton-mill workers in Vercelli in 1888. He was also instrumental in the strike of leather goods workers in April of that year He constantly worked to radicalise and spread the actions, then drawing in mechanics again, as well as porters and bakers. This spread to include women textile workers. In June he was heavily involved in the strike of 2,000 cotton workers. However, repression forced him to leave the area and move to Nice in France.

Moving from his tactic of entry into unions he began to prioritise coordination between labour activists and specific anarchist groups. He began to criticise the functionings of formal organisations, and this was later to develop into a distrust of all formal organisations, anarchist included and formed the basis of his future anti-organisational anarchist communism.

In 1890 he was forced to move to Switzerland. Here he made friends with Herzig and Dumartheray, and Jacques Gross, who introduced him to works by Kropotkin and Brousse, and to Elisée and Elie Reclus who were then living on the shores of Lake Geneva, from whom he learnt much. This reinforced his particular outlook on anarchist communism.

After prison sentences and constant harassment, and spells outside Italy, Galleani was eventually forced to move to the United States. It was here that he established a predominantly working class movement.

As Wellbrook writes:" While they were vocal in their criticism of trade unionism, Galleanisti could be regularly found bolstering picket lines, delivering speeches amongst striking workers, and raising money for jailed strikers. It is also important to be clear that although Galleani held a strict line of anti-organisationalism, his ideology should not be classified as anarchist-individualist, desiring instead spontaneous, cooperative structures among workers that would emerge during periods of crisis. Neither was this desire necessarily unrealistic, as organising unions carried huge risks, and recognition struggles were met with fierce opposition. As a result, spontaneous industrial action was not uncommon and had been a common occurrence in many parts of the country during the upheavals of 1877. In January 1916, at such a strike in Coddage, Galleanisti (and Galleani himself) gave speeches praising the workers' decision to refuse the offers of affiliation from the AFL or the Industrial Workers of the World (IWW)."

Indeed, unlike some individualists, Galleani had no time for the ideas of Nietzsche, who in vaunting the individual, rejected the view that life fulfilment was characterised by a social and collective relations, saying "how absurd it is to deduce even the most hybrid and distant affinity with anarchism".

Galleani advocated communism throughout his life – "communism because, as everyone must contribute to social production, each should benefit according to their own needs... anarchy because we do not want any yoke of authority, feeling that we are capable of governing ourselves by ourselves..." (Cronaca Sovversiva, 6th May 1905). He summarised anarchist communism thus: "As the ways and measure of the satisfaction of needs vary from person to person, according to their development and to the particular environment in which they live, while the right to satisfy them in the manner which each person, the sole judge, deems convenient, remains equal for all; equality and justice could not receive a more real and sincere sanction than that which is given by the libertarian communist conception of society. All have an equal right to live a full life – the strong and the weak, the intelligent and the dull, the capable and the inept; and, without regard to the contribution each one may have given to the total production of society, they all have the same right to satisfy their needs and to reach the superior forms of higher development." (The End of Anarchism, 1925, p.23).

Thoroughly orientated towards the workers' movement and to strike action and the advocacy of the general strike, Galleani coupled this with a call to armed action against State and Capital, always defending individual responses to repression, and supporting the acts of those like Ravachol, Czolgolz, Angiolillo, etc. As Wellbrook notes: "Anarchists would come to widely criticise and condemn the methods of the Galleanisti (and other anarchists over this period). Terrorist and clandestine tactics would later become practiced by small Marxist-Leninist groups, but never again in the anarchist movement. Ultimately, the organisational strains of anarchism would win over and the Spanish revolution, in particular, would serve to legitimise this strategy to a global audience of militants." (ibid.)

Galleani in his anti-organisationalism demonstrated a profound mistrust of the ideas of Malatesta and Fabbri around an "anarchist party", with an unwillingness to believe in the power of effective organisation and delegation. Writing in the End of Anarchism, he was to state that "Organisationalists are, if we do not err, those anarchists who deem it desirable, necessary and possible to organise systematically, on the basis of previously agreed programmes, as a political party, distinguishable from all other proletarian parties, and able, whenever the opportunity appears, to make itself heard in bargainings, alliances and coalitions that might be suggested by the necessities of the moment, the circumstances of the struggle against the ruling class, against any intolerable misdeed that might have occurred.

Other anarchists call themselves organisationalists, not only because they promote the specific establishment of a political party, but also because they believe that the basis of anarchist movement should be the existing labour organisations and, even more, those that would arise under their auspices, with their stimulus, and have an open revolutionary character.

To these two trends, which differ only by degree, and whose action should always be collective in character, Merlino – if we do not misunderstand his thought – opposes those anarchists who prefer individual activity both in the field of propaganda and revolutionary action.

Modestly, but firmly, we are opposed to those anarchists who call themselves organisationalists, whether they wish to organise an anarchist party politically, or whether, in order to strengthen it, they aim to base it on labour organisations as they exist now, or on other ones they might organise that correspond more to their aims.

A political party, any political party, has its programme; i.e., its constitutional charter: in assemblies of group representatives, it has its parliament: in its management, its boards and executive committees, it has its government. In short, it is a graduated superstructure of bodies a true hierarchy, no matter how disguised, in which all stages are connected by a single bond, discipline, which punishes infractions with sanctions that go from censure to excommunication, to expulsion."

During the post-WW1 ferment in Italy, these anti-organisationalist positions seemed archaic with the greater emphasis on constructing an effective territorial organisation, the Unione Anarchica Italiana. Instead, Galleani advocated merging "with the anonymous crowd" "a decisive force that cannot be organised" and criticised delegation and the passing of resolutions at the UAI Congress of July 1920. At least Galleani's criticisms of the UAI were measured and expressed in reasonable tones, unlike those of the individualist Renzo Novatore. Both the organisationalists and the anti-organisationalists were to be defeated by the rise of Mussolini, and Galleani was to spend most of the rest of his life in prison or under house arrest, often in ill health, finally passing away in 1931.

Luigi Fabbri (1877-1935)

Luigi Fabbri, born in 1877 at Fabriano near Ancona, came from the middle bourgeoisie. His father was a pharmacist. Becoming a republican at the age of fifteen, he was then influenced by meetings with an individualist anarchist, Virgilio Condulmari, at his father's shop, a year later. Condulmari provided him with his first libertarian texts and Fabbri was to write in his diary on 1st August 1893 that "From today I feel that I am an anarchist socialist". His new found convictions soon won him the attention of the police. In 1897 he started publishing a little news sheet at Macerata called La Protesta Umana. This was the same year that he met Malatesta for the first time which had a profound effect on his political convictions. Up to then favourable to individualism, and to the optimistic outlook of Kropotkin, and seeing anarchism as a natural law, his meeting with Malatesta changed all of that. Malatesta discussed with him an article entitled Natural Harmony that the latter had written. By the end of the meeting over two days, Fabbri had become a convinced Malatestian.

Fabbri was often seen as the "son" of Malatesta, continuing his work and ideas. At the same time, there were profound differences between the two. Whilst Malatesta continued his life as a "man of action", with its roots in the Mazzinianism of his early youth, and in Bakuninist ideas, Fabbri, whilst capable of delivering revolutionary speeches, rejected the role of orator and tribune, preferring lectures which developed and clarified ideas to the simplified communication of oratory. Another major difference was in the writing of the two, Malatesta preferring direct and propagandistic articles, whilst Fabbri preferred detailed exposition. In addition, Fabbri was not just concerned with developing libertarian ideas in the field of politics and the workplace, but on a cultural level as well, which included his interest in birth control, freethought, and libertarian education, whilst being careful not to dilute the revolutionary essence of anarchist communist ideas.

As a fluent speaker of French, Fabbri was able to translate and publish texts from Faure, Grave, Pouget, Reclus and Kropotkin in the pages of the magazine that he edited together with Pietro Gori, Il Pensiero (Thought) from 1903. With the absence of Malatesta from Italy after his sensational escape from the isle of Lampedusa in 1899, Fabbri developed a propaganda which clarified the social bases of anarchism and argued very firmly for strong anarchist organisation and for the development of workers' organisation. In doing this he had to polemicise very sharply against the individualist ideas, whether Stirnerite or Nietzschean, within Italian anarchism, that he regarded as deviations as much as the Ravacholism of a previous decade. In a series of articles between 1906 and 1907, which later were gathered together in a pamphlet, Bourgeois Influences in Anarchism, he waged a campaign against these ideas. He was thus able to marginalise individualists like Libero Tancredi (real name Massimo Rocca) who were to evolve towards nationalism and from there to fascism.

Fabbri, like Malatesta, believed in the "anarchist party", conceived as a grouping of conscious militants convinced of the need for specific libertarian propaganda and action. He was one of the most determined militants in favour of the creation of an anarchist organisation. In 1901 anarchists in Rome had adopted an Anarchist Socialist Programme which they hoped to be adopted by the whole movement in Italy. As a result, regional federations were constructed in the Lazio and Marches but a national congress convened in Rome was not possible until June 1907, partly impulsed by the forthcoming international congress in Amsterdam later in the year. This was attended by over one hundred militants representing 37 groups. At Rome, Fabbri presented two texts, one a report on the standing of the Italian anarchist movement, and another on anarchist organisation, which concretised his ideas on the subject. As the text on anarchist organisation noted: "The anarchist organisation must be the continuation of our efforts, of our propaganda; it must be the libertarian adviser which guides us in our action of daily struggle. We can base ourselves on its programme, to diffuse our action in the other camps, in all the special organisations of particular struggles in which we can penetrate and carry our activity and action: for example in the unions, in the anti-militarist societies, in the anti-religious and anti-clerical groups, etc... Our special organisation can also serve as a ground for anarchist concentration (no centralisation!) of agreement, understanding, and the most complete solidarity possible between us. The more united we are, the less danger there will be that we will be drawn into inconsistencies and deviate from the spirit of struggle..."

As a result, the Anarchist Socialist Alliance was created, which remained active until the outbreak of the First World War.

At the Amsterdam Congress later in the year Fabbri contributed to the debate between Malatesta and Pierre Monatte. Always an advocate of a mass workers' movement, his positions on the question of syndicalism was more nuanced than those of Malatesta and in many ways he represented a halfway position between his old mentor and Monatte. He thus voted in favour of both motions from Malatesta and Monatte at the Amsterdam congress, explaining that in the Monatte motion, the affirmation of the class struggle was explicit, which was lacking in Malatesta's motion. On the other hand, Malatesta gave an explicit affirmation of the insurrectional character of anarchism, lacking in Monatte's motion. In addition, syndicalism had to break with reformism and become revolutionary in order to ensure the success of the social revolution. The development of a mass workers' movement had to be in tandem with the creation of a specific anarchist organisation. He continued to be active in creating this mass movement, participating with the anarchists Borghi and Dinale at a union conference at Bologna in 1905, subsequently being involved in the organisation of metal workers in that city and in the important union congress there in 1909. He remained a ferocious opponent of the parliamentary tendencies within the Italian revolutionary syndicalist movement.

In order to express the relationship between the mass movement and the specific anarchist organisation, it was necessary to develop an anarchist communist programme.

As a strong partisan of the specific organisation, he worked towards the foundation of the Unione dei Communisti Anarchici d'Italia (UCA d'I – Union of Anarchist Communists of Italy)) founded at a congress in Florence on 12th to 14th April 1919. Malatesta himself joined this organisation at the end of 1919 with his return from abroad to Italy. Fabbri seems to have acquiesced to Malatesta's drive for anarchist unity which saw that organisation transform into the Unione Anarchici Italiana (UAI, Italian Anarchist Union). He contributed heavily to its programme. He strongly criticised the individualists and the Galleanists, both advocates of anti-organisationalism. Unlike them he saw the growing danger of fascism in Italy, whilst some individualists downplayed the threat of Mussolini's march on Rome and saw the fascists as no more dangerous than the reformist socialists. He developed these ideas on fascism and its deadly threat in his The Preventive Counter-Revolution written in 1920, an acutely perceptive document. He placed the anarchist specific organisation in the front line of organising against fascist violence and repression and of developing the struggle towards anarchist revolution without subordinating itself to antifascism and losing its identity.

Both he and Malatesta saw clearly that a new class was emerging with the Leninist bureaucracy in the Soviet Union. These insights were articulated at the November 1921 conference of the UAI in Ancona, where the Bolsheviks were seen as the main enemy of the Russian Revolution.

Forced to flee from fascist Italy, Fabbri ended his days in Uruguay in 1935.

Bifolchi, Berneri

Unlike Fabbri and his associates, Giuseppe Bifolchi was one of the few Italian anarchists who rallied to the Platform. Originally an individualist anarchist, he later moved over to anarchist communist positions. He attended the international meetings convened by the Platformists and later signed, with others, an Anarchist Communist Manifesto of the First Section to Adhere to the International Anarchist Communist Federation. There was little support for this, and the problems at home in Italy and in exile led to this initiative being stillborn (see https://libcom.org/history/bifolchi-giuseppe-1895-1978).

Camillo Berneri was a thinker of anarchist communism with a refreshing outlook in the generations after Malatesta and then Fabbri. Born in Lodi in 1897, and profoundly influenced by his mother, a primary school teacher with progressive views, he first became active in a socialist youth group in 1912. Increasingly critical of the Socialists, he abandoned them at the age of 15 after three years of intense activity.

This disaffection came after the riots in Reggio Emilia following a meeting of the pro-war ex-socialist Cesare Battisti. He became increasingly frustrated by the Socialist Party's fudging position on the War, an equivocal "Neither for Nor Against".

Determinedly anti-war, Berneri became influenced by the anarchist bookbinder Torquato Gobbi. He was to meet and marry the sixteen year old anarchist Giovanni Caleffi and became active in the movement. Drafted in 1917, the War cemented his anarchist communist convictions.

Berneri worked with Malatesta on the paper Umanita Nova at the end of the War. He became a member of the UAI and served for a time on its national committee. Forced to flee from Florence, where he had settled, he moved to Umbria, and then, because of increasing fascist persecution, decamped to France.

Berneri constantly sought to make anarchist communism a movement that could be effective, could implant itself socially and with that aim in mind, he rejected anarchist purism and dogmatism. He engaged in polemics with the developing Leninist current, moving from initial support for the Revolution to a trenchant critique of Bolshevism and applied a sharp criticism to the current anarchist movement. He wrote:

"'Pure' anarchism, closed with absolute intransigence towards political life, is out of time and space, a categorical ideology, a religion, a sect. On the outside of parliament, of the municipal and regional institutions, it neither knows nor wants to fight actual struggles and obtain some consensus from time to time; it does not know how to raise questions that concern most citizens. (...) The anarchist movement has excluded itself from an infinity of battles, always blinded by the vision of the "City of the Sun", always lost in the repetition of its dogmas, always confined by its strictly ideological propaganda."

Berneri argued at the 3rd UAI congress in 1921 for a minimum programme and for effective organisation. As he said:

"There remains on the discussion table the question of the constitution of our movement as a party. It is necessary, on this and other issues, to define the meaning of the word, giving it a clear meaning in order to avoid the eternal, useless discussions for or against... What do we mean by party? What is the significance, the limit and the mission?... I cannot see the danger of centralisation, of authoritarianism that many see in an organisation that is ever more solid and coordinated at group, provincial union or regional federation levels. Has individual or group atomisation been useful? Is our movement not by nature and definition refractory to the negative influence of a badly understood party discipline? Why should a libertarian movement crystallise as it becomes a party and degenerate into some form of authoritarian centralism, as some fear and prophesise? I believe we need to gather our forces, to join together and coordinate, but I do acknowledge there are many contrasting positions in the movement on this matter."

Berneri wrote a number of essays on the problems of communism, including his I Problemi della Produzione Communista (The problems of communist production) and concluded that communism had two main enemies, the State and individualism.

He contributed to the USI paper founded in 1914 and edited by Armando Borghi, Guerra di Classe, (Class War) and later himself edited its continuation as a newspaper in Spain. In the pages of that publication, he engaged in an analysis of syndicalism and its validity as a form of revolutionary struggle.

He consistently polemicised against the scourge of individualism within the Italian movement, in particular in debates with the individualist Renzo Novatore and persistently defended a pro-organisational position. In favour of the creation of the UCAI and then the UAI, he was convinced that only an organisation with a certain coherence could realise the hopes for social transformation.

Forced to move from country to country after his flight from Italy, Berneri ended his days in Spain. There, in the pages of Guerra di Classe, he was to analyse and critique the unfolding Spanish Revolution. He polemicised against the militarisation of the militias, opposed the institutionalisation of the war and counterposed guerrilla warfare to one of the symptoms of that institutionalisation, trench warfare. He called for anti-imperialist campaigns in the Spanish colony of Morocco, in order to undermine an important bulwark of

Francoism, the Moorish troops. He denounced the involvement of CNT and FAI leaders in Republican governments. Above all he emphasised that the war and the revolution were intertwined and that the former could not be won without the strengthening and deepening of the latter. His valuable insights earned him the hostility of the Stalinists and he was murdered by them during the May Days in Barcelona in 1937.

The Libertarian Communist Federations

Silvano Fedi was an important anarchist communist during the Mussolini period. Born in 1920 in Pistoia, he became politically active at the high school he attended. Here in 1939 along with other students he organised a group to struggle against the fascist regime. He was arrested on the 12th October of that year along with Fabio Fondi, Giovanni La Loggia and Carlo Giovanelli by the secret police OVRA. They were sentenced to a year in prison for communist activity by a Special Tribunal.

Silvano Fedi returned to Pistoia after prison and took up anti-fascist activity again. By now he was calling himself an anarchist or, as he preferred, a libertarian communist, thanks to conversations with other Pistoian anarchists. The older generation of anarchists made contact with the student group which included Fedi and with several factory workers and technicians and with the group of Bottegone. The enthusiasm of the high school students galvanised the Pistoian anarchist movement and the Federazione Comunista Libertaria was set up in that city, growing and confronting and competing with the underground Communist Party.

Fedi was again arrested by the police in January 1942. With the fall of fascism and the armistice of Italy with the Allies, he was among the first to go to the main piazza (square) and address the crowds. On the 26th July 1943 he was addressing a factory gate meeting at the San Giorgio factory and called on the workers to strike. He was arrested by the police of Marshal Badoglio. On hearing of his arrest, a large crowd gathered outside the Palace of Justice and demanded his release. The authorities were forced to free him a few hours later.

Fedi now set up the most important partisan unit in Pistoia and its immediate vicinity. It was formed of peasants, workers, students and ex-soldiers, for the most part anarchists or influenced by libertarian ideas.

The unit initially consisted of 50 partisans and was called the Squadre Franche Libertarie. It did not hide in the mountains, but moved incessantly between the city and the countryside, carrying out several spectacular actions which relied primarily on surprise.

Fedi made it clear that he was not prepared to disarm when the Anglo-American forces arrived and that the armed resistance must lead on to social revolution. However, his plans were cut short when he was caught in a German ambush on 29th July 1944 and shot. The circumstances of his death are still not clear to this day, and the facts point to a betrayal.

Fedi represented developments within the clandestine anarchist movement in Italy under Mussolini. Strongly influenced by the experiences of Italian anarchist volunteers in Spain, where the concept of a realised libertarian communism was very much on the agenda, Libertarian Communist Federations were formed in different parts of Italy. One, the Federazione Comunista Libertaria Alta Italia (FCLAI, Libertarian Communist Federation of Upper Italy), held its first conference in Milan on 23rd to 25th June, 1945. This concretised the work of two secret conferences in 1944. After the Liberation of Italy several Libertarian Communist Federations were created. There were 28 sections of the FCLAI with 1200 members alone in Milan. Similarly, the Libertarian Communist Federation of Liguria, was also set up and formed a component of the FCLAI. The Ligurian Federation was set up as early as 1942 and included seasoned veterans lie Emilio Grassini, who had experience within both the USI and the anarchist movement, and was an "advocate of a class conception of anarchism, advocate of the workers' organisation founded on the councils," according to Guido Barroero.The following organisations attended the 1945 conference: In Lombardy, the Milanese Libertarian Communist Federation, the Lombard Libertarian Communist Federation, the Libertarian Communist Youth Federation of Milan, the Libertarian Communist Group of Legnano, the Bergamo Anarchist Group and the Libertarian Communist Group of Erba. Piedmont was represented by the Piedmontese Libertarian Communist Federation and the Piedmontese Anarchist Youth Federation, Veneto by the Libertarian Communist

Group of Verona, Liguria by the above-mentioned Ligurian Libertarian Communist Federation and the Ligurian Libertarian Communist Youth Federation, Tuscany by the Libertarian Communist Federation of Tuscany, the Tuscan Communist Federation of Florence, the Livorno Libertarian Communist Federation, the Libertarian Communist Federation of Carrara, and the Libertarian Communist Federation of Piombino, Emilia Romagna by the Imola section of the Italian Anarchist Federation, the Camillo Berneri Group of Sant'Arcangelo di Romagna, the anarchist group of Piacenza, and the Marche by the Marchese Anarchist Federation. Leading lights of the FCLAI included Ugo Fedeli, Mario Mantovani and Alfonso Failla.

The 1945 conference discussed the enactment of libertarian communism in the political and economic spheres, agitation within the workplaces and the recently formed Factory Commissions, the development of a youth movement and the progression of press and propaganda. The FCL brought out a weekly paper Umanita Nova. It was decided that, "despite the fall of fascism, the capitalist and monarchist framework has not even been affected and that therefore the anti-bourgeois struggle must continue more intensely by exploiting all the possibilities that present themselves". As a result of FCL activity young militants in the Communist Party like Arrigo Cervetto and Lorenzo Parodi came over to anarchist communism.

However, instead of continuing as a specific anarchist communist organisation, the various sectors of the FCLAI attended the founding conference of the Federazione Anarchica Italiana (FAI) on 14th to 20th September 1945 at Carrara where they agreed to unite with other anarchist currents in the creation of what was essentially a synthesist organisation, with the adoption of the Associative Pact of Malatesta.

At the end of 1945 members of the Lombard Libertarian Communist Federation, including Antonio Pietropaolo, Mario Perelli, and Germinal Concordia broke with the FAI, and founded the Federazione Libertaria Italiana (FLI, Italian Libertarian Federation) who wished to unite with dissident elements within the Communist Party. It set up a paper l'Internazionale and campaigned in 1946 in the referendum for a republic in Italy. It subsequently supported the Italian Socialist Party of Proletarian Unity (Partito Socialista Italiano di Unità Proletaria, PSIUP) in the elections that year. Following the expulsion from the government of the parliamentary left, and the split in the Socialist Party occasioned by its decision to jointly campaign with the Communist Party in the 1948 elections, a new grouping which rejected this, the Socialist Party of Italian Workers (Partito Socialista dei Lavoratori Italiani, PSLI) was formed.

Mario Perelli then joined the PSLI, along with Carlo Andreoni. Pietropaolo retired from political activity, later condoning the Soviet crushing of the Hungarian uprising in 1956. Germinal Concordia founded the National Communist Party, a pro-Titoist grouping, in 1949. The FLI fell apart, and many of its other members returned to the anarchist movement.

However, tensions soon arose with the anti-organisationalist Galleanists around Adunata dei Refrattari at the second congress of the FAI in 1947. Under their influence the National Council set up at the 1945 Congress was replaced by a Correspondence Commission which was a mere "mailbox" rather than a body undertaking the day to day running of the FAI. The influence of individualists like Cesare Zaccaria, opposed to permanent organisation and programmatic politics, should also not be underestimated. Also significant was the return from exile of Armando Borghi. Originally basing himself on syndicalist and class positions, (indeed the secretary of the USI and editor of its paper Guerra di Classe) Borghi had evolved into a defender of "ideological" anarchism and counselled against the reconstruction of the USI and involvement in the CGIL. The FAI turned further and further away from class positions.

The GAAP

A profound disquiet about this situation was expressed by old organisationalists like the worker Lorenzo Gamba of Savona and the young intellectual Pier Carlo Masini. Born at Cerbaia in the province of Florence, in 1923, Masini's youth was spent in the anti-fascist student circles which sprang up in Florence at the end of the 1930s. He joined the liberal-socialist movement of Tristano Codignola, and was a driving force in its youth group around the magazine Argomenti. He was arrested for "conspiratorial" activity on 21 June 1942 and condemned to three years confinement at Guardia Sanframondi in the Matese mountains in southern Italy. Released on 19th May 1943 he returned to Tuscany and there grew close to the Communist Party.

During the last phase of the war and the immediate post-liberation period, Masini moved towards the Anarchist movement, with what he saw as the compromises of Togliatti, the Communist Party leader. Under the influence of the anarchist veterans Alfonso Failla, Umberto Marzocchi (who had fought with the Anarchist militias during the Spanish Civil War) and Mario Mantovani, Pier Carlo became enthused with the ideals of anarchism from August 1945.

Two of the first Anarchist papers to appear in Tuscany in the months following the Liberation were edited by Masini-Passione Rivoluzionaria, organ of the Tuscan Anarchist Youth, and Alba dei Liberi (Dawn of the Free).

Masini's relationship with the anarchist movement was not easy. Pier Carlo was full of dynamism and enthusiasm, but he often came up against comrades advanced in years, exhausted by the long struggle against fascism and often isolated and marginalised within the workers movement by the hegemony of Marxism. Masini set out to consciously revive the movement, creating a political and cultural network that reached out far beyond the movement itself.

He put the first stage of this plan into operation with the magazine Gioventa Anarchica (Anarchist Youth) which appeared between 1946 and 1947, jointly edited with Carlo Doglio. Despite its brief life of 14 issues the magazine had a great influence on the renaissance of Italian anarchism, with articles covering many political and cultural issues, including important articles on cinema written by Doglio. Masini, through the magazine, entered into dialogue with other reviews and the tiny Bordigist and Trotskyist organisations.

Within the Italian Anarchist Federation (FAI) Masini was initially occupied with its Antimilitarist Commission, then becoming editor of the FAI weekly paper Umanita Nova in 1948. A magnificent and energetic editor, he was also a superb orator.

In Genoa, a group of young militants began producing the bulletin Inquietudine (Apprehension, Inquietitude) which expressed their concerns about the trajectory of the FAI. They included ex-partisans like Lorenzo Parodi and the Savonese Arrigo Cervetto, as well as Casimiro, Aldo Vinazza, Aldo Panzieri, Alberto Mondani, Rubino, Bruno De Lucchi, and Renata Lovarini. Eight issues of the bulletin appeared between March 1949 and January 1950. This group quickly established links with Masini.

The internal conflict within the FAI between the youth grouped around Masini and the more traditional elements came to a head with the Livorno congress of 1949 and the Ancona congress of 1950. Concern over the orientation of the FAI was also expressed by Arrigo Cervetto at the conference of the Ligurian Anarchist Federation in Genoa in March 1950, and he also expressed these concerns in the pages of the Milanese paper Il Libertario. At the third congress of the FAI in 1949 in Livorno Ugo Scattoni, Renzo Sbriccoli, Parodi and Masini argued for organisational efficacy. In the aftermath, a magazine contributed to by Rome militants like Scattoni, Marcello Cardone, Tancredo Maroncelli and Masini, and by Genoese and Livornese militants was established in September 1949. It was entitled l'Impulso (Impulse) subtitled Anarchist News from Lazio and Tuscany. The magazine proposed the intensification of local work, the strengthening of the FAI and a fight against revisionist and anti-organisational tendencies. It affirmed the class nature of anarchist communism and called for organisational efficiency. In a later issue the FAI was referred to as a "heterogeneous heap, held together by old and scarce reserves of sentimentality".

A polemic between Masini as editor of Umanita Nova and the individualist Zaccaria as editor of the L'Impulso magazine ended in the resignation of Masini from Umanita Nova. The fourth FAI Congress 1950 saw the triumph of Borghi's positions against the re-establishment of the USI and intervention in the CGIL. The proposal for an anarchist organisation with an anarchist theory and practice adapted to the new economic, political and social reality of post-war Italy, with an internationalist outlook and effective presence in the workplaces was rejected and this led to the secession of others and the creation of the Gruppi Anarchici d'Azione Proletaria (GAAP, Anarchist Groups of Proletarian Action) on 24th and 25th February 1951. There Cervetto put forward the thesis "the Liquidation of the state as an apparatus of class." In this thesis he argued that, "the social revolution, that installs a classless society, is accomplished with the simultaneous liquidation of the bourgeoisie as a class and the liquidation of the state as an apparatus of class," and that, "it's the task of the proletarian mass organisations (factory councils, agricultural community, people's committees) to expropriate the capitalist system of its facilities and to take on direct and collective management." Cervetto also developed analysis of the Soviet Union as state capitalist in the pages of l'Impulso.

Meanwhile at its Fifth Congress in 1953, the FAI rejected both the individualists and class struggle anarchism, setting the pattern for the next few decades.

The GAAP allied themselves with the similar development in France, the Federation Communiste Libertaire. These two groups were the main components of the Libertarian Communist International (ICL) in 1954, along with a small Spanish section and informal links with the British movement via the militant Ken Hawkes, and the FDSA (Social Anarchist Federation of Germany).

The GAAP now sought to set up a front with other groups, the Bordigist Internationalist Communist Party of Onorato Damen, Azione Communista, a group of dissident ex-Communist Party members led by Giulio Seniga, who had been on the PCI central committee, the Trotskyists of the Revolutionary Communist Groups led by Livio Maitan, in a cartel called the Movement of the Communist Left. They held a joint demonstration in Milan.

Cervetto began to develop an analysis of the Soviet Union, defining it as "state Capitalism" in a series of articles for l'Impulso.

Three tendencies developed within the GAAP as expressed within their internal bulletin l'Agitazione (Agitation), the first one of organisational anarchist communism, the second around Masini which looked for a synthesis of anarchism and Marxism, and the third around Cervetto and Parodi evolving more and more towards Leninism. In 1956 the GAAP changed its name to the Federazione Comunista Libertaria at its fifth congress held in Milan on 13th to 15th October 1956. Cervetto and Parodi pushed for the acceptance of the notion of the dictatorship of the proletariat.

On 16th December 1956 the first National Conference of the Communist Left took place in Livorno. It sought a unitary position for the different groups, facilitated by an Action Committee. Soon the Bordigists and the Trotskyists left the cartel. In May 1957 there was a joint communiqué from Azione Communista and the FCL sanctioning the merger of the two organisations. With this the history of the GAAP/FCL ended. Cervetto and Parodi had now developed openly Leninist views and called for the formation of a class party.

As Masini wrote in a letter to Fontenis, "nostalgists for paleolithic Leninism and second-hand Leninists" seized control of Azione Comunista and forced out or discouraged the anarchists. Masini made the decision to join the Socialist Party (PSI) at the end of 1958, joining a tendency within it that had internationalist, classist and anti-Togliatti positions. He remained with these social-democratic views for the rest of his life. Seniga also joined the PSI. Lorenzo Gamba returned to the anarchist movement. Azione Comunista ceased publication in 1966 and Parodi and Cervetto then founded the group Lotta Comunista.

The 1960s

The 8th Congress of the FAI in Carrara in 1965 saw the tensions between the Galleanists and the organisationalists come to a head, with the former seceding after the affirmation of the old Associative Pact of the UAI was approved. The seceders, who included Borghi founded the Gruppi di Iniziativa Anarchica, and upheld Galleanist positions until their dissolution in 2011.

The ferment that began with 1968 led many young Italian anarchists, like their counterparts in France and Britain, to rediscover the Organisational Platform of the Libertarian Communists.

A first manifestation of this was the 1st National Convention of Anarchist Workers in Bologna in August 1973, assembling around thirty groups. This was followed by the expulsion of platformist elements from the FAI. The first regional conference of the Apulian Anarchist Organisation (OAP, Organizzazione Anarchica Pugliese) attended by groups expelled from the FAI, took place in Bari in 1974. It was founded on the Platformist principles of theoretical and tactical unity and collective responsibility. It had groups in all the important cities in Apulia, set up liaisons in the high schools and universities and neighbourhood committees. It sought unity with other regional groupings of expelled Platformists.

In 1976 it changed its name to the Organizzazione Rivoluzionaria Anarchica (ORA). In 1978 it convened its first National Congress at Bari, where in addition to the Apulians, groups from the Emilia,

Lombardy and Campania attended. Later groups from the Marchese, Veneto and Piedmont joined and the ORA was able to transform itself into an Italy-wide organisation. A leading light in the ORA was the militant Donato Romito (1954-2018).

Alongside this development was the emergence of the Unione dei Communisti Anarchici della Toscana (UCAT, Anarchist Communist Union of Tuscany) set up in 1978. It was formed from a fusion of the Anarchist Communist Group of Florence and the Organizzazione Communisti Libertaria (OCL) of Livorno. Other groups that emerged were the Organizzazione Anarchici Ligure (Anarchist Organisation of Liguria) which evolved into the Organizzazione dei Comunisti Libertari (Libertarian Communist Organisation) of Genoa and which included the important working class militants Franco Salomone (1948-2008) and Guido Barroero (1946-2015). In addition, there was the Organizzazione Anarchica Marchigiana (OAM, Marchese Anarchist Organisation) made up of anarchist communists who had left the FAI in 1972, the Movimento Anarco-Comunista Bergamasco (Anarchist Communist Movement of Bergamo) and the Gruppi Kronstadt (Kronstadt Groups) of Naples. All of these upheld positions of class, anarchist communism and adherence to the Platform.

In 1980 a national congress of the ORA was held in Modena, and as a result of disagreements, Modena anarchists left to found the Partito Anarchica Italiana (Italian Anarchist Party, PAI).

The ORA began to be heavily involved in workplace activity, in addition to its social agitation in the neighbourhoods.

The FdCA

In 1981 the 5th Congress of the ORA took place and it was proposed that a National Connection of Anarchist Communists be set up to coordinate the different regional groupings. This was duly set up, including the PAI, the OCL of Livorno, the Federazione Communista Libertari Ligure (FCLL) and the UCAT. However, unity was only forged between the ORA and UCAT which came together in 1985 to found the Federazione dei Comunisti Anarchici (FdCA)

At the Third Congress of the FdCA in 1992, it was reinforced by merger with the OCL of Livorno, which brought with it its magazine Comunismo Libertario.

But an extraordinary congress of the FdCA in 1994 saw the emergence of a tendency which wished to turn the organisation into a synthesist organisation like the FAI. This group around Comunismo Libertario departed after their defeat at the congress and became a FAI circle in Livorno.

In 1997 the FdCA relaunched itself with its Minimum Programme of the Anarchist Communists. It joined the SIL (Solidarité Internationale Libertaire) set up by the French UTCL) and brought out a paper, Alternativa Libertaria.

Thanks to the entry of a wave of young people into the FdCA, as well as old militants like Franco Salomone, the organisation was able to re-galvanise in 2004. The previous seven years had seen a numerical and geographical expansion An FdCA website was set up and the FdCA had sections in Emilia-Romagna, Fano-Pesaro, Liguria, Lombardy, the Northeast, Puglia, Rome and Sicily. The 9th Congress of the FdCA in 2014 saw a name change to Alternativa Libertaria/FdCA. In 2017 the group around the new run of Comunismo Libertario in Livorno and Lucca decided to join the FdCA.

References

Manfredonia, Gaetano. La Lutte Humaine: Luigi Fabbri, le mouvement anarchiste Italien et la lutte contre le fascism. Paris (1994).

Santos, Francisco Madrid. Camillo Berneri: un anarchico Italiano (1897-1937) Rivoluzione e contrarivoluzione in Europa (1917-1937). Pistoia (1985)

Senta, Antonio. Luigi Fabbri: the most dangerous anarchist in America (2020).

Fabbri, Luigi. L'Organisation Anarchiste: https://fr.theanarchistlibrary.org/library/luigi-fabbri-l-organisation-anarchiste

Wellbrook, C. Seething with the Ideal: Galleanisti and class struggle in late 19th century and early 20th century USA

https://libcom.org/history/seething-ideal-galleanisti-class-struggle-late-nineteenth-century-early-twentieth-centur

Entry on Emilio Grassini: http://www.bfscollezionidigitali.org/entita/13643-%E2%80%8Bgrassini-emilio/

http://www.comunismolibertario.it/gaap.html

https://books.bradypus.net/sites/default/images/free_downloads/organizzazione_anarchica_marchigiana_no_images.p

Chapter Thirty Six
Anarchist Communism in Bulgaria

Hristo Botev, elevated to the stature of 'National Poet' by the Stalinist regime and still held in great esteem in Bulgaria, was to fall under the influence of the Russian anarchist Mikhail Bakunin and was probably the first to introduce anarchist ideas into Bulgaria with his distribution of Bakunin's Statism and Anarchy there. He founded the first Bulgarian libertarian group at Brăila, across the border in Romania.

In the decades to come and after the independence of Bulgaria from the Ottoman Empire was established in 1877, socialist and libertarian propaganda began to be spread within the country. Spiro Gulaptchev established the first socialist publishing house, Skoropetchatnitsa (Rapid Printing) at Ruse. Most of the contributors were anarchists, with a number of Marxist writers also contributing. Among the libertarian contributors were Nicolai Stoinov, Varban Kilifarski and Paraskev Stoyanov (the founder of surgery in Bulgaria).

Stoinov and Kilifarski helped form the first peasant unions in Bulgaria and Stoinov also participated in the founding of the Union of Teachers, the first union in Bulgaria in July 1895.

Kilifarski and Stoinov founded the Bezvlastie (Acracia – no rule) publishing house in 1908 which published all the essential texts of anarchism. This allowed the greater spread of libertarian ideas so that by 1910, there was already talk of an anarchist federation to coordinate the activities of local groups.

Mikhail Guerdjikov founded the paper Probuda (Awakening) in 1912 with the aim of organising the nascent movement. Two years later, other anarchist publications appeared: the paper Rabotnikcheska Missal (Workers' Thought) and the magazine Osvobodenye (Liberation). The Ruse group attempted to set up an anarcho-syndicalist movement with a programme and aims and principles and a publishing house of the same name.

The wars in the Balkans and the First World War brought anarchist publishing activity to a halt. However, the number of people refusing military service grew considerably. This period was characterised by bold acts of armed struggle by some anarchists, epitomised by the dashing and romantic revolutionary, Georgi Sheytanov. They proved to be a serious threat to the State. The amount of propaganda increased in volume. It was indicative of the development of the movement that Sheytanov turned away from armed action towards the building of a mass movement.

Rabotnikcheska Missal reappeared in 1919 and took the initiative to call for the founding conference of an anarchist federation. This took place in Sofia between 15th and 17th June where more than 150 delegates from different towns and villages attended. The congress decided to establish The Anarchist Communist Federation of Bulgaria (FAKB). A large number of groups were now formed in nearly all towns and the biggest villages. The movement attracted workers, students and high school students, as well as teachers, white collar workers and various professionals. Many conferences and meetings took place and Probuda became the official organ of the FAKB.

When it was closed down by the authorities, underground and other still legally published papers took its place. The next three conferences of the FAKB took place in secret. Finally, a legal conference took place at Yambol in 1923, attended by 104 delegates and 350 observers representing 89 local groupings. The conference reported that Rabotnikcheska Missal had a print run of 7,500 copies, distributed in 140 localities. There were four publishing houses and 16 pamphlets had been published in this period. The conference attracted the attention of the authorities and subsequent repression, resulting in the murder of 30 anarchists by the authorities on 26th March 1923 and a subsequent military coup on 9th June.

Subsequent risings in September were bloodily put down.

The establishment of a repressive regime with the King at its head led eventually in 1926 to the setting up of a 'democratic' government, which gave the anarchist movement a little leeway and allowed for the publication of several papers and magazines. However, the movement as a whole still had to exist underground and was only able to hold one national congress in secret at Kazanlik in August 1927. Because of the difficulties of illegality and the repressive regime there were problems of disorganisation in this period. This prompted moves towards greater organisation within the FAKB. Bulgarian anarchism had always rejected individualism and revolutionary syndicalism and above all defined itself as anarchist communist, citing Bakunin, Kropotkin, Malatesta, Faure, etc. However, from 1926 anarchosyndicalists began discussing how to organise workers in the towns and cities. This was at the instigation of Pano Vasiliev from Lovech, who had returned from Argentina. A good orator, polemicist and writer, Vasiliev and some of his followers, including former Marxists, organised large-scale propaganda, publishing their ideas in several newspapers and magazines. Anarcho-syndicalism in Bulgaria was itself split between mainstream anarcho-syndicalists and those influenced by the Organisational Platform. The first current organised itself around the paper Rabotnik (Worker) and the second around the paper Probuzhdane (Awakening) and an organisation, the Federation of Workers and Peasants (FRS).

Partisans of the Organisational Platform of the Libertarian Communists now had a certain popularity in Bulgaria. In fact, the Dielo Trouda group had arranged a meeting with Polish and Bulgarian anarchists in late 1926 which proved fruitful, with wide agreement over the question of organisation. Several senior members and functionaries of the FAKB, who had been imprisoned during the repressive period came under the influence of the Platform and pushed these ideas within the organisation. There was a resulting clash within the movement. The magazine Thought and Activity, expressing Platformist views, was set up in Sofia in 1930, edited by Boris Markovensky from March 1930 to February 1931. From June 1932 up until April 1934 in Sofia, under the editing of Petar Bukurestliev, Probuzhdane was published with 50 issues. Originally, it had defended the traditional line of the FAKB but moved to platformist and syndicalist positions. Other editors included G. Yordanov, Hristo Todorov and Hristo Nikolov.

On March 1, 1932 the Bulletin of the Federation of Workers and Peasants was set up in Sofia, representing the specifically Platformist tendency, under the editorship of Angelov. The FRSists believed in the creation of syndicalist unions alongside that of a specific anarchist communist organisation.

There was fierce polemicising between these two tendencies, leading to mutual hostility. Both set up clubs in Sofia, each numbering about 50-60 people, and were involved in supporting strikes in this period.

However, they both remained minorities within the Bulgarian anarchist movement, with the majority of the FAKB holding to their original positions. In addition, the maximalist positions of both the syndicalists and FRSists had little resonance among striking workers.

The FRS in an article "Among the Masses" fulminated against anti-organisationalism and stated "Enough dogmatism. It leads to wear and tear, to alienation from the people, to sectarianism." In another article, The Organising Problem, the FRS commented that: "Anarcho-syndicalists are the bearers of the anarchist idea in the labour movement. This is the mass wing of anarchist-communism, its agent in working class circles." It was recommended that anarchists merge with the masses without losing their ideological lines.

The pure anarchosyndicalists accused the FRSists of seeking to create another political party, and posited the need for revolutionary syndicalist unions free from the influence of all the political currents, including the anarchists.

The FAKB anarchist communists acted strongly against the attempts by the syndicalists to capture the movement. They wished to affirm that the main role in a revolution would be by specific anarchist communist ideological groups. They convened a conference in summer 1928 near the Shipka monastery that united 40-50 militants. The main topic discussed was the state of the movement after the April 1925 pogroms and how to re-establish the movement.

A quite considerable number of anarchist militants established themselves in southern France and in Paris, having taken a joint decision to move there in 1927 whilst in exile in Yugoslavia during the period of repression in 1925. The group in Toulouse, numbering 35 and in conjunction with comrades in Paris and Beziers, supplied support to the comrades back home, while at the same time, formulating a new platform and programme for the FAKB. The group included Alexander Sapundzhiev, Dimitar Balkov, Hristo Manolov, Vladimir Vodenicharov, Vasily Denchev, and Georgi Hadzhiev (real name Georgi Grigoriev, also later known as Georges Balkanski). This new platform was inspired by the Organisational Platform. They had studied and analysed the Platform over a period of three years (1928-30) and had adapted it for their own platform and draft programme. These returned to Bulgaria following an amnesty and constituted a group of twenty based in Sofia. They then worked towards the convening of a secret conference in a forest near Lovech in August 1932. This was attended by 90 delegates. There were four items on the agenda of the conference: 1. "The ideology of the anarchist organisation" 2. "Union movement" 3. "Cooperative work" and 4. "Peasant trade unions".

The conference was a major step in the reconstitution of the FAKB. Unanimity was achieved, the papers of the different tendencies were suspended and Rabotnikcheska Missal was established as the united paper of the FAKB. However, this unity was short-lived as the pure syndicalists, sceptical of a specific anarchist organisation, withdrew from the FAKB after several months, as did those who had developed a platformist-syndicalist approach, who were to maintain the FRS.

At a meeting of anarchists near the Dryanovo Monastery, fierce arguments broke out between the syndicalists and the FRSists. The nub of the matter was the differences over organisation, the FRSists believing in a strict disciplined organisation (later on they added the submission of the minority to the majority) whilst the syndicalists believed in the construction of unions imbued with anarchist ideas (the FAKB majority anarchist communists, on the other hand, saw anarcho-syndicalism as one of several tactics to be employed). The syndicalists regarded ideological anarchists as representing intellectualised elements and that only one movement was needed, that of anarchist unions that represented a genuine anarchist communism.

For their part the majority anarchist communists called the FRSists 'anarcho-Bolsheviks'.

A follow-up conference held secretly in the mountains near Maglitch in 1933 affirmed the need for a specific organisation, for tactical and ideological unity, and for a programme of action. Local groups federated into five regional organisations within the FAKB. This was named the sixth congress of the FAKB. It took a decision to transcend the factional struggles and to proceed with reorganisation. It also recommended that the groups be cleansed of supporters of factional struggles. Delegates from Sofia spoke out against the syndicalists and FRSists, who they did not regard as anarchists at all. In addition, the conference decided against any united front alliance with the Stalinists and "an independent and uncompromising struggle". A federal secretariat was elected but this attempt to rebuild the FAKB failed, with the factional struggles continuing. Various groups expressed the need to work together and disgust at the "hostility and mutual destruction", stressing that there was still scope for common work.

Despite this, with consistent propaganda, the FAKB developed everyday agitation among workers and peasants with organisational work, the establishment of cooperatives, cultural groups, free schools and libraries. This period of relative liberty nevertheless involved the arrest of militants and the closing down of publications. Another coup took place on 19th May 1934 and the movement once more had to go underground.

The majority of anarchists (anarchist communists, the FRS, and some anarcho-syndicalists) rejected proposals for joint action and a common front against reaction in Bulgaria. In a manifesto to the Bulgarian people, the FAKB states that "the capitalist system in Bulgaria sees in fascism its last support". At the same time, they refused to cooperate with other anti-fascist forces because they were against all power, and rejected the popular front as an alternative to the development of political life in Bulgaria. "The Popular Front is the new, most dangerous illusion for the Bulgarian workers".

Some anarchists, mainly anarchosyndicalists and the FRS, allowed for joint action with anti-fascist organisations, primarily the Bulgarian National Agrarian Union and the Social Democrats, but not a united front with them, action only being predicated on a class base, based on joint work of the different unions. They regarded the work of the Communists and other organisations as opportunistic.

There was support for the Spanish Revolution in 1936 with 30 comrades managing to get to Spain. The dictatorship and the subsequent period of Nazism during World War Two limited much activity. The Bulgarian Communist Party itself, whilst also underground, had no liking for anarchists, as witnessed by its murder of the anarchist resistance fighter and agronomist, Radko Kaitazov, on the day of the liberation from Nazism in 1944.

The Spanish Revolution brought temporary unity between the three different anarchist currents, with joint solidarity work. The anarcho-syndicalists, in imitation of the Spanish anarchist movement, initiated the National Labour Confederation (NCT) with a magazine entitled Class Struggle. The FAKB and the FRS also stepped up their activity. The FRS brought out a mimeographed Bulletin whilst the FAKB produced a pamphlet about Spain.

When the Fatherland Front was founded in July 1942 at the instigation of the Stalinists, with the participation of the left of the Agrarian People's Union, the left of the Social Democratic Party, etc, as a front against fascism the FAKB at first accepted the tactic of "support and cooperation" in the fight for the destruction of fascism. Soon though, the FAKB anarchist communists began to openly criticise and reject the Fatherland Front, in opposition to the syndicalists and FRSists who continued to support it. The FRSists at this time had Lalo Marinov (Lamar), D.K Madzhov, and Hristo Arnaudov as leading lights.

In 1945 the anarcho-syndicalists and the FRS convened a joint conference. This was attended by about 20 people, with attendance from members of the FAKB, who denounced the organisers as tools of the Communist Party. The conference decided that the two groups would form the Union of Workers and Peasants. In a report to the delegates entitled

"Our attitude toward the Fatherland Front, war, trade and cultural and educational organisations" it was stated that "the ideal of communists and anarchists is one and the same. The dispute is only about the ways of its realisation. "Anarcho-syndicalists express support for Bulgaria's participation in the "defeat of fascist Germany ".

"The War, which is now waged by the Bulgarian people, is an anti-fascist war" the report said. "Our opponent is fascism. That's why we anarchists… we cannot stand indifferent in the war." Moreover, both syndicalists and the FRS were positive about the Red Army's liberation mission and the Soviet Union. "The Antifascist War spread between the peoples of Europe the spirit, the benefits of the largest ever social revolution – the Russian Revolution". Anarchists were urged to take part in the activities of the various organisations of the Fatherland Front. However, some delegates disagreed with this statement and it is not clear whether it was accepted.

The Sofia organisation of anarcho-syndicalists recommended "waiting" and "looking for the right time" and until then should work within the committees of the Fatherland Front. They advised working in these organisations, but "avoiding raising the maximum slogans" and not being a "ruthless opposition". The views of the FAKB on the other hand were expressed through their paper Rabotnikcheska Missal. Opposition to the new government were expressed, and in some places anarchist communists started open public activity, with propaganda both indirectly and directly criticising the Fatherland Front.

A new Stalinist regime, carried through by a military coup with the support of the Soviet Army, took place on 9th September 1944. For a while the legal existence of the anarchist movement was possible, allowing the holding of a conference in October of that year in Sofia.

Rabotnikchetska Missal was once again published for four issues before it was shut down again by the authorities. The activities of local groups continued, leading to a well-organised secret conference on 10th March 1945 near Sofia. This had come about as the result of a joint meeting between the FAKB and part of the anarcho-syndicalists earlier in the year, where it was agreed on a merger of the two groups. The March 10th conference was attended by 90 delegates. In conference statements, opposition to the Fatherland Front were voiced. However, the secret police conducted a raid and arrested all the delegates who were then placed in a concentration camp. Fortunately, circumstances within the new Stalinist regime led to their liberation and the publishing of four issues of the paper. The print run shot up from 7,000 to 30,000, and if there had not been paper rationing, there would have been 60,000 printed! However, the occupying Red Army subsequently suspended the paper because its soldiers were reading it and were starting to come under the influence of anarchism.

Rabotnikcheska Missal published the Platform of the FAKB agreed at the March 10th Conference. The publication of the Platform went openly and actively against the Communist Party and the Fatherland Front. They campaigned against involvement in the projected elections of November 18th, 1945. Seeing that the Communists were orienting propaganda towards Bulgarian youth, they called for the restoration of anarchist youth organisations. For their part, anarcho-syndicalists around the paper called for support for the Fatherland Front in the elections.

Those members of the FAKB who were imprisoned were told by a leading light of the Communist Party, Russi Hristozov, that:" It is clear to the Party that if we give you freedom of agitation and propaganda, you will become a force that we can never cope with. This determines the attitude towards you". At a Party plenum, Tsola Dragoycheva states: "If we give the anarchists freedom of organisation, propaganda and printing, all our revolutionary cadres will go to them."

Meanwhile the Platformists of the FRS decided to enter the Bulgarian Communist Party with the excuse that they would work secretly within it "until the storm passes". This failed to materialise, and the ex-FRSists were offered high positions and scientific titles and were completely co-opted by the Stalinists.

The regime now instituted a new period of repression, with anarchists being interned in concentration camps. Another secret conference took place in Sofia in August 1946 with 400 groups represented. An underground duplicated bulletin replaced the banned FAKB paper. A further wave of repression was carried out in December 1948, two days before the fifth congress of the Communist Party. More than 600 anarchists were arrested and detained in concentration camps. Many militants escaped abroad, the exodus starting in 1946 and continuing up until 1951. These militants established the Bulgarian Anarchist Union in exile, working within the anarchist international organisations of the International Workers Association (IWA-AIT) and the International of Anarchist Federations (IAF-IFA).

With the fall of the different Stalinist regimes throughout Eastern Europe, the Bulgarian anarchist movement re-emerged from clandestinity and established the Bulgarian Anarchist Federation, which exists to this day.

References

Balkanski, Gr. Histoire du Mouvement Libertaire en Bulgaria. (1982)

Hadzhiev, Georgi, History of Anarchism in Bulgaria: https://ru.theanarchistlibrary.org/library/georgi-hadjiev-istoriya-anarhizma-v-bolgarii http://obuch.info/vvedenie.html

(It is interesting that the online History of Anarchism in Bulgaria by Hadzhiev/Balkanski/ Grigoriev in a Russian translation of the Bulgarian original, specifically mentions that the Bulgarian anarchists in Toulouse studied the Organisational Platform and were influenced by it, whereas the French translation leaves this out. Could this be due to the antipathy of the French publishers, Groupe Fresnes-Antony of the Federation Anarchiste, towards Platformism?)

Daskalov, Doncho. Anarchism as Ideology and Movement: an introduction to anarchism: http://obuch.info/vvedenie.html

Daskalov, Doncho. Anarchism in Bulgaria (Sofia: Univ. Ed. St. Kliment Ohridski, 1995).

Chapter Thirty Seven
Anarchist Communism in Latin America

Anarchist communism was brought to Latin America in the aftermath of the First International by Italian, Spanish, Portuguese and German immigrants, some of whom were temporary refugees from political repression in Europe, like Malatesta, some who became permanent residents. It entrenched itself in the newly emerging industrial centres and with anarcho-syndicalism, became one of the main currents within the workers' movements there, only losing influence to Leninism in the aftermath of the Russian Revolution in the 1930s. The most industrialised of the Latin American countries was Argentina and here a large anarchist movement was to emerge.

Argentina

"To start talking about anarchism in the early twentieth century in Argentina, we have to separate what is anarcho-syndicalism and what is anarchism as union policy. The development of FORA in Argentina tends to be identified as anarcho-syndicalism, however, anarcho-syndicalism is a late conjunction. What we know as anarchist unionism at the beginning of the century, is an original experience that has not had a similar one in Europe. FORA is a political-union organisation. It organises workers, but not as workers but as anarchists, committed to the 'purpose' of Anarchist Communism." Fernando Lopez Trujillo, 2004.

Malatesta's sojourn in Argentina had an important influence on the workers' movement there. There were already existing Italian, Spanish and Spanish language sections of the First International in Argentina, that had been established in the 1860s but it was not until 1876 that some of these became attracted to Bakuninist ideas and a section in Buenos Aires affiliated to the 'anti-authoritarian' International.

In the 1880s some Belgian immigrants from the Verviers region introduced anarchist communist ideas to Argentina. Among these was Emile Piette. These were reinforced by the French militant Jules Alexandre Sadier and Alexandre Falconnet. Piette set up a bookshop in Buenos Aires in 1884 and distributed the anarchist communist paper Le Révolté as well as Le Père Peinard and set up an anarchist club. In June 1884, 18 Italian internationalists set up the Circolo Comunista Anarquico in the capital and in 1885 V. Mariani also distributed Le Révolté whilst the Catalan carpenter Juan Vila translated Kropotkin's Conquest of Bread and distributed it in Buenos Aires.

In 1887 the Italian Ettore Mattei began to publish El Socialista, an anarchist communist weekly. In 1909 he was to write about the appearance of Malatesta in Argentina, who had fled imprisonment in Italy in 1885:

"Communist and anarchist propaganda intensified when, after two or three months of the arrival in Buenos Aires of our comrade Malatesta, a Círculo de Estudio Sociales was formed with great enthusiasm, located in 1375 Bartolomé Mitre Street, where Malatesta and other comrades gave the first anarchist communist public speeches, later published in Italian in La Questione Sociale. In the following years other circles and clubs of "estudios sociales" were formed, some of them anarchist communist.... In 1887 Errico Malatesta cooperated with other anarchist comrades in the permanent organisation of the Sociedad Cosmopolita de Obreros Panaderos, giving speeches at their meetings."

In fact, Mattei had initiated the founding of this bakers' union and had asked Malatesta to write a charter and programme for it. Mattei edited its paper, El Obrero Panadero and this bakers' union became a major foundation stone of the emerging workers' movement. Its successful strikes galvanised the Buenos Aires workers. "His and Mattei's roles in the union were fundamental; they fought so that the union would be an authentic society of resistance, an organisation that moreover could be labelled as "cosmopolitan", instead of yet another mere mutualist society" (The influence of Italian immigration on the Argentine anarchist movement, Osvaldo Bayer). The ten day strike of January 1888 initiated by Mattei and Malatesta resulted in a 30% pay rise and inspired other strikes among shoemakers, rail workers, metal workers and building workers.

Malatesta was never convinced that strikes alone could significantly alter the economic situation, but became more favourably disposed to such workplace agitation "because Argentina lacked the "industrial reserve army" that enabled employers to replace strikers in Europe, and because the strikes in Buenos Aires helped the anarchists enlist workers in their ranks" (Nunzio Pernicone, Italian Anarchism,1864-92).

As a result of the joint work of Mattei, Malatesta and other European anarchists four anarchist communist manifestoes appeared between 1886 and 1889, the first of which was issued on 13th December 1886 to protest against a resolution of the Public Hygiene Commission in relation was to the cholera epidemic that was hitting the city at the time. As a consequence of the appearance of this manifesto, Ettore Mattei and three other anarchists suffered short jail terms. The second manifesto was published in November 1888 and made reference to the Chicago Martyrs. The third and fourth manifestos were produced in 1889.

It also appeared that Malatesta was able to smooth over the controversies between collectivists and communists that afflicted the anarchist movement in other countries. Unfortunately, after Malatesta's return to Europe in 1889, and the arrival of anti-organisational anarchist communists who had arrived in 1888 and 1889 from Spain, this truce was to end. Disputes flared up between the new arrivals and the Catalan collectivist Antonio Pellicer Paraire. The latter, from his own experience in Spain, was a proponent of the development of workers' organisation. A skilled print worker, he contributed much in publishing and organising in Argentina. He wrote "...we need to organise and to create a force that is greater than that of the governing classes. This force resides in each of us, the oppressed. But this power is meaningless without association, without organisation. Therefore, if we have the goal, we must organise to realise our objective."

Paraire advocated an anarchist workers' organisation that was federated nationally. He published a series of articles titled La Organización Obrera (The Workers' Organisation), where he argued against individual action and called for the setting up of sociedades de resistencia (resistance societies) on a local basis. These would then federate to form craft federations, which would fight to improve economic and social conditions, and then form local federations, which would deal with all organisational matters. The arrival in 1898 of the Italian anarchist communist Pietro Gori reinforced this drive towards the creation of a libertarian workers federation, through his speeches, articles and pamphlets. In Our Utopia, Gori went beyond his originally Kropotkinian belief in the inevitability of revolution and argued that it was necessary to be involved in everyday struggle as a means of building anarchist communism which implied anti-parliamentary positions.

As noted by Emanuela Minuto, Gori and Malatesta "set out a programme that contrasted individualism, terrorism, and spontaneity with an entry into the world of work and an operational strategy that set aside the revolutionary framework. The main tool to propagate this programme became the weekly L'Agitazione, founded in Ancona in March 1897, in which the voices of Malatesta, Gori, and other organisationists outlined guidelines for a people's strategy focused on economic campaigns and legal battles for civil liberties based on an agenda modelled on the existing order." (Pietro Gori's Anarchism: politics and Spectacle, 1895-1900). Gori advocated a move away from individualism and terrorism towards a concentration on building working class organisation.

Gori's propaganda efforts linked with those of Paraire and of the cabinet maker Inglan Lafarga who had, in 1897, set up what was to become the most important anarchist paper in Argentina, La Protesta Umana (Human Protest).

In 1901 fifty delegates from socialist and anarchist organisations founded the Federacion Obrera Argentina (FOA, Argentinean Workers Federation). This uneasy coalition was at first dominated by anarchists who were in the majority, and the FOA advocated the general strike as a weapon, and rejection of political (i.e., parliamentary) means to liberate the working class. At the same time, it accepted collective bargaining, but not with the government as a medium. At first the FOA numbered only 10,000 workers. Socialists left the FOA after a year, with anarchists now in full control. A period of intense class struggle began in that year, continuing until 1908, with many general strikes, and increasing State violence to quell the unrest.

Virginia Bolten and the Anarchist Communist Women's Movement

Virginia Bolten was the daughter of a German street vendor. She was born in Uruguay, either in San Luis, according to some, or in San Juan, according to the researcher Placido Grela, and moved to Rosario in Argentina.

Rosario was known as the "Barcelona of Argentina" at this point in time because of its concentration of industries, the radical ferment there and the political influence it had over the rest of the country. She worked making shoes for workers and then later in the Refineria, the huge sugar factory that employed thousands of workers, many of them European immigrants and many of them women. She married Juan Marquez, an organiser of a shoe workers' union and a fellow Uruguayan.

Bolten became associated with El Obrero Panadero which had become one of the first voices of anarchism in Argentina, with many bakery workers attracted to anarchist ideas. It had a key role in organising the first May Day demonstrations in 1890. In 1889 she helped organise the seamstresses' strike in Rosario, believed to be the first strike of women workers in Argentina.

Juana Buela, in her autobiography Historia de una ideal vivido por una mujer, remembered the strength and tenacity of Virginia in propagating anarchist ideas including in the pages of the anarchist papers La Protesta Humana and La Protesta and especially in La Voz de la Mujer, (Woman's Voice, 1896-97). This was a paper which explicitly described itself as anarchist communist, with a subtitle "Dedicated to the advancement of anarchist communism". It was the first publication edited by women for women in the whole of Latin America, fusing class struggle anarchist ideas with the liberation of women. Supported by the meagre wages of Virginia and her women comrades in the shoe and sugar industries. It was an anarchist publication that was typical of the period, small and ephemeral and semi-clandestine. Its descriptive subtitle summed it all up: Appears when it can. Only nine issues appeared, although it is believed that Virginia edited another issue in Montevideo. Issues 1-4 had a print run of one thousand copies, which went up to two thousand for the following four issues whilst the last appearance of the paper merited a print run of 1,500. Other leading anarchist women activists involved in the paper included Teresa Marchisio and Maria Calvia.

La Voz de la Mujer published many articles from Spanish anarchists on the subject of the liberation of women. Contributors included the

Louise Michel by Clifford Harper

great anarchist organiser Teresa Claramunt, Soledad Gustavo, etc. The support of Emma Goldman and Louise Michel was actively sought and secured. It deplored the action of the anarchist F. Denanbride in shooting his lover five times because she was leaving him. This woman, Anita Lagouardette, was a contributor to La Voz de la Mujer and miraculously survived the attack. La Voz de la Mujer railed against the hypocrisy in male anarchist ranks where freedom was denied to women: "When we women, unworthy and ignorant as we are, took the initiative and published La Voz de la Mujer, we should have known,

Oh modern rogues, how you would respond with your old mechanistic philosophy to our initiative. You should have realised that we stupid women have initiative and that is the product of thought. You know – we also think... The first number of La Voz de la Mujer appeared and of course, all hell broke loose: 'Emancipate women? For what?' 'Emancipate women? Not on your nelly!'... 'Let our emancipation come first, and then, when we men are emancipated and free, we shall see about yours'. "

Virginia undertook speaking tours throughout Argentina speaking at meetings in San Nicolás, Campana, Tandil, Mendoza and many other towns. The police intervened on many occasions to stop her speaking. Her main topics were the situation of the working class and in particular the various oppressions suffered by working class women. In November 1900 she and Teresa Marchisio organised a counter procession against the parade of the Catholic establishment in Rosario, the procession of the Virgen de la Roca. She and Teresa were arrested with four other anarchists.

In the same year she was actively involved in the setting up of the Casa del Pueblo (the House of the People) with other anarchists. This housed political, social and cultural events with many conferences, debates, discussions, poetry readings and theatre pieces; it had an orchestra and a library of 380 books. She was one of the speakers at its inauguration. On the 20th October 1901 she was arrested for distributing anarchist propaganda outside the gates of the Refineria in the course of a strike. During this incident, she witnessed the cold blooded murder of the immigrant worker Come Budislavich by the police. She helped set up an anarchist women's group with other anarchist militants like Lopez and Teresa Deloso that year.

In 1902 she was one of the main speakers at the First of May rally in Montevideo using it as an occasion to denounce the situation in Argentina. In 1904 she was forced to move to Buenos Aires where she was active in the Comité de Huelga Femenino (Women's Strike Committee), which with the Federación Obrera Argentina organised the women workers in the port fruit market of Buenos Aires and brought them out on strike. Her intensive activity began to affect her health. The comrades of the anarchist theatre group Germinal issued an appeal to all libertarian groups, unions and societies to take part in a benefit to aid her. The great Italian anarchist Pietro Gori introduced her to anarchist intellectual circles in Buenos Aires and helped her found an organisation of anarchists and socialists focused on attacking legal marriage and other authoritarian concepts.

The failure of the civil-military uprising of Hipolito Irigoyen against the conservative government in 1905 was used as a pretext to attack the workers' movement. Despite the fact that the anarchist movement had no kind of alliance with Irigoyen its principal activists were arrested, prosecuted and even deported. Virginia was arrested along with her partner and detained for two days. Marquez was expelled to Uruguay under the new Residency Law.

In 1907 she was one of the initiators of the Centro Femenino Anarquista (Anarchist Women's Centre) and through it was one of the principal organisers of the tenants' strike of that year. Following her speech during this strike, she became the first woman to be deported under the Residency Law, which was used to deport her to Montevideo in Uruguay, where she was reunited with Marquez and their young children.

The FORA

In 1905, the FOA changed its name to the Federacion Obrera Regional Argentina (FORA) to emphasise its internationalism. At the same time, it recommended to its membership to propagandise "the economic and philosophical principles of anarchist communism" among the working class. This led to the departure of any remaining social democrats. The FORA was thus a specifically anarchist communist mass workers organisation, as opposed to a revolutionary syndicalist body like the CNT for some of its existence, or the "neutral" unions as advocated by Malatesta. Its activists often emphasised that it was an anarchist communist workers' organisation rather than an anarcho-syndicalist body. Furthermore, it stated that "We... must not forget that a union is merely an economic by-product of the capitalist system, born from the needs of this epoch. To preserve it after the revolution would imply preserving the capitalist system that gave rise to it." This was a clear difference with both revolutionary syndicalism and anarcho-syndicalism which saw the unions as key administrative organs in a new future society.

FORA's unions always operated under the name of Societies of Resistance and functioned as associations of trades. Industrial federation was frowned upon as a step towards centralisation. There were no paid officials and direct action and combative strikes were stressed.

The FORA member Eduardo Colombo has left a helpful summing up of the positions of the FORA: "We can summarise FORA's objections to unionism as a doctrine in three points:

1. Syndicalism cannot be sufficient on its own because the revolutionary finality (for the FORA, anarchism) is a necessary condition for the proletariat to go beyond the simple demand for wages, or the standard of living in the sense economic.
2. The concept of the economic unity of the class is false because a minimum of awareness of the situation of the oppressed and of the society that one wishes is essential to join a revolutionary union.
3. The conception of the union as an organ of the future society is unacceptable because it contains a concealed statist proposal, and authoritarian, if it is understood as "all power to the unions". The Resistance Society is a response to today's capitalist system; the new society will have to create its own non-authoritarian institutions". (Anarchisme et syndicalisme. En quoi la FORA a-t-elle été différente? Le Monde libertaire, no 1109, 5-11th February 1998, also online at https://ml.ficedl.info/spip.php?article3465).

The leading Italian anarchist communist, Luigi Fabbri, then in Buenos Aires, and close to Malatesta on the advocacy of neutral unionism was to comment: "I do not want to be a bad prophet, but I am afraid that sooner or later this tactical error will be hard paid for by our movement in the Argentine Republic. (The union organisation), in order not to be dogmatic or authoritarian, must avoid any affirmation that may divide the proletarian mass according to special party concerns... It is equivalent to saying to the workers that they do not think like us".

The FORA experienced a rapid growth, reaching a membership of 30,000 by 1906. However, the pure syndicalist current within it was to depart in 1909 and to set up the Confederacion Obrera Regional Argentina (CORA) with the participation of socialist unionists. The CORA believed in negotiating with the employers, rather than adopting tactics of direct action. It began to grow, and started to call for reintegration with the FORA. Then at its 1914 conference the CORA decided to dissolve and for its members to go into the FORA en masse. This devious manoeuvre came at a time of internal disorganisation within the FORA. As the bulk of the CORA was not particularly disposed towards anarchism this disturbed the equilibrium within the latter organisation. The result was that at the ninth congress in 1915, the hold of anarchist communists over the FORA was loosened and the commitment to anarchist communism was rescinded, with the FORA preferring to adopt the revolutionary syndicalist position of the Charter of Amiens. The anarchist communist current departed to set up the FORA-V (after the fifth congress where anarchist communism had been adopted as the ultimate goal). The FORA majority (FORA-IX, after the ninth congress) merged with other autonomous unions in 1922 to form the Unione Sindical Argentina (USA). This described itself as revolutionary syndicalist, and some anarcho-syndicalists operated within it, as did socialists and Communists. It declared itself anti-State and anti-parliamentary. The USA was strongly influenced by the founding of the Unione Sindicale Italiana (USI) in Italy. But the FORA-IX took an increasingly reformist outlook, calling on the State and the police to intervene in labour disputes and in 1918 rejecting the general strike as a weapon and renouncing any revolutionary aspirations. It eventually merged with the Argentinean Workers Confederation (COA) to create the Confederacion General del Trabajo (CGT) in 1930.

Meanwhile the FORA-V, due to its combative attitude, and the events of the Tragic Week of 1919, with a State massacre of workers, and continuing industrial unrest, had reached a peak of 200,000 by 1922.

The Russian Revolution caused great damage to the Argentinean movement, as it did elsewhere in Latin America and around the world. The FORA-IX was affected, as was FORA-V, where a pro-Bolshevik faction was expelled in 1921 and subsequently moved to join the USA.

These "anarcho-Bolsheviks" favoured the dictatorship of the proletariat based on the unions as opposed to the Party. Like many anarchists in other countries, they were initially dazzled by the Russian

Revolution. They were organised around papers of wide circulation like Bandera Roja (Red Flag) El Communist, Cuasimodo and Via Libre. For example, Bandera Roja, financed by port workers, had a run of 20,000 on a daily basis. The editor of Via Libre, Santiago Locascio, brought out a pamphlet named Anarchism and Bolshevism (Marxism). There, he referred to the soviets in Russia as the equivalent of the anarchist communist idea of the commune, which would federate both nationally and internationally to form a new society. Leading lights among the Anarcho-Bolsheviks included Enrique García Thomas and Eva Vivé. They were influential in the Red Triennium strike movement that began in November 1918 and ended in late 1921 and in the Red Summer of 1919-20. They gained the upper hand within FORA-V at the 1920 congress when there was a name change to FORA (Comunista). However, the following year, more and more disturbing news reached the Argentinean workers' movement about the nature of the Communist regime in the USSR, often transmitted via the same Russian immigrants who had earlier so enthusiastically cheered the Revolution. The anarcho-Bolsheviks were expelled from the FORA, not least for their contact with Soviet envoys who visited both Argentina and Uruguay with the aim of affiliating unions to the Red Trade Union International (RTUI). The concept of the dictatorship of the proletariat was rejected and the FORA returned to its old name.

The anarcho-Bolsheviks were leading enthusiasts for the creation of the USA and in January 1923 they founded a federation of affinity groups, the Alianza Libertaria Argentina (ALA) as well as the Asociación Argentina de Colonos y Arrendatarios (AACA, Argentine Association of Settlers and Tenants) whose aim was to carry out activity in rural areas. They led movements such as the Red Summer of 1919-20 and the Bomb Strike of March 1920.

The anarcho-Bolshevik enthusiasm for the Russian Revolution led them to support USA entry into the Red Trade Union International (RTUI) controlled by the Bolsheviks. This caused much internal controversy within USA, with a battle between the "autonomists" and the "Muscovites". This led in the long term to the death of the USA. There were controversies within the ALA itself. In 1924 some of its militants began to move away from it, like the writer Rolando Martell and the young intellectual Luis Di Filippo. At the end of that year Garcia Thomas and his grouping departed and set up the ALA II. Both groupings went into decline after this, with ALA I upholding anarchist ethics and with a weak influence in the USA, and ALA II turning to "revolutionary pragmatism" and the organisation of day labourers and tenant farmers. By 1930, the current hardly existed, with many turning to anarcho-syndicalism or orthodox anarchist communism, among the latter Juan Lazarte, Luis di Filippo, and Hermenegildo Rosales. By 1932 both ALAs no longer existed.

The FORA was, according to Santillan, still strong in the 1930s. The Uriburu coup resulted in the outlawing of the FORA, and its buildings were closed down. The FORA was more or less underground now until early 1945. Santillan argued that the main reason for the coup was the growing strength of the FORA, although this is debatable. The fact that anarchists suffered more under the Uriburu dictatorship certainly reinforces his view.

The chief theorists of the FORA were Diego Abad de Santillan and Emilio López Arango. They developed their ideas in the pages of La Protesta. Founded in 1897, this paper had close links with the FORA. It is interesting to read a rejection of class struggle in a joint work by Santillan and Arango, El Anarquismo en el movimiento obrero (Anarchism in the Labour Movement). They write: "The notion of class strikes us as a contradiction of the principles championed by anarchism. We consider it the last refuge of authoritarianism, and while fighting to liberate the workers' movement from m the political parties, we are, if we assert the notion of class, preparing the ground for a new dominion. The fact that revolutionaries emerge almost exclusively from the ranks of the oppressed and exploited does not mean that the revolution i s a class affair: for those oppressed and exploited who d o their bit for the task of transforming society have arrived at an egalitarian outlook on life that rules out the narrow interests of the revolutionaries themselves, taken as a particular group. The proletariat as a class is an abstract invention... In actuality, the proletariat is a motley collection which in part passively endures the blights of society, in part enters into tactical or express alliances with the bourgeoisie and the reaction, and in part also bands together to fight for Freedom and Justice..." Thus, like Malatesta they turn away from the fundamental class tenets of revolutionary anarchism, developed within the First International. On the other hand, they reject pure syndicalism and state that: "the Syndicate is, as an economic by-product of capitalist organisation, a social phenomenon spawned by the needs of its day. Clinging to its structures after the revolution would be tantamount to clinging to the cause that spawned it: capitalism." They argued for the purging of all traces of Marxism from anarchism which had persisted since its origins or had been introduced by syndicalism.

A number of distributors of La Protesta were arrested or killed within a year of Uriburu's ascension to power. Moran, leading light of the anarchist influenced Maritime Federation, independent from the FORA, "disappeared", whilst some of the more individualistic anarchists, and advocates of assassination and expropriation like Severino di Giovanni, were executed. Protesta ceased publishing and an underground newspaper Rebelión took its place.

Ironically, the Uriburu coup led to the roundup of as many as 1,200 anarchists, and these were concentrated in the Devoto prison. During August, September and August 1931 these anarchist prisoners from different tendencies and currents were able to carry on in-depth discussions, which they had never done before. This ongoing conference applied itself to self-criticism of the movement. It was concluded that sectarianism and internal strife had so weakened the movement that it was unable to resist the coup.

The idea of a unitary congress was mooted. By 1932 the anarchist movement was not as numerically strong as it had been, but was widespread in that it had organisations and groups in practically every town in Argentina. The 1932 congress at Rosario decided to construct a specific organisation and created a regional committee for anarchist coordination to facilitate this. No reference was made to the previous specific organisation, the ALA, as it was seen as being tainted by the discredited idea of anarcho-Bolshevism. Finally, after intermittent waves of repression, the Federacion Anarco-Comunista Argentina (FACA) was formally established in 1935. This merely acknowledged a fait accompli as a press commission, with a paper, Accion Libertaria, was already functioning. It also had a strong insertion within the reformist unions, as it had been decided to carry out activities there as well as within the FORA. It increased its internal importance within the Argentinean anarchist movement due to the decline of the FORA.

But alongside the birth of the FACA, was the emergence of another organisation in Buenos Aires, the Spartacus Alianza Obrera y Campesina Spartacus Worker Peasant Alliance). This organisation was heavily influenced by the ideas of the Organisational Platform of the Libertarian Communists and by the Spartakist movement in Germany. It was founded by Horacio Badaraco, just out of prison, together with Domingo Varone and Antonio Cabrera. Its slogan was: "workers, peasants and soldiers to fight for socialism". The great construction strike in 1935-36 was carried out under the influence of Spartacus. During support work around the Spanish Revolution, Spartacus collaborated with the FACA and both leading lights of the FACA like Jacobo Maguid, José Grunfeld and Jacobo Prinz, as well as Badaraco, went to fight in Spain. Spartacus expired in 1940.

In 1942 the FACA developed its union activity via the CORS (Workers' Commission for Union Relations) in alliance with the reconstituted USA which had re-emerged after a split in the CGT in 1935 and had rallied some independent anarchist unions to it.

The FACA became the Argentine Libertarian Federation (FLA) in 1955, but like its predecessor organisation was never able to gain a mass following. In 1985, the FLA replaced its newspaper Acción Libertaria with a new political journal called El Libertario.

The phenomenon of Peronist populism swept away most of what was remaining of the anarchist movement. However, at the end of the 1960s, new anarchist groupings began to emerge like Resistencia Libertaria (RL), Linea Anarco Comunista (LAC), Accion Directa, and Movimiento Anarquista. These groupings were based primarily among students. They were influenced by the May/June events in France in 1968. They had little or no continuity with the FLA or the FORA. They discussed "proletarianisation" with the aim of inserting themselves within the working class by taking jobs, for example, in the shipyards of La Plata, like the Tello brothers. The LAC talked about the construction of an Anarchist Party that was nothing other than the specific organisation of anarchists that would "work to structure the conditions for the social seizure of power." RL was an absolutely clandestine organisation, conditioned as it was by coup after successive coup during the 1960s. It conceived of a "dynamic agent of the proletariat, but not a leader."

In 1972 at Mar de la Plata there was an attempt to unify these new groupings. In 1974 there was another attempt at unification, impelled by RL, Accion Directa, and Organización Anarquista, an organisationalist split from Movimiento Anarquista, with the aim of establishing a specific organisation at the national level.

This proved to be a failure, though OA and RL were able to get agreement on setting up a front, Resistencia Anticapitalista Libertaria (RAL). It also resulted in a split in Acción Directa, with some joining the RAL and others dedicating themselves to the establishment of the Revolutionary Anarchist Organisation (OAR). As to LAC, the bulk of its members moved over to the RAL.

The coup of 1976 was to sabotage these various organisational moves. For example, 80% of the most active militants of RL were "disappeared" (kidnapped by State forces), and in the long term 20% remained "disappeared", that is, murdered. At the end of 1977 a factory occupation involving RL militants, ended up with the factory surrounded by tanks, and the disappearance of more RL members.

In response RL created political and military wings. It counted upon a hundred active members between 1976 and 1978 which carried out clandestine activities.In 1978 the full force of State repression was unleashed with heavy losses for the RL.With the end of this terrible period in 1985 the anarchist movement reemerged in Argentina. The FORA was reconstituted and new groups began to emerge.El Libertario, the paper of the Federazione Libertaria Argentina, began publishing.

The uprsing in 2001 in response to the economic crisis saw a heavy involvement of new groups like the Organisacion Socialista Libertaria (OSL) and the AUCA. The OSL had its origins in a group of young anarchist sympathisers, CAIN, who had started meeting in late 1996, in Buenos Aires and who then began propaganda and culturral activities. The paper En La Calle (In the Street) began to appear in November 1997. In the same year the AUCA group (Auca is the Mapuche word for rebel) emerged in La Plata, as well as the OAR (Anarchist Organisation of Rosario). Steady work was undertaken in the neighbourhoods, unions and among the unemployed. This led on to the founding of the OSL at the end of 2000. Both AUCA and CAIN stressed the need to be involved in struggles, and they both proposed organisational, tactical and ideological unity in the tradition of the Platform. CAIN had its origins as an anarchist group within FORA. The AUCA emerged in 1997 in La Plata.

AUCA, CAIN and OAR jointly produced En La Calle and participated in student and anti-repression struggles. This alliance lasted until September 2000 when AUCA disappeared into the Peronist movement. But at the same time the OSL was founded and continued with the publication of En La Calle.

In the post-crisis period the OSL carried out work with the piqueteros movement and from 2002 inside the Unemployed Workers Movement (MTD).However, the OSL was to dissolve in 2009.

However some former OSL members, as well as others involved in the unemployed workers movement began meeting in 2012 and formally announced themselves as the Accion Socialista Libertaria in November 2015. The ASL has groups in Buenos Aires, La Plata and Cordoba. Like the OSL before it, the ASL believes in the construction of a specific organisation and insertion within the class struggle.

The Uruguayan Experience

In neighbouring Uruguay, the Federacion Obrera Regional Uruguaya (FORU) was set up in 1905. It had evolved out of the Resistance Societies that had been created in the 1890s and which echoed their similar development in Argentina. In the decade before World War One, the anarchist current was predominant within the workers' movement in Uruguay. Alongside these anarchist unions were centres and groupings like Agrupacion Nueva Idea, which published La Accion Obrera (Workers' Action) which carried much workplace news.

The FORU was at first under the influence of Bakuninist collectivist ideas, but as with Argentina across the river Plate, anarchist communism soon overwhelmingly superseded Proudhonian mutualist and Bakuninist collectivist ideas. The FORU maintained an explicit anarchist communist line. Like the FORA, it described itself as "finalist", that is, it openly declared that its aim was the establishment of an anarchist communist society. The FORU stated that "our organisation is purely economic and is unlike and opposed to all bourgeois and worker political parties in that they are organised to take over political power while our aim is to reduce the existing legal and political state forms to purely economic functions and to replace them with a free federation of free associations of free producers".

Deported from Argentina in 1907, Virginia Bolten collaborated with Juana Buela in 1909 in the anarchist feminist newspaper La Nueva Senda (The New Path, 1909-10). In early April 1911 she was involved in the setting up in Montevideo of the Asociación Femenina-Emancipacion she which sought to unite all anticlerical women in Montevideo. She and Maria Collazo were influential in this organisation. It appealed to working class women and held its meetings at the offices of the Electrical Workers Union. It made strong efforts to organise among telephone operators, at this time made up mostly of native women workers. It rejected the overtures of the reformist Pan-American Federation, Virginia speaking out against appeals for female suffrage.

Unlike other countries in South America, Uruguay was known as a stronghold of bourgeois democracy and social reform. Under its President Battle y Ordonez, a whole raft of legislation was introduced in the mid-1910s. This disoriented some elements within the fairly strong anarchist movement in Uruguay. In the process sections of the Uruguayan anarchist movement were neutralised.

This episode referred to as "Anarcobatllismo" caused the first important rift within the anarchist movement in Uruguay. Virginia Bolten and other anarchists like Francisco Berri, Adrian Zamboni, Orsini Bertani, and Clerici organised around the anarchist communist paper Idea Libre began to give critical support to the regime of President Batlle y Ordonez.

During his second term in office in Uruguay Batlle initiated a huge reform programme. This was not just far-reaching for Latin America but on an international level. He separated Church from State, banned crucifixes in hospitals, removed references to God and the Bible from public oaths, gave widespread rights to unions and political parties and organisations, brought in the eight hour day and universal suffrage, introduced unemployment benefits, legalised divorce, created more high schools, promised and practised no residency laws against exiled anarchists and other radicals, opened universities to women, and led a campaign to take away the control of industry and land from foreign capitalists (the British capitalists had huge influence in Uruguay) and nationalised private monopolies.

The emerging Socialist Party had supported Emancipacion but now turned against it. Their paper El Socialista attacked Virginia Bolten in July 1913, reproducing alleged statements from her in which she praised Batlle as 'progressive' and 'unlike anything we have ever had in this country'. By the end of the year El Socialista had heightened its critical tone, insisting that Virginia and her associates had betrayed the workers' movement, that workers reorganise their movement and "send anarchism to the devil". This brought about the collapse of Emancipacion and the working class women's movement in Uruguay, as well as doing damage to the anarchist movement and bringing about the ascendancy of the Socialist Party.

Despite this, the FORU could count on a membership of 90,000 in 1911, though this started to fall in the coming years. Despite the activities of the Socialist Party and after the Russian Revolution, the Communists, the FORU remained the dominant workers' organisation into the late 1920s and early 1930s.

The Russian Revolution affected the Uruguayan anarchist movement as it affected other similar movements worldwide with some orientating towards a défense of the dictatorship of the proletariat and "anarcho-Bolshevism". This had repercussions within the FORU and the anarchist movement.

The anarcho-syndicalists and revolutionary syndicalists who adopted an "anarcho-Bolshevik" line and had originally organised within the Comité Pro Unidad Obrera (Committee for Workers Unity) broke away from the FORU, and together with a Communist minority, established the Unione Sindical Uruguaya (USU) in 1923, which began to grow quickly.

Meanwhile, a Comité de Relaciones de Agrupaciones Anarquistas was set up in 1919 in El Paso del Molino, a working class neighbourhood of Montevideo, involving 20 groups, and seeking to develop a specific anarchist communist organisation alongside the FORU. On 20th March 1926, a plenary meeting of the Comité decided on the setting up of the first Federacion Anarquista Uruguaya (FAU), after a long period of discussion and debate. A Federal Committee was established and the FAU in its Declaration of Principles described its goal as "Communism to replace the exploitative practices of the bourgeoisie, and Anarchy as a unique way and means of social agreement".

The FAU was highly active in campaigns around the Italian-American militants Sacco and Vanzetti, condemned to death in the USA, and publicised their plight in the pages of their paper, Volonta (Will).

The Terra coup and dictatorship of 1933 dealt a heavy blow to the Uruguayan movement with the deportation of the vast majority of foreign comrades – Italian, Spanish, Argentinian, etc., and though the FAU carried on it was further weakened by the murder of a leading militant, Pedro Tufro, by the Stalinists in Spain in 1937. The FAU disappeared in 1941 whilst the FORU also faded away around the same time.

Between 1948 and 1954 the working class in Uruguay was comparatively well off, with good conditions and pay, in a country presided over by a ruling class with a liberal outlook. This all changed between 1955 and 1959 with an increasing cost of living. Inflation began to rise sharply and strike waves broke out. A wage freeze was introduced, The Army broke strikes and emergency laws were

Sacco and Vanzetti by Clifford Harper

introduced. The excuse for this was the supposed threat from the leftist guerrillas of the Tupamaros, but in reality, to repress the agitation in the workplaces.

Bordaberry came to power in 1971 and gave increasing powers to the Army in the fight against the Tupamaros. In 1973 political parties were banned, congress was closed down, public meetings were banned and constitutional rights were suspended. The employers dropped their liberal outlook and banned the National Workers' Convention (CNT) which federated many unions, when it called a general strike. Wages were driven down by 35% whilst inflation rose by 80%.

The second FAU

The Federacion Anarquista Uruguaya (FAU) was set up in 1956. Militants within it like Juan Carlos Mechoso began to agitate for the creation of a specific anarchist organisation as opposed to the anarcho-syndicalists who thought that work in the unions was enough to bring about radical social change. As Mechoso later said in an interview: "I was in favour of a specifically anarchist organisation, a given scheme of political work different from that of the anarcho-syndicalists who held that trade union work was enough to bring about emancipation of the workers and subsequently reorganise social life." At first the FAU had been an alliance of different anarchist currents, from the anarcho-syndicalists on one hand, through those who believed in setting up anarchist communities in the here and now, traditional anarchist communists on to the group around Mechoso, Gerardo Gatti and Leon Duarte.

The major reference points for the FAU were Malatesta and Bakunin, the former for his advocacy of organisation and refutation of individualism, the latter for his advocacy of developing close links with the workers' movement. They were also influenced by Uruguayan advocates of specific organisation like José María Fosalba, and also by the writings of the Bulgarian anarchist communist Balkanski (real name Georgi Grigoriev) on anarchism and organisation. The Organisational Platform had no influence as it was not extant in Uruguay in this period (the FAU did go on to establish relations with the French Platformist ORA).

Controversy had already arisen in the international movement over the increasingly reformist ideas of Rudolf Rocker. One of the pioneers of anarcho-syndicalism, he had taken a principled stand against the First World War and was interned in England as a result. However, by 1945, after his support for the Allies in WW2, Rocker began to reject class-based notions of anarchism, moving in an increasingly liberal direction. In this he had the support of other German anarchists like Augustin Souchy, and elements within the Spanish CNT in exile like Abad de Santillan. Nevertheless, it was people like Souchy who adopted a critical approach to the Cuban Revolution, along with the Cuban anarchists themselves, who directly experienced repression from the Castro regime. Within the FAU itself there was intense debate over the Castro regime between 1961 and 1965 with Mechoso, Gatti and co. supporting the Cuban regime. This led to a split in the FAU in late 1963 with the Gatti/Duarte/Mechoso faction retaining the FAU name and symbols, affirming the class struggle nature of anarchism, but also giving critical support to Cuba. The minority around Luce Fabbri, the daughter of Luigi Fabbri, and the Comunidad del Sur group formed the Alianza Libertaria Uruguaya (ALU). The FAU now began to incorporate elements from different currents of Marxism, calling for a synthesis between Marxism and anarchism, whilst referring to Poulantzas and Althusser, and later Gramsci. It increasingly broke with the anarcho-syndicalists by moving from the need for a specific anarchist organisation to talk of a Party. It set up the Student-Worker Resistance (ROE), which was meant to be a broad class struggle front, and began to seek out alliances with the Tupamaros and other leftists. As a result, many students influenced by 'revolutionary Marxism' began to join the ROE, accelerating the move away from anarchism. The writings of Che Guevara became popular and influential within this broad movement. The FAU established its own armed wing, OPR-33, in the late 1960s.

There was an increasing spiral of repression and counter-attack by the FAU/OPR-33, and many militants lost their lives in gun battles. By 1974 the US security forces launched Operation Condor in collaboration with the dictatorships now reigning in Argentina, Uruguay, Chile and Paraguay. Uruguayan and Argentinian security forces worked in tandem to kidnap FAU militants and many were imprisoned in a torture camp, where after many months of terrible agonies, they were murdered. Gatti, Duarte and Alberto Mechoso (Juan Carlos's brother) were among those murdered.

OPR-33 was seen as to be firmly under the control of the FAU and was meant to relate its actions to the workers movement in Uruguay itself. However, in the final analysis its actions had the same effect as those armed groups influenced by Castroism. FAU/OPR-33 lost a large number of militants. At the same time Gatti had pioneered the setting up of the People's Victory Party (PVP) whilst in exile in Buenos Aires in 1975, along with Ruben Prieto, Pablo Anzalone and others. The PVP was a heterodox mixture of anarchism and Castroism/Guevarism.

The deaths of Gatti and co. accelerated the move of the PVP away from anarchism. It participated in the creation of the Broad Front-Frente Amplio – a coalition of over a dozen political groupings as well as unions and community groups and in 1980 began to take part in its electoral activities and today is just another leftist parliamentarian party.

What was left of the FAU re-established its structures in 1986 after the fall of the dictatorship. It remains active in work in the unions and the neighbourhoods. As one French observer noted: "The FAU, like a number of other organisations, fell headlong into the political cracks opened up by the Cuban revolution and backed it for years, even if it had become plain that that revolution was turning into a bureaucratic dictatorship and even after Cuban anarchists had been rounded up and executed... The FAU eventually distanced itself from that betrayed revolution and withdrew its support from it, though it does not appear to mean that it is prepared to risk blunt criticism of the current Cuban regime". This observer notes a sympathy for the leftist FARC guerrillas in Colombia and the Guevarist MRTA in Peru, putting the anti-imperialism of the FAU down as underpinning this sympathy "which is very probably bound up with a lack of critical information about such authoritarian movements".

Brazil

The anarchist movement in Brazil was fed by waves of immigrants from Portugal, Spain, Germany, Russia, and Italy. The first Brazilian anarchist communist newspaper O Despertar (Awakening) appeared in Rio de Janeiro between October and December. Later, one of the first and chief propagandists of anarchist communism in Brazil was the Italian Oreste Ristori, commencing in the early years of the 20th century. Ristori was also active in Argentina and Uruguay.

Many anarchists in Brazil were under the influence of Malatesta and Kropotkin but there was a concentration on developing mass workers unions rather than specific anarchist communist organisations. The chief protagonist of this strategy was Gregorio Nazianzeno de Vasconcelos (1878-1920), better known as Neno Vasco, and born in Portugal. There was opposition to this strategy from some anarchist communists, wary of the tendencies of unions towards reformism and routinism, and from those who wished to transform the unions into pure anarchist ideological bodies. In the end Vasco's broad syndicalist strategy won out. Vasco's ideas on the unions were similar to those of Malatesta on the subject, in that he believed that anarchists should involve themselves in the unions, but not create specifically anarchist unions. Anarchist influence among the masses far outweighed that of the socialists, and in 1906 the Confederação Operária Brasileira (COB, Brazilian Workers' Confederation) was founded, engaging in militant activity. Alongside this there were a number of anarchist publications, at one time as many as one hundred, with four being dailies, as well as various educational centres, schools and theatres set up by anarchists. Thus, the Brazilian movement approximated more closely to the Spanish movement than it did to the movement in neighbouring Argentina, and there were fewer internal disputes than in the latter country.

Some anarchist communists changed their position over their attitude towards the unions. For example, José Elias da Silva, in 1913 served as the Secretary General of the Federação Operária do Rio de Janeiro (FORJ, Rio de Janeiro's Workers Federation). But three years later along with two other anarchists, Manoel Campos and Antonio Moutinho he severely criticised anarchist participation in the unions, in a pamphlet O anarquismo perante a organisação sindical: para desfazer mal entendidos (Anarchism before the union organisation: To undo misunderstandings). But again, with a rise in industrial struggle in 1917, he returned to the unions. We shall see later how this mercurial character performed further gyrations.

Attempts were made to develop specific organisations as with the Anarchist Alliance of Rio de Janeiro (Aliança Anarquista do Rio de Janeiro), founded in 1918 with the aim at working within the unions to maintain anarchist influence there. This played an important role in anti-war activity during World War One, as a result of the decision by the Brazilian government in October 1917 to enter the conflict on the side of the Western Allies. A general strike that year had been met with violent repression, and the Brazilian State used its entry into the war to declare a state of emergency. The ensuing clamp down led to the end of the Alliance.

On March 9th 1919, the Partido Comunista do Brasil (PCdoB) was founded by some anarchist communists, Edgar Leuenroth, Florentino de Carvalho, Antonio Cadeiras Duarte, Helio Negro, Astrojildo Pereira, and José Oiticica. Similar to contemporary developments in France and elsewhere, it declared that its members were "irreconcilable enemies of Collectivism and State Socialism, which, tending to destroy capitalist privileges, inevitably create bureaucratic privileges."

Both the Alliance and the Communist Party represented organisational currents within Brazilian anarchism. But, as the true nature of Bolshevism emerged, anarchist communists began to distance themselves, leading to the demise of the Party in 1920. In any case, because of its anarchist character, it failed to obtain the endorsement of the Comintern.

The PCdoB's first act was an organisation of a May Day rally, attended by large numbers, followed by the writing of a Communist-Anarchist programme by Oiticica, and the setting up of a newspaper, Spartacus. In addition, a Sao Paulo branch, the Libertarian Communist Party, was set up.

Pereira now became highly critical of anarchism, and the struggle between him and libertarian militants like Leuenroth and Oiticica intensified.

In 1922 another Communist Party, the Partido Comunista do Brazil, was founded, this time by eleven ex-anarchist communists like da Silva, Pereira, Octavia Brandão, Bernardo Canelas, and one socialist, but this time, it rapidly bolshevised. Elias da Silva and Pereira were to declare that year that on the day they took power they would decapitate every libertarian they could get their hands on. Despite this, the Comintern was again wary of the PCB, and suspicious of the anarchist past of many of its members.

Anarchism remained a powerful force in Brazil well into the 1930s. Oiticica continued to argue for specific organisation, warning in 1923 that the anarchists were too involved in the unions to the detriment of ideological activity. He argued for the creation of "anarchist federations outside of the unions". Oiticica advocated closed groups, with a defined programme of action. He believed that the "centralisation" of anarchist forces in the struggle against the ruling class was necessary. Two things were necessary for the effectiveness of anarchist activity: "selection of militants and concentration of forces", saying that "Only this will give us unity of action".

In Sao Paulo, which continued to be a bastion of working class anarchism in the 1930s, a Federação Comunista Libertária (Libertarian Communist Federation) was set up, closely connected to the explicitly anarchist union, the Workers' Federation (FOSP), and whose main functions was the dissemination of anarchist communist ideas.

The Vargas regime in the 1930s culminating in the dictatorship of the Estado Novo (New State) established on corporatist and fascist lines, dealt a very serious blow to the workers movement. As Thomas E. Skidmore noted in a review of a book on anarchism and communism in Brazil "The Anarchists were too divided and too lacking in organisational discipline to build on their early strike victories. The Communists, on the other hand, were all discipline and no mass support." (Hispanic American Historical Review [1975] 55 (1): 132-35). Whilst, unlike the Communist Party, the anarchists had a widespread influence within the working class, they were unable to fully capitalise on this due to their failure to develop long-lasting specific organisations.

The overthrow of the Vargas dictatorship by the military in 1945 saw a much-depleted anarchist movement re-emerge. Over the years, the deportation of many immigrant anarchists from Brazil, the murder of others by the regime and the total clamp-down on the workers' movement had dealt severe blows.

Organisational anarchist communists grouped around the magazine Ação Direta in 1946, and included Oiticica but the movement had been depleted by the previous decades and numbered only a few hundred. The 1964 military coup also presented problems. However, the militant Ideal Peres, himself the son of a militant, continued activity within the Circle of Libertarian Studies (CEL) and in the 1980s affirmed a re-engagement with social struggles and encouraged a new generation of young militants.

By the 1990s the Brazilian movement was heavily influenced by the especifismo politics of the FAU in Uruguay, as a result of a dialogue between the FAU and the CEL. This led to the creation of the Organização Socialista Libertária (OSL) in 1997, self-defined as an especifist organisation, and lasting until 2000. Organisationalists created the Forum of Organised Anarchism (FAO) in September 2001 with the purpose of creating an organisation at the national level. This culminated in the creation of the Coordenação Anarquista Brasileira (CAB, Brazilian Anarchist Coordination), in 2012. The CAB includes a large number of local and state-wide organisations, including the Anarchist Federation of Rio de Janeiro (FARJ) itself founded in 2003.

Mexico

The role of founder of anarchism in Mexico is often given to the Austro-Greek Plotino Rhodakanaty. However, his views combine an admiration for Fourier with influences from Proudhon, and he seems never to have completely renounced his Mormon beliefs! Certainly, he had an important influence on the emerging working class movement in Mexico between the 1860s and 1880s, in particular the National Congress of Mexican Workers. His mixture of Fourierist phalansterism and Proudhonist mutualism meant that he was opposed to revolutionary change, believing in a peaceful transition to socialism, and he had an elitist conception of the role of the intellectual in social change.

Rhodakanaty believed that socialism would be founded on the creation of artisan workshops, workers' collectives and agrarian communes. The coming of these together in a vast federation would lead to the establishment of socialism.

The coming to power of the Diaz regime in 1880s led to repressive measures against unions, mutualist societies and cooperatives. The repression led to Rhodakanaty's return to Europe in 1886.

The group which had coalesced around Rhodakanaty which included Francisco Zalacosta, Santiago Villanueva and Hermengildo Villavicencio, began to organise mutualist societies and unions among both urban and agrarian workers. Gradually these mutualist groups began to evolve towards Bakuninism.

In Mexico there was little evidence of Marxist groups before the twentieth century, and there was a lack of any significant social-democratic formations.

A more militant and combative current emerged within the Mexican workers' movement beginning in 1900 with the introduction of anarchist communist ideas.

One of those who seized on these ideas was the radical liberal Ricardo Flores Magon. Born in 1874, the son of an Army officer and landowner in the southern state of Oaxaca. He became involved in the student movement against the dictatorship of Porfirio Diaz in 1892 and was imprisoned for a month. He read Kropotkin at an early age. By 1900 he was calling himself an anarchist. In that year he helped produce an anti-Diaz paper, Regeneracion. Repression led to the closure of the paper in 1903 and Ricardo and his associates crossed over to the United States to continue the struggle against Diaz from across the border.

Regeneracion then reappeared in 1904, published from San Antonio. Due to harassment by the local authorities Magon and his circle moved to St Louis in Missouri. It was here that they founded the Partido Liberal Mexicana (PLM) on 25th September 1905. Ricardo, his brother Enrique, and Librado Rivera were increasingly moving in a more radical direction, after having met with Emma Goldman and the Spanish anarchist Florencio Bozora, whilst other Liberals like Juan Sarabia remained as reformists, and Antonio Villareal adopted an orthodox socialist outlook. The PLM leadership decided not to push its anarchist convictions in order to develop a broad body of support in Mexico. Nevertheless, the PLM, despite its continuing to retain the same title, started to transform itself into an anarchist communist organisation. The Magonistas began to smuggle Regeneracion into Mexico and massive agitation took place among the workers and peasants.

This had a huge influence on events in Mexico, and in 1906 the circulation of Regeneracion went up to 30,000 copies. In that year the PLM had organised 44 guerrilla units as well as Liberal clubs throughout Mexico. They became involved in the Cananea Copper Company strike in the state of Sonora that year. The strike provoked an intervention by Arizona Rangers, who crossed the border with the encouragement of the Cananea bosses and state officials in Sonora. In the end the State governor crushed the revolt by threatening mass conscription of workers. Between thirty to one hundred workers died during the five days of fighting. As a result, the Diaz regime became increasingly unpopular, partly because of the American intervention. The strike encouraged workers unrest throughout Mexico and both the Diaz regime and the US government now looked towards smashing the PLM.

Another PLM-inspired insurrection followed in 1908, again brutally repressed. For their part, the USA interned some of the PLM leadership in 1907 for conspiracy and violation of the laws of neutrality between Mexico and the USA. When Madero, a typical modernising member of the bourgeoisie, whose aims were solely the departure of Diaz and the introduction of democracy called for an uprising against Diaz on 20th November 1911 the PLM mobilised its forces for an uprising. They were in favour of a tactical alliance on the ground with the Madero forces against Diaz, but were categorically against a political alliance with them. Indeed, the PLM hoped to win elements of the Maderistas over to more radical positions. Unfortunately, the Madero uprising failed, and it was only in late December that the movement renewed itself. PLM forces under Praxedis Guerrero crossed the border and marched through the state of Chihuahua. The PLM rose up in nine other states in Mexico, orchestrating joint military activity with the Maderistas and inflicting big defeats on the old regime. In Baja California the PLM seized Mexicali and this deeply disturbed the regime. The PLM hoped in the long run to expropriate the big landowners there, but in the meantime, forced them to hand over large sums of money. The PLM, in addition, hoped to use Baja California as a base from which to support other PLM units.

PLM units gained many victories, in contrast with the poor military record of the Maderistas. Internationally, support began to grow for the PLM, with many socialists, syndicalists and anarchists supporting their cause.

Thanks to Silva, a PLM guerrilla commander, Madero returned to Mexico from the States, but on the following day, declared himself commander in chief of the insurgent forces, and after another PLM commander came over to his side, arrested Silva for refusing to recognise his authority. The situation was compounded by the split between the leadership in exile in the States, clearly anarchist communist, and some of the PLM membership in Mexico, not as politically developed, and leading to compromises with Madero. For his part Madero denounced PLM militants to both the US and Mexican governments, and profited from lack of communication to peddle the myth that the two movements were in alliance. This destroyed PLM unity, leading to splits towards Madero. Madero had eight leading Magonistas arrested in Chihuahua and 147 members of their units were disarmed. At the same time a campaign of slander began against the PLM on both sides of the border. On the American side they were portrayed as mere bandits, on the Mexican side they were portrayed as tools of American interests. This situation was facilitated by the large number of American volunteers swelling PLM ranks, be they socialists, anarchists or IWW.

Madero finally came to power on 21st May, signing a treaty with Diaz. Officially, the Revolution was over, and everyone was to lay down their arms. The PLM refused this, and saw that a social revolution was continuing within Mexico. However, many insurgents now thought that the Madero regime would lead progressively towards greater social justice. The American Socialist Party withdrew its support from the PLM, and transferred it to Madero. Only a section of the IWW and the anarchists continued to support the PLM.

Despite these setbacks Regeneracion released a new manifesto to replace that of 1906, calling for struggle against authority, the Church and capitalism, and for the establishment of a free society. However, some influential members of the PLM, including Jesus Flores Magon, had rallied to Madero. And, in June 1912, Ricardo and other important PLM militants were arrested by the US government and sentenced to 23 months in jail for breaking the neutrality laws.

Peace only lasted a few weeks after the signing of the treaty and several movements, including that of Zapata, took up the cry of Land and Liberty. Madero himself was murdered by the reactionaries and a new phase of unrest began. When Ricardo Flores Magon came out of jail in January 1914 he renewed his agitation. Criticising the successive regimes, he denounced the manipulation of the masses by the different factions of the bourgeoisie. He castigated Pancho Villa for acting as their servant, but praised the Zapatistas for maintaining their principles and behaving as anarchists whilst not using this title.

However, repression was falling more and more upon the PLM. Ricardo and Librado Rivera were again arrested by the US government and sentenced respectively to 20 and 15 years in jail! In 1922 Ricardo died in prison, with strong indications that he had been murdered by the US authorities. Released in 1923 Rivera returned to Mexico where he was a leading light in the anarchist group Hermanos Rojos (Red Brothers), maintaining his convictions until his death in 1932.

The PLM put the military and insurrectional question before the political education of its militants. As a result, there was a lack of ideological unity, as witnessed in the succession of splits and defections. The 1906 and 1908 insurrections had resulted in the deaths or imprisonment of many of the most active and politically advanced militants. The PLM in its progression towards anarchism began to accentuate the importance of the working class over that of the peasantry. However, the working class in Mexico was still in development and too weak and numerically small to have a decisive influence. For its part propagation of PLM ideas among the peasants was hindered to a certain extent by widespread illiteracy. Recruitment to the PLM had been difficult, and the influx of foreign volunteers had distorted the situation. The leading lights in the PLM had in the main remained in Los Angeles when they should have been on the ground in Mexico. They had believed that the production of Regeneracion, enabled by being in the States, was of first importance. This removal from the scene clouded their judgement and their lack of clarity led to a debate on the international level as to whether or not they were truly anarchist, (they certainly were) robbing them of a certain amount of international solidarity. The PLM suffered from lack of finances, whereas Madero, for example, was able to call on millions of dollars.

Finally, to end positively on the PLM, they had influenced the struggles of both workers and peasants with their anti-authoritarian ideas, radicalising them from the Zapatistas in the south to the formation of unions heavily under the influences of anarchism. Today still in Oaxaca, the PLM has inspired the present-day Magonistas.

References
Hart, John M. Anarchism and the Working Class, 1860-1931. (1987)

Chapter Thirty Eight
Cocks crowing in the dark: anarchist communism in China

Anarchist communist ideas were brought to China by students who had gone to France or Japan to study. They used the used the term Wu-Zheng-Fu Gong-Chan (literally Without Government Common Production) to translate the term Anarchist Communism.

The Paris group, organised by Zhang Ji, Li Shizeng and Wu Zhihui, all but the latter from the wealthy classes, looked towards the modernisation of China and sought out radical ideas in Europe, understanding anarchist communism as propounded by Kropotkin to be a "scientific" doctrine and that China needed both a political and cultural revolution. This distinguished them from the Tokyo group of anarchists, who looked back to traditional ideas of Daoism to justify their positions. Indeed, Li Shizeng was to remark: "Anarchism advocates radical activism. It is the diametrical opposition of quietist nonaction. Anarchism does not only advocate that imperial power does not reach the self; it also seeks to make sure that it does not reach anyone else".

Leading lights in the Tokyo group which existed between 1907 and 1910 were Liu Shipei and his partner He Zhen. Liu started out as a straightforward scholar of Confucianism. He maintained his admiration for Confucianism and Daoism even after his conversion to anti-Manchu nationalism in 1903 and then anarchist communism. He maintained that Lao Zi, the founder of Daoism, was equally the founder of Chinese anarchism. He looked towards the Daoist tract of Bao Jingyan, which attacked the concept of rulership and the division between rich and poor as an example of pioneering anarchist communism. Liu Shipei returned to China in 1908 where he supported the Qing regime, serving in various posts in different parts of China including Sichuan, where the Qing official Duan Feng repressed republican revolutionaries in 1911. With the establishment of the Republic, Liu served under the warlord Yan Xishan and then supported Yuan Shikai, a former Qing general. There are allegations that he acted as an agent provocateur for the Qing dynasty. He died of TB in 1919. His speedy return to conservative views quickly invalidated the positions he had adopted on the relationship of Daoism and anarchism in the eyes of his peers.

He Zhen has in the past been overshadowed by Liu Shipei. In actual fact, she appears to have been the moving force behind the magazine Tianyi Bao (Journal of Natural Justice), the organ of the Society for the Restoration of Women's Rights, and to be responsible for its more radical aspects. The Tokyo group also established the Society for the Study of Socialism (Shehui zhuyi jiangxihui). Within the 'traditional' approach of the Tokyo group, its anti-modernist outlook and its vaunting of agrarian society, there were contradictions. The magazine was one of the first Chinese anarchist journals to discuss the nature of labour, and the need for equality where "everyone has work and everyone has labour". Equally forward looking was the emphasis of the Tokyo group on the absolute need for the equality of women. The first Chinese translation of the Communist Manifesto first appeared in Tianyi Bao, and this was supplemented by He Zhen's What Women Should Know about Communism. There she wrote, "Think of all the things in the world. They were either produced by nature or by individual labour. Why can rich people buy them but poor people cannot? It is because the world trades with money. It is because people seize the things they have bought with money for their own exclusive use. If every single woman understands that nothing is more evil than money and they all unite together to cooperate with men to utterly overthrow the rich and powerful and then abolish money, then absolutely nothing will be allowed for individuals to own privately.... This is called communism". He Zhen argued strongly for the centrality of women's liberation in the social revolution. By issue No.8 of Natural Justice, the aims of destroying contemporary society and instituting equality had been changed to read: To destroy national and racial boundaries to institute internationalism; resist all authority; overthrow all existing forms of government; institute communism; institute absolute equality of men and women.

Precisely because of the publishing of the Communist Manifesto, Tanyi was shut down in 1908, to be replaced by Hengbao (Equality), dedicated to "anarcho-communism, anti-militarism, the general strike, reports about the people's suffering, and links with the international revolutionary labour unions." Whilst Liu Shipei referred more often to Tolstoy than to Kropotkin, the series of articles on the peasant question, which appeared in Hengbao seemed to be more strongly influenced by the latter, and they may well have been written by Zhang Ji, now seeking refuge in Japan, whilst Liu and probably He Zhen had returned to China.

In 1906 the Paris group founded the World Society, Shiejie she. In 1908 the World Society published a Chinese weekly version of Temps Nouveaux, (New Times) the anarchist communist paper edited by Jean Grave, called Xin Shiji, and La Novaj Tempoj in Esperanto. Both Li and Zhang were compromised by the fact that they owned profitable businesses and continued to do so, and they and Wu by their links to the Chinese Nationalist Party (Guomindang-GMD) led by Sun Yat-sen. Indeed, in the 1920s they became "Elders" of the GMD, and took the side of Chiang Kai-shek in purging it of leftists and communists. Wu, Zhang and Li attended the special meeting of the GMD supervisory committee in April 1927 which initiated a chain of events which led to the massacre of thousands of Communists, trade unionists and rank and file workers in Shanghai (the White Terror which was unleashed claimed according to the GMD, 5,000 deaths, according to the Communists 50,000 whilst an independent source gives a figure of 12,000). As the young militant Hui Lin wrote in a letter to Zhang, "the moment Li and Wu entered the Guomindang they as good as stopped being anarchists." As Dirlik notes, "At no time in his [Wu's] life did he totally accept the Kropotkinist anarchism he claimed to adhere to".

Liu Shifu, later known as Shifu, and in Esperanto as Sifo, born in 1884 to the educated class described himself as an anarchist communist and founded the Society of Anarchist Communist Comrades. He was radicalised during a stay in Japan, and took part in the progressive republican and anti-colonialist movement led by Sun Yat-sen, the Tongmenghui (Revolutionary Alliance), precursor of the GMD. This movement was influenced by the People's Will group in Russia and advocated the use of terrorist tactics, including the assassination of leading figures of the ruling regime. He then took part in the Assassination Corps of that movement and attempted to kill Li Zhun, a tyrannical governor of Canton Province, on June 11th 1907. The bomb which he hoped to use to kill Li exploded before it could be used, wounding him in the head, chest and limbs. Arrested by the police, his left arm was subsequently amputated. He was imprisoned in appalling conditions, and there probably contracted the TB that was later to kill him. He avoided execution thanks to the influence of his father. He became an anarchist communist after the failure of the May 1911 rising and his disillusionment with republicanism. Shifu was now to reject terrorist tactics, and look towards the distribution of propaganda and attempts to create a mass movement, including the organisation of both workers and peasants.

Shifu founded the Cocks Crowing in the Dark Society, Huìmíng Xuéshè, at Xiguan in Guangzhou (Canton) province in May 1912, together with his partner Ding Xingtian, and others. Over the next year the Society put out 10,000 leaflets, often reproducing texts from the best articles in New Times, and distributing them throughout China. Shifu had obtained a small press for this, and used this to publish the group's paper, People's Voice (Minsheng). In summer 1913 the paper carried articles in Chinese and Esperanto that were strongly anti-militarist. As a result, People's Voice was suppressed and Shih Fu fled to Macau, then ruled by the Portuguese. There he attempted to republish the paper, but was prevented by the Portuguese authorities.

After six months he moved to Shanghai and founded an anarchist communist group there, the Society of Anarchist Communist Comrades – Wu-Zheng-Fu Gong-Chan Zhuyi Tongzhi Hui.

The Manifesto of the Anarchist Communist Party produced by the group in July 1914 advocates the creation of "a society without landowners, without heads of families, without leaders, without police, without courts of law, without law, without religion, without marriage" and that, "the implementation of anarchist communism depends on the strength of our party. If we wish to increase our party's strength, uniting as a whole body and advancing together is our most important task today. Wherever they are, all our comrades should unite with those who share the same purposes and establish groups in free association."

However, the advancing ravages of TB led to his death on 27th March, 1915 at the age of 31. China was thus deprived of a leading exponent of anarchist communism. His polemics with the social democrat Juang Kanghu helped publicise anarchist communism, which now became also known as "pure socialism".

Shifu was a sharp critic of Zhang and co, addressing himself to Zhang thus, "You formerly were an advocate of anarchism. Anarchism absolutely does not recognise politics as something of benefit to society. Your going helter skelter into politics means that you have changed from your former anarchism." He followed this up by remarking: "Recently there have been those who have talked about "semi- [banmian] socialism" and who constantly say that you can use politics to arrive at the objective of socialism. This kind of heterodox theory is a blot on socialism. Zhang Ji and Wu Zhihui have been the foremost advocates of anarchism. A few years ago, when writing in the New Century, they were very passionate [in advocating anarchism]. Now Zhang Ji has become a senator. Wu Zhihui sometimes consorts with the Guomindang and daily becomes closer to the political parties which is the same as daily becoming more estranged from the socialists and anarchists."

The Guangzhou group around Shifu produced many important militants like his brothers Liu Shixin and Liu Kefei, Xie Yingbo, Ou Shengbai, Liang Bingxian, Yuan Zhenying, Zhe Peigang and Huang Lingshuang. In Shifu's home town of Xiangshan, anarchist communism was also strong, and a militant there, Lang Ou, published Tie Sheng, an anarchist communist journal from May 1920 into 1921. It organised workers in unions, especially among forestry workers, and circulated as far as Malaya, Singapore and Thailand. The Guangzhou group made great efforts to organise workers, in particular Xie Yingbo, an old associate of Shifu, organised a mechanics' union, and Liu Shixin and Huang Lingshuang were also highly active in labour organising. These unions were the first labour unions in China, and in the mid-1910s there were about 40 of these in Guangzhou. In fact, between 1905-23 a total of seventy anarchist communist papers were published and there were 92 anarchist communist societies in mainland China between 1919 and 1923. For example, Liu Shixin, Fu Wumen and Liang Bingxian published the weekly paper The Workers in Guangzhou. Anarchist communism remained the major radical current in China at least until 1925.

Another development was the founding of the Socialist Party in 1911 by Jiang Kanghu. Jiang had read both anarchist and socialist texts and the original platform of the Party included praise for anarchist communism and anarchy as the ultimate goal but it was a highly heterogenous body. When Jiang moved it firmly in a reformist direction at its October 1912 Congress, this resulted in a breakaway Social Party- Shehui Dang around the young medical student Sha Gan, Lu Daren and the young Buddhist monk Taixu, sometimes known as the "pure socialists". The new grouping published five issues of Social World- Shehui shijie in 1912.Its programme was openly anarchist communist; as Dirlik notes it sought to ," (1) abolish class divisions created by differences in wealth (hence communism), by distinctions between high and low (hence respect for the individual), by distinctions on the basis of intelligence (hence educational equality); (2) eliminate all divisions among people on the basis of state, family, and religion (which Taixu and others identified with ancestor worship and the lineage system)." This attracted the attention of Yuan Shikai, the militarist and first President of the new republic and resulted in a banning of the group in December, less than a year after its foundation, and its retreat to the extraterritorial asylum of the French Concession in Shanghai. During the Second Revolution which started on July 12th, 1913, Sha Gan set up a Dare to Die Corps -Gan si dui- to fight Yuan, was arrested and shot. Former members of this group were to be core members of the anarchist communist Masses Society (Qun She) in Nanjing.

The Comintern encouraged the establishment of Marxist study groups in China and the Comintern delegate in China, Voitinsky, went on to urge the founding of the Chinese Communist Party from March 1920. This was finally founded on 23rd July, 1921, including intellectuals like Chen Duxiu, Li Hanjun and Li Dazhao in its leadership. There were barely fifty Communists in China at the beginning of 1921, but soon the Party grew to a thousand members. At first the Communists courted the anarchist communists, but upon entry into the GMD and agitation in its left wing in late 1922, the Communists soon forgot about their former "allies".

At the beginning of 1922 anarchist communists began to look towards linking up the various societies they had founded throughout China. This resulted in the meeting of 50 militants in spring of that year in Guangzhou where an Anarchist Federation was founded. However, with the departure of several key activists overseas this soon fell apart. Other attempts to create a viable organisation also foundered. Following the events of May 30th 1925 in Shanghai the Communists were able to use their superior organising abilities to grow their Party to 50,000, eclipsing anarchist communism in China (British police fired on workers and students protesting against the clampdown on strikes in Japanese-owned textile factories and in this and ensuing riots at least 30 workers were killed. This initiated the anti-imperialist May 4th Movement).

Ba Jin was among those who criticised the lack of organisation and cohesion that had helped enable the rise of the Communist Party. Part of a new generation of anarchist communists, Ba Jin was born Li Feigan in 1904 in Chengdu in Sichuan to a high-up official's family. His youth was marked by the convulsions that shook China, with the fall of the Emperor and the proclamation of the Republic in 1912. In 1919, there was a wave of strikes and social unrest and young Li Feigan joined the Chengdu anarchist communist group, the Equality Society. He took the name Ba Jin from the first syllable of the anarchist Bakunin and the last from Kropotkin in tribute to them. He was deeply impressed by the work of Kropotkin, especially his An Appeal to the Young, and of Emma Goldman, and he entered into correspondence with her. He was the most active member of the group, involved in distribution of propaganda and the setting up of a reading room in the building of the local anarchist paper. He later moved to Shanghai where he continued to be active. After the Shanghai massacre of 1927, he moved to Paris.

There he was active in the anarchist movement and acted as a liaison between the European and Asian movements. He translated Kropotkin's Ethics into Chinese, and continued to write for the Shanghai anarchist magazines. He met many anarchists in France, including Alexander Berkman, whose ABC of Anarchism he later translated into Chinese as From Capitalism to Anarchism. Whilst in Paris, he involved himself in the debate around the Organisational Platform. A week before he arrived in Paris, a meeting of Russian, French, Spanish, Italian and Polish libertarians, met to discuss the Platform. Also present was the Chinese militant Wu Kegang (1900-99) who used the alias Chen.

Wu Kegang was a young student in economics at the Sorbonne with whom Ba Jin became acquainted on setting foot in Paris. It was Wu

Kegang who came to meet Ba Jin when he got off the train. Above all, Ba Jin intervened in the debate on the "Platform" by a written contribution that was intended for the interim committee on which Wu Kegang sat. For reasons which will become clearer later, the report remained unpublished, except for a long passage he confided hidden behind the pseudonym Renping to Pingdeng (Equality), a Chinese magazine of anarchist persuasion, based in the United States, in San Francisco, under the title "Chinese Anarchism and the question of organisation". He launched a plea in defence of organisation but never referring, at least in the published part, to the Platform.

Ba Jin's support for the Platform seems to have been limited to this written contribution. Wu Kegang was among those arrested by the police at the Cinema Les Roses conference on 20th March, and became the subject of a police investigation. After that he was served a notice for deportation.

Another activist of the new generation was Lu Jianbo was for many years one of the most active anarchist communists in China, speaking for class struggle, effective organisation, and against compromise with the nationalist Guomindang. Like his better known comrade Ba Jin, he hailed from Sichuan in southern China. In fact, Ba Jin described him as "a young man full of energy" "endowed with great fortitude" "shows great talent" "is a revolutionary ready to devote himself to his ideal".

Lu Jianbo was born in 1904 near Luzhou. He was radicalised by the May 4th Movement that commenced in 1919. He joined an anarchist group in Chongqing. Lu founded an anarchist paper, Helian (Black Billows). Later he helped set up the Minfeng she (People's Vanguard Society) in Nanjing in 1923 along with his wife Deng Tianyu and Mao Yibo (1901-96). Both Lu and Deng were keen Esperantists, Lu having discovered it for himself in 1920.

Their paper Minfeng (Vanguard) advocated class struggle anarchism, revolution carried out by the masses of both town and country, and effective organisation. In 1925 Lu and the Minfeng Society relocated to Shanghai and there their Society founded two others, the Society for the Study of Syndicalism (Gongtuan zhuyi yanjiu hui) and the Federation of Young Chinese Anarchist Communists (Zhongguo shaonian wuzhengfu gongchan zhuyizhe liangmeng, usually abbreviated to Shaolian) in 1927. When Lu arrived in Shanghai, he shared living quarters with Ba Jin. Lu later put together a collection of Ba Jin texts. Lu and Ba Jin launched the Shanghai anarchist magazine Minzhong (Masses) in September 1925.This aimed to act as a liaison between anarchists in southern China as well as providing information on both native and foreign anarchist groups.

In 1928 Lu had to flee from Shanghai to escape the persecution of the Guomindang. This was a result of his and his associates' sharp criticisms of any sort of alliance with the GMD, as advocated by some anarchists. Lu had established a friendship with Ba Jin, who, whilst disapproving of collaboration himself, adopted a middle position of cooperation between both anarchist currents, and they fell out over this although their friendship was later mended.

In late 1927 the GMD anarchists had established the influential Labour University in Shanghai. The Minfeng she agitated among both teaching staff and students at the University, calling for struggle against the GMD and Lu recalls a meeting held there "with tens of individuals" attending. These activities contributed to his eventual flight.

One of the accusations thrown at Lu and his anarchist current was that they were "Bolshevised". Lu demonstrated the falseness of this accusation in his articles on the dictatorship of the proletariat in three issues of the magazine Xuedeng (Light of Learning) in 1924, where he stated that: "Facts tell us: the inner lining of the dictatorship of the proletariat is the dictatorship of a single party – the Leninist party. The Soviets have already been captured by bureaucratic socialists".

The prophecies of Lu and his comrades proved correct when the GMD turned on its anarchist supporters in 1929, branding them Communists and shutting down their societies and workplace unions. The proscription of the movement led to its extinguishing, with only individual activists able to act in a limited way over the coming years.

When the war with Japan broke out in 1937 Lu and other comrades were able to start publishing Jingzhe (Spring Festival) at Chengdu in Sichuan when the GMD moved there in retreat from the Japanese army. They advocated a popular war against the Japanese. At the same time, they publicised the Spanish Revolution, for example printing articles on Durruti. Another way Lu sought to spread anarchist communist ideas was via the Esperanto movement and via his concept of "proletarian culture".

Lu had an emancipated position on the liberation of women, writing articles for the feminist magazine Xin Nuxing (New Woman) writing Tan Xing (On Sex) in a 1928 issue. He also contributed other articles on the role of women, Tan Xing Ai (On Sexual Love) for Huanzhou (The Mirage) in 1926. He actively supported Deng's participation in anarchist propaganda work.

By 1944 he was professor of the history of ancient Greece and Rome at Chengdu University, where he initiated Esperanto classes. In 1945 he established (or maintained) links with overseas libertarians in Japan, India, France and the USA. In this period, he assisted Ba Jin in bringing out the complete works of Kropotkin in Chinese, as well as attempting to set up a Kropotkinist Association.

The coming to power of the Communist Party in 1949 curtailed Lu's activities. He was eventually pressurised to join the Party, although it always appears he maintained his old beliefs. He died in 1991 in Chengdu.

One young man, Ma Schmu, (Ma Shimou) was in contact with him and he later in the 1960s he had an important influence on introducing several young people into libertarian ideas. These were to become was founder members of the 70s Front, in Hong Kong, in the mid-1970s.

The 70s Front was a group made up of Hong Kong Chinese and refugees from the Cultural Revolution. It was a contradictory grouping, incorporating many influences, including those of the historic anarchist movement in China, Situationism, American Leftism and counter-culture, as well as Trotskyism from some of its older members. It maintained contact with the ORA/AWA in Britain and with the French ORA.

Despite its effectiveness in organising various mass actions and a popular biweekly magazine, Minus, it imploded due to the internal contradictions between its libertarian and Trotskyist components. After July 1973 the magazine stopped regular publishing. Some of its members were involved in grass roots organising into the 1980s but others moved to reformist positions.

References

Gilmore Clifford, Paul. The Intellectual Development of Wu Zhihui: A Reflection of Society and Politics" In Late Qing and Republican China: https://core.ac.uk/download/pdf/161529315.pdf

Chapter Thirty Nine
Anarchist communism in Japan

A pioneering role in introducing anarchist communism to Japan was taken by Kotoku Shusui. Born in 1871 he began working as a journalist in Tokyo in 1893. He started moving from liberalism to social democracy and was one of those who attempted to set up a Social Democratic Party in Tokyo in May 1901. It was immediately banned by the government.

During the war with Russia in 1904-05 he took part in an anti-war paper Heimin Shinbun (Common People's Newspaper), which finally collapsed under government pressure in January 1905. The paper was the first to publish the Communist Manifesto in Japanese, and again it was banned with Kotoku and his associate editor Sakai Toshihiko receiving heavy fines. In February 1905 Kotoku served a prison sentence of five months for offences related to the publication of Heimin Shinbun. Whilst in prison he read Kropotkin's Fields, Factories and Workshops and he became a convinced anarchist communist. The Japanese social democrats failed to question the Imperial institution for reasons of expediency, but Kotoku realised that the Emperor and his court were the mainstays of capitalism in Japan.

Upon his release Kotoku decided to take a break of six months to the USA. He read Kropotkin's Memoirs of a Revolutionist on the ship taking him to California. He also read Kropotkin's Conquest of Bread whilst in the USA. Kotoku was further influenced by the industrial unionism of the Industrial Workers of the World, with which he had established contact. He was also influenced by the terroristic tactics of the (non-anarchist) Russian Social Revolutionary Party (the SRs).

Eventually a clandestine edition of one thousand copies of Kotoku's translation of Appeal to the Young was published in March 1909 and was widely distributed among students and workers.

On his return from the USA, Kotoku addressed a large public meeting, on 28th June, 1906, speaking against parliamentarianism and for the general strike. He affirmed these views in subsequent articles.

A new Socialist Party had been formed in Kotoku's absence. He correctly described this as a coalition of "Social-Democrats, Social

Revolutionists, and even Christian Socialists" and went on to write that "it is not because they are assuredly convinced which is true, but because of their ignorance of Anarchist Communism." Under Kotoku's influence, the Party dropped its legality clause of "operating within the limits of the law of the land". This led to the banning of the Party, and a split between social democrats and libertarians in its ranks.

Anarchist communists began to propagandise their ideas. One such militant was Akaba Hajime (1875-1912), previously noted for his anti-war activities, who wrote a pamphlet addressed to Japanese peasants, Nomin no Fukuin (The Farmer's Gospel) where he exhorted peasants to "send the land robbers [landlords] to the revolutionary guillotine and return to the "village community" of long ago, which our remote ancestors enjoyed. We must construct the free paradise of 'anarchist communism', which will flesh out the bones of the village community with the most advanced scientific understanding and with the lofty morality of mutual aid". Akaba was forced to go underground, but was captured, imprisoned and died in Chiba prison in 1912 after a hunger strike.

As open agitation and propaganda were subject to severe repression, as was any attempt at organising associations of workers, it was of little surprise that there was a turn to the advocacy of replying to State violence with defensive violence, in order to catalyse a popular uprising. When four militants were arrested in May 1910 in possession of bomb-making equipment, State authorities used this as a pretext to arrest hundreds of activists and to fabricate a case of plotting to assassinate the Emperor against 26 of them.

The trial in December 1910 led to all defendants being found guilty and all bar two sentenced to death, including Kotoku. Twelve of these had their sentences commuted whilst the other twelve were hanged in January 1911. The Japanese State had succeeded in destroying many of the leading activists of the movement, and followed this with a draconian banning of papers, meetings, and general harassment of militants.

Osugi Sakae was the most accomplished surviving activist, and during this "winter period" which continued until 1918, he advocated syndicalist methods inspired by the French CGT. Anarchist communism had suffered in Japan because of Kropotkin's position on the First World War, and syndicalism filled the temporary gap that had been created by this. Osugi and Arahata Kanson was able to use the magazine Kindai Shiso (Modern Thought) to discuss syndicalism under the guise of philosophical discussion, and to organise meetings under the aegis of the Syndicalism Study Group between 1913 and 1916. The authorities overlooked these activities because they attracted young intellectuals rather than workers. Nevertheless, this allowed a certain space for ideas.

Things began changing in summer 1918 with the rice riots, triggered by inflation, and huge rises in the price of Japan's staple food, rice. A small demonstration by fisherwomen in Toyama Prefecture set off a whole chain of protests spreading across the country and involving tens of thousands in direct confrontation with the police, and the army being called out. This resulted in a dissipation of the repressive atmosphere, although laws still remained on the books, ready to be employed.

This opening allowed the appearance of anarchist papers and magazines. Alongside the riots in 1918 had come labour unrest, with 66,000 workers involved in disputes throughout the year. This enabled the creation of anarchist labour unions, notably among the printworkers. Others who organised in anarchist unions were watchmakers, general labourers, tram workers, shipyard workers, engineering workers and communications workers.

As elsewhere, the Russian Revolution brought complications for the libertarian movement. Arahata Kanson, who had been Osugi's co-editor, and Yamakawa Hitoshi, who had been a close associate of Kotoku, were among those who founded the Communist Party of Japan in 1922. Osugi, whilst at first prepared to cooperate with the Bolsheviks, began to translate and publish articles about the suppression of the Kronstadt uprising. The consequential estrangement saw the Bolshevik controlled unions combining with reformist unions against the anarchist unions' advocacy of a decentralised federation. This would eventually result in the setting up of the first nationwide federation of libertarian unions, the Zenkoku Rôdô Kumiai Jiyû Rengôkai (All-Japan Libertarian Federation of Labour Unions) in 1926.

In 1923, after eastern Japan was hit by a massive earthquake, resulting in the death of 90,000, the resulting fires were blamed on revolutionaries, resulting in the lynching of Korean immigrant workers and the murder by the military police of Osugi and his partner, the prominent anarchist and feminist Ito Noe. This dealt a severe blow to the movement, and in the aftermath, other anarchists involved in retaliatory attacks against the State authorities also met their deaths.

In 1926 a resurgence in the movement began, with the emergence of the above-mentioned All Japan Libertarian Federation of Labour Unions) often known under the abbreviation in Japanese as Zenkoku Jiren, and the Kokushoku Seinen Renmei (Black Youth League) usually known as Kokuren. Zenkoku Jiren in its 1926 charter recognised the class struggle, rejected all political movements and focussed solely on economic action, endorsed libertarian federalism, opposed imperialist aggression and affirmed the international solidarity of the working class. Anarchist communists were active in both these formations, although they encompassed other anarchist tendencies. Relations between the two groupings were close, with Kokuren militants turning out to bolster the strikes led by Zenkoku Jiren. Kokuren was founded on the following positions, the emancipation of the workers must be the task of the workers themselves, libertarian federalism. The destruction of all political (i.e., parliamentary) movements, the denunciation of all proletarian political parties, the eradication of all trade union corporatism, and repeal of the harsh security laws.

Two noted theorists and propagandists of anarchist communism now came to the fore, Hatta Shûzô and Iwasa Sakutarô. Both of these individuals, the flamboyant Hatta and the quieter Iwasa had harsh criticisms of the syndicalists and indeed of the Japanese labour movement. They appealed to both tenant farmers and workers and popularised the ideas of anarchist communism. "When the anarchist communists talked about converting by revolutionary means the miserably impoverished farming villages into flourishing, self-supporting communes, their message seemed directly relevant to the tenant farmers in a way in which the predominantly urbanised, industrialised and unionised approach of the anarchist syndicalists could never be" (John Crump, the Anarchist Movement in Japan 1906-96, 1996). Hatta and Iwasa represented museifukyosan (libertarian communism) or junsei museifushugi (pure anarchism).For them, the future society could not be based on the trade union or the industrial union, but taking their cue from Kropotkin, on the commune. As agrarianists and anti-urbanists, this commune would be above all the rural commune.

Hatta argued that anarcho-syndicalism reproduced the power relations found under capitalism, and perpetuated the division of labour, and that, by adopting a form of organisation which mirrored capitalist industry, anarchist syndicalism would perpetuate the division of labour. He stated: "In a society which is based on the division of labour, those engaged in vital production (since it forms the basis of production) would have more power over the machinery of coordination than those engaged in other lines of production. There would therefore be a real danger of the appearance of classes".

In the process Hatta and Iwasa erroneously rejected the concept of class struggle as the way forward for anarchists. They justified this by saying that the relationship between the millions of tenant farmers who lived in miserable conditions and the landlords from whom they rented was closer to feudalism than to capitalism. Hatta was to say: If we understand... that the class struggle and the revolution are different things, then we are forced to say that it is a major mistake to declare, as the syndicalists do, that the revolution will be brought about by the class struggle. Even if a change in society came about by means of the class struggle, it would not mean that a genuine revolution had occurred.

Hatta envisioned a future society based on "small societies" (communes) which would engage in agricultural and small-scale industrial activity. An article in the Kokuren paper Kokushoku Seinen (Black Youth) stated in 1929 that: "The anarchist movement is progressing a great deal in Japan at the present time. In other countries we find an anarchist movement which links up with the syndicalists. But in this country we do not approve of them, driving them away just as we do the Bolsheviks. We are even against anarchist syndicalism and we adhere to anarchist communism".

In fact, the syndicalists within Kokuren had at first grouped around the paper Han Seitô Undô (Anti-Political Party Movement) in June 1927, and then departed from the organisation. This split was followed by one in Zenkoku Jiren, with the syndicalist minority departing from the second congress in March 1928. These splits were replicated within the other spheres of libertarian influence, including the lively artistic and cultural movement heavily influenced by anarchist ideas.

One would have assumed that these ruptures between the two currents would have been disastrous. However, the now largely anarchist communist Zenkoku Jiren had a total membership of 16,300 in 1931, twice as large as in its founding year of 1926. It remained a combative federation of unions, involving itself in several important struggles. But it stressed the importance of going beyond fighting for better wages and conditions and for the establishment of a new society. Peculiarly perhaps, as both Zenkoku Jiren and Kokuren were composed mainly of urban dwellers, they emphasised the importance of the tenant farmers as a force for change. It should be remembered that the latter still vastly outnumbered the urban working class in Japan.

But now the Japanese State, pursuing imperialist policies in China, decided to crush opposition at home. Kokuren was closed down by the authorities in 1931, whilst both Zenkoku Jiren and the anarchosyndicalist union, Jikyô, suffered severe repression, leading to a severe haemorrhaging of membership. As a result the two federations were united under the force of circumstances in January 1934, when Jikyô dissolved itself and most of its membership and unions rejoined Zenkoku Jiren. But the continuing pressure of the State saw that federation shrink to 2,300 members in 1935.

Some anarchist communists responded by attempting to organise in the countryside. They created the Nôson Seinen Sha (Rural Youth Society), usually abbreviated to Nôseisha in February 1931. Its founders were Aki Yagi and her partner Miyazaki Akira, Suzuki Yasuyuki and 11 others. In their Appeal to the Peasants they called on farmers to disregard the cities, refuse to pay taxes and ignore all State authority, and organise a federation of rural communes based on anarchist communism and self-sufficiency. They were advocates of extreme decentralisation in their own organisation, both for prefigurative reasons and for security from the State. This advocacy of extreme decentralisation went up to the point that they made a decision to dissolve the organisation in September 1932, although they were also mindful that most of their members in Tokyo were arrested earlier in the year following an expropriation to raise funds, and so moved to save themselves. They carried on work at an informal level in the countryside, but the dissolution of Nôseisha failed to save them from the State repression that was to come. At the trial of Nôseisha in

1935 stiff sentences were handed out, Aki Yagi receiving two and a half years imprisonment, Akira and others to three years imprisonment. Nevertheless, the influence of Miyazaki Akira was seen in unrest among farmers, particularly in the mountains of central Honshu and in the prefecture of Nagano. There an uprising involving several hundred people took place in 1934-35. It was put down, and this contributed to the State feeling that it must repress Nôseisha.

Another response by other anarchist communists was the establishment of the Museifukyosanto (Anarchist Communist Party) in January 1934.This had emerged from the Nihon Museifukyo Sanshugisha Renmei (Anarchist Communist Federation) and involved a small number of militants. They were all around thirty years old and numbered among the new generation within the movement. Perturbed by the divisions within the movement, they called for unity. The growth of Japanese militarism also disturbed them, and they felt that all the radical and progressive movements were under threat. From this, they formed the opinion that a secret organisation had to be created to resist repression.

This organisation was organised on a pattern of Leninist-style discipline, with a restricted membership. It infiltrated its members into larger groupings. One example of this was their virtual takeover of Jiyu Rengo Shimbun (the Libertarian Federation Newsletter), voice of Zenkoku Jiren, where they agitated for its reunification with Jikyô.

Secretive organisation most often fosters an atmosphere of distrust and paranoia. This ended with one member shooting another, because he suspected him of being a police spy. This was followed by a botched expropriation at a bank. As a result, one of the leading members of the Anarchist Communist Party, Akira Aizawa, was arrested, and under torture, revealed the existence of the Party.

This was the excuse the State authorities needed to come down heavily on the whole movement. Some four hundred militants were arrested, Zenkoku Jiren was closed down, and a stronghold of anarchist communism, the Tokyo Printers Union, had almost one hundred of its members arrested. The police then concentrated on pursuing members of Nôseisha, which had been dissolved in 1932. The dissolution of Nôseisha did not stop the police arresting another 300 militants in May 1936. Futami Toshio, who had killed the fellow Party member, received a death sentence, although this was commuted to twenty years in prison. Others, like Aizawa received six years. Whilst the repression could not be compared to the death sentences handed out to Kotoku and the murders of Osugi and Ito Noe, in other ways it was worse, with heavy pressure and persecution of the movement forcing all organised activity to end by the end of the year.

The war against China and then Japan's involvement in the Second World War followed. Many anarchists did not survive these grim years and the capitulation of Japan in August 1945 brought with it occupation by the U.S. armed forces. The US occupying authorities were wary of allowing any legalisation of radical movements and were wedded to anti-Communist policies, which included anarchism in its ambits.

Nevertheless, the Nihon Anakisuto Renmei (Japanese Anarchist Federation) was founded in May 1946. This united both anarchist communists and anarchosyndicalists, and was created in an atmosphere of fresh enthusiasm. However, the organisation failed to grow. It was harassed by the occupying authorities and it was divided by the continuing disagreements between anarchist communists and anarchosyndicalists. It was hindered from growing in the workplaces by the strong presence of the Communist Party there. The support that could be counted on among the peasants was no longer there, with a wholesale desertion of the countryside for the cities, partly occasioned by land reform legislation after the war, which eliminated the tenant farmers as a class.

Differences within the Federation erupted with the creation of the Anaruko Sanjikarisuto Gurūpu (Anarchosyndicalist Group) in May 1950. In October that group left and the Federation was dissolved. The anarchist communists regrouped in the Nihon Anakisuto Kurabu (Japanese Anarchist Club) in June 1951. The Club lasted until March 1980 but never grew beyond its circle of veterans. None of these groups made any credible links with the student radicalism and the New Left of the late 1960s onwards, remaining isolated and marginalised, keepers of the flame.

Today only a few small groups survive in a society that has promoted conformity and obedience. The only hopeful sign of a fresh wave of radicalism has been the anti-nuclear movement that emerged after the earthquake and tsunami of 2011 triggered the Fukushima nuclear disaster.

Chapter Forty
Anarchist Communism in Korea

"... anarchism in Korea has been notable for the extent to which it has been permeated by nationalism and also for the Korean anarchists' readiness over many years to engage in conventional politics. The immediate reason for these peculiarities of Korean anarchism would seem to lie in Korea's colonial subjugation by Japan from 1910 to 1945 and the division of the country after 1945" (John Crump, *Anarchism and Nationalism in East Asia*, 1995, p.45).

Anarchist ideas were first introduced to Korea from both China and Japan. There were few Korean translations of major anarchist texts until well into the twentieth century, but educated Koreans could understand Chinese and/or Japanese. Korean students and intellectuals discovered anarchist ideas whilst in China or Japan. Sin Chaeho read texts from Kotoku Shusui and others during the late 1900s. When Japan annexed Korea in 1910, he went into exile in Shanghai where he published a paper, Sin taehan, in Korean and Chinese, where he introduced anarchist ideas. Na Kyŏngsŏk encountered anarchists like Osugi Sakae whilst studying in Japan.

But whilst anarchist ideas circulated in Korea, it was not until the 1910s that there was an attempt at organisation, and then at first in exile in China and Japan. As a result, the ideas that were imbibed were predominantly anarchist communist. In the 1920s many newspapers and magazines began being published, when the Japanese occupiers began relaxing censorship laws. As well as this, there was a circulation of pamphlets and books in Chinese and Japanese, Kropotkin's Appeal to the Young and Mutual Aid being the most popular, as well as excerpts from Fields, Factories and Workshops, and the Conquest of Bread and other Kropotkin writings.

The Japanese occupation of Korea had a huge influence on how radical ideas were being formed among the intellectuals and the youth. As a result, anti-colonial nationalism had a huge sway over them, and while anarchist communism as an idea became highly popular, those who described themselves as anarchist communists were in danger of quickly slipping into outright nationalism.

Yu Rim organised the first organisation, the Jo-sun gong-san mu-jung-bu ju-eu-ja yun-meng (Korean Anarchist-Communist Federation) in 1929, and became a leading light among Korean anarchist exiles in China.

However, the growth of Leninist groups in Korea, backed by the Comintern, meant that many anarchists crossed over, as for example Chŏng T'aesin, Song Yŏng, and Yi Kiyŏng.

Yu Rim, who was a leading light in the China branch of the General League of Anarchists, Yu Ja-Myeong of the Korean Revolutionist Federation and Korean Anarchist Federation in China served as assembly members "as representatives of anarchist forces" in the Korean Provisional Government in exile in Chungking in China in 1940. The following year, other anarchists like Jeong Hwa-Ahm and Park Kee-Seong became members of the assembly. In 1945, Yu Rim was elected to the cabinet. At the same time, anarchist guerrilla units were integrated into the Provisional Government's armed forces.

At the end of the war, Yu Rim participated in the anarchist congress that took place in Anwi in 1946. Anwi was the home town of another anarchist Ha Ki-Rak, who was chair of the Free Peasant Union Committee of Anwi. The congress was attended by 60 people from the Free Social Constructors League, the Korean General League of Anarchists, the Black Friend League and the League of Truth and Fraternity and was meant to be the founding congress of a united organisation. There Yu Rim put forward the idea that anarchists should organise a political party. He argued that "The situation in Korea is a very special one. Under such conditions, even anarchists are bound to respond to the urgent desire of the Korean people to build their own country and to set up their own government. Therefore, the anarchists must create their own political party, and play a positive part in building a new Korea." The Congress voted to accept his proposal and later that year set up the Dok-lip no-nong-dang (DNN, Independent Workers and Farmers Party).

The DNN was quickly hamstrung by the succession of authoritarian governments that were set up in South Korea in the 1950s. All left, Communist and Anarchist groups were criminalised by the Syngman Rhee regime and forced underground. The DNN collapsed, only maintaining two groups. When a period of liberalisation came in 1956 it re-emerged. However, the military rule of Park Jung-hi in 1961 soon closed the DNN down. Yu Rim died that year, bringing an end to this failed experiment.

In 1987 Ha Ki-Rak and his comrades refused to take part in the mass demonstrations of students and workers against the military dictatorship. Earlier they had called for Koreans to work with the American army of occupation to end industrial unrest. Ha Ki-Rak was to write in 1986 "…a 'government of non-governing'. Non-government means non rule and non-exploitation and government means the social management of human lives by the people themselves, namely independent self-government. Therefore there is no contradiction between the two conceptions of non-government and government" and that "it seems that the word 'anarchism' has been used as being synonymous with 'non-government' in Korea. But it's a misinterpretation of 'anarchism' by Japanese scholars. To tell the truth, 'an-' means 'without or not', and 'archi-' means 'boss or chief, that is compulsory power'. Therefore anarchy means 'absence of compulsory power or control.' I am an anarchist who rejects compulsory power, but not a non-governmentist who objects to an autonomous government. An anarchist objects only to a heteronomous government."

Many young radicals hold the Korean Anarchist Federation in contempt, believing that it represents a nationalist rather than anarchist current, that Ha Ki-Rak and his associates were Anarchist in name only, and then only because during the Japanese occupation they advocated propaganda by the deed.

John Crump argues that the South East Asian colonised countries have not had a history of strong libertarian movements, apart from Korea, and that if they had, there would have been far more cases of them degenerating into radical nationalism. This was certainly the case in India, where a movement autonomous from nationalism was unable to emerge, and where those who did enunciate anarchist ideas quickly became subsumed into the nationalist movement.

References
Anarchism and Culture in Colonial Korea: Minjung Revolution, Mutual Aid, and the Appeal of Nature Sunyoung Park, University of Southern California

Park, Sunyoung. 2018. "Anarchism and Culture in Colonial Korea: Minjung Revolution, Mutual Aid, and the Appeal of Nature." Cross-Currents: East Asian History and Culture Review (e-journal) 28: 93-115. https://cross-currents.berkeley.edu/e-journal/issue-28/park.

Anarchism in Korea: Independence, Transnationalism, and the Question of National Development, 1919-1984, by Dongyoun Hwang. "Anarchism and Nationalism in East Asia" Anarchist Studies, 1996, vol. 4, no. 1

Chapter Forty One
The future

The history of anarchist communism has been marked by many setbacks. Whilst it emerged as one of the better achievements of the First International, the following period, after the crushing of the Paris Commune and general repression throughout the planet, was marked by a turning in on itself and a reliance on disconnected and small affinity groups and a distrust of effective organisation, breaking with the prescriptions of Bakunin. A period of individual attentats against various figures of authority did little to better the situation. This was rectified to a certain extent by the turn towards mass workers organisations in the 1890s; however it was still not reciprocated by the building of specific anarchist communist organisations. A trend towards this that started to develop in the 1910s was short-circuited by the coming of the First World War.

Of course, that too, brought a crisis, with one of the leading theorists of anarchist communism, Kropotkin, along with others, deserting the colours of internationalism and precipitating a damaging rift within the movement. The coming of the Russian Revolution brought its problems too, as the Russian anarchist movement saw itself politically out-manoeuvred by the Bolsheviks. Whilst anarchist communists in Ukraine constructed a mass movement, known as the Makhnovshchina, to resist first the Austro-German invaders and their puppets, and then the White armies, they were eventually militarily defeated by the Reds.

Some of those who had participated in the Russian Revolution, like Makhno, Arshinov and Mett, sought to learn the lessons of the defeat of the anarchist movement and produced the Organisational Platform of the Libertarian Communists. It proved to be a controversial document and brought forth condemnations from many in the old guard of anarchism. Its insistence on a class-based anarchist communism brought on the opposition of those who had adopted a vague humanist approach to anarchist theory. As a result it had little influence on a worldwide scale, with the exception of France and Bulgaria, where it did have an impact on the movements there.

The anarchist communist movement, and anarchism in general, had been sorely weakened by the repercussions of the Russian revolution. A parody of communism was now the State monopoly of the Soviet regime and they exported it worldwide. As a result, Communist Parties, some of them on a mass scale, under the sway of the Soviet-controlled Comintern had been established throughout the world, and an important number of anarchists crossed over to them, many of them to remain there, to eventually drop out of political activity, or in a few cases, return to the movement. In addition, the First World War had engendered disillusion among many, whilst countless militants who had been conscripted or who had rallied to the colours, were decimated in the slaughter. In Spain, there still remained a mass anarchist movement but this too was to be savagely annihilated with the establishment of the Franco regime throughout the country. The coming of the Second World War and before that the establishment of authoritarian regimes in Portugal, Germany, Italy, and Hungary had also contributed towards the rout of anarchism.

It certainly looked like the end. However small groups of surviving veterans and young people radicalised during the Second World War, began to organise and re-group. The growth of a worldwide culture of resistance, began to develop as a result of the disaffection of a layer of radicalised youth, uneasy with the new consumer society, affrighted by the threat of nuclear annihilation, and inspired by phenomena like the civil rights movement in the USA, the anti-apartheid struggles in South Africa, and the various anti-war movements that developed, as well as new countercultural trends in the arts and music. The crushing of the Hungarian Revolution of 1956 brought disillusionment with the Soviet system and its monopoly of what passed for opposition to capitalism. The U.S. intervention in Vietnam brought a further radicalisation, shortly followed by the rise of militancy among black people in America, and the explosion of social discontent that was April-May 1968 in France. Co-existent with this was the development of radicalism in sexual politics, with the emergence of both the women's liberation and gay liberation movements.

However, whilst strengthened to a certain extent by the repercussions of 1968, lack of effective organisation once again showed that the anarchist movement was at a disadvantage with Trotskyist and Maoist movements who were able to fill the vacuum brought about by an increased disenchantment with the Communist Parties. Once again, the Platform was rediscovered and anarchist communism began to re-emerge as a visible though small current in various countries around the world.

The collapse of the Soviet Union and the increasing turn of China towards a market capitalism controlled by the State, as well as the repression unleashed with the Tienanmen Square massacre, brought about the collapse of many Communist Parties, and crises within both Maoist and Trotskyist groups. The various social-democratic parties, including the Labour Party, revealed more and more that they were on board to manage capitalism and to enthusiastically take part in vicious attacks on the working class with their austerity measures. Leninism in all its forms has been revealed as completely bankrupt in offering any alternatives to capitalism.

And this is what is sorely needed now, a credible alternative to capitalism, which continues its death march with wars, famines, the increasing gap between rich and poor, the obscene spectacles of billionaires flaunting their wealth, the deepening problem of global warming and species extinction, the move towards greater and more authoritarian control of the masses.

Anarchist communism is increasingly being seen as that alternative. The republishing of Kropotkin's Conquest of Bread and of his Anarchist Communism in Penguin's cheap Great Reads series is one indication of this, as is the increasing tendency by anarchists to specifically describe themselves as anarchist communists. This book has been written to assist in this process of rehabilitation.

There is an image in Frans Masereel's great graphic work The Idea of a number of men gathering around the female figure symbolising the Idea, rolling on the floor in laughter or urinating on her. In their belittling of anarchism Stalinist historians like Hobsbawm, who wrote that there was 'no real intellectual room for anarchist theory', other historians like Irving L. Horowitz who derided anarchism as 'a religious expression, a messianic critique', or ex-anarchists like George Woodcock, who dismissed anarchism as a lost cause', fulfil the role of Masereel's scoffing men.

But far from being utopian or a lost cause, anarchist communism is beginning to be seen as the only way out of the appalling situation that capitalism has brought us to.

The history of anarchist communism has been full of many defeats, of scissions and failures. Yet is has perennially renewed itself, attempting to learn from the mistakes of its past. The self-isolation of the 1880s, the failures of the movement during the Russian Revolution, the Fontenis experiment, the lack of perception in terms of the national liberation movements, which led to support of dubious groupings like the Algerian FLN, these and other mistakes have to be rectified and transcended if anarchist communism is once more reveal itself as an inspirer and galvaniser of social struggle.

Anarchist Communism was the Idea that impelled women and men to take up that struggle in the past. They gave up their time to spread that Idea, standing on draughty street corners, agitating in their workplace and neighbourhood, creating cultures of resistance, writing, speaking and acting. Sometimes they gave up their lives, suffering hangings, shootings, guillotining, garrotting, beheadings and being burnt alive.

If this book has even a minimal role in convincing its readers of the viability of and indeed urgent necessity for Anarchist Communism, then it will have been of worth.

If the human race is to survive, it has to look towards a free society based on need and not profit, where production is geared to our essential needs and is socially useful, where we live in peace with nature rather than at war with it, where the expression and development of the individual is framed within the solidarity of all, where all the old hierarchies are trampled down, where State, Capital and Patriarchy are monoliths that have been tumbled. A society of community and individual fulfilment, Anarchist Communism.

Appendix One
Anarchist Communist Manifesto

Anarchist-communists are unanimous in affirming that the principle of authority which today's institutions are based on is the fundamental cause of all social ills, and it is therefore for this reason that they are today, tomorrow and forever, unyielding enemies of political authority (the State), of economic authority (Capital) and of moral and intellectual authority (Religion and Official Morality).

In short: anarchist-communists are against all the dictatorships of political, economic, scientific or religious derivation; on the other hand they are sincere partisans of a form of social organisation which is based on the free association of producers and consumers with the aim of better satisfying the various needs of the new society.

They are communists, because having carefully examined the social question in all its facets they are of the opinion that only a society based on libertarian communism will be able to guarantee every one of its members the greatest well-being and freedom.

They are revolutionaries, not for any fanaticism for glory in blood, but because they have observed that reforms are illusory and at the mercy of the whim of the ruling powers. These powers, even if they are democrats, are activated by reactionary despotic financial forces, evident or hidden, and only an Anarchist Revolution can put an end to the government and exploitation of man over man.

They are individualists, not in the sense of an exaggerated respect for the individual which, however it may be disguised, is a form of authoritarianism, but because they are supporters of communism for the very reason that it guarantees every individual the greatest physical, intellectual and moral development.

They are educationalists, because they believe that the best chance that the Revolution has of arriving sooner and having greater effect is directly linked to the level of revolutionary social education of every individual. They are convinced that the Revolution will be the logical natural product of the large-scale explosion of collective revolt, rendered conscious by a widespread understanding of the injustice of the present capitalist social system. Education of this type excludes the contemplative, fatalist, passive education which is an end in itself.

Social Program

Anarchist communism, indispensable for the realisation of a society without exploiters or exploited, is based on the free cooperation of individuals in order to satisfy each other's economic, intellectual and moral needs, since it is only right that the organisations born from within the working class should regulate social functioning after the Revolution.

Inspired by the formation and development of an ever-growing number of associations in all fields of human activity, anarchist-communists have seen that the spirit of association and federalism is ever more predominant due to the fact that political and economic centralism is providing ever more mediocre answers to the new needs of technical, scientific and social progress.

Encouraged by a similar libertarian tendency, anarchist-communists continue to be supporters of a social organisation which will develop into the Commune, a local demographic agglomeration which is large enough to be able to practice social solidarity effectively by organising the production in a rational way and, in its every act, taking into account the inviolable liberty of individuals and associations.

The libertarian Commune, in the way anarchist-communists understand it, is not a version of the present-day municipal councils nor is it a representation in miniature of any government, but a moral and material pact which unites the inhabitants of a given area in a common project in the economic, intellectual and moral field which can allow every individual of whatever sex and age to enjoy the right to freedom and to well-being, as far as the possibilities of production permit, naturally.

Relations between different Communes can be managed without useless, even dangerous interference from the central, national and international powers, in the knowledge that federalism is a basic condition for the safeguarding of the principle of freedom upon which the new communalist society will rest.

Without wishing to go into long, bothersome detail which is almost always rendered null by tomorrow's reality, anarchist-communists, as a large part of their pre-Revolutionary program, consider it sufficient to hold to the general lines of the libertarian Commune based on federalist or sovietist cooperation, sovietist in the sense of decentralisation and as a spontaneous, conscious emanation of the technical and political capacity of the working class.

Organisation

The proletarian coalitions for defence and attack against the constituted powers which have as their specific aim the maintenance of the present state of exploitation and oppression are not recent creations. They are the natural result of a painful centuries-long experience, given that individual revolt, though always appreciable for its courage, nobility and the spirit of sacrifice of the iconoclast, can never affect the organisms of oppression which are solidly organised and can never come close to effecting any social improvement or transformation.

It is for this reason that anarchist-communists are not content with proclaiming the goodness of their libertarian principles, but rather they unite in groups, in federations, in national unions and in the international union, in order to better resist and bring about the single moral and material front against the powers of repression and exploitation. It is in this way that they can provoke, in the near future, the vast, tragic and painful epilogue to this uninterrupted class war, the libertarian Revolution, to bring about a definitive end to the existence of all classes.

History brims with examples of the repression of such unions carried out in every place and time by governments of all types, but the sole fact that they constituted a single, constant target which is stronger than the capitalist violence (and will continue to do so), encourages anarchist-communists to persist in their path, the only one capable of channelling the forces of the exploitation towards the emancipating Revolution.

With regard to organisation, the present generation of anarchist-communists are certainly unanimous in recognising that thus far their predecessors have done precious little to realise it, given the bitter, continuous reaction they were victims of and anarchism's lack of an ideological unity which could permit their physical unity without which, and despite popular disgust with the parliamentary farce and the undeniable decomposition of bolshevism, anarchism will be unable to find its way into the hearts of the working masses, the only ones who can bring about the Revolution.

But after the war, fascism and above all the painful lessons of the Russian Revolution of 1917-19 (where anarchism only played a secondary role from the social point of view, despite its considerable intellectual development and its innumerable sacrifices and owing to its chronic disorganisation, both in its constructive and often in its destructive programs according to the most involved libertarians in the Russian movement), there arose among anarchist-communists from all countries a concrete idea of the necessity and the aims of anarchist organisation, based on single, universal ideological and tactical principle, excluding the reluctance that smells of byzantinism and certain ideological and tactical reservations which are the most marked characteristics of bourgeois socialist democracy.

Let this tendency develop and triumph, since, if we seek further development of anarchism as a current of popular liberation and emancipation, it is right to wait until anarchist-communists are able to oppose the authoritarian coalitions with a strong, tenacious libertarian coalition with a homogeneous program of destruction and reconstruction and homogeneous tactics.

Only in this way can there be the full participation in society of all those among the working masses who have been fooled by the daily lies of the bourgeois press and by certain revolutionary demagoguery and who continue to be ignorant of, misunderstand and even scorn the ideal for which so many have sacrificed and continue to sacrifice their lives, their freedom and a happy life.

1st Italian Section of the International Anarchist Communist Federation (Written in late 1920s by Giuseppe Bifolchi and others)

Appendix Two
Platform of the Anarchist Communist Federation of Bulgaria (1945)

Basic Positions

We reject the present social system of State and capitalist centralisation, as it is founded on the principle of the State which is contrary to the initiative and freedom of the people. Every form of power involves economic, political or spiritual privilege. Its application on an economic level is represented by private property, on a political level by the State and on a spiritual level by religion. These three forms of power are linked. If you touch one, the others are changed and, inversely, if you keep one form of power, it will inevitably lead to the re-establishment of the other two. This is why we repudiate the very principle of power. We are supporters of the abolition of private property, of the State and of religion, and of the total suppression of every form and institution of constraint and violence. We reject every teaching and every social, political and economic-political movement aimed at maintaining the State, private property, the church, and constraint and violence in social relations. We repudiate fascism, which is a historic attempt to restore absolutism, autocracy and the strength of the political form of power with the aim of defending the economic and spiritual dominance of the privileged classes. We reject political democracy, as it does not foresee the disappearance of the principle of power, and drives the masses to bewilderment by leading them, through lies and illusions, into fights which are against their interests, and corrupts them through the exercise of power and the maintaining of the appetite for domination.

Political democracy, furthermore, shows that it is totally incapable of solving the great social problems and that it fosters chaos, contradictions and crime as a result of its social foundations based on the centralised State and capitalism. We repudiate State socialism as it leads to State capitalism – the most monstrous form of economic exploitation and oppression, and of total domination of social and individual freedom. We are for anarchist communism or free communism, which will replace private property with the complete socialisation of lands, factories and mines, and of all goods and instruments of production. The State will be replaced by a federation of free communes regionally, provincially, nationally and internationally united. The church and religion will be replaced by a free individual moral and a scientific vision. Unlike all other socio-economic and political concepts and organisations, Anarchist Communism is federalist. The new social organisation that will replace the State will be built and run from the bottom upwards. All the inhabitants of any given village will form the local free commune, and all the local free communes will unite regionally, provincially, nationally and internationally in unions and federations and in a universal general social confederation. The new organisation of society's production will be formed by a tight network of countless local agricultural enterprises, artisans, mines, industry, transport, etc., united on a regional, provincial, national and international level in production unions and federations as part of a general confederation of production. Society's new organisation of exchange, consumption and supply will likewise be represented by a dense and complex network of regional, provincial and national organisations, unions and federations, grouped in a general confederation of exchange and consumption for satisfying the needs of all inhabitants. All human social activity and all transport, communications, education, healthcare, and so on, will be organised in a similar fashion. With this organisational system of all the functions of the various aspects of social life, there will be no place in society for the power of one individual over another or for the exploitation of one by another. The basic principle of production and distribution for the building of the new social system will be: everyone will produce according to their possibilities and everyone will receive according to their needs.

Tactics

The realisation of this social ideal of equality, solidarity and freedom can only be brought about by the united workers and peasant masses, inspired by anarchist communism and organised into ideological, professional, exchange and consumption, cultural and educational groups. Anarchist communism, while repudiating the State, rejects the involvement of the workers in the administration bodies and institutions of the State, in the parliament and in any vote for the official management of the State. As the sole means of efficient struggle, as a defence of the immediate interests of the working masses, and for the realisation of the full ideal of humanity's freedom, anarchism recognises only the direct action of the workers themselves, initiated by their economic organisations and expressed through strikes, sabotage, boycotts, general strikes, insurrections and the social revolution. In consequence, anarchism rejects all forms of organisation and struggle by political parties, considering them sterile and ineffective, unable to respond to the goals and the immediate tasks and to the interests of the workers in the towns and villages. The true strength of the workers is in the economy and their economic organisations. Only there lies the terrain where capitalism can be undermined. Only there lies the true class struggle.

Organisation

The radical social re-organisation demanded by anarchist communism requires the organisational action of all the forces on whom this historical task is incumbent. It is above all necessary for the partisans of anarchist communism to be organised in an anarchist communist ideological organisation.

The tasks of these organisations are:
- to develop, realise and spread anarchist communist ideas;
- to study all the vital present-day questions affecting the daily lives of the working masses and the problems of the social reconstruction;
- the multi-faceted struggle for the defence of our social ideal and the cause of working people;
- to participate in the creation of groups of workers on the level of production, profession, exchange and consumption, culture and education, and all other organisations that can be useful in the preparation for the social reconstruction;
- armed participation in every revolutionary insurrection;
- the preparation for and organisation of these events; in the use of every means which can bring on the social revolution.

Anarchist communist ideological organisations are absolutely indispensable in the full realisation of anarchist communism both before the revolution and after. These organisations are formed on a local level. Every local organisation chooses a secretary, whose task is to keep in contact with other similar organisations. The secretaries of all the organisations of one locality with a certain number of inhabitants constitute the general organisation of the locality. All the local organisations unite, by region and province, in regional and provincial unions. Contact between the unions is assured by the respective secretaries. All the provincial unions of the country are united in the Federation of Anarchist Communists of Bulgaria. Activities are co-ordinated by the federal secretariat. The members of each secretariat form part of the local organisation in their area of residence, and it is obligatory for every initiative of theirs to pass through the local organisation, and therefore be considered an initiative of the latter. The secretariats are merely liaison and executive bodies with no power. Only anarchist communists can be members of the anarchist communist ideological organisations. A second type of organisation is the workers' syndicate, also based on the federative principle, organised by workplace or by trade, and united into production or trade unions in a general federation of workers' syndicates. These organisations, created with the participation of anarchist communists, adopt the tactic of direct action and reject the struggles of political parties and all interference by political parties in the workers' organisations.

Their tasks are:
- the defence of the immediate interests of the working class;
- the struggle to improve the work conditions of the workers;
- the study of the problems of production;
- the control of production, and the ideological, technical and organisational preparation of a radical social reconstruction in which they will have to ensure the continuation of industrial output.

All workers who accept their structure, tactics and tasks may be members of these organisations. When conditions do not permit the existence of such organisations, anarchist communist workers join other independent syndicalist workers' organisations, while defending their concept of direct action and their anti-party position... such an organisation today. A third type of organisation must group the peasantry. This is the locally-created agricultural labour organisation, united on a regional, provincial and national level in a general federation which, together with the federation of workers' syndicates, make up the national confederation of labour.

The tasks of these agricultural labour organisations are:
- to defend the interests of the landless peasants, those with little land and those with small parcels of land;
- to organise agricultural production groups, to study the problems of agricultural production;
- to prepare for the future social reconstruction, in which they will be the pioneers of the re-organisation and the agricultural production, with the aim of ensuring the subsistence of the entire population.

The agricultural labour organisations are built on the basis of sector and reject all struggles by political parties and their interference in the organisations. They apply the tactic of direct action, whenever possible, in their specific conditions, including refusing to pay taxes, boycotting the State, production strikes, etc. The members of these organisations can be landless peasants, those with little land and those with small parcels of land, who work the land themselves without the use of wage labour. When the conditions to create such organisations do not exist, anarchist communist peasants join other similar labour organisations, with the aim of promoting within them their vision of direct action and struggle against political parties and the tactic of peasant direct action… is the co-operative. Anarchist communists participate in all types of co-operatives, bringing to them the spirit of solidarity and of mutual aid against the spirit of the party and bureaucracy. Agricultural production co-operatives today merit special attention, as they will become more important and will play a decisive educational role in the future construction of an anarchist communist social system. Another type of organisation are those of young people, women, temperance groups, Esperantists and other cultural organisations whose members support the ideas and the struggles of the anarchist communist ideological and economic organisations of the working people. Relations between the aforementioned organisations are on a functional basis, that recognises the full freedom and independence of the members and the organisations, and excludes all external interference and all subordination of one organisation to another. The reciprocal dependence between the various types of organisation can only be based on their ideological commonality and unity, the common goal to which they all aspire. Organisational decisions within anarchist communist organisations are made unanimously, and not by majority. The decision of the majority is not binding on the minority; persuasion should always be sought. In practice, the minority generally rallies to the decision of the majority, which reserves the right to express the correctness of its position, once it has been demonstrated in fact. Thanks to this principle, which is widely applied within the anarchist movement, splits, enmities and arguments are rare. However, within the mass economic organisations and the other organisations, decision is taken by majority vote and are binding, as only in this way can unity be achieved, unity that is absolutely indispensable in mass organisations. But in certain cases where there is profound disagreement, the minority may be freed from the obligation to apply a general decision, on condition that it does not prevent the execution of such a decision. All the aforementioned organisations share the common task of preparing the radical social reconstruction throughout the country. During the social revolution, they will each carry out (within their own domain) the expropriation and socialisation of the means of production and of all goods.

Immediate tasks
At present, the Federation of Anarchist Communists of Bulgaria has adopted the following slogans:
- The creation of free worker and peasant local councils and committees elected directly and not as representative of political parties, organised and controlled by the people. These councils and committees must take completely in hand, or control, the political direction of the country.
- The role of these councils and committees is to express the wishes of the working masses and of co-ordinating the efforts of all in order to construct a complete social system and ensure its functioning. They are united on local, regional and national levels and represent the whole people's political force, thought and will.
- The adoption by Bulgarian workers and peasants of the International Workers' Association, to defend the worldwide interests of all working people and impede any forthcoming war.
- The clear and categorical rejection of all forms of class collaboration.

- Recognition of the right of workers to struggle freely to defend their material interests, to improve their conditions and to strike.
- Workers' control of production and a share of the benefits.
- The reduction of wage differences between the various categories of civil servants, State workers and private sector workers, tending towards the introduction of a family wage.
- Exemption from all taxes for workers, low-level employees, small peasants and all low-paid levels of society. Free and voluntary agricultural co-operative associations.
- Free and voluntary co-operation between small artisan enterprises.
- Progression towards a complete co-operative system of exchange, food supply and consumption, and towards co-operative development to include domestic and foreign trade and social security.
- Increases in the prices of agricultural production up to an average level and a reduction to the same level of the prices of industrial products, based on real retail prices and a just and egalitarian remuneration for labour in the towns and countryside.
- Organisation of the struggle against speculation and the black market by the labour associations, producers' associations, exchange and consumption associations and by the public naming of all speculators and traffickers.
- The creation and development of regular, high-quality commercial relations throughout the country, with the rapid satisfaction of needs with regard to basic essentials, such as clothing and footwear, through foreign imports.
- The financial stabilisation of the country with a streamlining of the bureaucratic apparatus, with a real (not provisional) State budget and economy, with the complete elimination of all unnecessary spending (such as the costs of war), and with a real increase (not just a demagogic one) in the national production.
- Complete freedom of speech, of the press and of organisation and assembly for all non-fascists. The suppression of all State and police control – left over from the fascist period – of co-operatives, trade unions and other organisations. The government must fulfil its promises in this regard.
- Opposition to all dictatorships of whatever name or colour.

- Suppression of the death penalty and of all special laws.
- The disappearance of all concentration and labour camps or workhouses with the aim of punishing; dissolution of the forced labour system, applied as a police method.
- Struggle against the remnants of fascism and vigilance against all activity against the people, under the aegis of the various labour, production and ideological organisations of the workers and peasants.
- The grouping of all worker and democratic elements into egalitarian military unions in order to resist strongly and effectively the growing reaction.
- War reparations to be made by war criminals.
- The dissolving of the army, the suppression of obligatory military service and the militaristic education of young people both inside and outside schools.
- The creation of a voluntary popular militia (not controlled by any party), recruitment to which will be solely effected from among the workers and peasants, and controlled by the worker-peasant organisations.
- Fully scientific teaching and education, free of all political party and class influence, widely available to the new generations.
- Free, widely available healthcare for everyone.
- The total exclusion of all religious interference from teaching and the family.
- Aid to the population under the control of the labour, production and ideological organisations of the workers and peasants.
- Bread, freedom, peace and jobs for all workers and the progressive layers of the Bulgarian people.

Long Live the International Solidarity
Of the Workers!
Long Live Anarchist Communism!

Friends of Just Books

Just Books is a self-managed not for profit worker run collective. Established in 1978 by the Belfast Anarchist Collective it is still ran by anarchists who believe self-education is an essential element in building a new world that can replace capitalism, states and oppression.

Currently we operate a library and reading room in Belfast, organise events, distribute anarchist and radical literature, and are heavily involved in the organisation of the Belfast Anarchist Bookfair. Currently the only anarchist bookfair on the island of Ireland.

This book, alongside our reprint of Constructive Anarchism, marks our first serious step into publishing. In the pipeline are a Belfast strike chronology, an updated history of anarchism in the north of Ireland by Maírtín O'Catháin (based on his Wee Black Booke of Belfast Anarchism), work by Jason Brannigan on the 1919 strike in Belfast and Glasgow, and more.

Our library is based on donations and the financial support of people like you. As is our ongoing publishing. In order to support our work we have set up the Friends of Just Books program. For £15 a month (more if you like!) for a minimum of three months you will receive a copy of every title we publish as long as your membership is active. All the money raised through FOJB will go into publishing new titles and maintaining and improving of our library and archive.

For details of how to become a Friend of Just Books contact us at justbooksbelfast@gmail.com or: P.O. Box 258, Newtownabbey, BT36 9FQ.